NORFOLK GEM

44 PRINTMAKERS EXPLORE THE CO

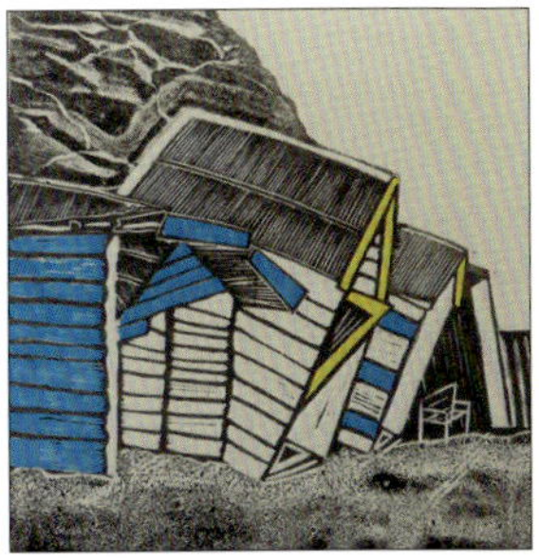
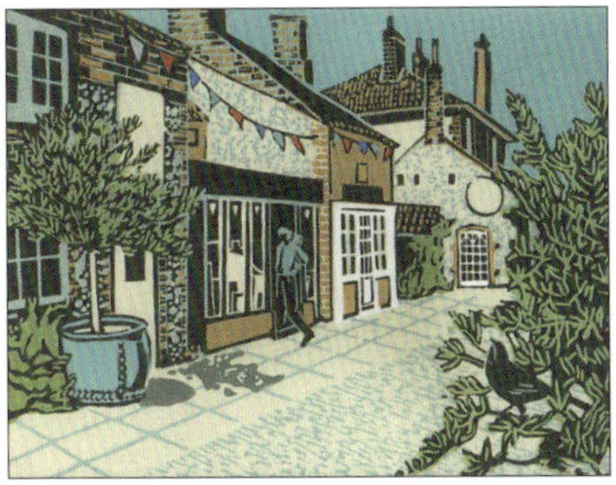
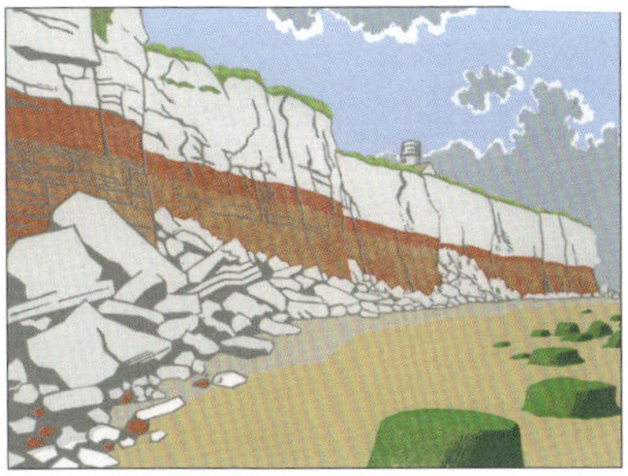
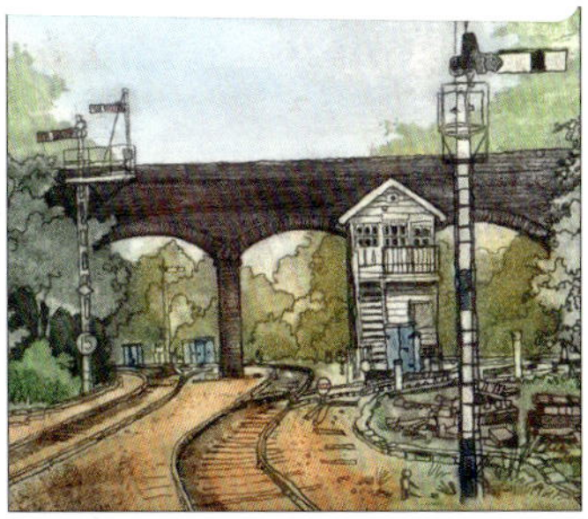
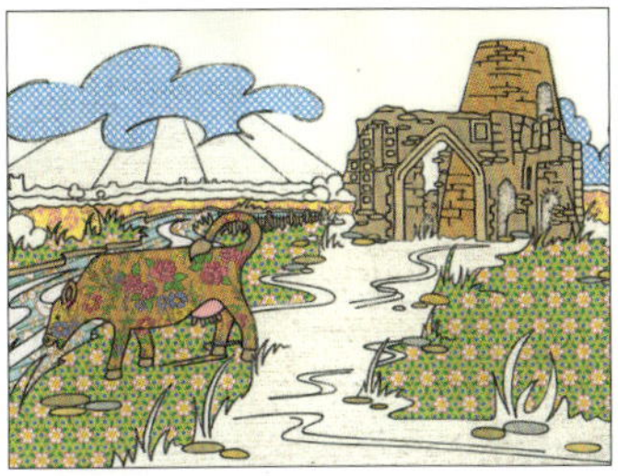
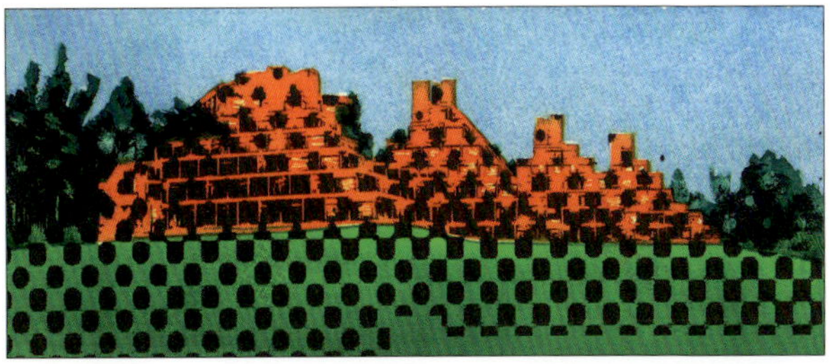
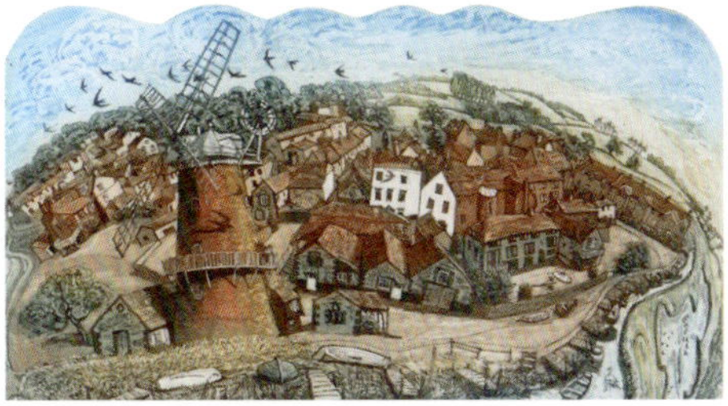
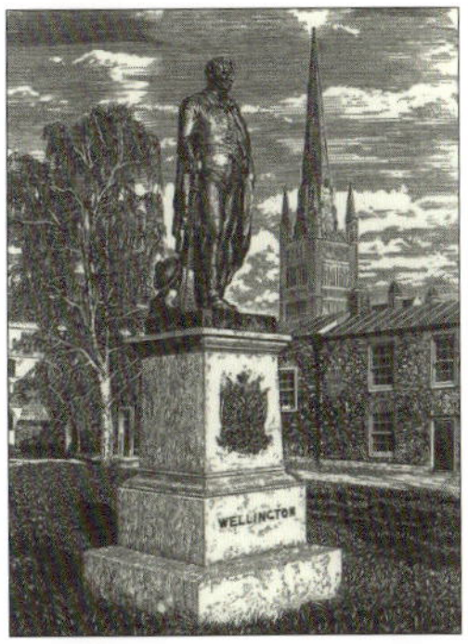
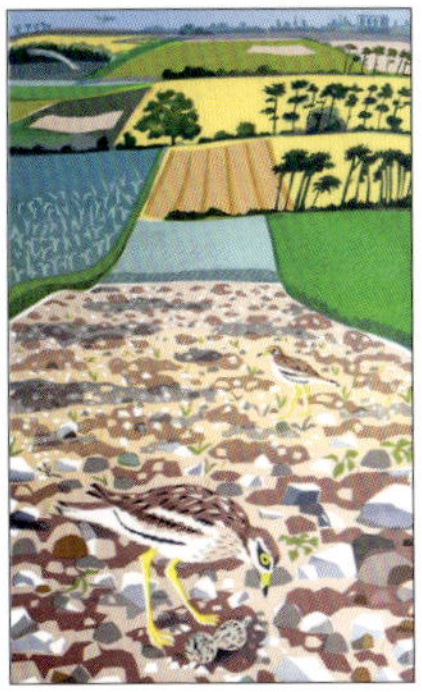
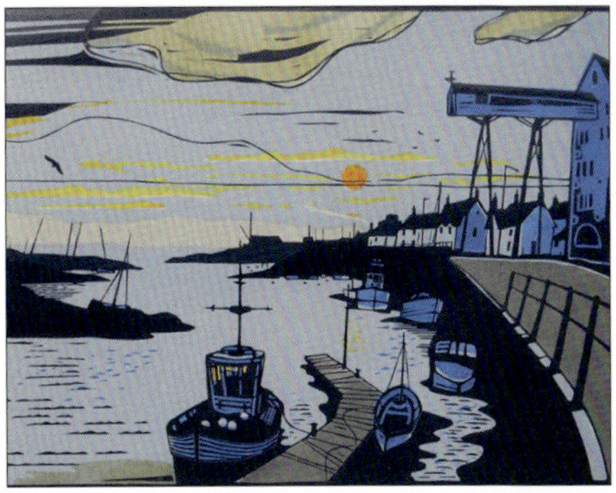
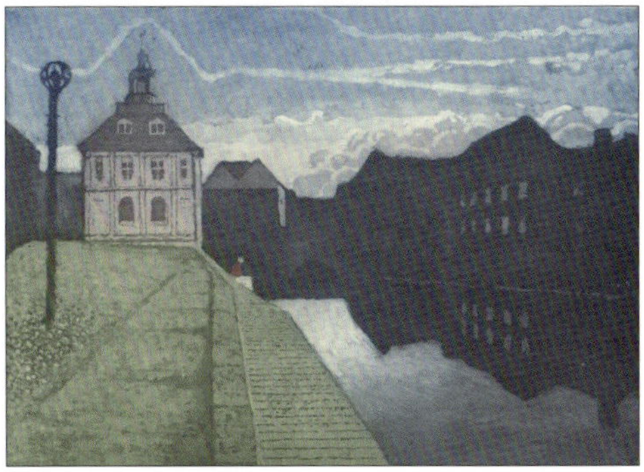
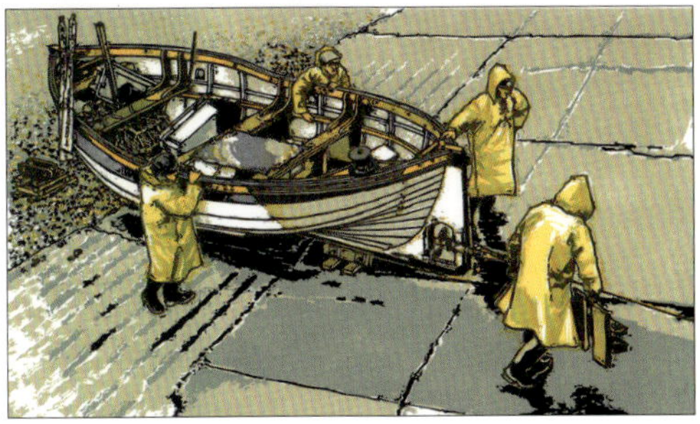
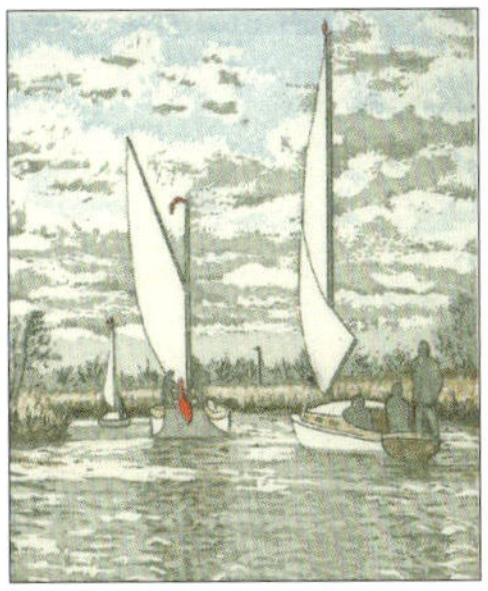
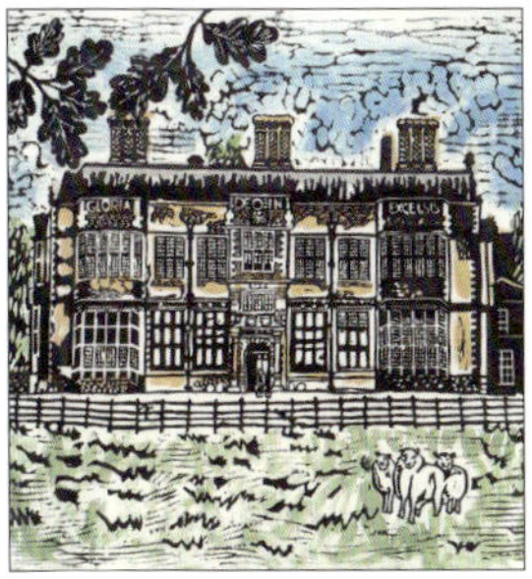
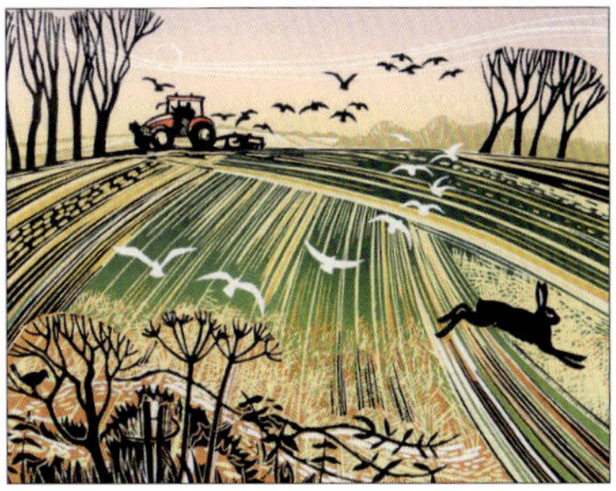

MADE IN NORFOLK BY MASCOT MEDIA

The Artists

Carry Akroyd (Northants) www.carryakroyd.co.uk
Max Angus (Kent) www.maxangus.co.uk
Rob Barnes (Norfolk) www.robbarnesart.co.uk
Sarah Bays (Norfolk) www.sarahbays.co.uk
Neil Bousfield (Norfolk) www.neilbousfield.com
Amelia Bowman (Norfolk) www.ameliabowman.co.uk
Stuart Brocklehurst (Yorkshire) stuartbrocklehurst@outlook.com
Gail Brodholt (London) www.gailbrodholt.com
Vanessa Burroughes (Norfolk) www.vanessaburroughes.com
Moyra Byford (Suffolk) www.moyrabyford.com
Colin Bygrave (Norfolk) www.norwichprintfair.co.uk
Fiona Carver (Rutland) www.fionacarver.com
Louise Davies (London) www.louisedavies.com
Jan Dingle (Norfolk) www.jandingle.co.uk
Anthony Dunigan (Suffolk) anthonydunigan156@btinternet.com
Andy English (Cambs) www.andyenglish.com
Chris Evans (Suffolk) www.norwichprintfair.co.uk
TM Fairbank (Norfolk) www.norwichprintfair.co.uk
Robert Gillmor (Norfolk) www.pinkfootgallery.co.uk
James Green (Yorkshire) jgprintworks@hotmail.com
Robert Greenhalf (Sussex) www.robertgreenhalf.co.uk
Kate Heiss (Herts) www.kateheiss.com
Sally Hirst (Norfolk) www.sallyhirst.co.uk
Lisa Hooper (Borders) www.hoopoeprints.co.uk
Richard Horne (Norfolk) www.elhorno.co.uk
Leanda Jaine Hughes (Norfolk) www.leandajaine.co.uk
HJ Jackson (Norfolk) www.norwichprintfair.co.uk
Jeremy James (Derbyshire) www.jeremyjamesceramics.co.uk
Clare Johnson (Suffolk) www.clarejohnson.co.uk
David Jones (Norfolk) www.davidjonesartist.co.uk
Ross Loveday (Suffolk) www.rossloveday.com
Vanessa Lubach (Norfolk) www.vanessalubach.co.uk
Martin Mitchell (Norfolk) www.norwichprintfair.co.uk
Colin Moore (Dorset) www.colinmoore.uk.com
Jenny Portlock (France) www.woodengravings.eu
Winter Rose (Suffolk) winterr@gmail.com
Laurie Rudling (Norfolk) www.laurierudling.co.uk
Valerie Sims (Cambs) www.valeriesims.co.uk
Louise Stebbing (Norfolk) louiseprintmaker@gmail.com
Annette Sykes (Northants) www.aesykesart.co.uk
Thelma Sykes (Cheshire) thelmasykes@tiscali.co.uk
Glynn Thomas (Suffolk) www.glynnthomas.com
Mandy Walden (Suffolk) mandywprintmaker@gmail.com
Janet Watson (Suffolk) www.janetwatsonart.co.uk

First published in Great Britain in 2017 by Mascot Media, Norfolk, England. 2nd printing 2022.
email: mascot_media@btinternet.com web: www.mascotmedia.co.uk

A CIP catalogue record for this book is available from the British Library.

ISBN: 978-0-9954651-6-9

Written and designed by Alan Marshall. Edited by Marion Scott Marshall.

Printed by Swallowtail Print, Drayton Industrial Park, Taverham Road, Drayton, Norwich, Norfolk NR8 6RL.
Email: contact@swallowtailprint.co.uk Web: www.swallowtailprint.co.uk

Made in Norfolk
by Mascot Media

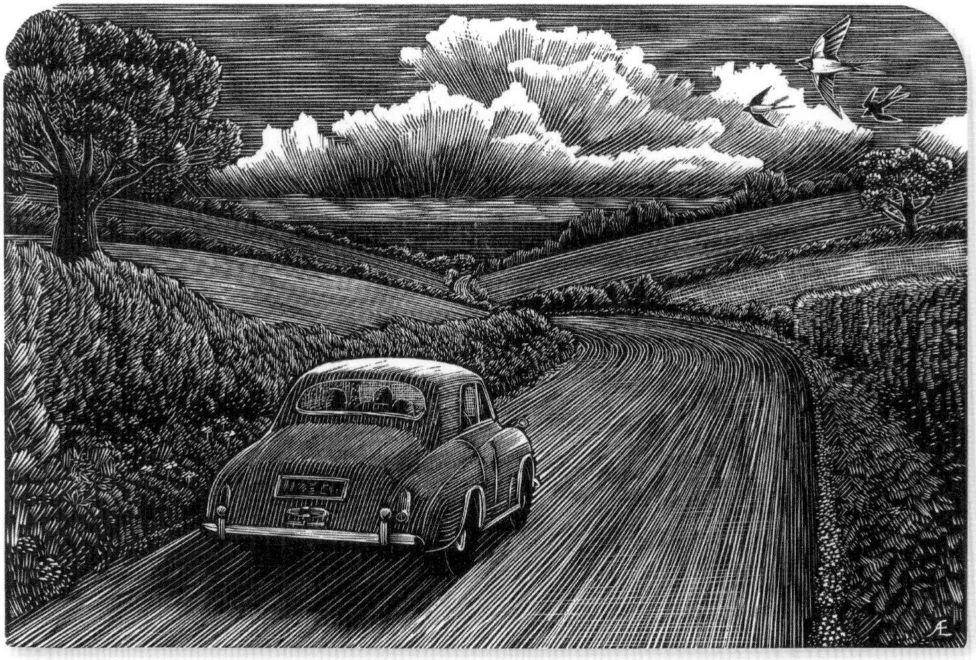

"I can see the sea"

captions

Front cover, from left to right, top to bottom: Moyra Byford – *Sunday Morning Yacht Racing* (Broads); Colin Moore – *Brancaster*; Anthony Dunigan – *King's Lynn Custom House*; James Green – *Cromer no. 1*; Leanda Jaine Hughes – *Fine City* (Norwich); Glynn Thomas – *Burnham Overy Staithe*; Laurie Rudling – *Old Warren Heath* (Brecks); David Jones – *The Forum* (Norwich); HJ Jackson – *Dry Dock, Wells*; Jan Dingle – *The Sail* (Broads).
Title page, from left to right, top to bottom: Annette Sykes – *Washed Away* (Cromer); Max Angus – *Good to see you* (Holt); Robert Gillmor – *Hunstanton Cliffs*; Chris Evans – *Reedham Junction*; Amelia Bowman – *St Benet's Abbey*; Clare Johnson – *Ziggurat* (UEA); Glynn Thomas – *Cley-next-the-Sea*; Anthony Dunigan – *The Iron Duke* (Norwich); Carry Akroyd – *Stonies' Plot* (The Brecks); Colin Moore – *Wells Morning*; Colin Bygrave – *Lonely in King's Lynn*; HJ Jackson – *Wet Slipway* (Sheringham); Jan Dingle – *Still Sails* (The Broads); Vanessa Burroughes – *Felbrigg Hall*; Rob Barnes – *Plough II*.
Above: Andy English wood engraving – *I can see the sea* (North Norfolk).
Back cover, from left to right, top to bottom: Martin Mitchell – *Erpingham Gate* (Norwich); Amelia Bowman – *Cley Windmill*; Chris Evans – *October Evening, Gorleston*; Kate Heiss – *Sails & Sea Campion* (Brancaster); Valerie Sims – *Saltmarsh* (Blakeney); Rob Barnes – *Back to the Quay* (Blakeney); Max Angus – *Cley Shingle Bank*; Gail Brodholt – *Indian Summer* (Cromer); Carry Akroyd – *Broadland Afternoon*; Vanessa Lubach – *Cley Windmill*.

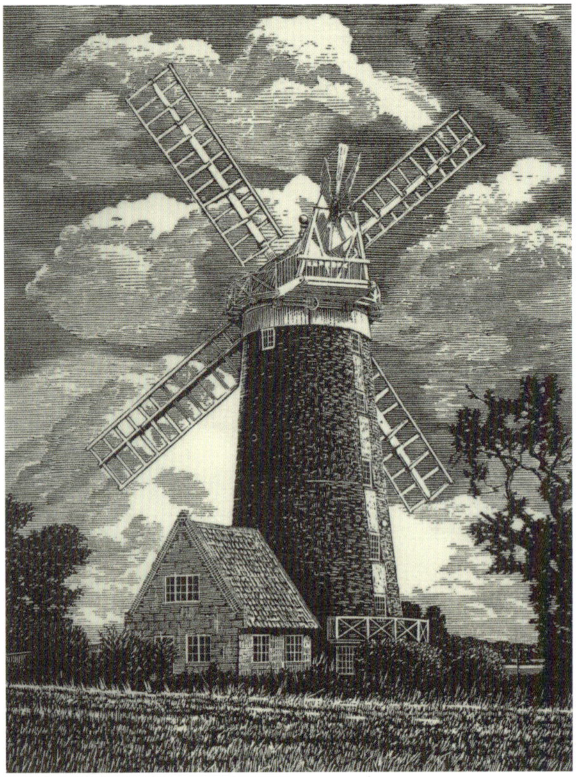

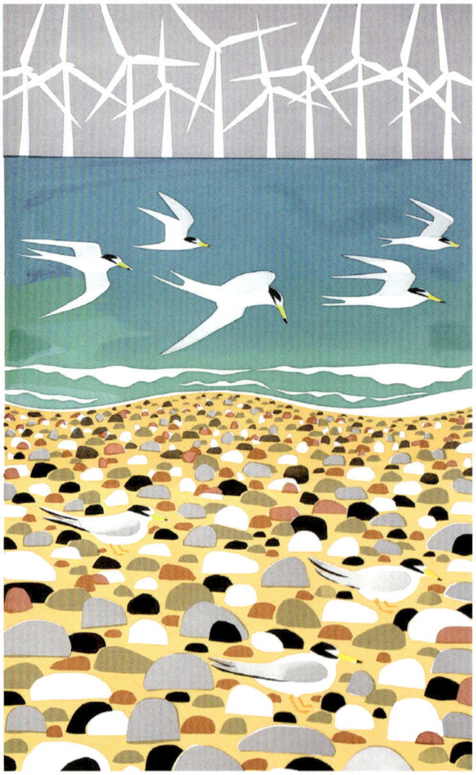

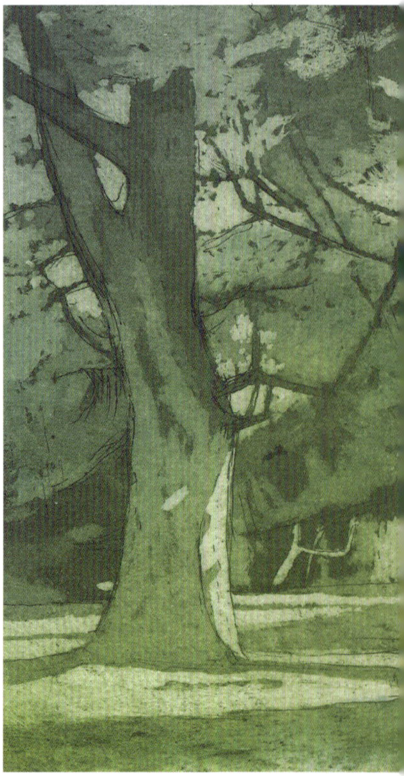

Norfolk is a county rich in both history and natural history. Its geography has been shaped by a farming heritage that extends back to the pre-Roman era, although the Romans laid the foundations for Norfolk's agricultural might.

As well as vast tracts of fertile farmland, both flat and rolling, the county claims more than 160km of coast and 320km of inland interconnecting waterways. Combined with the appeal of its ancient buildings and a wealth of wildlife, these features draw millions of visitors every year.

An average 166 people occupy each of Norfolk's 5,370 sq km, compared with 195 people in Suffolk and 417 in Essex. Some 40 per cent of residents are based in Norwich, Great Yarmouth, King's Lynn, Thetford and Dereham. The rest are spread thinly around England's fifth-biggest county, occupying hundreds of small towns and villages.

The 413,000 residences in Norfolk include more than a fair share of flint-fronted cottages, converted barns, ancient farmhouses, former rectories and grand stately homes. Norfolk plays part-time host to the Royal Family, thanks to Her Majesty The Queen's estate at Sandringham in the west of the county.

Famous sons and daughters range from the heroic, such as Horatio Nelson, Robert Kett, Edith Cavell and Elizabeth Fry, through the political (Sir Robert Walpole) and theatrical (Sir John Mills, Rupert Everett), to the literary (Henry Rider Haggard, Philip Pullman and Stephen Fry).

Norfolk's landscape rises gently from east to west, with an abrupt decline to the flatlands of the Fens bordering Cambridgeshire and Lincolnshire. The low-lying coastline provides numerous stunning sandy beaches and a smattering of quaint seaside towns.

To the east of the county is a wide, flat and rather wet landscape known as the Norfolk Broads, created through the flooding by nature of extensive peat excavations dating back to the Middle Ages.

Britain's biggest protected wetland, it attracts two million visitors a year, who come in pursuit of peace, wildlife, fishing or to participate in a relaxed and extended waterborne pub crawl.

The Iceni first occupied the lands that were to become Norfolk, from the 1st century BC to the end of the 1st century AD. They revolted against the Romans, led in AD 60 by Boudica. They lost, and the triumphant Romans built roads and ports, as well as introducing effective farming and land management practices. By the 5th century AD the Angles were in charge, splitting to become the North Folk and South Folk and creating the two neighbouring and rival counties of Norfolk and Suffolk that are divided forever by football...

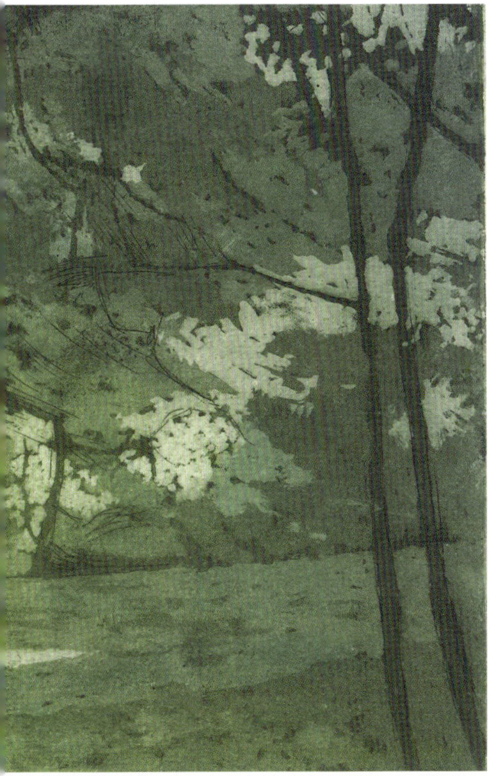
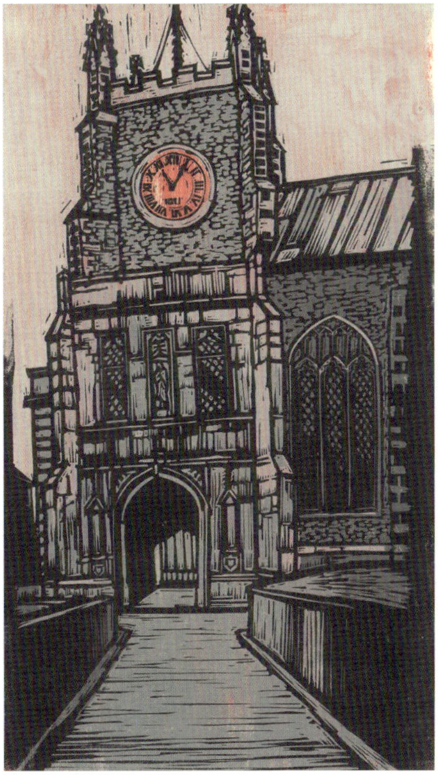
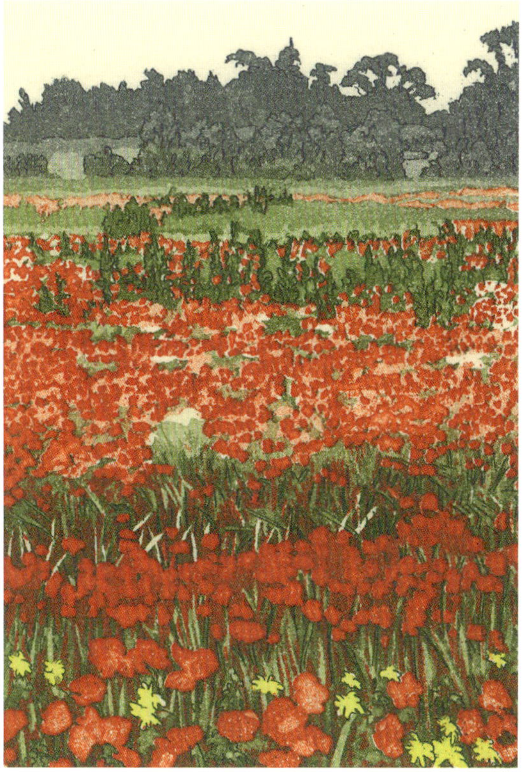

After the Danes moved in, the eastern wetlands began to be drained and used for farmland. Migration rose sharply, and by the time of the Domesday Book this was one of the most densely populated parts of Britain – numbering 148,000 people. Agriculture was joined by the wool trades, creating wealth and spawning a church-building programme that has resulted in a legacy of vast numbers of grand and ancient places of worship. Norfolk has 659 surviving medieval churches, more than the rest of the British Isles combined.

By the 16th century, Norwich was the second-biggest city in Britain, but the ravages of plague wiped out a large part of the population. When the Industrial Revolution was leading to boom times elsewhere, Norfolk ploughed its lonely agricultural furrow and economic decline continued.

Fishing boomed and then busted in Great Yarmouth and across the border in Lowestoft. Railways came and went. Offshore gas provided a relatively short-lived boost, while the growth in whirling wind farms has provided some benefits as well as changing the coastal outlook forever.

Nature has made several attempts to wash the county away, with a particularly vigorous effort in 1953. As Norfolk is conspicuously low lying and has limited coastal protection, the North Sea can find its way inland rather easily. Storm surges in recent years have provided a painful reminder of the county's vulnerability in the north and east, with the landscape once again shifting to reflect the power of the sea and the lack of investment in protecting people, property and wildlife.

Norwich may no longer be the major centre of population and influence that it once was. However, almost every nook is crammed full of history, and the city retains great cultural significance.

Norfolk's artistic pedigree is enviable, with great originators such as Seago, Stannard and Cotman still inspiring new generations of painters. Renowned pop artist Colin Self is Norfolk-born and trained, a contemporary of Norwich-based printmaker HJ Jackson whose work appears in these pages.

The annual Norfolk & Norwich Festival is one of the oldest surviving arts festivals in the UK (its origins date back to 1772); while Norfolk & Norwich Open Studios is one of the biggest events of its type, providing temporary access for the curious each year to more than 250 garrets, sheds and otherwise secret places. And then there's The Norwich Print Fair, which celebrated its 20th year in 2015 and continues to draw big crowds

From left: Anthony Dunigan – A Norfolk Scene (wood engraving); Carry Akroyd – Big Turns & Little Terns III (serigraph); Colin Bygrave – Sunlit Clearing (aquatint); HJ Jackson – St Michael at Pleas (linocut); Jan Dingle – Still Blaze (etching)

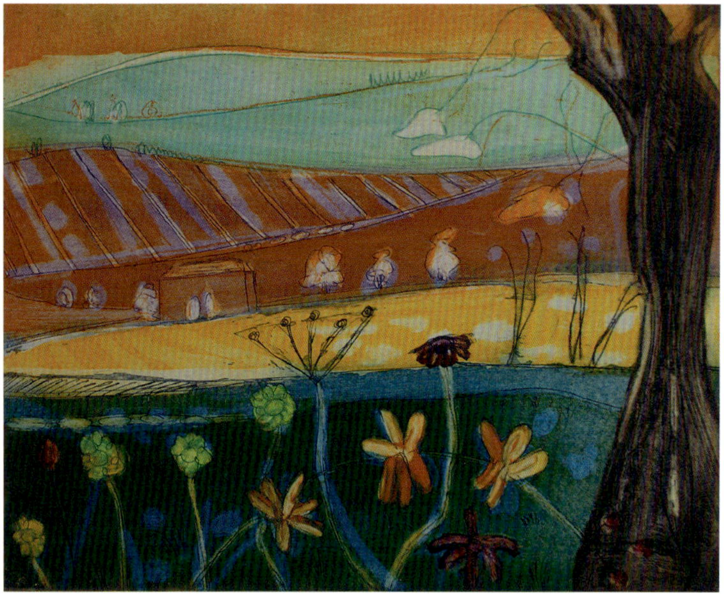

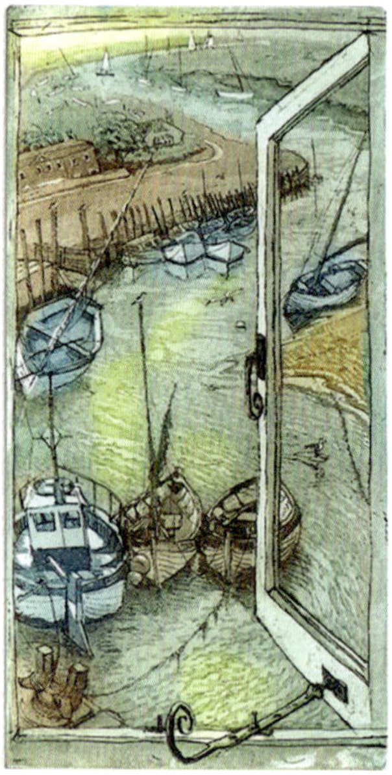

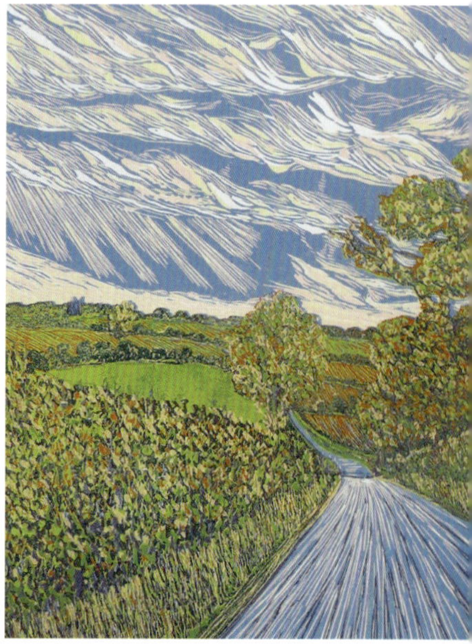

during its September parade of printmakers.

Given the number and variety of artists located in the county, it is no great surprise that this book brings together a dazzling array of styles. As an artistic destination, Norfolk has become increasingly important for wildlife, landscape and even abstract painters and printmakers. This volume is a compilation of contemporary printmaking organised by location, taking readers on a journey from the south-east to the north-west of the county.

We cannot promise that you will find your favourite place among these pages. Artists are proudly independent and notoriously free-spirited. Their subjects are seldom chosen solely for commercial appeal, and they will often avoid the more predictable locations.

Norwich, of course, has enduring appeal, and the portfolio of images paying tribute to the city is particularly large and diverse. Even here, there are remarkably few repetitive interpretations of the most obvious locations such as the Anglican Cathedral, Norwich Castle or the 17 surviving medieval churches.

It will come as no great surprise that the long and spectacular span of north Norfolk coastline attracts the most artists. Both the Brecks, a vital natural environment crossing into Suffolk to the south of Thetford, and the Broads also provide the basis for many linocuts, etchings, collagraphs and wood engravings.

Common to this book and its sister volume *Suffolk Jewels* is a desire to showcase a remarkable diversity of printmaking approach. Even within the main disciplines – woodcut, linocut, wood engraving, etching, mezzotint, drypoint, engraving, screen printing, collagraph, lithograph and monoprint/monotype – there are great variations of technique and style.

There are plenty of people who still do not grasp the concept of the original print. Many printmakers smile through gritted teeth when asked by potential customers if the original is available, as they prefer not to buy 'copies'. In fact, the quality and beauty of some printmakers' inked lino blocks and acid-etched copper plates would look perfectly lovely hung on the wall, but these are the 'originals' rather than a painting that is being copied photo-mechanically for so-called 'limited edition' sale.

The beauty of the various printmaking processes is that they, by definition, create a number of originals. In the case of monoprints, the clue is in the name and there will be only one. This is a very 'painterly' technique, and if you are fortunate enough to own the original you will not see another one quite like it.

More typically, prints will be editioned from the blocks or plates created in the studio using a variety of hand tools, acids and inks. Presses of various sizes will be wielded, or hand-burnishing implements applied. High-quality handmade paper will be used for the prints, and the purchaser will be able to spot the differences in every print made.

Edition sizes will vary, dependent on the size/complexity of the block(s) or plate(s), the preference of the artist or the fragility of the medium. Some materials will not cope with repeated applications of the press, etc.

Unlike photo-mechanical reproduction of an original painting, the printmaker will have spent hours/days/weeks or even months etching or carving his or her way through wood, metal or lino, before applying the inks and pressing the block or plate on to the prepared paper surface.

Multiple applications can mean individual ink colours combine to create new ones. There are challenges with registration so that the image from each block or plate lines up perfectly. After a lengthy process of inking,

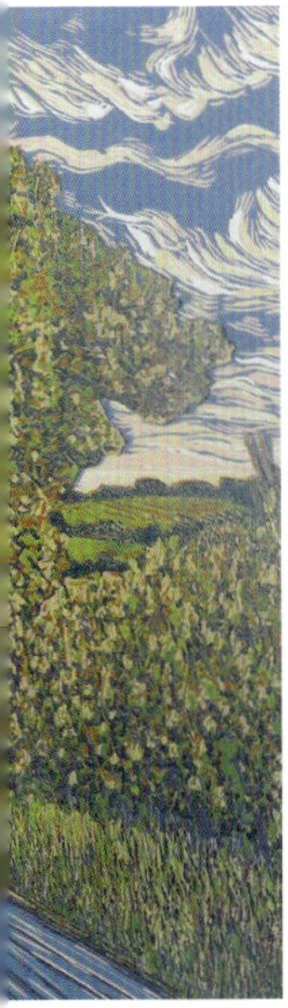

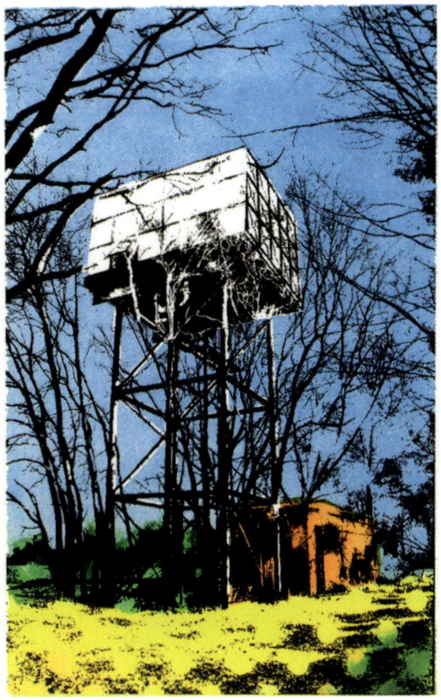

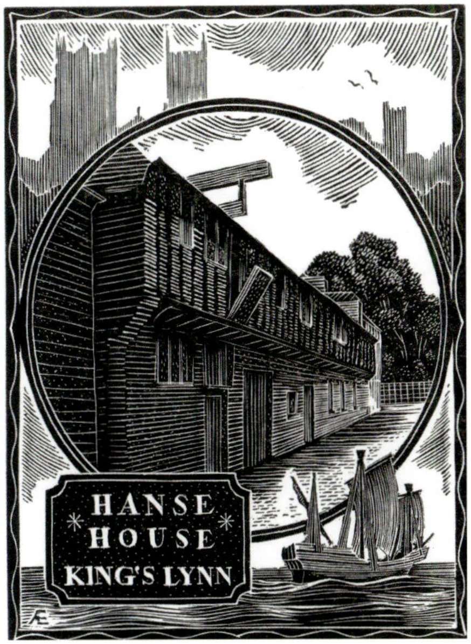

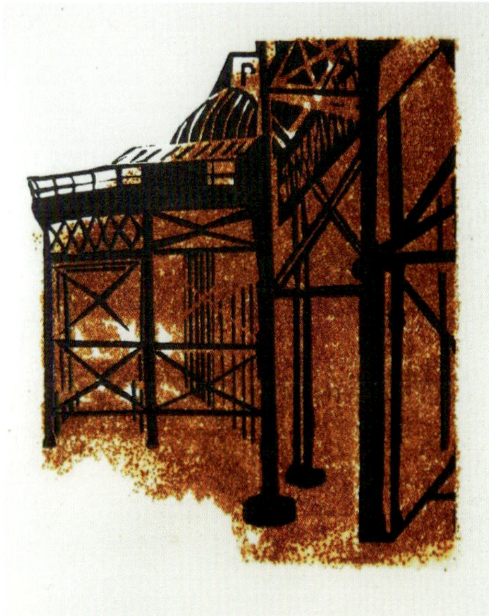

wiping, burnishing or the use of a press, the print will be allowed to dry and then be hand-numbered and signed.

There is a great deal of 'craft' involved in most forms of printmaking that demands skill with tools, precision, organisation, dexterity and/or strength. In many cases, beautiful detailed drawings form the basis for the engraving, etching or linocut. The artists often have the added challenge of working in reverse, as the printmaking process requires a 'negative' to be transformed into a 'positive' during the printing phase.

It clearly isn't necessary to understand the technique involved to appreciate a framed picture on a gallery wall. The reaction to art is much more complex and often emotional. It won't always be appropriate to analyse the artist's methods and abilities before deciding upon a purchase. However, it is a good idea to know what you are buying. Just because there is an edition number and a signature does not mean it is necessarily an original print. Always ask if the picture is a reproduction of an original painting (therefore a copy), or if it is a handmade individual print produced by the artist from blocks, plates or similar masters.

We would argue that more enjoyment can be derived from any artwork if the owner understands the process used and learns a little about the person behind the frame. We will therefore be introducing the artists who provided the images for *Norfolk Gems*.

Around 20 of the artists featured in this book practise one of the younger forms of printmaking. Linocuts are a form of 'relief print' made by cutting the image out of a flat surface. The remaining raised areas then form the relief block to which ink is applied by means of a roller.

The medium emerged in the early 20th century in the hands of the German Expressionists. Linoleum at that time was a robust mixture of linseed and cork that was backed with a canvas sheet. When used in the place of traditional hardwood blocks, it could be carved more easily and quickly into relief designs that could take black or coloured inks. A sheet of suitable paper is then pressed against the inked surface, using either a printing press or some form of hand burnishing. Only the raised part of the block deposits the inked image on to the paper.

Some eight decades later, linocut artists have seen relatively few changes in the basic process. The majority of contemporary linocut printmakers eschew the delicate, fragile woodblock-style Japanese papers in favour of thicker, more robust hand-made stock that takes the ink well; can deal with rougher handling; and is less likely to ripple when the ink is still wet.

Tools are very similar to the originals, with most artists using only a couple of sizes of cutter. Ink rollers may be made differently, but do much the same job. Hand-burnishing techniques have varied remarkably little, with a simple tablespoon still as likely to be employed as an original Albion press from the Victorian era.

As regards the process, there are still two main approaches to the creation of linocut prints. One is the multi-block method favoured by the majority of artists, who apply their own tweaks and twists to the process for perfect alignment, etc. Separate blocks are cut for individual colours, with each colour often being printed separately. On occasions, one block may be used to print more than

From left: Louise Davies – Country Hedgerows (etching); Glynn Thomas – Blakeney Channel (etching); Louise Stebbing – Rolling Countryside (linocut); Clare Johnson – Babes in the Wood (monoprint); Andy English – Hanse House (wood engraving); Sally Hirst – Weathered (collagraph)

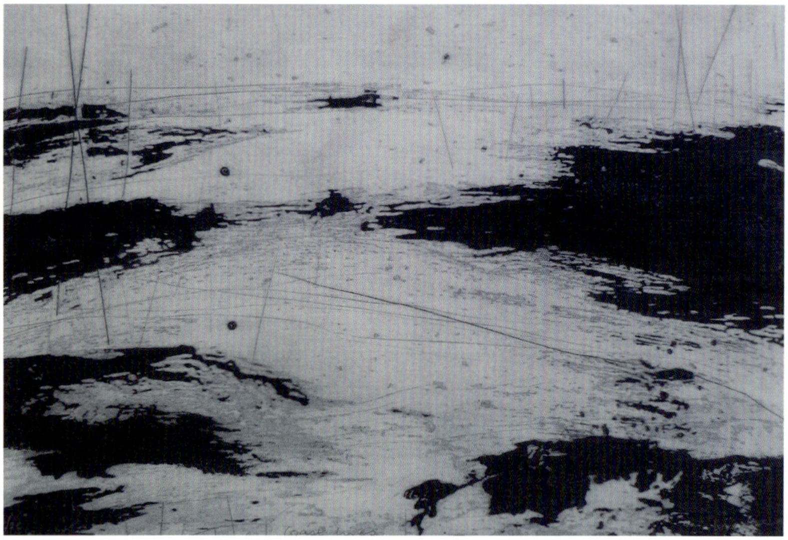

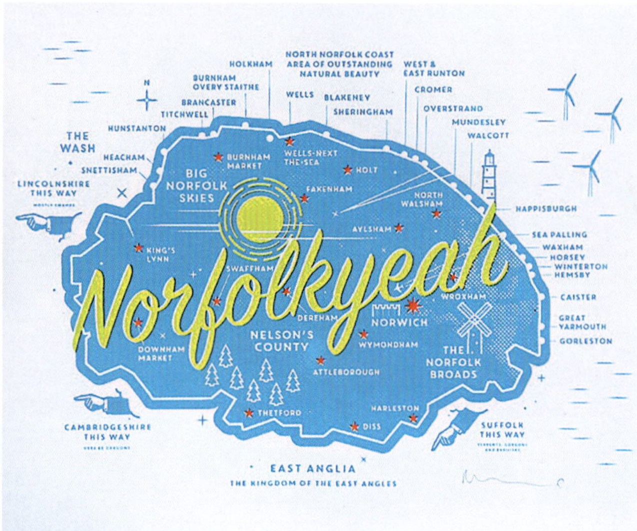

one colour. Each section is inked separately, and the block reassembled and printed in one operation. As the inks used are transparent, further colours can be achieved by over-printing one with another.

The other approach to producing linocuts is the so-called reduction, or reductive, method, nicknamed the 'suicide' process as it is extremely unforgiving and errors can seldom be remedied. Picasso fought the corner for this method, and it still finds favour with plenty of printmakers today.

One block is used for the entire print. The complete edition is printed in the first colour, which may use the whole block or show areas of white (depending on the colour of the paper being used). More of the block is then removed and a second colour is printed on to the first, carefully registering one upon the other. This process is continued until the final printing is complete.

Veteran printmaker HJ Jackson has a number of complex linocuts reproduced in these pages that rely upon the multi-block method. In spite of working regularly on a large scale, the artist eschews the use of a press and hand-burnishes using an elderly tobacco tin. Some of his earliest prints are found in the Great Yarmouth section of this book, while a new linocut of fishing boats in Sheringham can be seen on page 136.

Fellow Norwich resident Vanessa Lubach is responsible for linocuts depicting Blickling Hall, Hickling Broad, Cley Windmill and Baconsthorpe Castle. She specialises in intricately carved, multi-layered linocuts often hand-burnished with a spoon. Her subjects range from the landscapes found here to cats, chickens and inanimate household objects.

While Colin Moore is Scottish by birth and a former architecture student in Glasgow, he has worked mainly as a painter and printmaker since 2004 and now lives in Dorset. This hasn't stopped him tackling a number of key Norfolk locations, with his linocut-based depictions of Brancaster, Holkham, Blakeney, Wells and Burnham Overy Staithe reproduced later in this book.

David Jones has produced a collection of Norwich architectural interpretations using a mixture of the linocut and woodcut processes. His experience as a museum curator and a continuing interest in history is evident in all of his work. David's prints often have prominent contemporary features but are still mindful of the past since the scenes recorded will soon become history. As well as a portfolio of familiar Norwich scenes, David has provided prints (linocut and woodcut) of Warham Camp, Binham Priory and Wymondham Abbey.

Rutland-based Fiona Carver has been creating things since she was a young girl – her artist grandmother would encourage her to draw elaborate chalk pictures on her kitchen floor. Having obtained a degree in Design & Applied Arts at Edinburgh College of Art, she began to experiment with printmaking and became fascinated by linocuts. She enjoys the different stages of sketching ideas, gouging and carving lino blocks – and, of course, inking and printing that she does with her antique cast-iron press. Her work is very much inspired by nature and her surroundings. The sea has always been an important part of her life, and she has spent a lot of time exploring the British coastline. Our collection here includes Holkham's long beach and sailing on the Norfolk Broads.

Another non-native drawn to Norfolk locations is Yorkshire-based James Green who has provided two linocuts of Cromer, the so-called 'gem of the Norfolk coast'. Both are two-colour prints using the multiple-plate method, and James is particularly fond of the area around Cromer's impressive pier.

Hertfordshire-based printmaker Kate Heiss combines multi-block linocuts with screen printing to create bold, colourful and highly individual artwork. She is inspired by her love of nature, especially the flowers and birds of local landscapes – including Norfolk. Prints

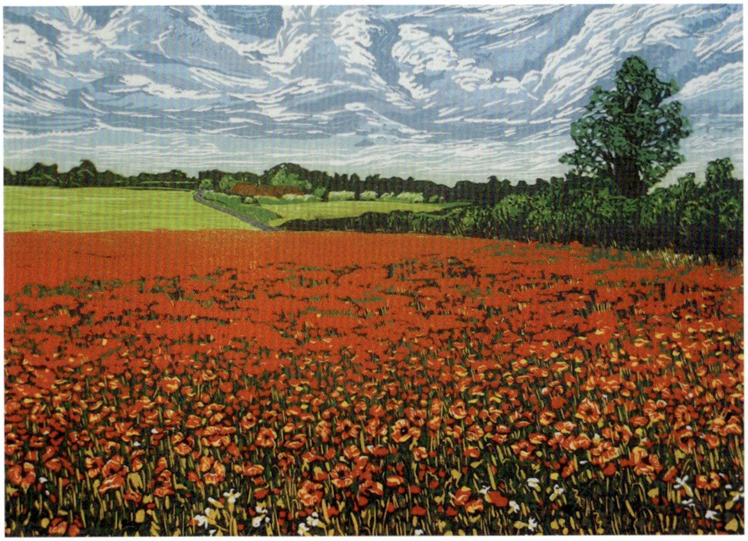

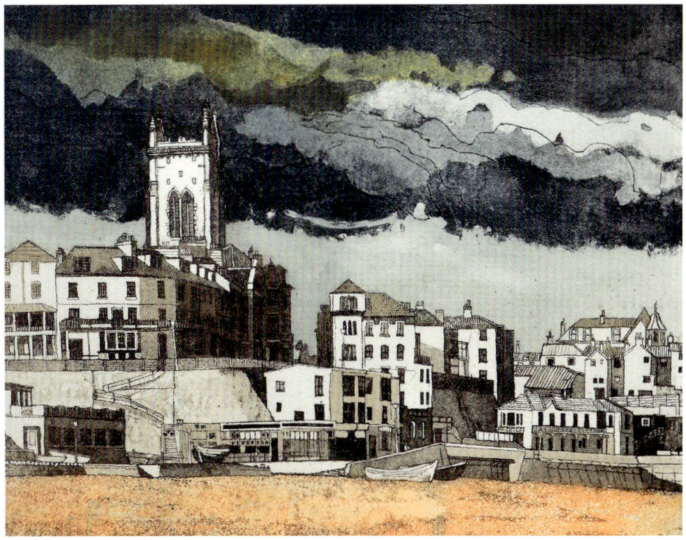

in this book feature Thornham, Brancaster, Holme and Holkham, influenced by her love of textiles, pattern and colour.

Several members of the Society of Wildlife Artists (SWLA) are either based in Norfolk or make it an essential stop during painting and printmaking trips. Some of them have provided prints for this book, including Max Angus, Thelma Sykes, Robert Greenhalf and Robert Gillmor MBE.

Max often combines landscape with birds and mammals, hence the appearance of Cley, Happisburgh, Stiffkey, Holme and Holt in this collection. Thelma has captured on paper and then lino a number of avian subjects along the north Norfolk coast. While the Norfolk Wildlife Trust reserve at Cley-next-the-Sea features as a location, she admits to feeling more at home farther west at Holme, Brancaster, Thornham and at the RSPB strongholds of Titchwell and Snettisham.

Cley resident Robert Gillmor has created a large number of wildlife-themed prints from his local patch. We have reproduced a few here, as well as his image of the spectacular cliffs at Hunstanton from a *New Naturalist* book jacket design.

Another wildlife-oriented artist Jeremy James has developed linocut printmaking as a sideline to his long-established clay modelling of hares, otters and numerous species of bird. We feature his black-and-white print of Broadland grebes and the brighter colours of his Sheringham divers in this book.

Landscape linocut specialist Rob Barnes is clearly inspired by his local environment, living close to the Norfolk/Suffolk border and creating large-format prints of locations in both counties. Inland scenes of farmland accompany more immediately identifiable coastal locations such as Blakeney.

Louise Stebbing admits to having become mesmerised by printmaking techniques since her art school years, and now uses a variety of techniques – most recently dominated by linocuts, such as her depiction above of "an amazing field of poppies" near Docking in the reduction linocut *Red Landscape*. She likes each print to evolve as she creates it, without working out too much detail in advance.

Annette Sykes adds carborundum and embossing to her prints such as storm-damaged beach huts at Cromer, while Janet Watson often uses her linocut images for the covers of hand-bound books.

Completing the lino line-up are evocative images of Cromer by London-based Gail Brodholt, Jenny Portlock's Swallowtail butterfly image, the striking Felbrigg Hall print from Norfolk-based Vanessa Burroughes, and Suffolk artist Moyra Byford's snapshot of sailing fun on the Broads.

Intaglio printmakers also abound in this collection, using sharp tools and chemicals to create often highly detailed and subtly coloured images. An intaglio print is made by cutting into a flat surface by hand or by using acid to burn into a metal plate in a process known as etching. Ink is rubbed into the hollows, and dampened paper is then placed over the inked plate and passed through a rotary press, forcing the paper into the inky hollows and leaving it embossed by the plate. The depth and density of the pits and hollows control the tone of the finished print.

Several variations involve inscribing directly into the surface of a copper, zinc, steel or even perspex plate with a sharp, pointed steel tool. With the drypoint technique, not only is a line inscribed into the surface but a burr is pushed up, similar to the furrow of a ploughed field. When the plate is inked and wiped, both the inscribed mark and the burr hold the ink, printing as a thick, velvety line.

Norwich-based Sarah Bays, Northants' Annette Sykes and Ross Loveday from Bury St Edmunds in Suffolk have all contributed

From left: Ross Loveday – Coastlines (drypoint); Richard Horne – Norfolkyeah (screenprint); Louise Stebbing – Red Landscape (reduction linocut); Chris Evans – Storm at Cromer (etching)

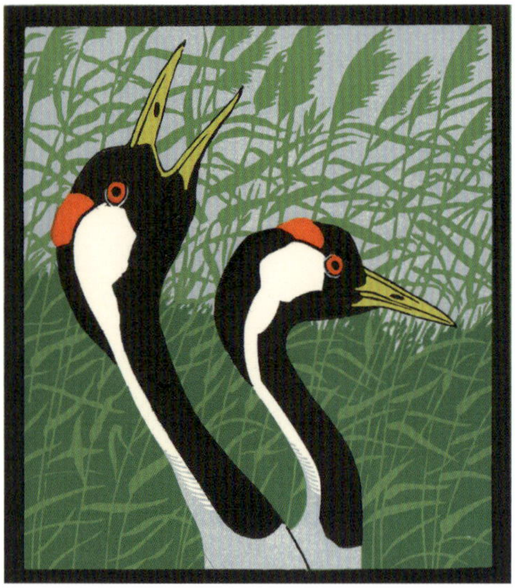

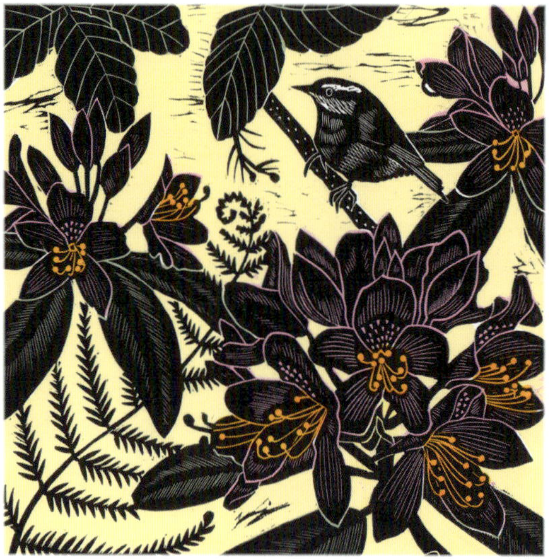

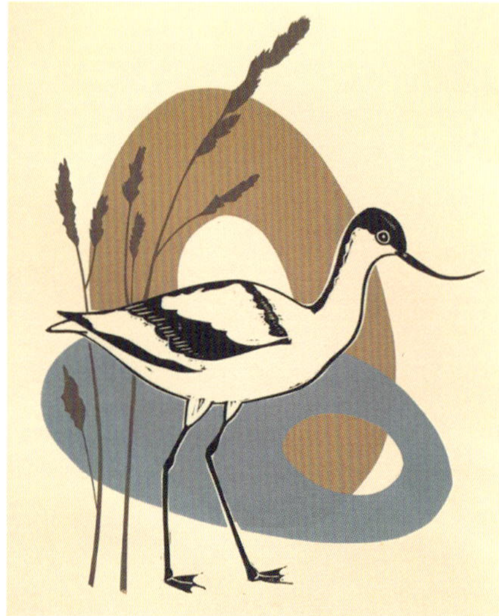

drypoints to this book. Sarah uses a small etching press on a tea trolley in the corner of her dining room. Sarah is also an exponent of the monotype print, of which more later.

Wells, Holkham, Sheringham, the Broads and the outskirts of Norwich provide subjects for Sarah's drypoint prints, while the more abstract north Norfolk-inspired compositions from Ross feature carborundum grits as a way of building tone, depth and texture.

Carborundum is also a feature of Annette's printmaking process, combined with drypoint as well as linocut. Her *Thornham Marshes* print is a drypoint on aluminium with carborundum for added texture.

Wildlife artist Robert Greenhalf works mainly in watercolour, oil, woodcut and drypoint. The drypoints are often printed in black and hand-coloured with watercolour. Robert's steel-plate etchings reproduced here date back to early north Norfolk visits from his home in Sussex.

With another intaglio printmaking variant, the mezzotint, a flat steel blade with a fine serrated edge (known as a rocker) leaves thousands of tiny indented holes spread evenly over the entire surface of a copper plate. This will print as a rich, velvety black, and an artist revelling in this technique is Norwich-based Martin Mitchell.

Working from dark to light, a tonal design is produced by scraping and polishing the surface of the indented plate with a scraper and burnisher. The deeper the indented areas remain, the darker they will print. Where the plate is polished smooth, no ink will adhere and so will appear as highlights. Martin's mezzotints of the Norwich locations Erpingham Gate and Bishops Bridge are reproduced here, plus newer works based on Whitlingham Broad and the Marriott's Way long-distance path.

In the case of etching, where our collection features Glynn Thomas, Chris Evans and Louise Davies, a flat metal plate is first coated with an acid-resistant ground consisting of beeswax, bitumen and resin. The plate is gently heated and the wax ground is melted on to the surface and spread evenly in a thin layer using a hard-wearing roller or dabber. The plate is allowed to cool, the wax hardens and it is then ready for the design to be scratched through the hardened coating, exposing the metal below. As an alternative, or complementary, technique, a bitumen-based stop-out varnish can be used to paint out the areas of the plate the artist does not wish the acid to affect. The whole plate is then immersed in the acid. This burns or etches only the exposed areas of the metal plate where the design has been drawn. The longer the plate remains in the acid, the deeper the lines are etched. The depth and density of the etched lines control the tones of the print.

London-based artist Louise uses two- or sometimes three-plate etchings along with a collagraph plate for some of her prints. Her work is very much based on landscape and her response to it, trying to evoke the seasons and atmosphere of a place. She uses hard- and soft-ground and works with zinc plates. The landscape outside Cromer, sandy beaches at Great Yarmouth, and north Norfolk's farmland appear in her prints.

In the case of Chris Evans, living on the Suffolk/Norfolk borders, his etchings are nowadays an exploration of landscape and architecture, with contributions including the mere at Diss, working boats at Gorleston and the railway junction at Reedham.

Glynn Thomas is perhaps East Anglia's best-known creator of intaglio landscape prints, using his etched copper plates to provide a highly individual interpretation of familiar places. He will devote weeks of work to capturing the tiny architectural detail of his locations, spinning around to provide a 360-degree view of places and the people who populate them.

Aquatint is used to etch large areas of even tone. When large areas are etched, the acid bites evenly over the open area, creating a dark line around the edge when the plate is

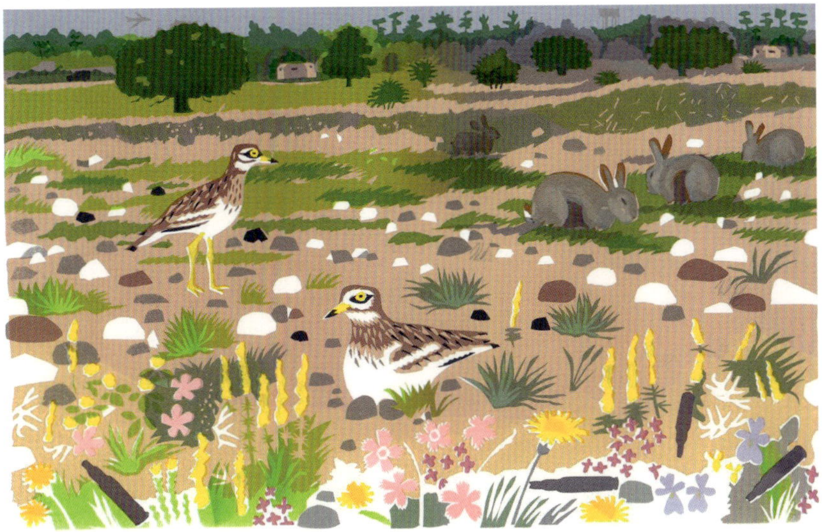

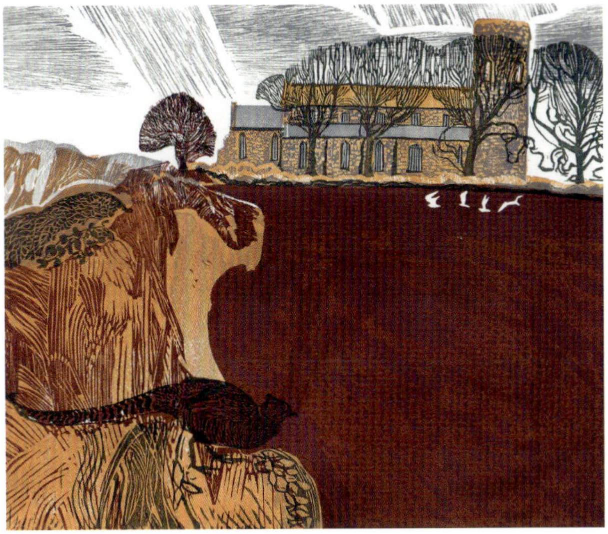

inked and wiped. To create the desired tone, a fine, even layer of acid-resistant powdered resin is dusted over the surface of the plate. When the plate is heated, the resin melts and fixes to the plate. Starting with the highlights, the design is painted out with acid-resistant stop-out varnish. The acid bites into the metal plate between the individual grains of resin. The tones are stopped-out and etched in stages; the longer in the acid the deeper the etch, therefore the darker the tones.

Norfolk artist Colin Bygrave's favourite subject for etching is landscape – he is fascinated by paths, lanes, tracks and occasionally roads. Trees are a major feature of many of Colin's prints. He likes the subtle colour range that comes with etching – which he views as a tonal rather than a colour medium. The images of Sheringham Park reproduced here are the perfect example of Colin's accomplished aquatint technique.

Trees and the Breckland landscape are captured in fellow Norfolk artist Laurie Rudling's classic copperplate aquatint etchings, which he describes as delicate tonal essays in light and atmosphere. His work is shown alongside that of another Norfolk etcher, TM Fairbank, whose work also celebrates the wooded Brecks landscape.

Jan Dingle, on the other hand, has more of a fascination with water – reflecting her location on the banks of the River Thurne in the Broads. All of her artworks are conceived as etchings. She likes to build up images of the landscape on the copper plates as she goes along, using the way the acid works on the metal to create her design nuances.

Although based in the Suffolk castle town of Framlingham, Winter Rose blends aquatint and photo-etching to create Norfolk images such as the Brancaster beach print reproduced in this volume. The photographic influence is always evident in Winter's work, as is a strong graphic element, and he is constantly exploring new ideas while perfecting the hybrid between photography and conventional printmaking techniques.

Two older forms of printmaking are featured in this book, namely wood engraving and woodcuts. Both use the same material, but are quite different. Wood engravings are worked into the end grain of a block of wood (usually box or fruit wood), in which very fine, detailed work can be engraved. Woodcuts are worked into the side grain or plank of the wood, with the cutting generally following the direction of the grain. The grain itself, if sufficiently pronounced, can be incorporated into the design.

Robert Greenhalf and Thelma Sykes are woodcut practitioners, among their other printmaking skills, and Cambridgeshire-based Valerie Sims has contributed several north Norfolk-themed woodcut prints that combine landscape and wildlife. Wood engravings are contributed by Andy English (also from Cambridgeshire), Suffolk's Anthony Dunigan and Norfolk's Neil Bousfield.

Andy's vintage view of a trip to the north Norfolk coast graces page 3, and his beautifully detailed work also encompasses Burnham Overy Staithe, Blakeney and King's Lynn. Anthony works on a much bigger scale, sometimes using engraver's plastic in place of wood, and packs plenty of detail into his prints of churches, mills, statues and other architectural subjects. Neil Bousfield has been working on a new series of engravings capturing the mystery of the lesser-known Norfolk Broads. Sadly, these hadn't been completed in time for inclusion here, but a sequence of Walcott studies discusses the threat of rising sea levels and the fragility of the north-east coast of Norfolk.

The remaining images reproduced in *Norfolk Gems* are screen prints (sometimes known as serigraphs), monoprints (or monotypes) and

From left: *Robert Gillmor – Clarion Crane (linocut); Kate Heiss – Nuthatch at Sandringham (linocut); Kate Heiss – Avocet at Thornham (linocut); Carry Akroyd – Secured Ground (serigraph); Robert Greenhalf – Norfolk Christmas 1974 (etching)*

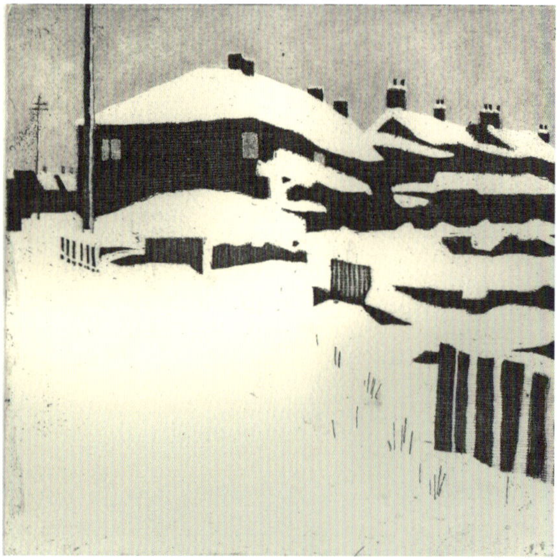

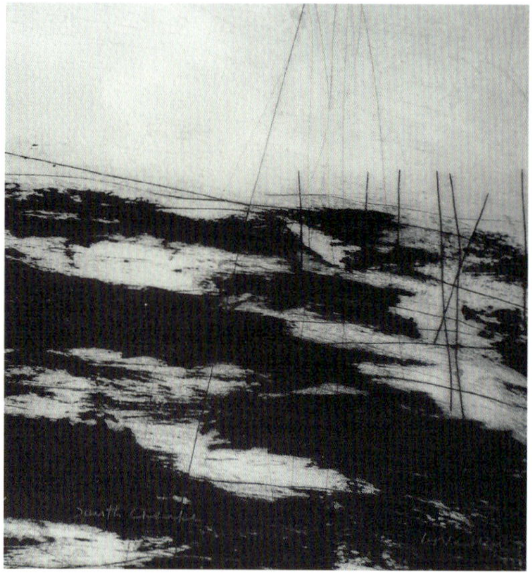

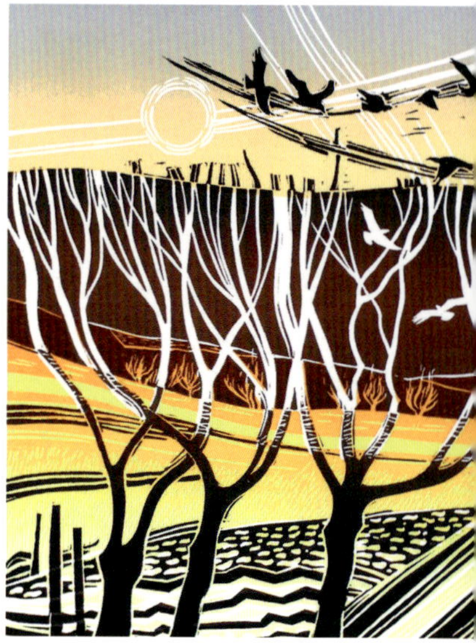

collagraphs. To produce a screen print, a fine woven mesh (originally silk, but today made from synthetic materials) is stretched tightly over a frame. Stencils are used to mask out the areas of the screen that are not to be printed. A sheet of paper is laid under the screen, then a flat rubber blade called a squeegee is drawn over it, forcing ink through the open areas not masked by the stencils.

The complete edition is printed in the first colour before proceeding to the second stencil, and printing, ensuring that the colours fit one upon another. This process is continued until the image is complete. Additional colours can be achieved by using transparent inks and overprinting one colour with another, thereby producing a third colour. The screen print is characterised by its uniform layer of colour and is an ideal medium for a design with large areas of flat colour.

Carry Akroyd, a Northamptonshire artist with a fondness for the Fens and East Anglia, provides large colourful serigraphs with landscape and wildlife themes, as well as using other printmaking methods such as linocuts. Her Norfolk portfolio of serigraphs covers the endangered Stone Curlews of Breckland, the contrast between locally nesting Little Terns and offshore wind turbines in the Brancaster/Burnham area, and her interpretation of the landscape around Hickling Broad.

Norfolk artist Leanda Jaine Hughes is well represented on these pages thanks to her large and growing portfolio of embossed screenprint-based images that provide an alphabetical tour of Norwich and beyond. Fellow Norwich Print Fair member Richard Horne is the creator of screenprints of 'Revolutionary Norwich', producing highly imaginative and colourful works; while another Norfolk printmaker Vanessa Burroughes has contributed collaged screen prints of the Grade II English Heritage registered Plantation Garden in Norwich and beach huts at Wells.

A collagraph is a print made from a collaged or textured board. There are two basic approaches to producing a collagraph plate (which is made from cardboard). The first is to work in relief, applying a variety of materials on to the surface of the card. These can include fabric, string, sandpaper, tissue and PVA glue. The second approach is an intaglio method. This is achieved by scoring lines into the surface and cutting away layers of card with a scalpel, thereby creating recesses that will hold ink. The finished plate can be sealed with varnish to form a tough, non-absorbent surface prior to prints being taken. The edition size is usually smaller due to the limited life of the cardboard plate.

Cley Windmill is one of the great north Norfolk landmarks, and is depicted by several artists in various forms in this collection. Without doubt, one of the more striking interpretations is by Norfolk artist Amelia Bowman, whose colourful collagraphs can be found throughout the book. Cley has become one of her favourite collagraph plates, with the surface area of the mill proving big enough to showcase her pattern designs to great effect. Cromer, Wells, Blakeney and Norwich also get the Bowman treatment.

Mandy Walden is Suffolk-based and boasts a large portfolio of strong Suffolk images. However, she occasionally flirts with Norfolk, and her collagraph of hares at Elm Hill in Norwich is a particularly memorable image.

Sally Hirst is another artist with a bold approach to familiar sights, often adding carborundum to her collagraph prints for extra texture. Her work has always reflected where she lives, the places she visits and the journeys she has undertaken. Her prints are inspired by the ravages of time and tide on man-made structures such as piers, bridges, abandoned gas towers, old fishing

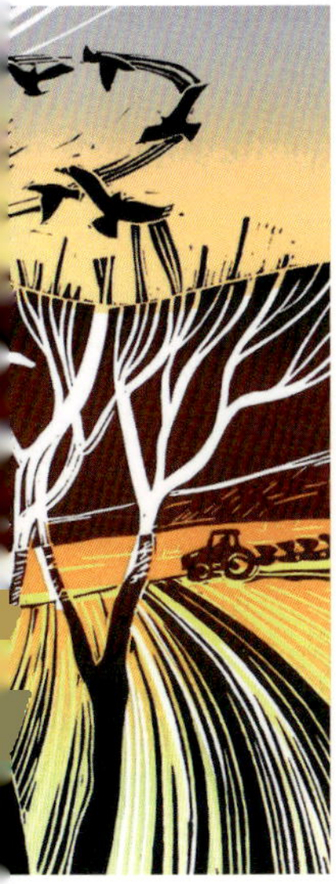
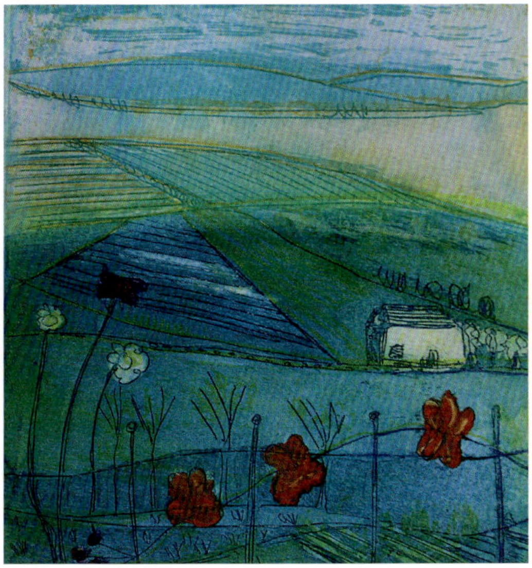
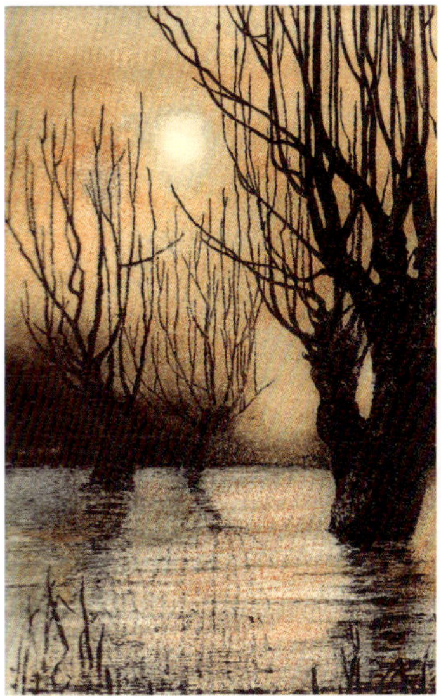
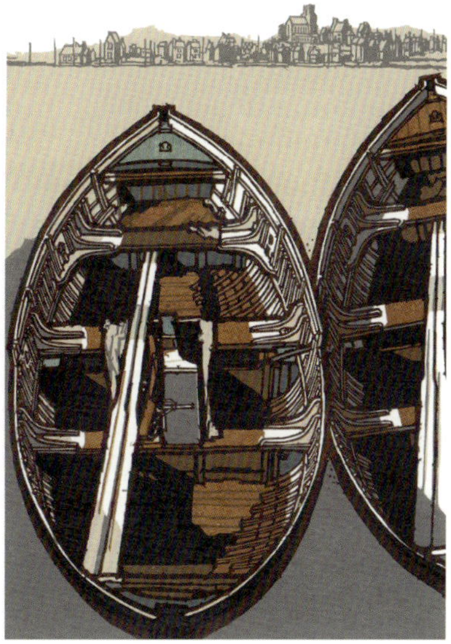

huts and boats. Each print incorporates a range of techniques, including collagraphy, carborundum and relief printing. In addition, she often includes rust by a process of oxidising iron filings.

Moving on to monoprints/monotypes, these are actually slight different, although some see the terms as interchangeable. Both are one-off print techniques in which an image, produced on a metal plate, sheet of glass or any other flat surface, is transferred to paper. The approaches are many, and the only limitations are the ingenuity and imagination of the artist. There are, however, two basic methods of working, using the subtractive and additive techniques.

In the subtractive approach, a metal plate or sheet of glass is inked up by means of a roller, and the image is produced by selectively wiping away the ink with rags, brushes, scrapers, etc. Paper is laid directly over the plate (at this stage a drawing can be worked on to the back of the paper lying on the inked plate). The print can be taken by either running it through a press or by hand-rubbing/burnishing the back of the sheet of paper.

In the additive approach, ink, paint or water-based media can be painted directly on to the plate, with the printing process the same as for the subtractive approach.

These basic methods can be used in combination with other print techniques, such as the use of stencils and masks; and opaque or transparent colours with over-printing.

Norwich's Sarah Bays is increasingly drawn to the painterly effects of monotype printmaking. Her portfolio of drypoints is therefore being enhanced and expanded by the 'new' method that encourages her to work in a slightly more abstract way, taking a remembered landscape as a starting point and adapting the image as she progresses.

Clare Johnson lives and works on the North Quay of Lowestoft dock, surrounded by cranes, forklifts and lorries, with views of industrial landscape to inspire her printmaking. Her subjects range from water towers and grain silos to the architecture of the University of East Anglia.

Influenced by vintage, hand-tinted postcards, Clare seeks to create something new and different. Photographs are transformed into screened black-and-white (dotty) images, tinted with a number of colour monotypes. Each print is uniquely coloured, with only the subject repeated.

This book is both a journey through Norfolk and a voyage of discovery in the world of printmaking. As with our earlier multi-artist printmaking titles, such as *The Printmaker's Cat*, *The Artful Hare*, *Fine Print*, *The Elegant Fowl* and *The Little Chicken Book*, this volume provides an opportunity to compare and contrast many different techniques and visual interpretations.

Given Norfolk's size, history and varying landscape, the county represents a great challenge for artists to avoid the obvious and to identify innovative ways of capturing its environment, buildings and wildlife.

Hopefully, *Norfolk Gems* will not only encourage the reader to explore the county, but also to examine more closely the work of the gifted individuals who have contributed to these pages.

Our thanks go to all of the artists who were prepared to loan us work for inclusion in this book, and for their insights into printmaking processes and the locations they have chosen as subjects.

From left: Colin Bygrave – Roofs (etching); Ross Loveday – South Creake (drypoint); Rob Barnes – Rooks Gathering (linocut); Louise Davies – Passing Clouds (etching); TM Fairbank – Misty Morning (etching); HJ Jackson – North Norfolk Beach (linocut)

A printmaking odyssey through Norfolk

Sweet was the walk along the narrow lane
At noon, the bank and hedge-rows all the way
Shagged with wild pale green tufts of fragrant hay,
Caught by the hawthorns from the loaded wain,
Which Age with many a slow stoop strove to gain...

William Wordsworth c.1790

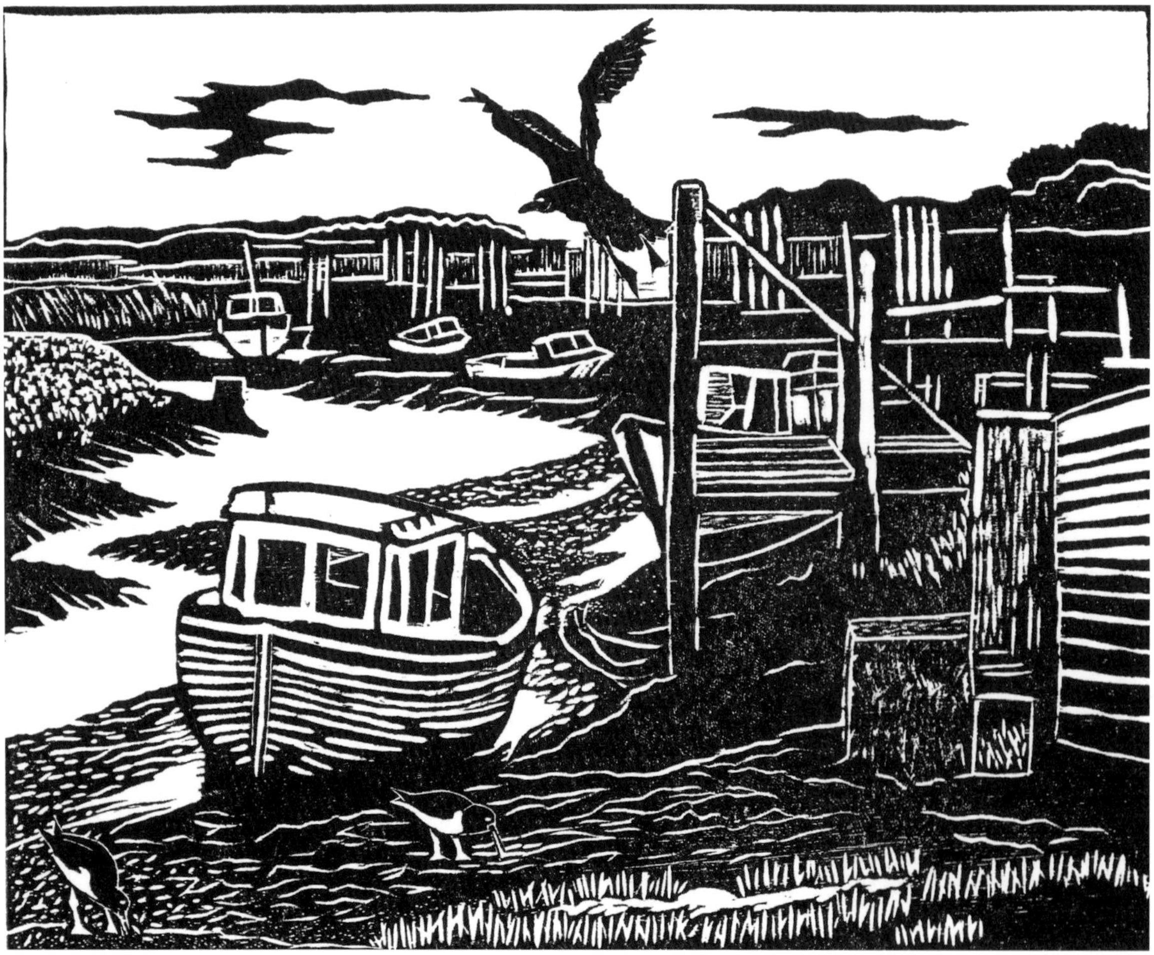

Valerie Sims – Oystercatchers (Thornham), woodcut

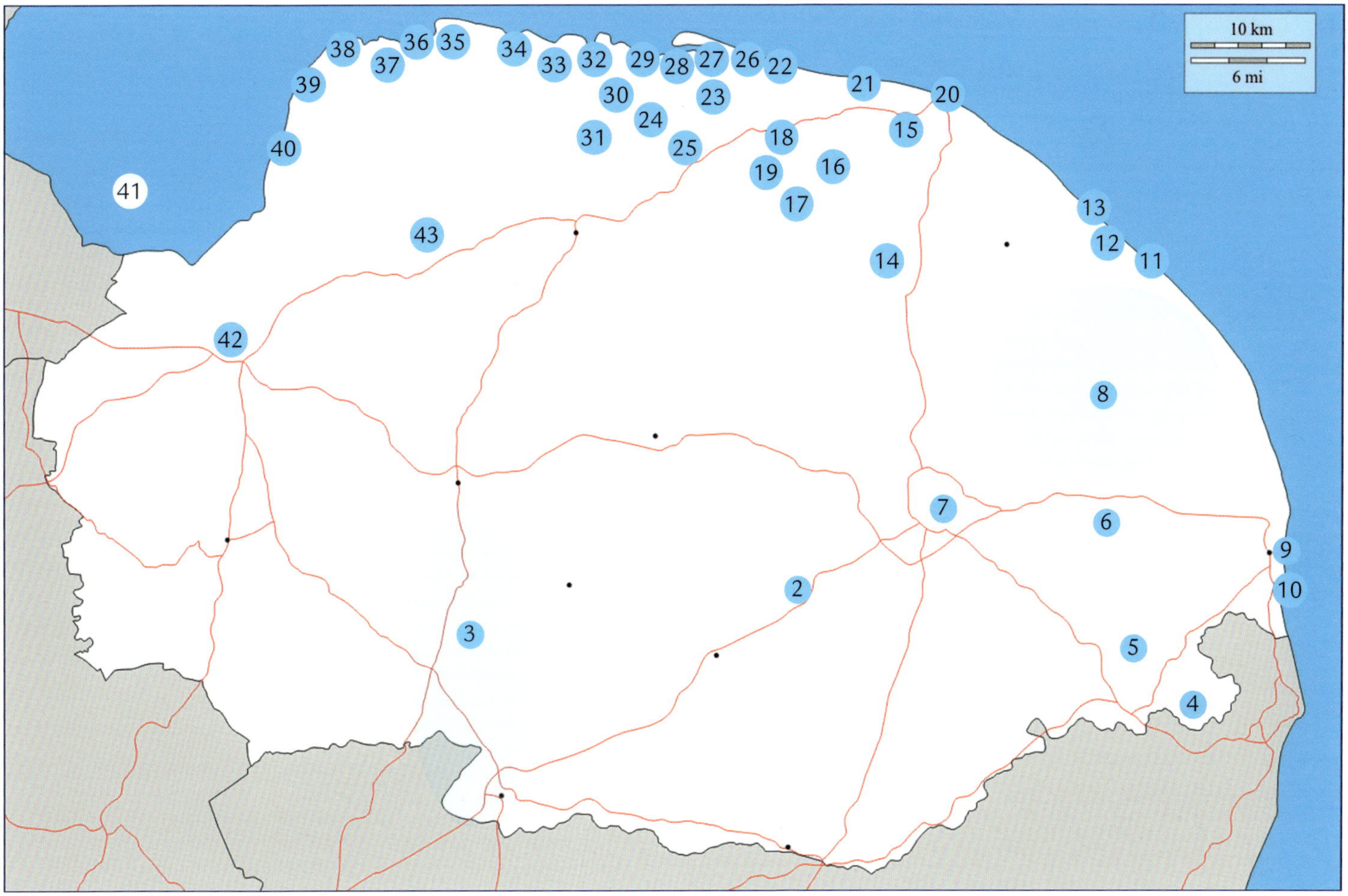

10 km
6 mi

Baconsthorpe Castle

This linocut print, completed just in time for inclusion in the book, is Norwich-based Vanessa Lubach's celebration of an attractive 15th-century ruin located not far from the Georgian town of Holt in north Norfolk.

Baconsthorpe Castle in Winter captures the season as well as the charm of the moated and fortified manor house built by prominent Norfolk family the Heydons.

Sir John Heydon probably built the inner gatehouse during the Wars of the Roses, and his son Sir Henry later completed the property. Over 200 years, successive generations of Heydons built, enlarged and finally abandoned the castle – which, in more peaceful times, housed a textile factory. The late addition of the turreted Elizabethan outer gateway was inhabited until 1920.

This 31cm x 41cm multi-block linocut was printed using Vanessa's Harry Rochat Albion press as part of an edition of 100.

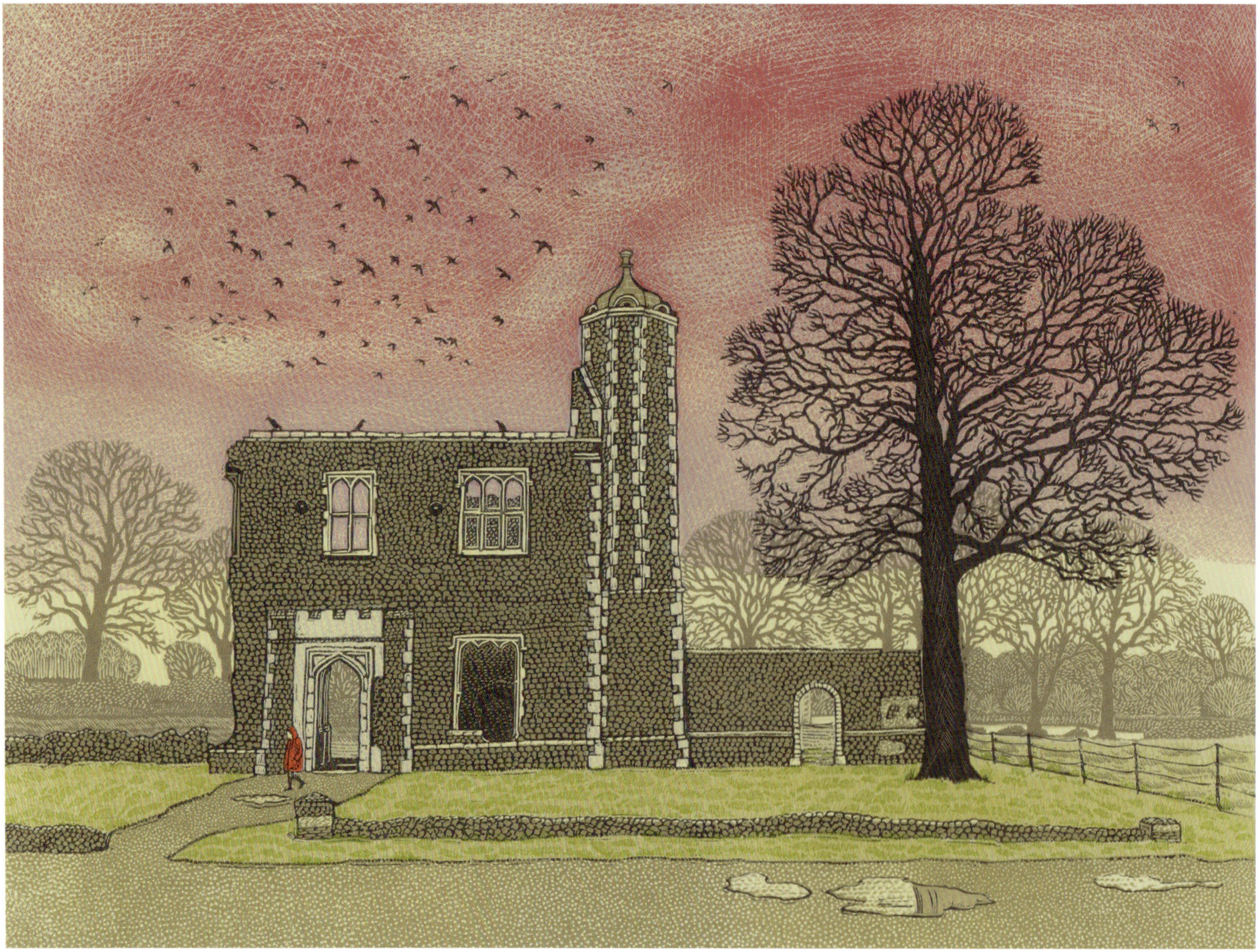

Bale Church

Once dwarfed by the 500-year-old Bale oak, recorded as having been of 36 feet in circumference before it was removed for safety reasons in 1860, All Saints Church in Bale is both compact and pretty. It is now surrounded by imported evergreen holm oaks that aren't in any way related to the original tree, but rumour has it that plenty of local furniture was made from the reclaimed wood of their predecessor.

Bale is a village within the civil parish of Gunthorpe, located on the north side of the A148 road some 23km west of Cromer and 14.5km east of Fakenham.

The church at Bale is thought to have been completed on the eve of the Black Death in the middle of the 14th century – although its oldest part, the chancel, dates back to around 1300. The nave, transept chapel and tower were either built or rebuilt some time before 1400.

All Saints was restored in 1862 by John Frederick Preedy, who contributed the roof cladding, stalls, pews and pulpit. Preedy did a great deal of work in this area, including a number of stained-glass windows in the neighbouring parish of Gunthorpe – which had been united with Bale.

There is a stunning collection of Norwich School stained glass in one of the south nave windows. This features all or part of five separate Annunciation scenes.

Colin Bygrave's aquatint etching *Bale Church* measures 39cm x 27cm. It is a great example of an intaglio printmaking method that is used to etch large areas of even tone by dusting a fine layer of powdered resin over the surface of the plate before heating.

The artist lives in Briston, near Holt in north Norfolk, and formerly taught art and design in Leicester. His garden studio plays host to a beautiful Hunter Penrose No 8 press that has been used to produce hundreds of his subtle and complex aquatints.

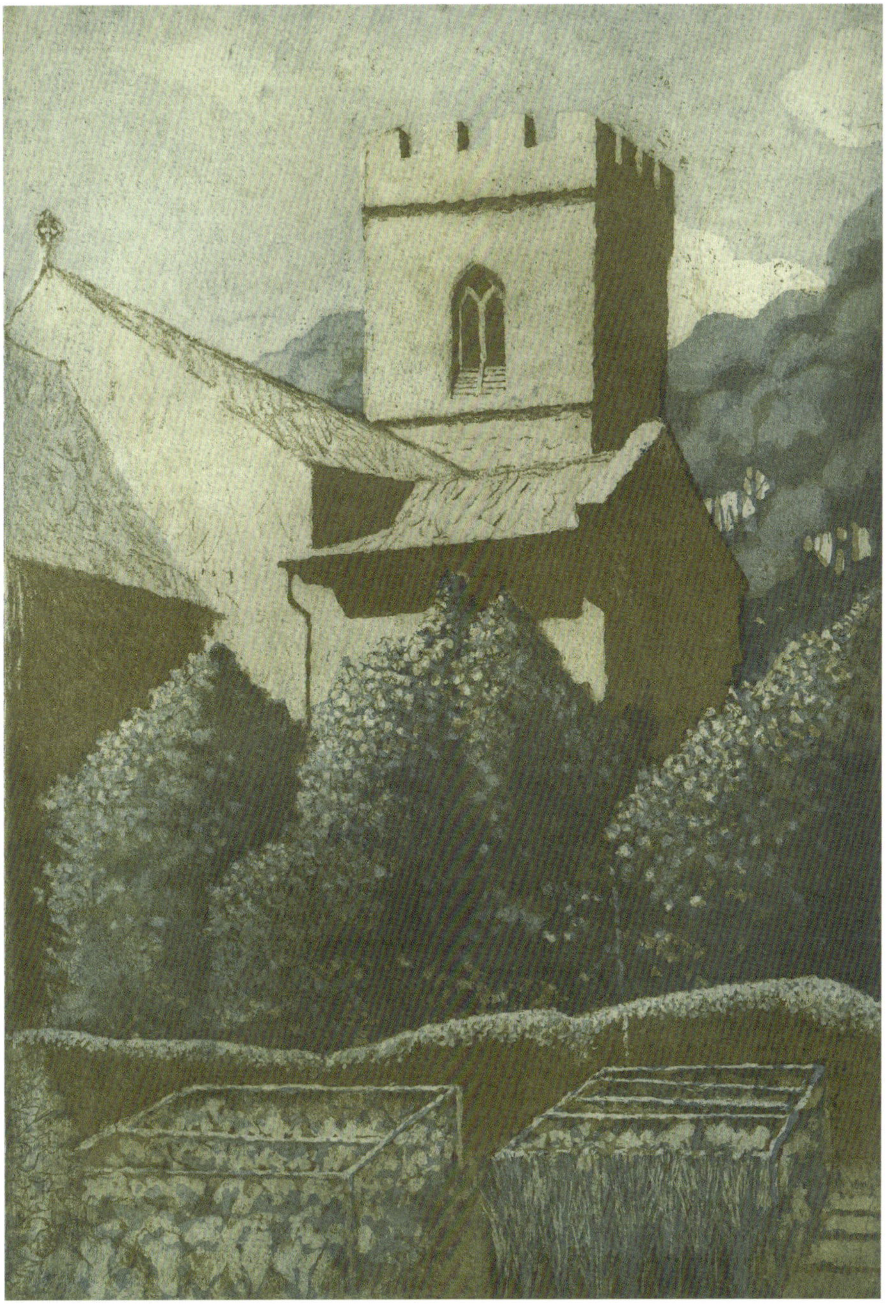

Binham Priory

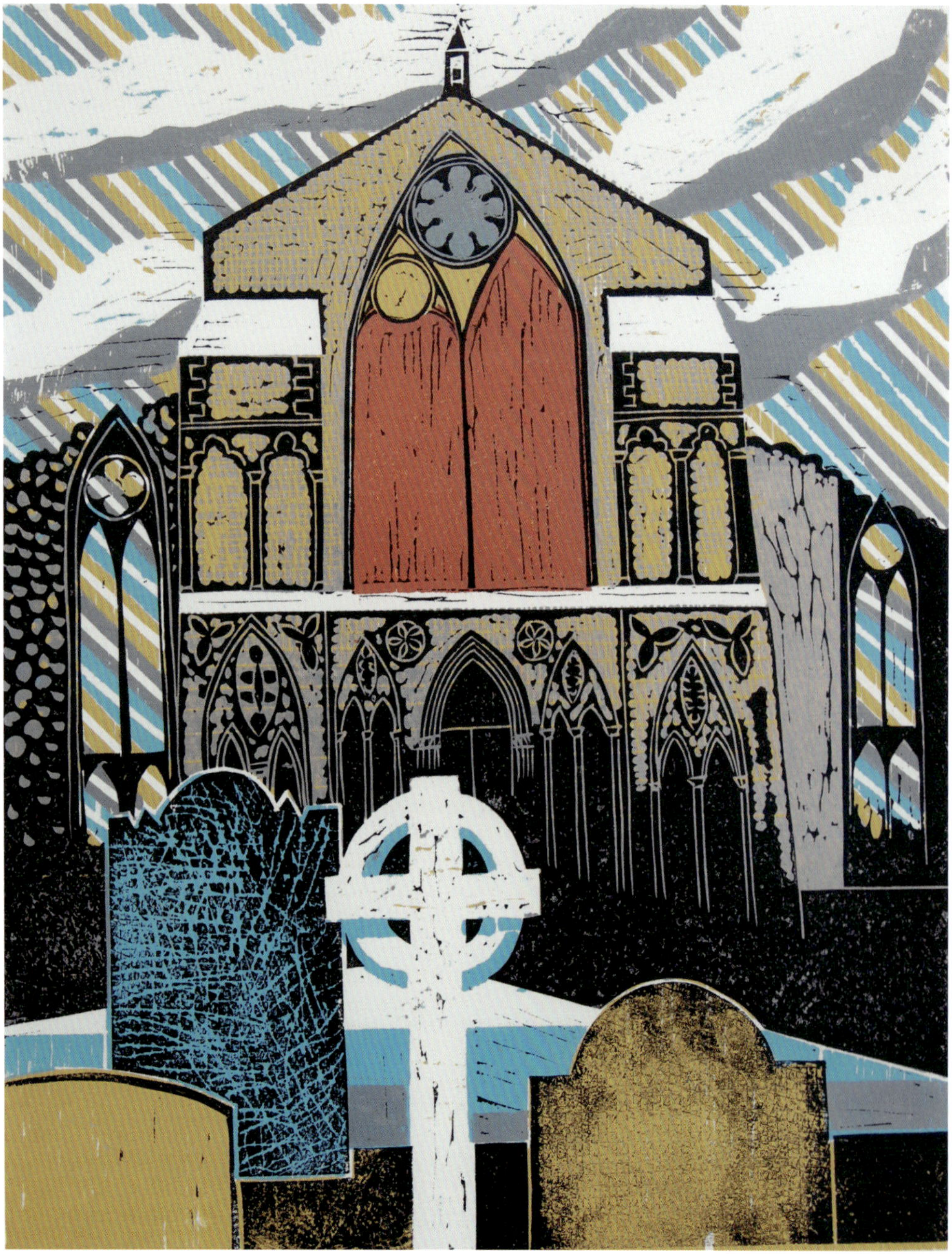

While Norfolk artist David Jones is perhaps better known for his large portfolio of Norwich locations and his depiction of the city's many bridges, his interest in architecture extends beyond the Norwich boundaries.

In this instance, he travelled close to the north Norfolk coast, where Binham Priory is located just inland from Stiffkey and east of Walsingham.

The Priory Church of St Mary and the Holy Cross is so named because the priory was dedicated to St Mary, and the church to the Holy Cross. What remains is the nave of the priory church that has always been used as the village church. It is built of local flint and Barnack limestone, brought from Northamptonshire by river and sea in barges, and up the river Stiffkey.

The west front is not the earliest part of the priory but is seen first and is of great architectural interest. According to Matthew Paris, the 13th-century monk and chronicler, this facade was built between 1226 and 1244 when Richard de Parco was prior. The facade is divided into three parts, the centre part containing the large west window. The latter could be the earliest example of bar tracery in England, and must have been magnificent before it fell into disrepair and was bricked up in 1809.

David's print *Binham Priory* is, like a number of his colourful prints, a mixture of linocut and woodcut. David's love of history is clear from his art. He was once a museum curator in Salford, Kidderminster and Norwich, specialising not in art but in social history.

Bircham Mill

This 13cm diameter etching from 2003 of *Bircham Mill* by Cambridge-born but Suffolk-based Glynn Thomas is a good representation of his 360-degree approach to many of his subjects. Glynn aims to capture the surrounding buildings, scenery and people in one two-dimensional image, and this circular 'fisheye' device is one of several used by the artist.

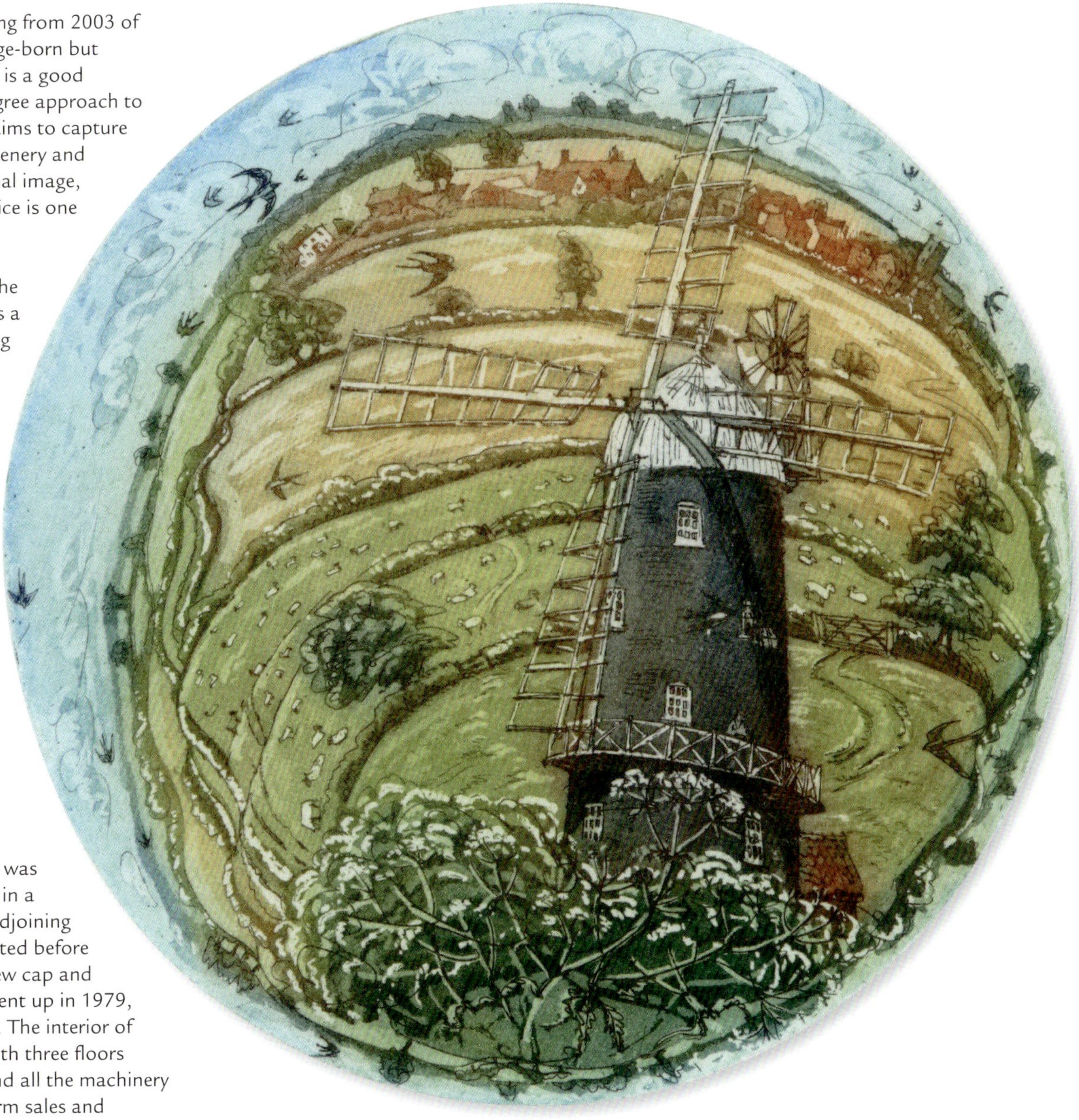

Towering over north-west Norfolk's undulating fields, the landmark at Great Bircham is a fine specimen of a functioning corn mill, looking much the same today as it did a century ago. Open to the public, it affords panoramic views over the countryside near the royal estate of Sandringham, as well as grinding the grain to produce flour for the on-site bakery and tearoom.

Visitors can climb the five floors up to the fan stage and, on windy days, watch the sails and the milling machinery in action.

The mill was built in 1846 and worked until the 1920s when the sails were removed and the tower abandoned. It was bought by the current owner in a very dilapidated state. Two adjoining cottages were initially renovated before it was decided to put on a new cap and begin restoration. The cap went up in 1979, followed by the sails in 1981. The interior of the mill was also restored, with three floors being completely replaced and all the machinery and stones gathered from farm sales and other derelict mills.

Blakeney

This small town on the North Norfolk coast was once an important commercial seaport, like neighbouring Cley-next-the-Sea, and was still active until the early 20th century. Areas of the village date back to the 14th century, such as the old Guildhall and its undercroft. Today the harbour is silted up, allowing only small boats to navigate their way past Blakeney Point into the North Sea.

Just two narrow streets provide entry to and exit from Blakeney Quay, both clogged with tourist traffic throughout the summer as visitors flock to view the picturesque estuary or stay at the Blakeney Hotel (seen in the linocut print below). Those keen to see the seals at Blakeney Point are better off heading for nearby Morston Quay, which provides regular open boat trips.

Accessible from either Blakeney or Morston, the three-mile spit of shingle and sand at Blakeney Point accommodates terns and seals in large numbers. Most people simply watch the seals from the comfort of their boat, while the seals return the compliment. You can, however, land and take a walk by the Old Lifeboat House

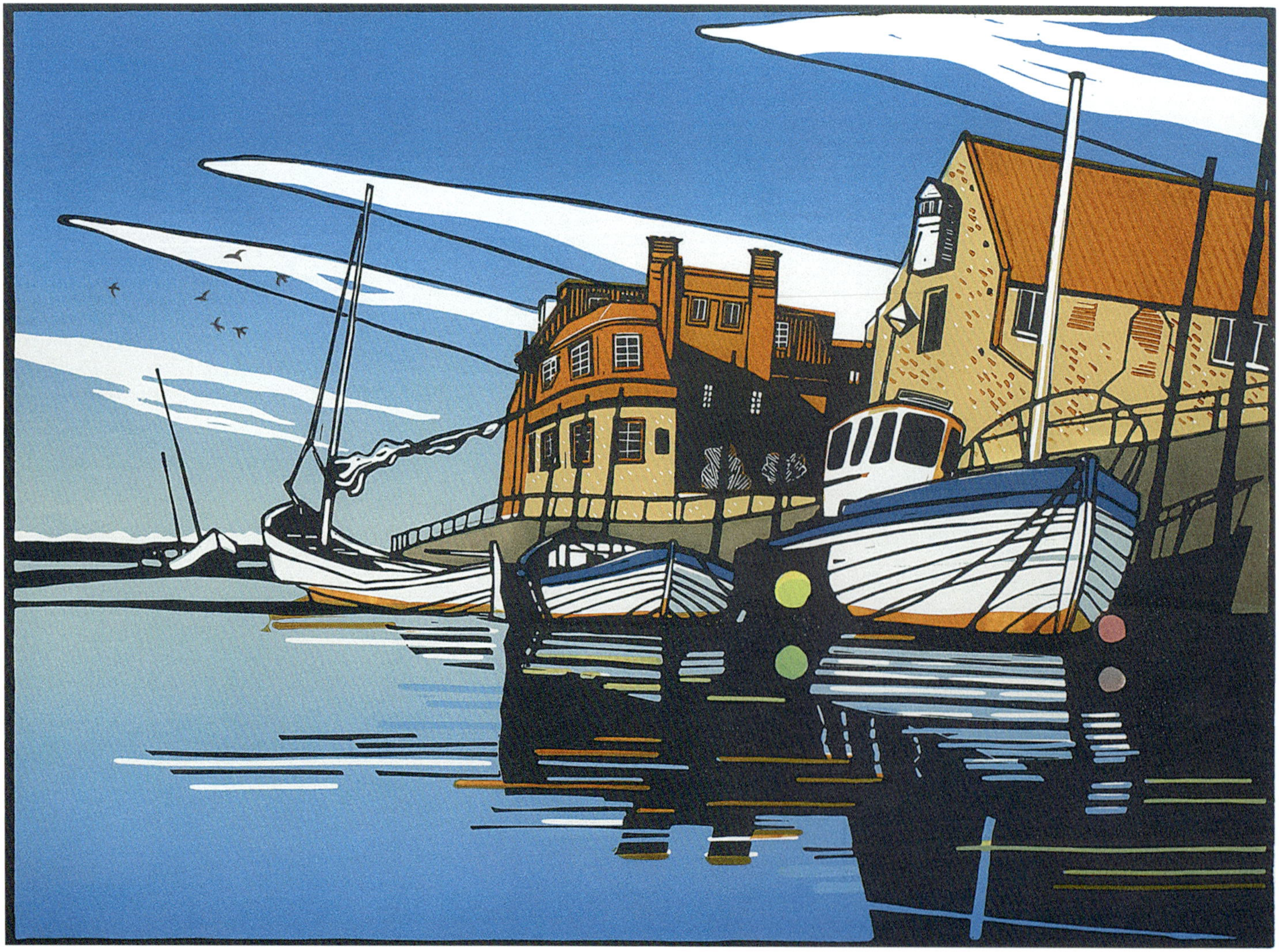

(see images on pages 22 and 24), now used by wardens and as an information centre.

Blakeney Point is one of the best places in the UK to watch and study seals. The colony is made up of Common and Grey seals, and numbers around 500. The Common seals have their young between June and August; the Grey seals between November and January. The seals usually bask on the sandbanks at the far end of the spit. During the summer months, Common, Sandwich, Little and Arctic Terns can also usually be seen.

The images left and below are by Colin Moore and Rob Barnes, respectively. Colin was born in Scotland where he studied architecture in Glasgow, but has worked mainly as a painter and printmaker since 2004. He currently lives in Dorset but has drifted as far as the north Norfolk coast to produce the large (59.5cm wide sheet size) 2015 3-block print *Blakeney Harbour* in an edition of 100.

"One of the challenges for the painter of coastal subjects is to find a view that shows the land, the sea and the relationship between

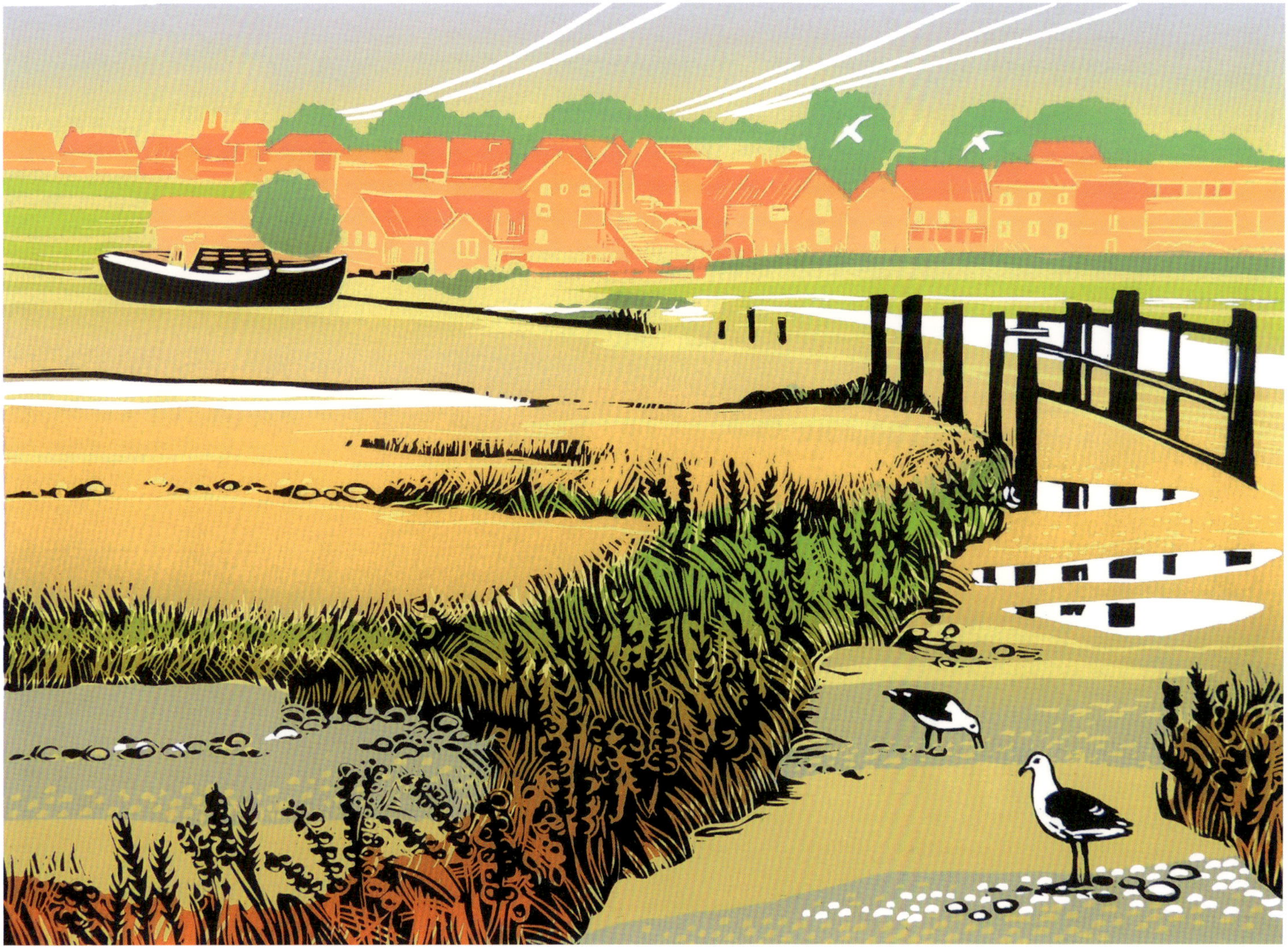

them. With its curving creek and charming buildings near the water's edge, Blakeney makes it easy," says Colin.

Norfolk-based Rob Barnes has entitled his linocut print *Back to the Quay* (44.5cm x 33cm). It looks back towards the town from the water's edge and a path that weaves through the saltmarsh and eventually out to the seals at Blakeney Point.

On the opposite page, far right, is *Blakeney II* (6cm x 14cm) by Glynn Thomas. Popular demand resulted in a revised etching of Glynn's view from the church at the very top of the town down to the harbour. In 2009, when the original print was conceived, Glynn had considered the view 'down' Blakeney from the church, but a brisk walk around to the saltmarsh opposite the hotel provided him with a much more effective perspective looking 'up' the town, giving the viewer a feel for the claustrophobic nature of the narrow thoroughfare from estuary to the main Cromer-to-Wells road.

Below is another of Glynn's prints, *Blakeney Point*, created in 2009 and measuring 8cm x 22cm. A newer etching, *Blakeney Harbour*, appears on the facing page, left.

Cambridgeshire woodcut specialist Valerie Sims provides the two images at the bottom of this page. *Saltmarsh* (bottom left) is from 2016 (18cm x 22.5cm) and *Staithe* (bottom right)

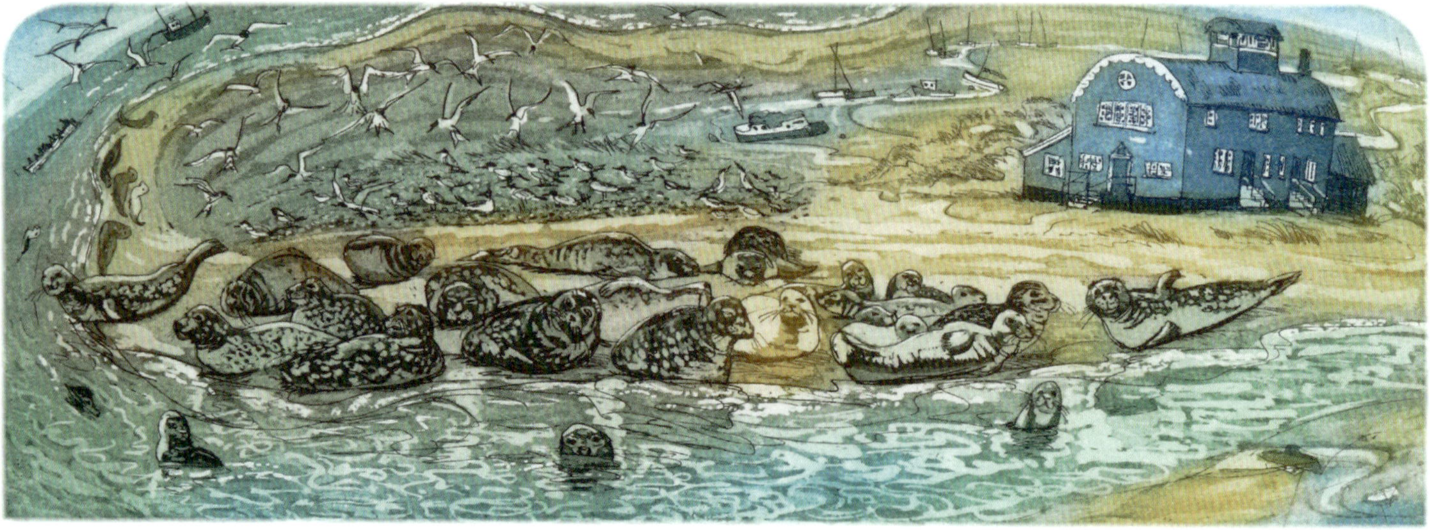

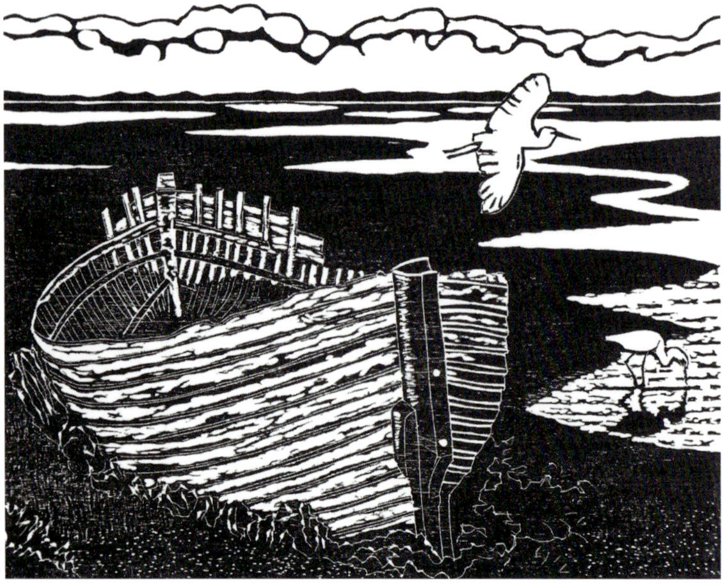

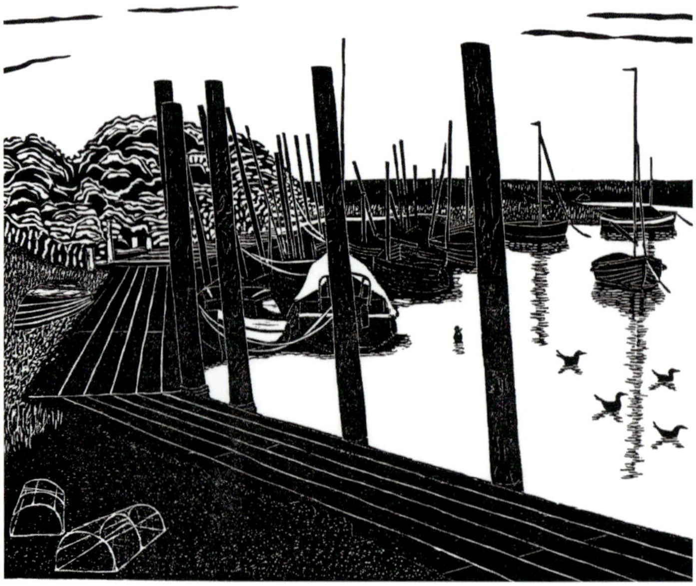

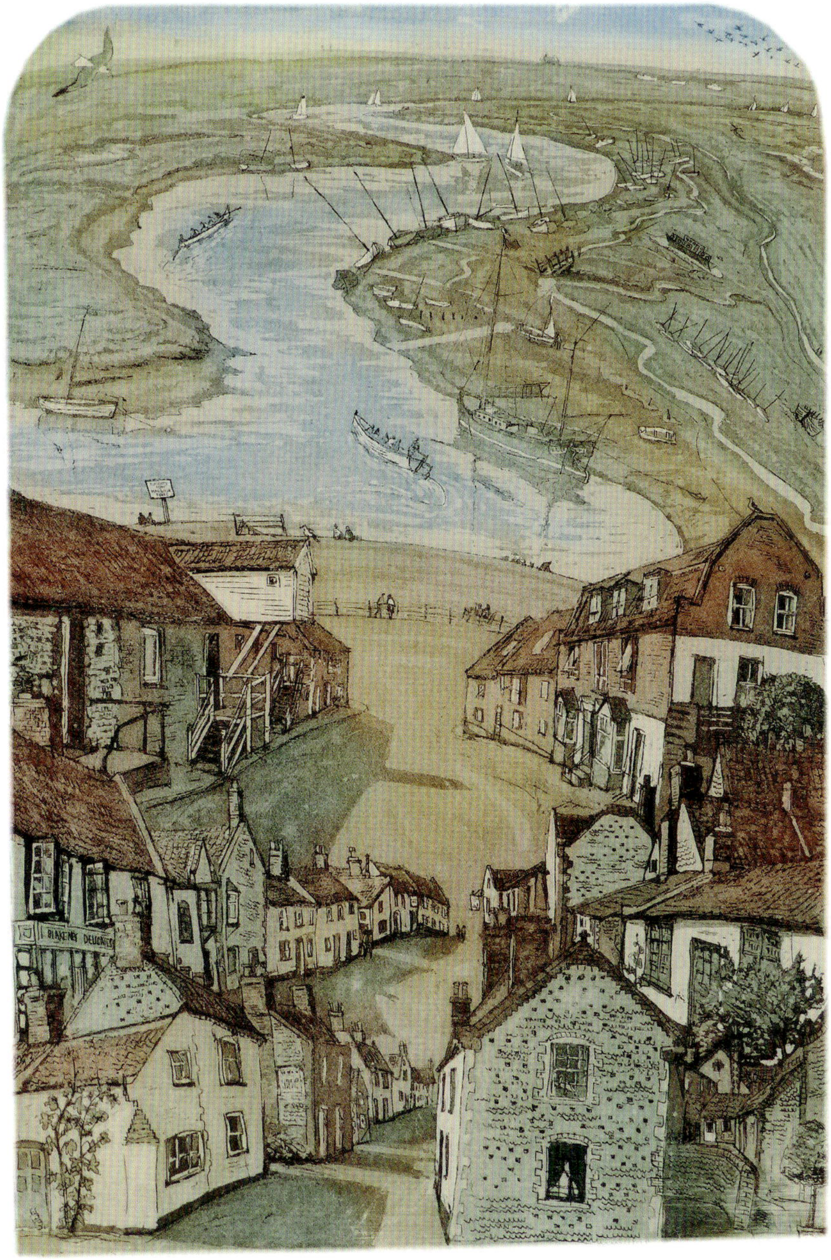

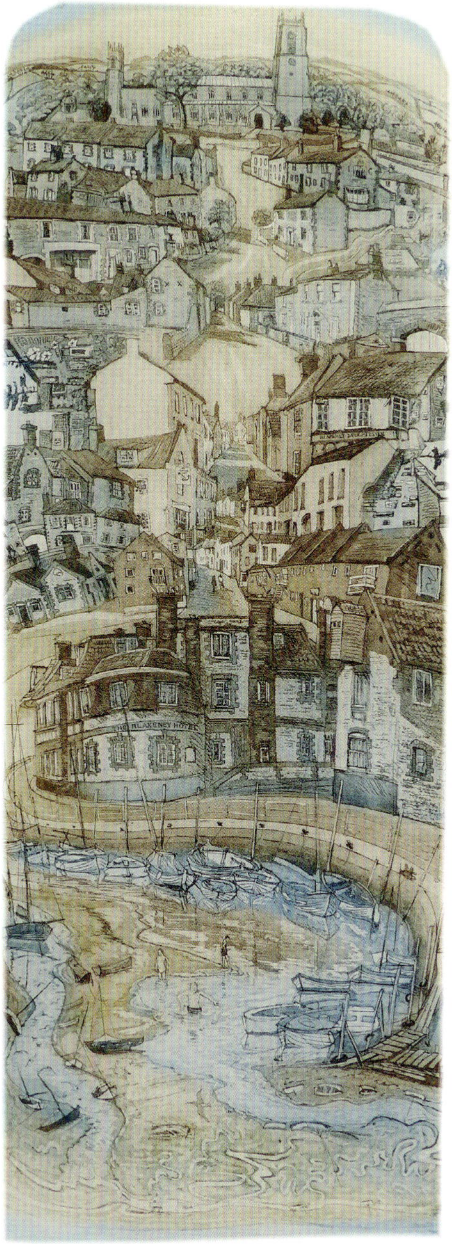

is from 2017 (26cm x 32cm). They are reproduced with *Jetty* (page 24, top right), a 2012 woodcut measuring 26cm x 32cm. All are editions of 20 prints.

Cambridgeshire wood engraver Andy English's 8cm x 10cm image of seals at Blakeney Point appears on page 24, while Norfolk-based Amelia Bowman is responsible for the colourful collagraph *Blakeney Lifeboat Station (Ixia)* on the same page. Wildlife artist Robert Greenhalf provided *Norfolk Reedmarsh*, a 1980 steel-plate etching (26cm x 29cm) of an autumn view looking west from the east bank at Cley towards Blakeney with the church in the background, which appears on page 25.

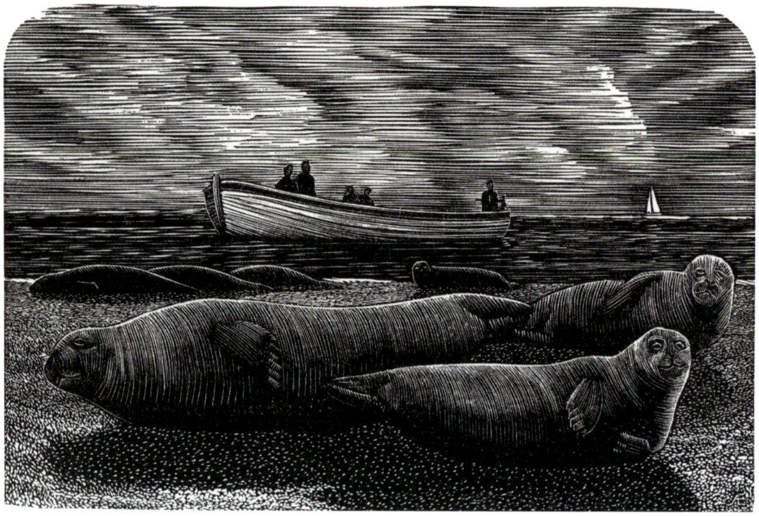

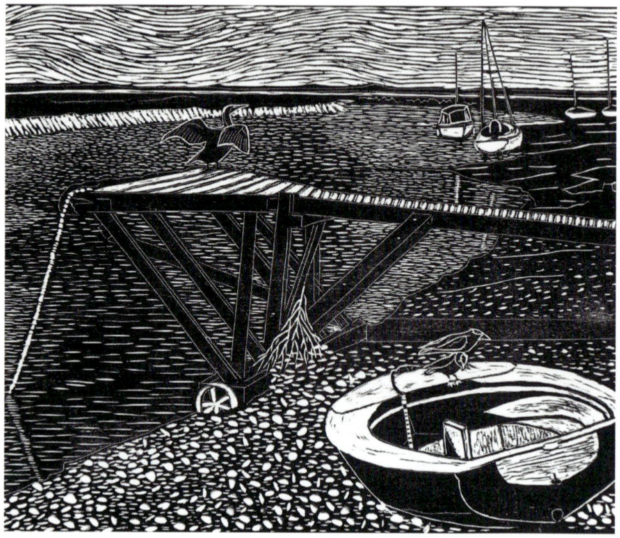

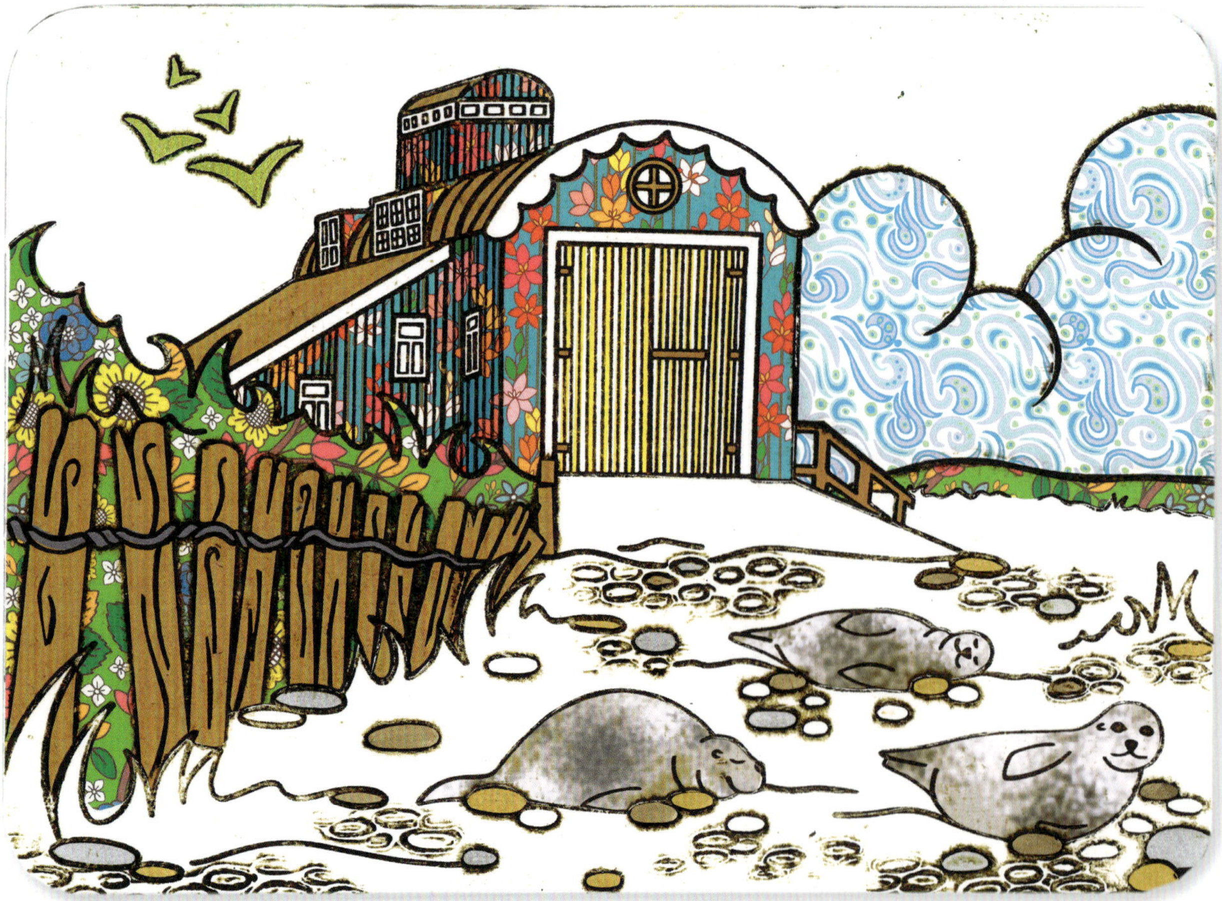

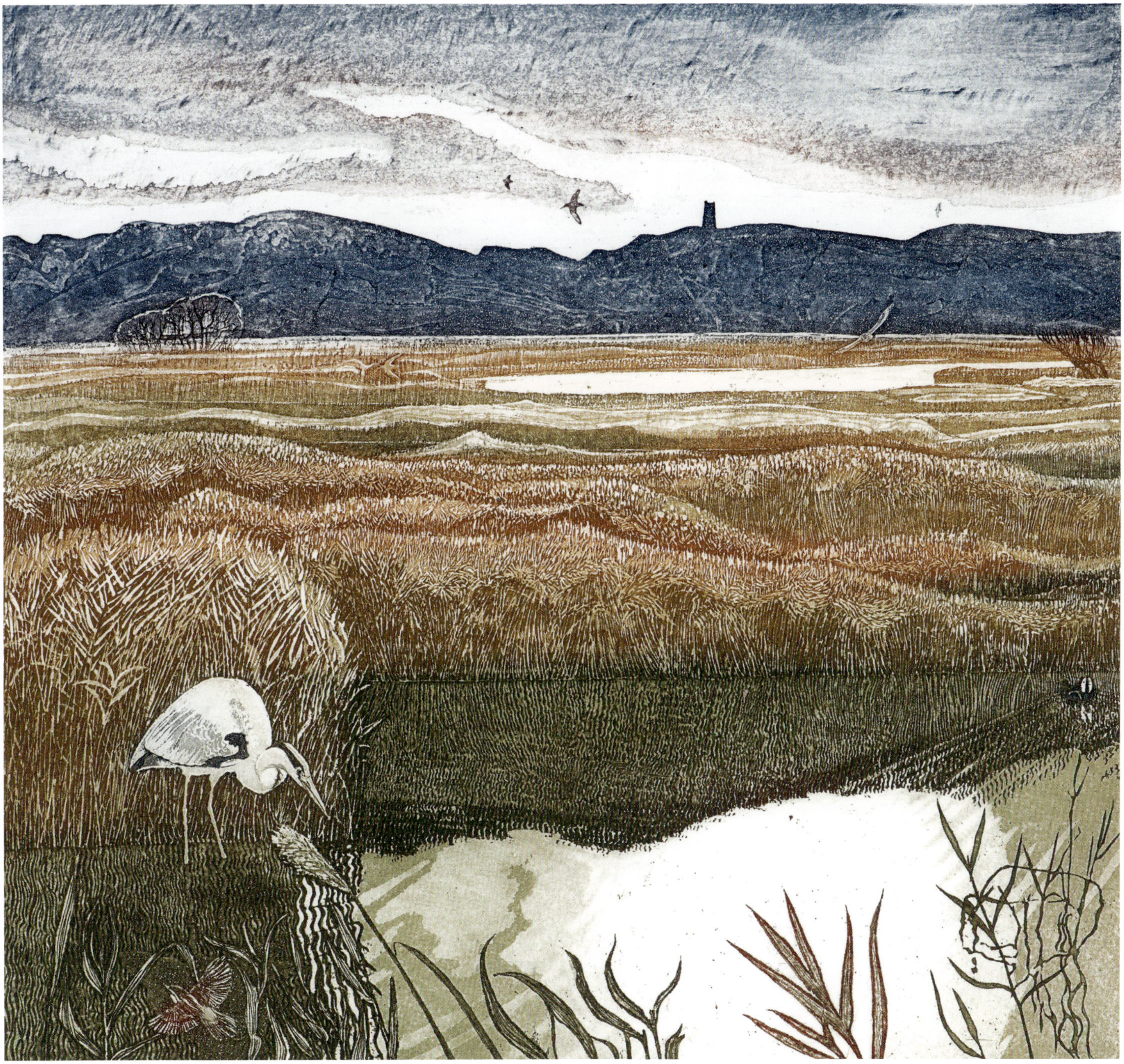

Top left: Andy English – Blakeney (wood engraving). *Top right:* Valerie Sims – Jetty (woodcut). *Left:* Amelia Bowman – Blakeney Lifeboat Station (Ixia) (collagraph). *Above:* Robert Greenhalf – Norfolk Reedmarsh (etching).

Blickling Hall

Blickling Hall, depicted here by two Norfolk artists Vanessa Lubach and Vanessa Burroughes, is a particularly attractive National Trust property on the outskirts of Aylsham.

The ancient manor of Blickling is recorded in the Domesday Book. Its owners have included Sir John Fastolf and Geoffrey Boleyn – grandfather of Anne Boleyn, one of King Henry VIII's less fortunate wives.

The present red-brick mansion was built during 1616-24 by Robert Lyminge (the architect of Hatfield House) for Sir Henry Hobart, 1st Baronet, Lord Chief Justice to King James I.

Relatively little is known about the long tenure of Lady Caroline Suffield and her husband. Despite inheriting Blickling in 1793, it wasn't until the late 1820s that she made her mark on the house.

The Blickling Estate and its owners have on occasion been very influential. It was Lord Lothian (who inherited Blickling in 1940) who persuaded Churchill to write the historic letter to Roosevelt that for the first time gave the United States

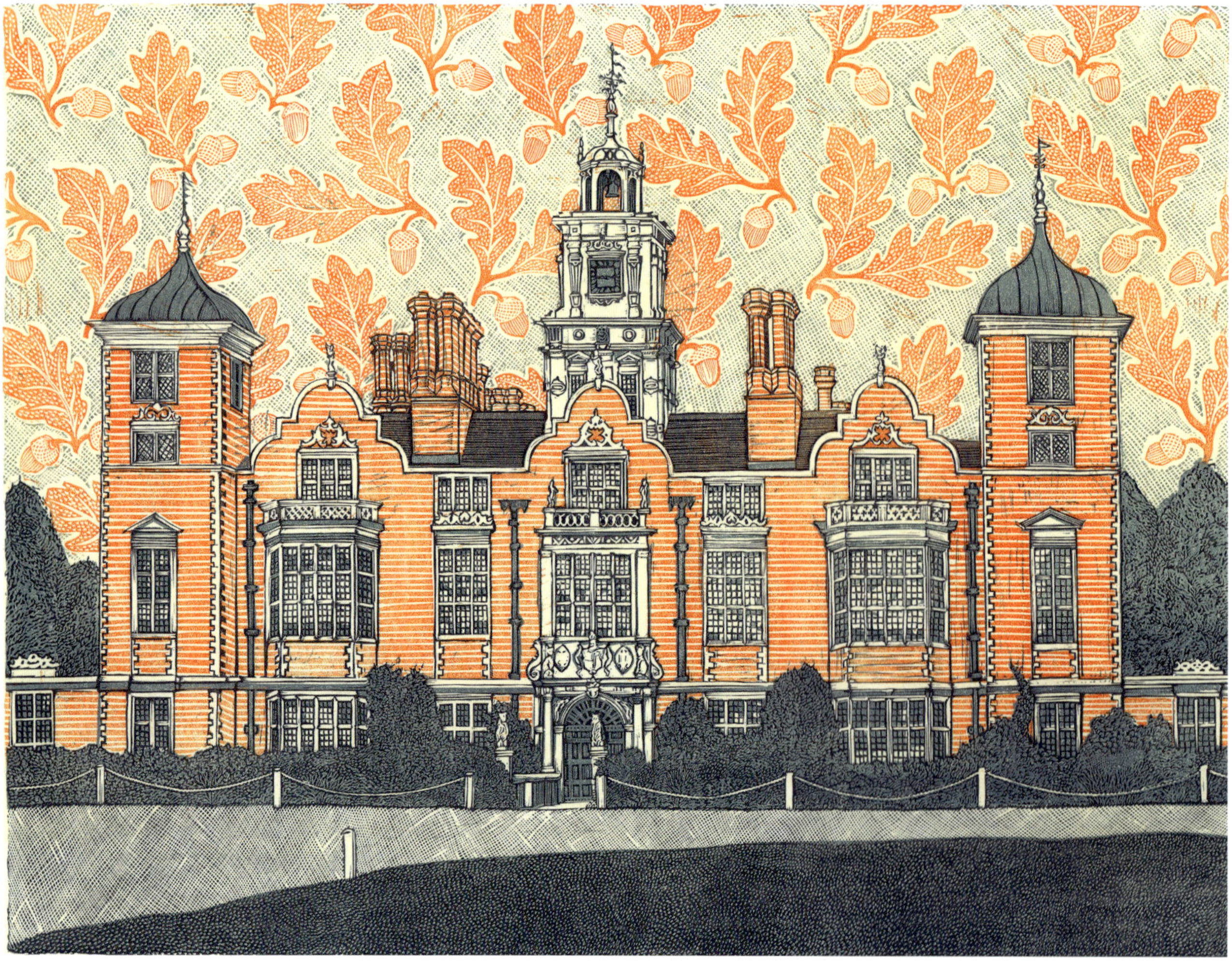

an unequivocal statement of Britain's depleted military strength during the early months of WWII.

During the war, the house was requisitioned and served as the Officers' Mess of nearby RAF Oulton. It was at this time that the house and its estate passed to the National Trust, under the terms of the Country Houses Scheme. RAF servicemen and women were billeted within the grounds in Nissen huts, while officers were housed within Blickling itself.

At the end of the war, the house was de-requisitioned. The National Trust again let it to tenants until 1960, when the Trust began work to restore the house to a style reflecting its history. The house and grounds were opened to the public in 1962.

The complex linocut print reproduced opposite is *Blickling in Autumn* by Vanessa Lubach, and measures 48cm x 63cm. It forms an edition of 50. The hand-coloured linocut below, *Blickling Hall*, was created by Vanessa Burroughes.

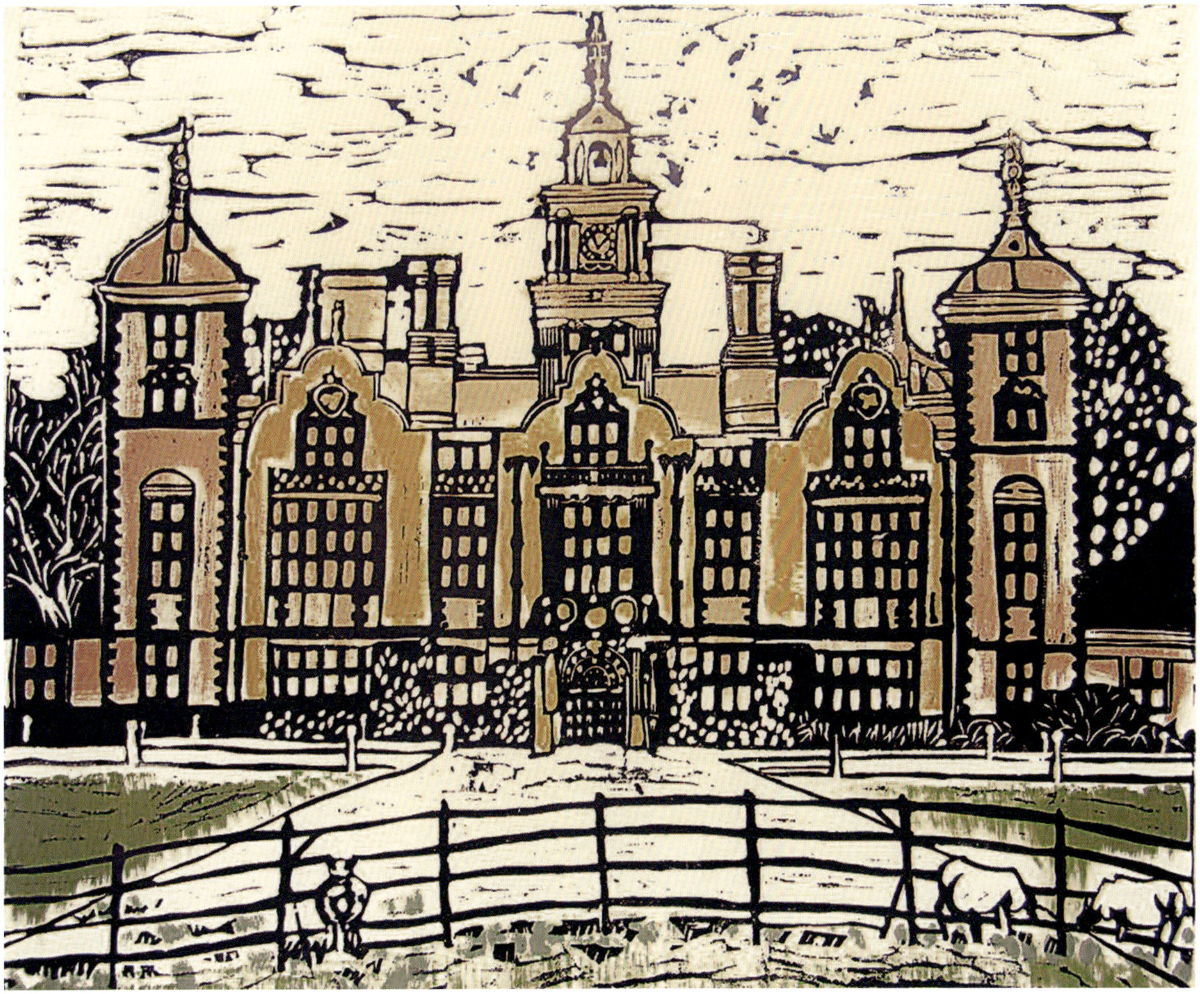

Blofield Church

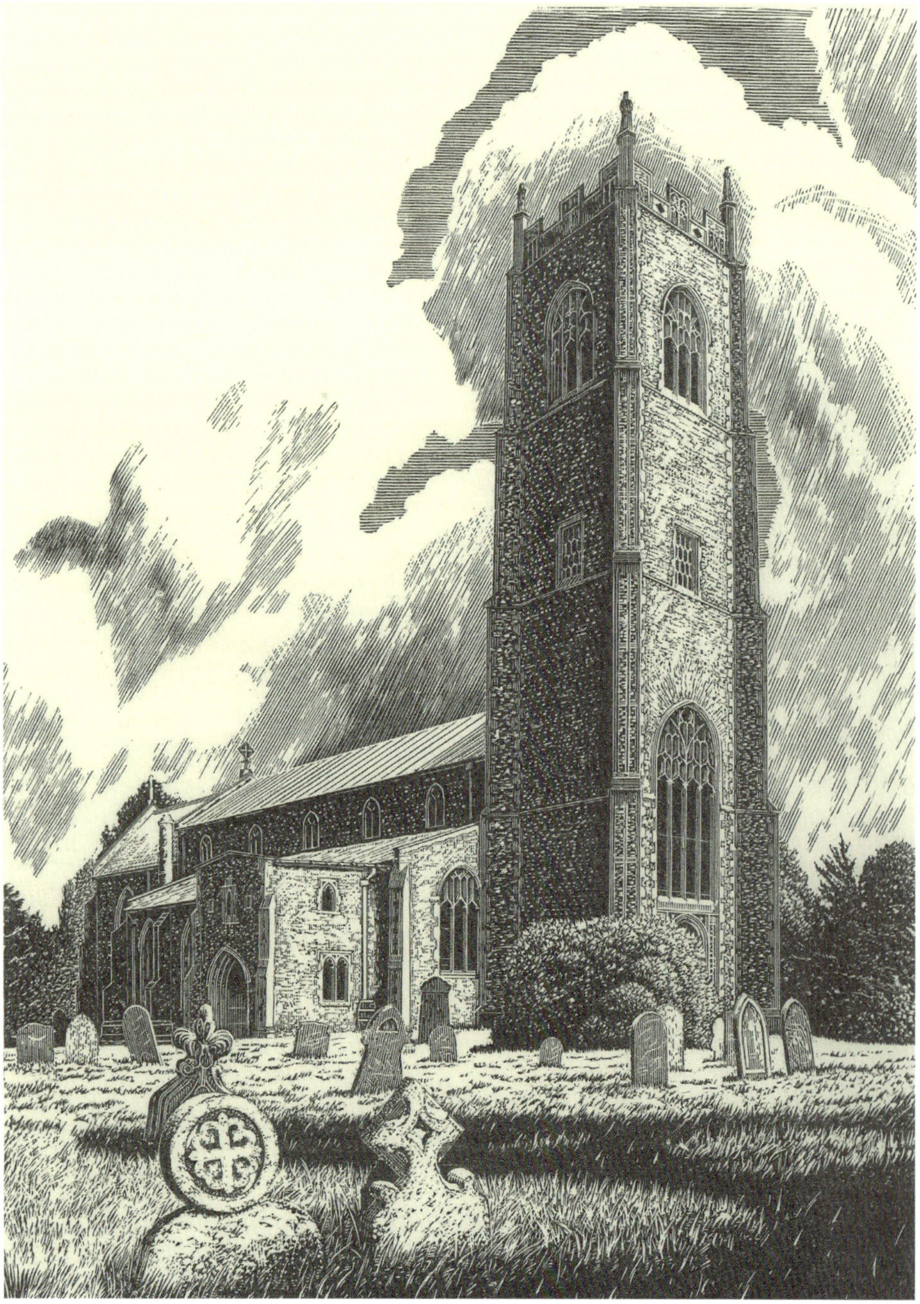

Churches are popular subjects for Suffolk-based wood engraver Anthony Dunigan, who includes a large number in his portfolio – several of which are featured in this book and in its companion volume, *Suffolk Jewels*.

Anthony's preferred method of working is to create a block with a darkened surface with the design traced on to it using a bright-yellow transfer paper. "I engrave on lemonwood or maplewood blocks or on engraver's plastic. All of my work is done by hand-burnishing."

St Andrew & St Peter, Blofield was consecrated in 1420 and finished in 1444. It is a large and rather grand wool church, paid for by the wealthy wool trade whose leading merchants sought to ease their way to heaven through the financing of spectacular places of worship.

Located close to the A47 between Norwich and Acle, Blofield Church has a perpendicular tower of 110 feet in height and contains eight bells that are rung regularly. Raised box pews at the rear of the nave are popular with families as children can see over the heads of those sitting in front. There are numerous ledger stones on the floors, and a marble monument to Edward Paston (1550–1630), a Norfolk gentleman, poet and musician.

The chancel is separated from the nave by the remains of a rood screen with painted panels of the Apostles. The north wall has a painted consecration cross, and the medieval font is unique with its eight sides depicting scenes from the Nativity through to the Ascension. The church contains Victorian and modern stained glass.

Anthony Dunigan is a member of the Society of Wood Engravers (SWE). His engraved print measures 38cm x 29cm and forms an edition of 40. "I drew the church at fairly close range, which meant shifting the perspective vanishing points in order to fit the drawing on to the page. This was engraved in 2006 on engraver's plastic."

A copy is in the SWE archive at Manchester Metropolitan University library.

Brancaster

Brancaster is one of those places that appeals to walkers, twitchers, golfers and sailors alike. The prints reproduced here showcase all of these aspects, beginning below with a large Colin Moore linocut (sheet width 59.5cm) created in 2016 in an edition of 100 produced from three blocks. The Dorset-based artist clearly couldn't resist the combination of working boats, mud, waders and sky.

Located at the western end of the north Norfolk coast, near Burnham Overy Staithe, Brancaster is a village and civil parish comprising Brancaster itself, together with Brancaster Staithe and Burnham Deepdale. The three villages form a more or less continuous settlement along the A149 at the edge of the Brancaster Manor marshland. Offshore is the Scolt Head Island National Nature Reserve.

Hertfordshire artist Kate Heiss is drawn regularly to this part of Norfolk, and it features in a number of her floral- and bird-themed prints. The first to appear in these pages is *Wild Rose at High Tide* (page 31), based on

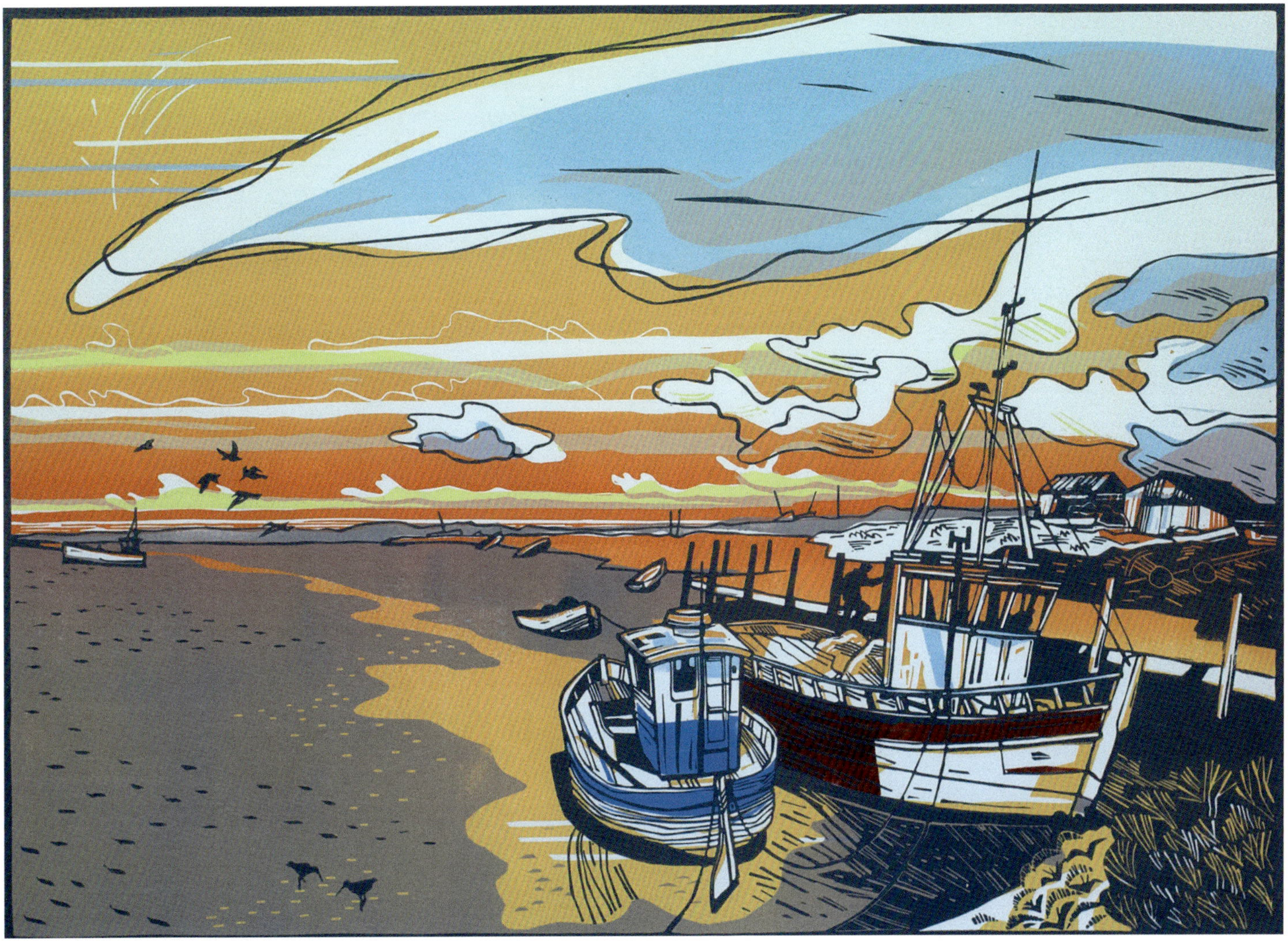

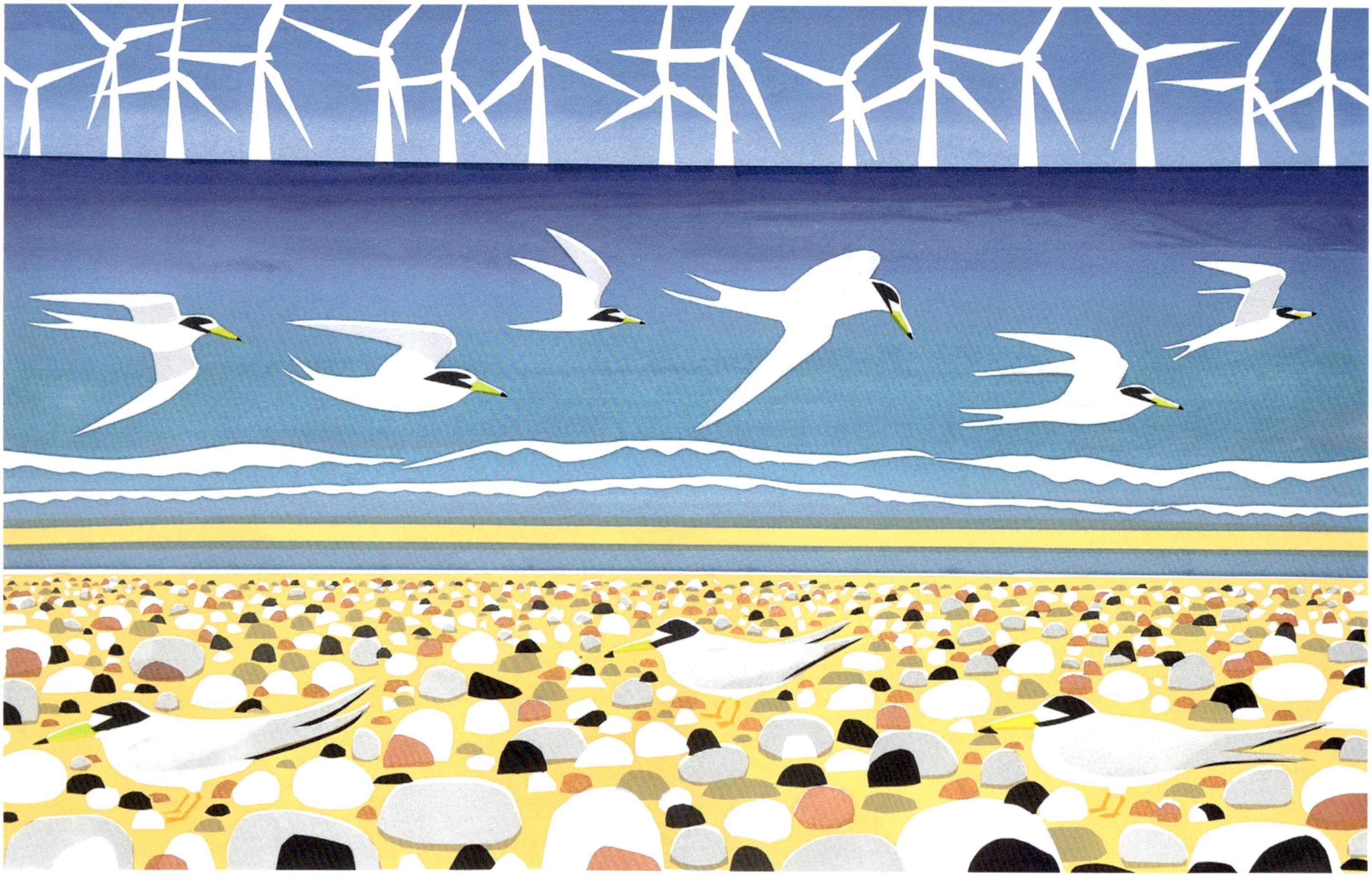

Scolt Head Island. The linocut and screenprint composition measures 40cm x 30cm, produced in 2014 as a variable edition of 30. The colours for this piece have been hand-painted directly on to the screen and printed. The details of the image are cut in lino and then printed over the top. This means the colours for each print are slightly different. Kate explains that the print is inspired by the exquisite wild red rose (Rosa rugosa) that grows in abundance on Scolt Head Island. "It has the most intense perfume and vivid bright pink flowers that turn into huge red hips in the autumn."

Facing Kate's roses, sailing boat and passing geese are some of Norfolk's growing population of wind turbines and the rather more endangered Little Terns. There are pockets of breeding birds around the Norfolk coast, with the Brancaster/Burnham area inspiring this serigraph (screenprint) by Northamptonshire artist Carry Akroyd.

Carry likes the juxtaposition of the natural world with the 'real' world of industry, commerce and population. The wind turbines may be controversial, but they aren't going away any time soon, so why shouldn't they be incorporated into art? The print *Big Turns and Little Terns II* from 2015 measures 50cm x 70cm. Carry admits that the title came first and a series of prints followed. While she associates the birds and the wind farm with this stretch of the north-west Norfolk coast, she allows that Little Terns and turbines are equally at home farther east in the county, along the stretch of coast between Great Yarmouth and Happisburgh.

Golfers are drawn to Brancaster thanks to the picturesque links course that adjoins

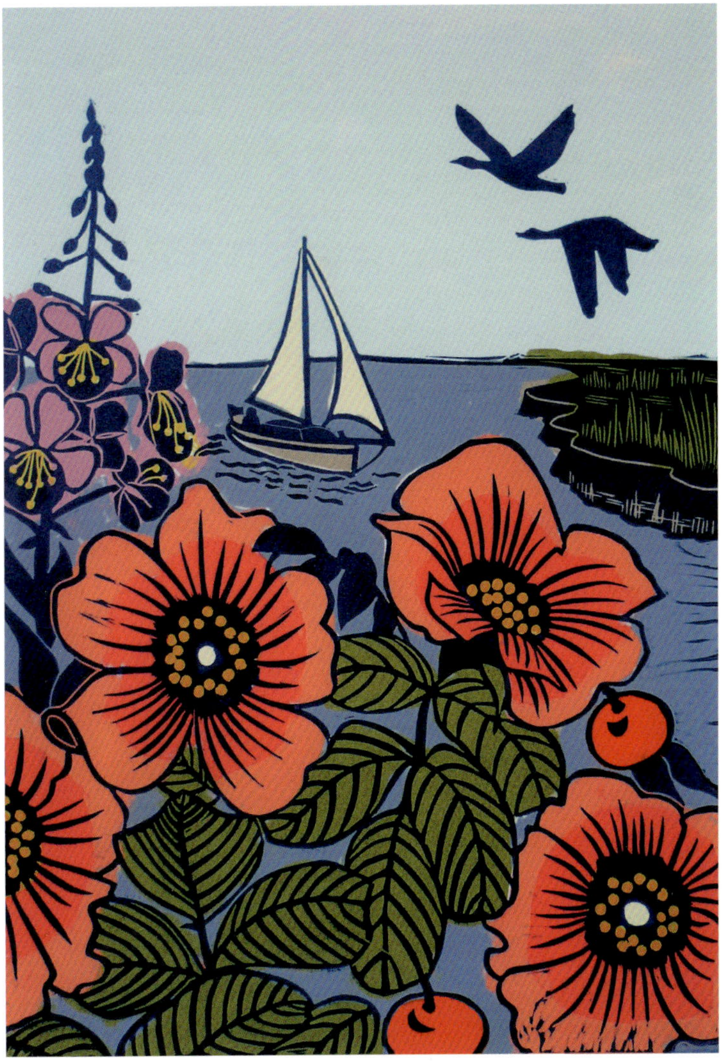

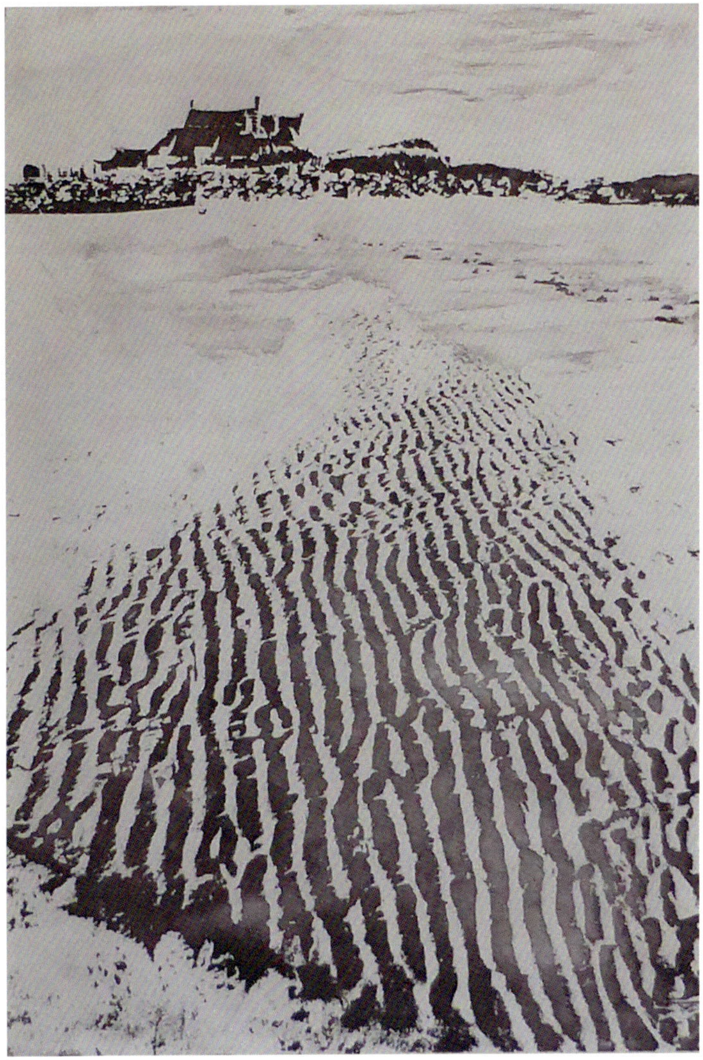

the spectacular sandy beach. Suffolk-based Winter Rose produced the print (far right) in 2015 as an edition of 25 using photo-etching and aquatint (39cm x 27cm). According to the artist,"the unusual rippled sweep of sand with the clubhouse behind stopped me in my tracks and I knew immediately this had to be a print subject".

The final Brancaster images are both from Kate Heiss. *Sails and Sea Campion* on page 32 is a linocut and screenprint (30cm x 30cm, edition of 30). "It was high tide at Brancaster Staithe when I pictured this print. As I walked between Brancaster Staithe and Burnham Deepdale, I collected Sea Campion and Rosebay Willowherb. The Reed Bunting was swinging on the stems of the reeds."

Evening Primrose at Brancaster (page 33) is a print of the same size and uses the same technique. Here Kate was attracted by the vibrant yellow of Evening Primrose framing the boats sailing on the creek at Brancaster Staithe. She includes the Stonechat sitting on a gorse branch to complete the composition.

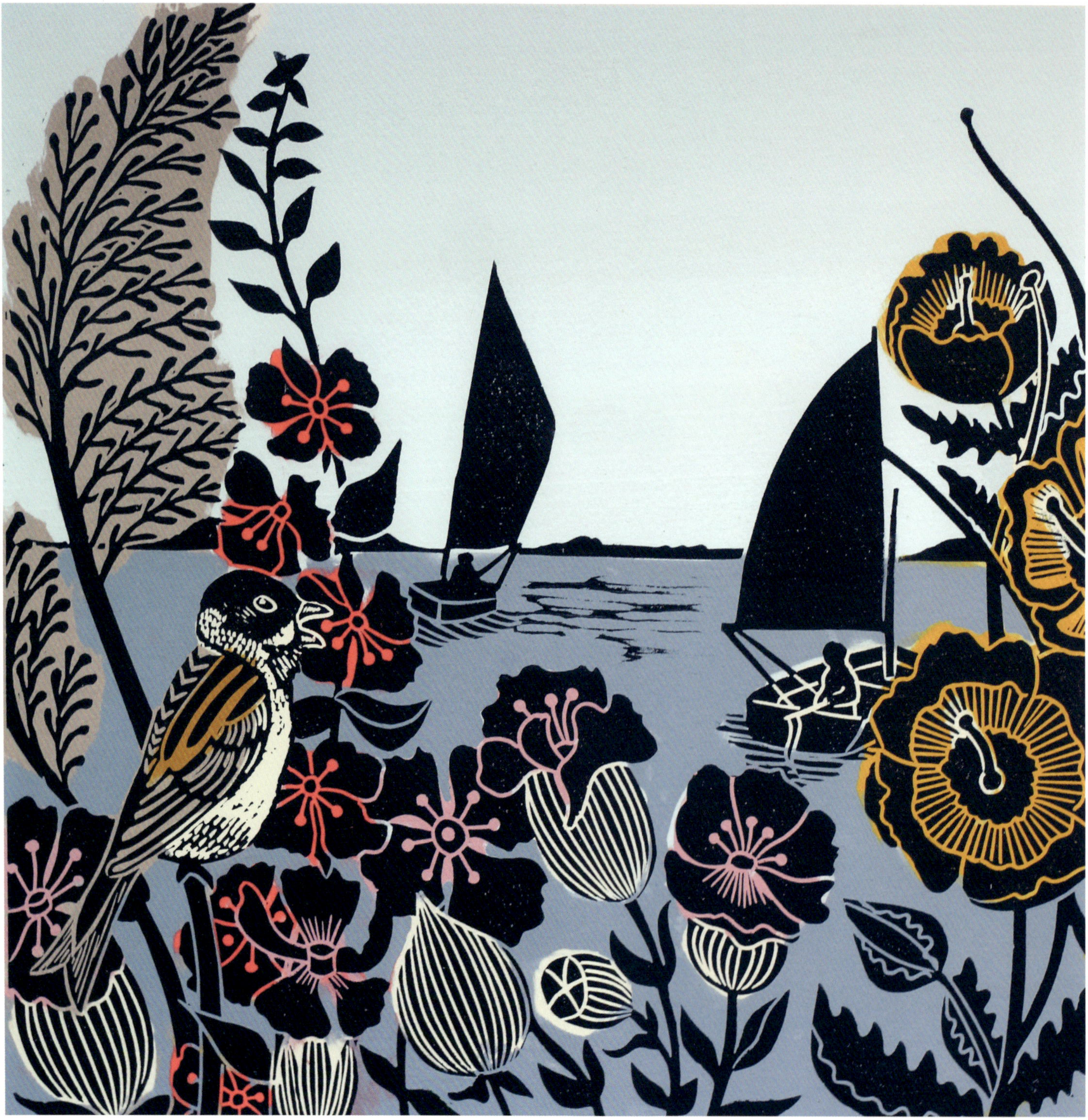

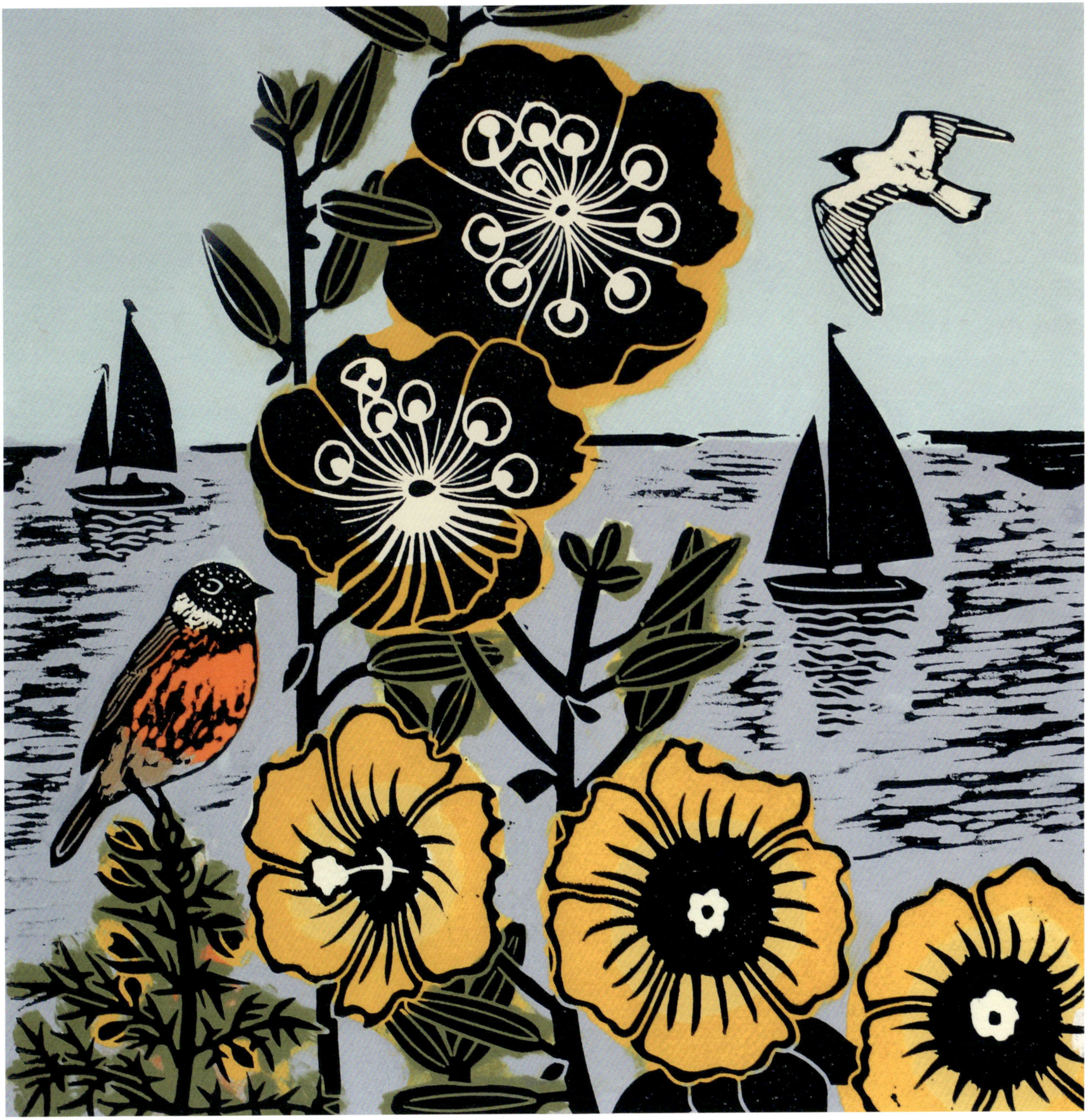

The Brecks

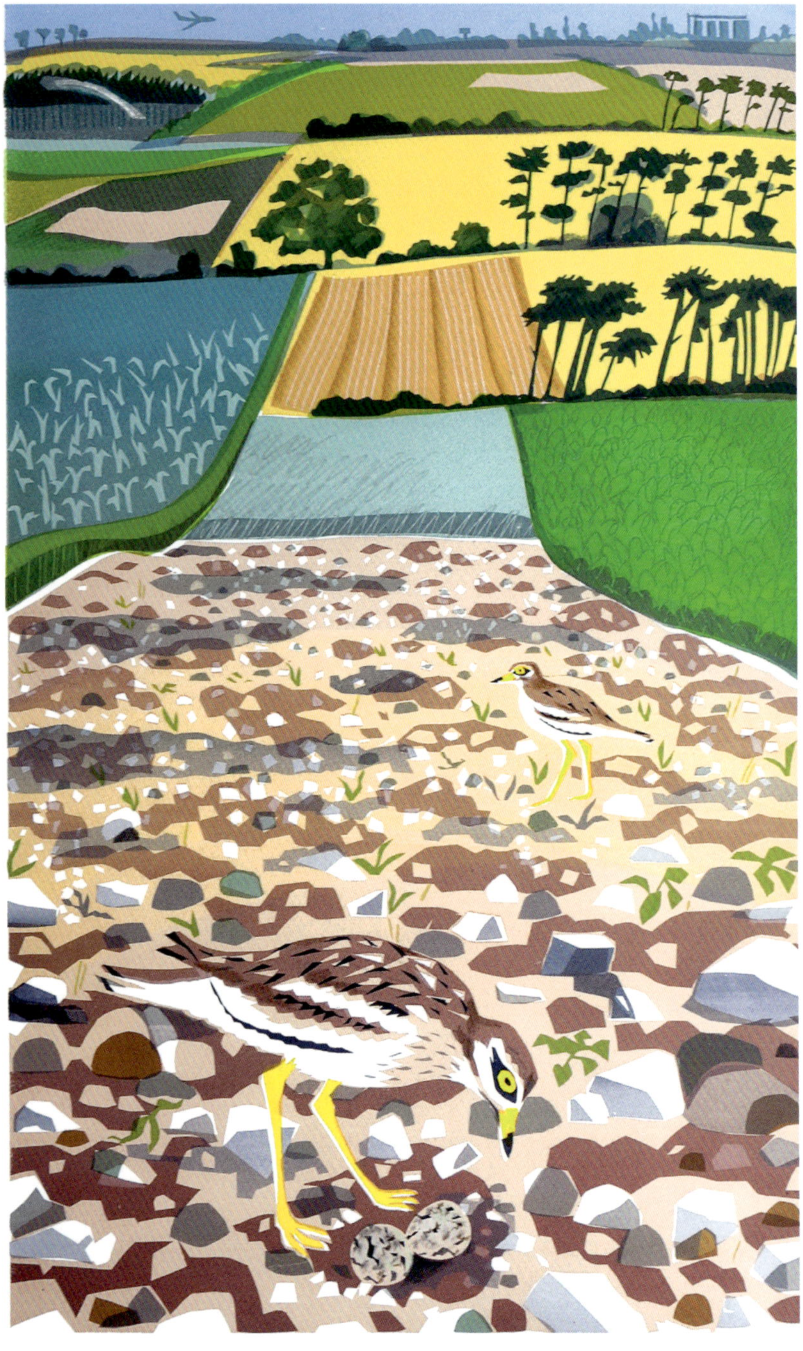

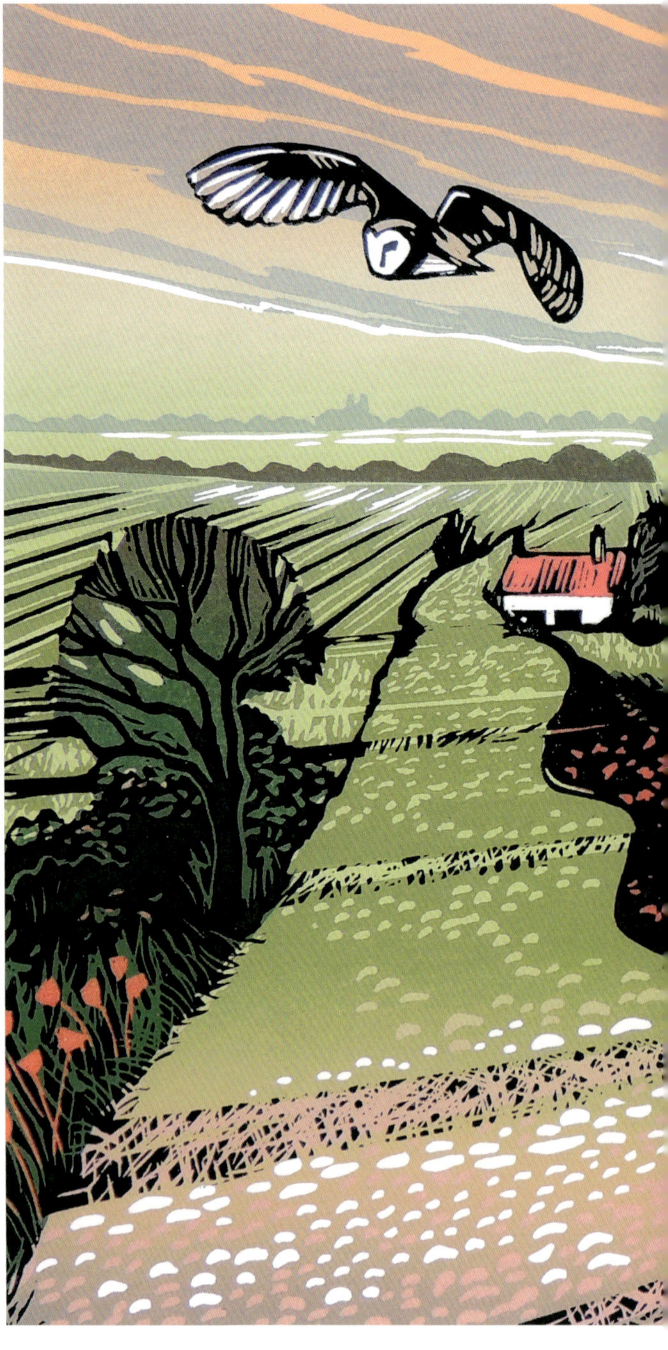

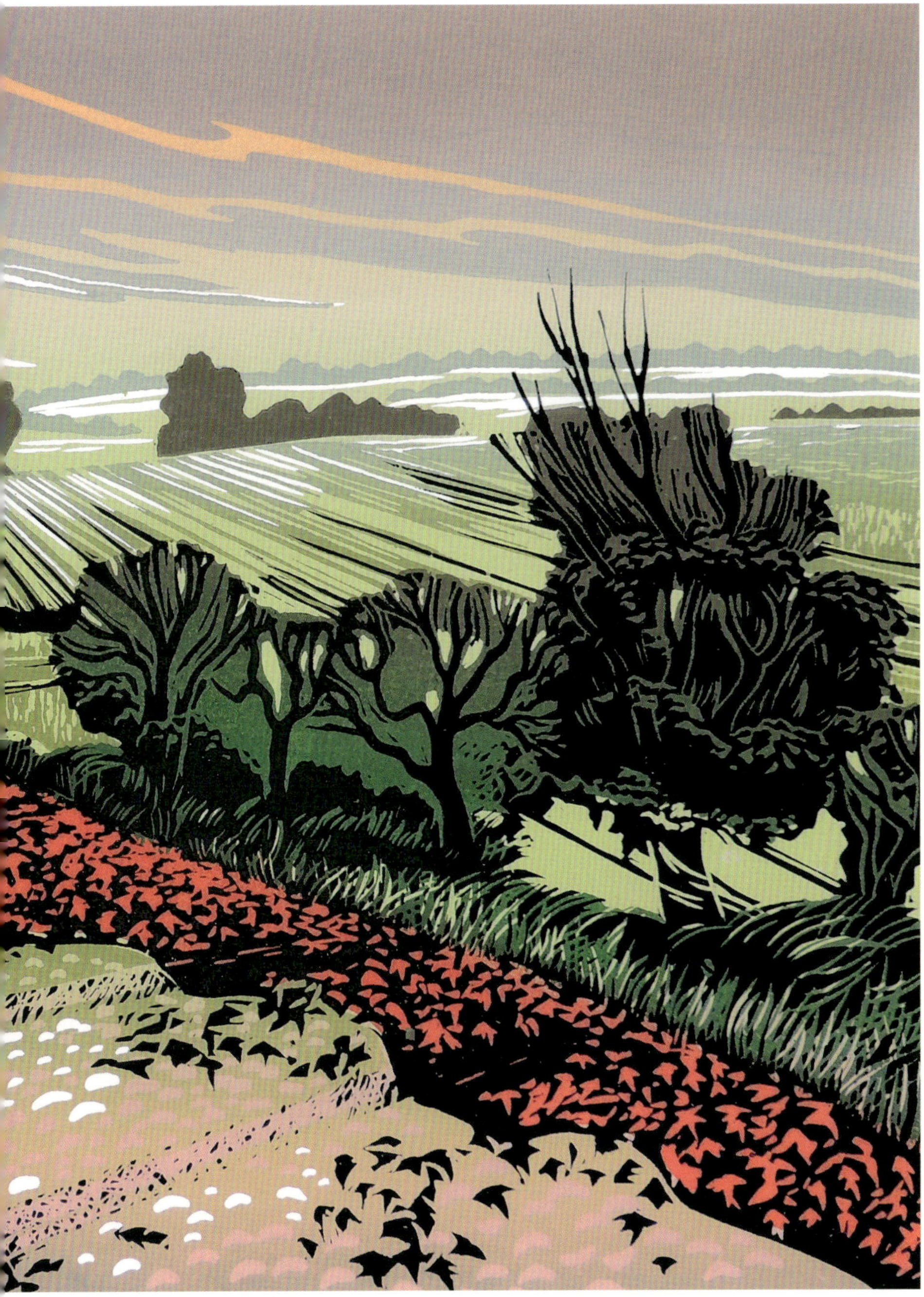

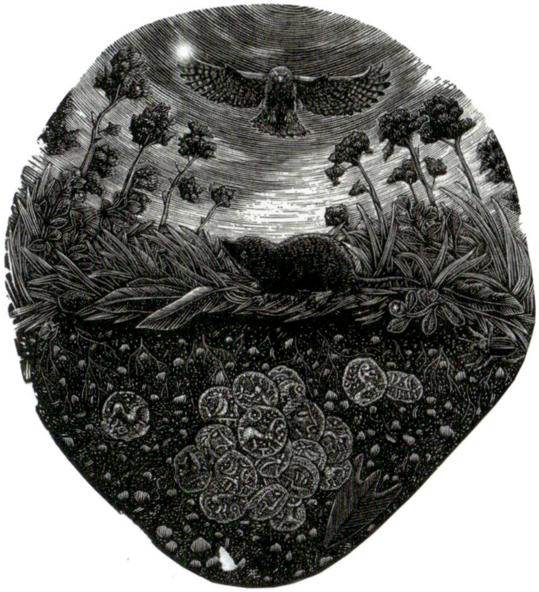

The Brecks is the name for an important area of natural habitat bordering Norfolk and Suffolk in the Dereham to Thetford area. As well as a refuge for the endangered Stone Curlew, the subject of the Carry Akroyd print on the far left, the region provides a home for many plant, tree, insect and mammal species.

Spanning more than 1,000 sq km, this is one of the driest parts of Britain that was once covered in ancient heathland created by prehistoric farmers, rabbits and sheep. The Brecks themselves were temporary fields cultivated for a few years and then allowed to revert to heath once the soil became exhausted. Through many centuries, the heaths, and the mysterious fluctuating Breckland lakes known as meres, became home to a distinctive range of plants and animals.

The large-scale pine plantations of Thetford forest and the use of modern farming technology have transformed much of the area into more productive land. The remaining stretches, and the more open parts of the forest, are now vital areas for wildlife conservation.

Carry's 2015 (70cm x 50cm) serigraph *Stonies' Plot* captures the environment and the rare species of bird. The soil of the Brecks is almost

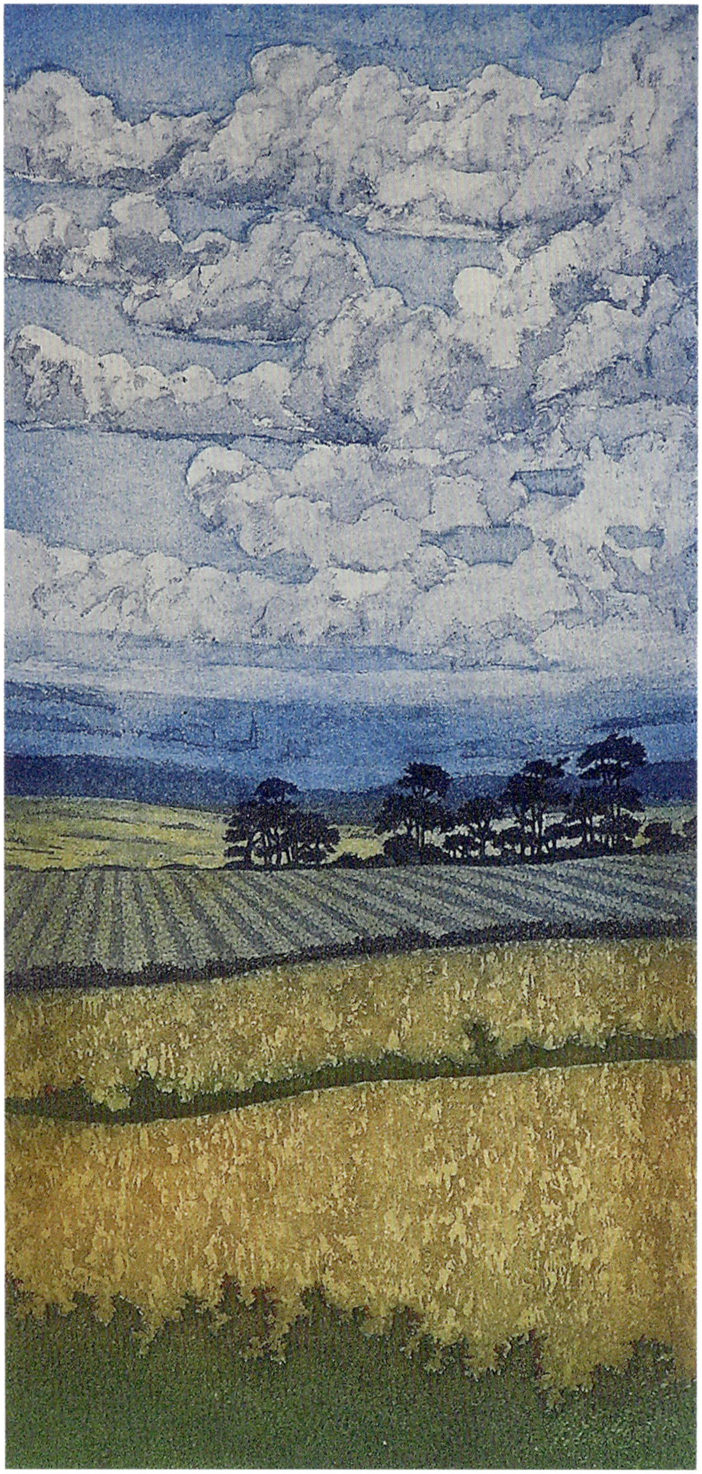

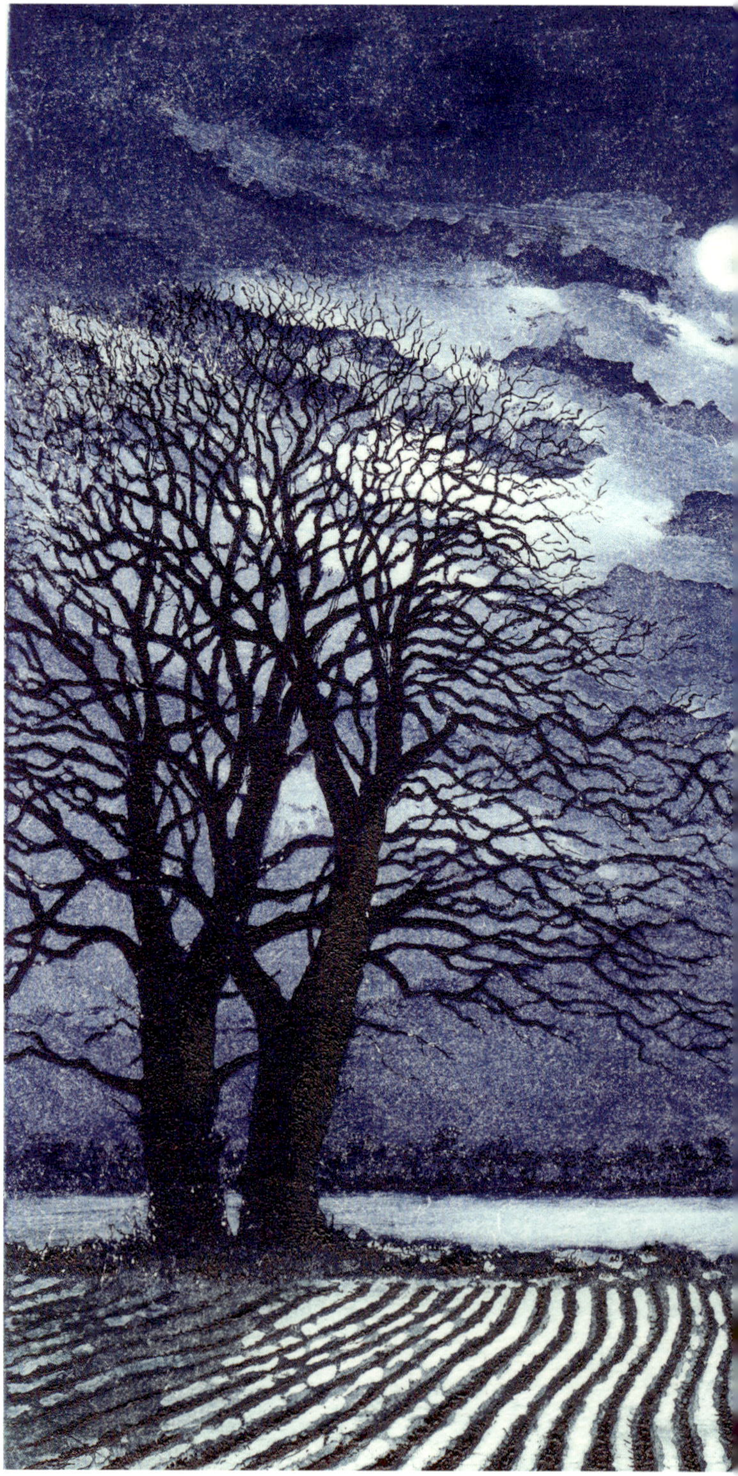

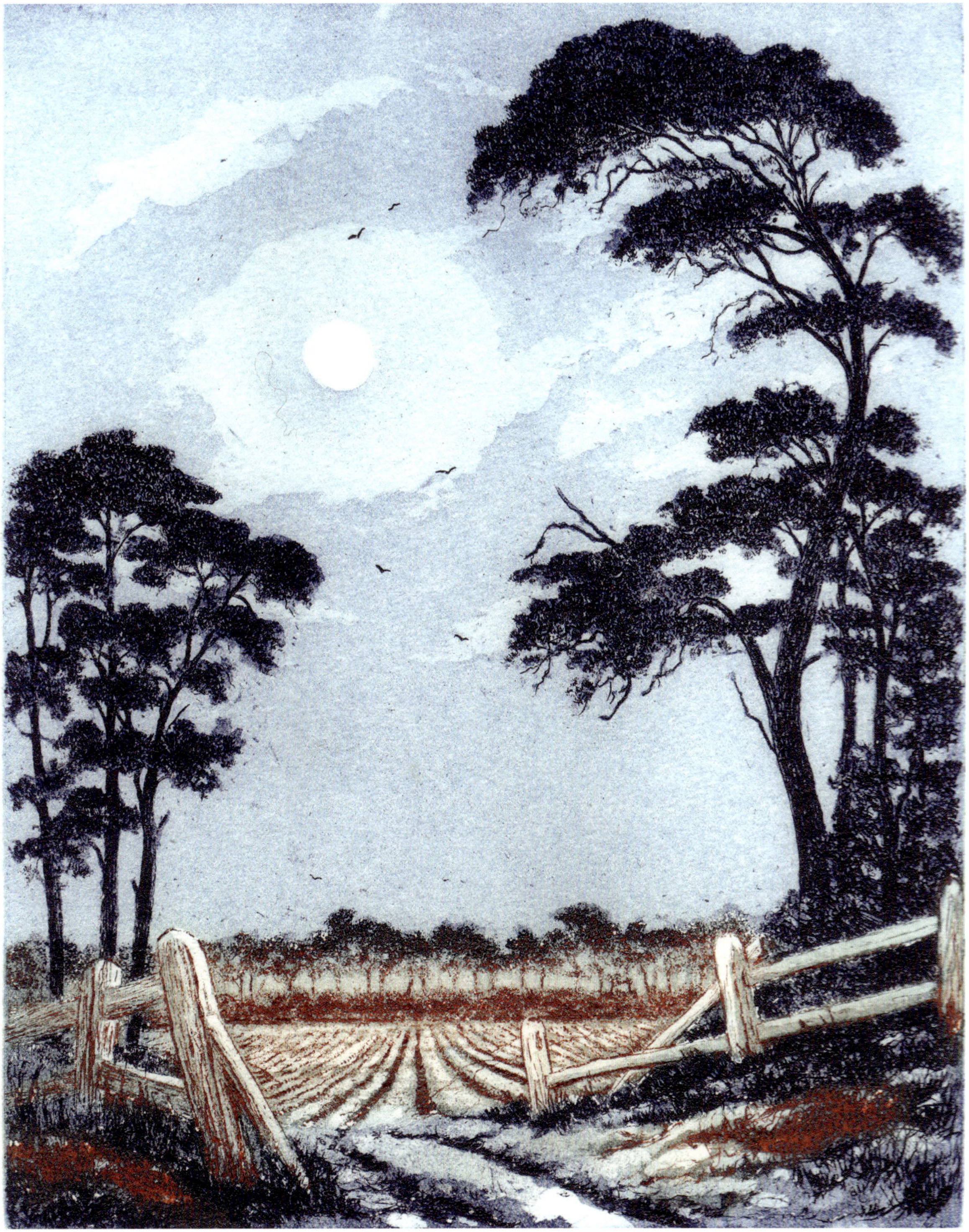

a sandy beach, says Carry. "Where a farmer deliberately leaves a bare section, the Stone Curlews have their ideal background to hide against. I wanted to convey their inconspicuousness, with emblems of the pine windbreaks typical of Breckland."

The linocut print *Daybreak* by Rob Barnes on pages 34-35 is another work that reproduces the Brecks landscape near Dereham, while the humorous little wood engraving by Andy English on page 35 considers the treasures left by our ancestors beneath the windswept soil.

Norfolk printmaker Laurie Rudling on page 36 provides the two-plate aquatint etching *Old Warren Heath* (40cm x 20cm), which he describes as one of his more interpretative landscapes. He also contributes the two prints below, *Before Dawn* (top, 15cm x 30cm) and *Shelterhouse Corner* (bottom, 17cm x 30cm). The

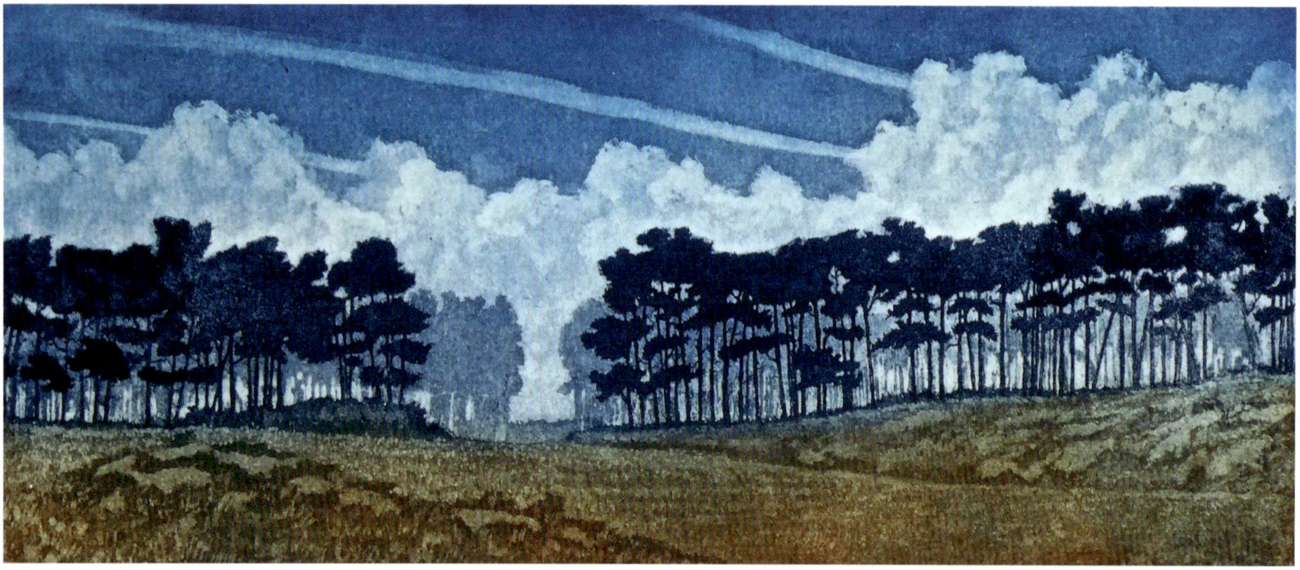

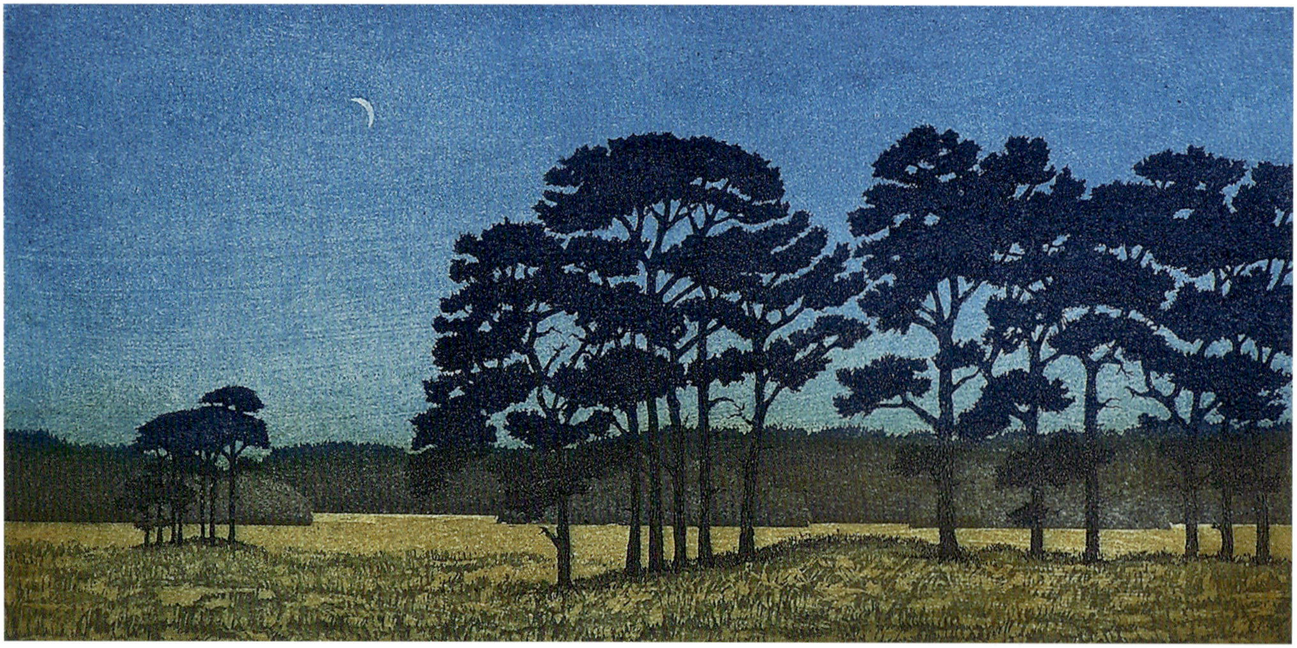

former is a two-plate aquatint etching from an edition of 40. The location is Wretham Heath, which straddles the A1075 north of Thetford. The second image is a single-plate aquatint etching (edition size: 40). "I discovered this on a winter mountain bike ride around Kings Forest to the south of Thetford. Riding down the bridleway beside Old Barnham Slip, one comes to a muddled area of old shelterbelts, slightly neglected fields and absolutely wonderful place names. Who could not warm to the sound of 'Barrow Clump Buildings', 'Summerpit Bottom', 'Dukes Ride' and 'Shelterhouse Corner'?"

TM Fairbank is the other contributor to our Brecks section, and has provided *The Ploughed Field* and *The Straight Furrow* (middle and right, pages 36-37) and *Five Oaks* (below). Her passion for etching originates from studying initially under her father, a freelance artist and prolific etcher. Like Laurie, Theresa has been attracted by the remote charm of the Brecks landscape, with her atmospheric aquatint etchings of trees capturing the sense of wide open spaces.

"The imagery inspiring my etchings relates to the beauty of the landscape on the Norfolk/Suffolk borders. The changing face of our fields has eliminated thick copses, leaving a thin elegant line of pine trees or a solitary oak marooned, denoting where dense hedgerows and woodland once gave cover for wildlife.

"My imagination responds to the relationship between line and form in these ancient places. Twisted trunks like dancing bodies from powerful roots to waving branches communicate stories, energy, change and wisdom."

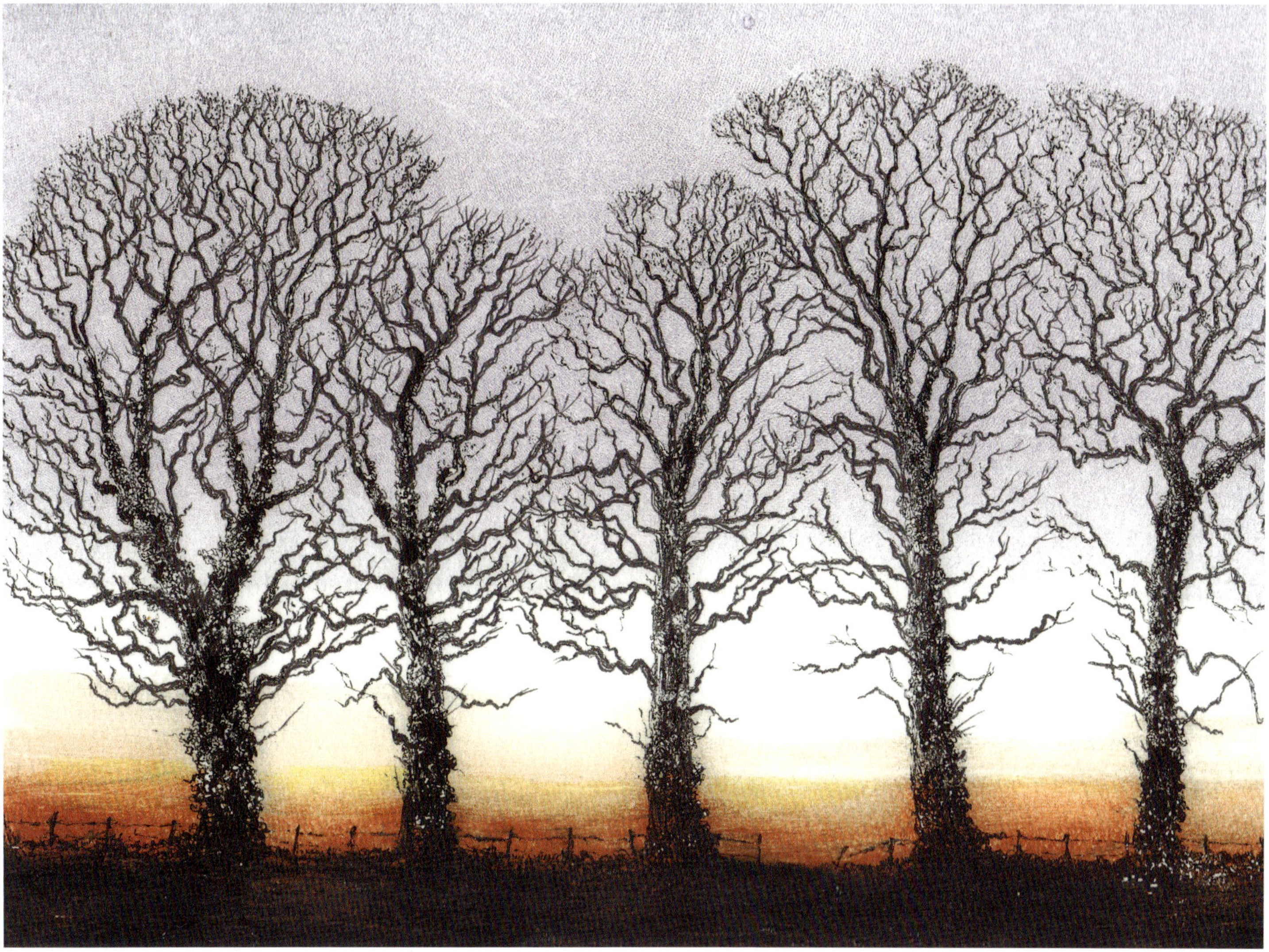

The Broads

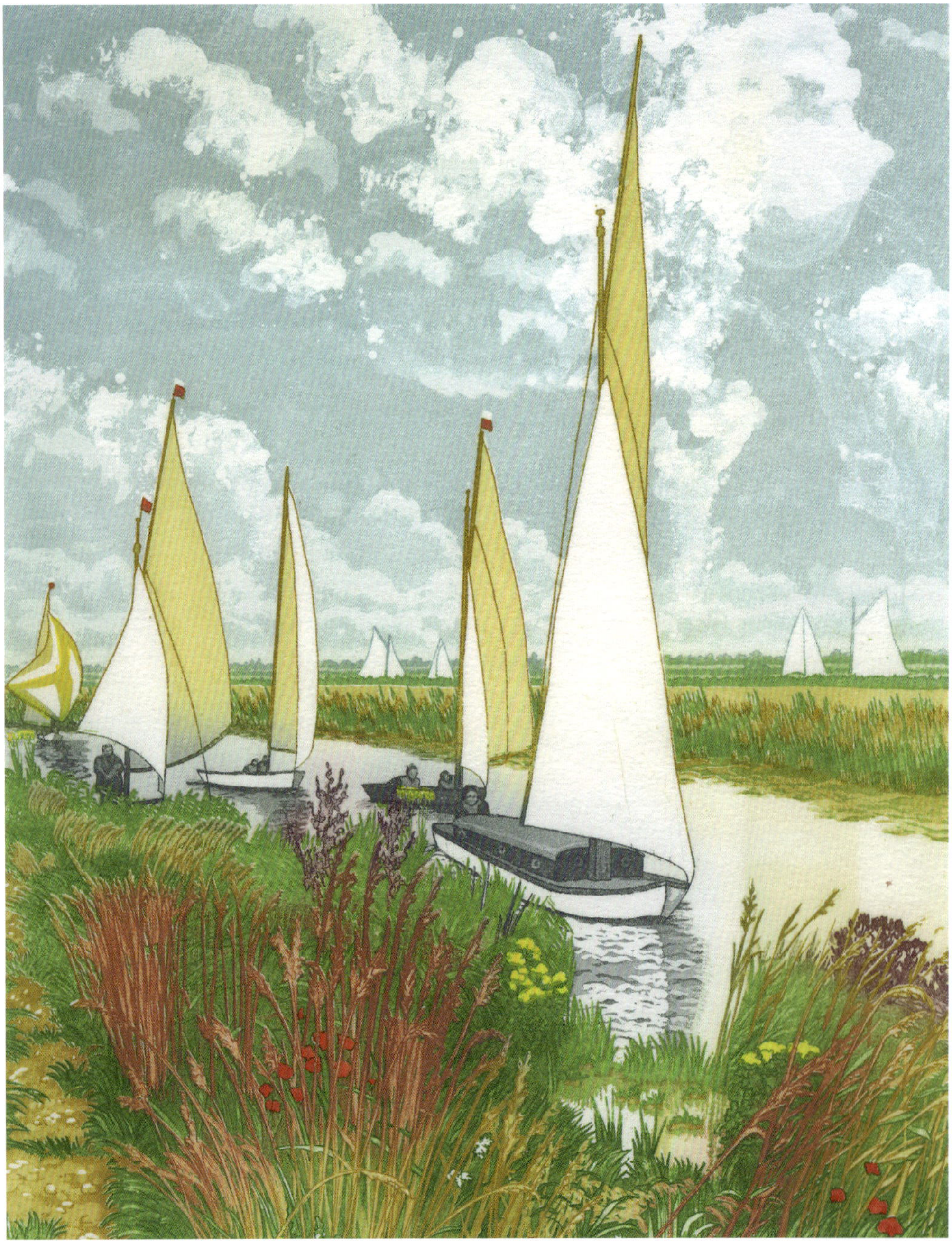

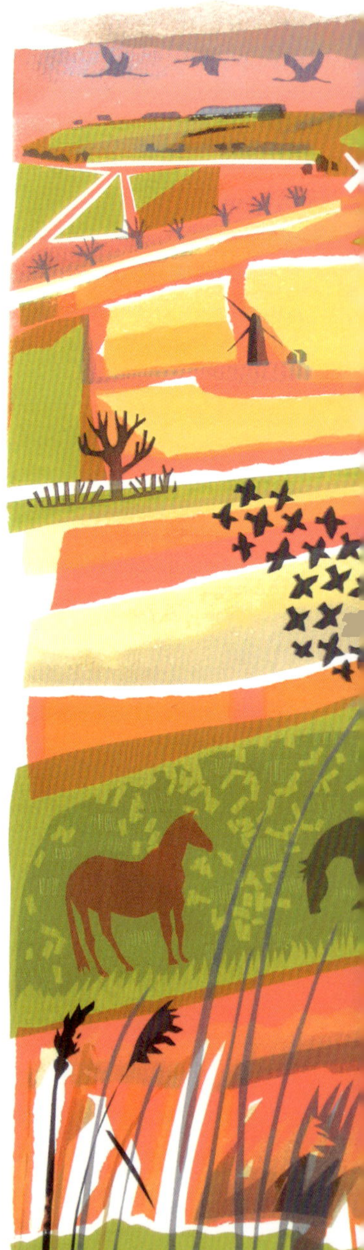

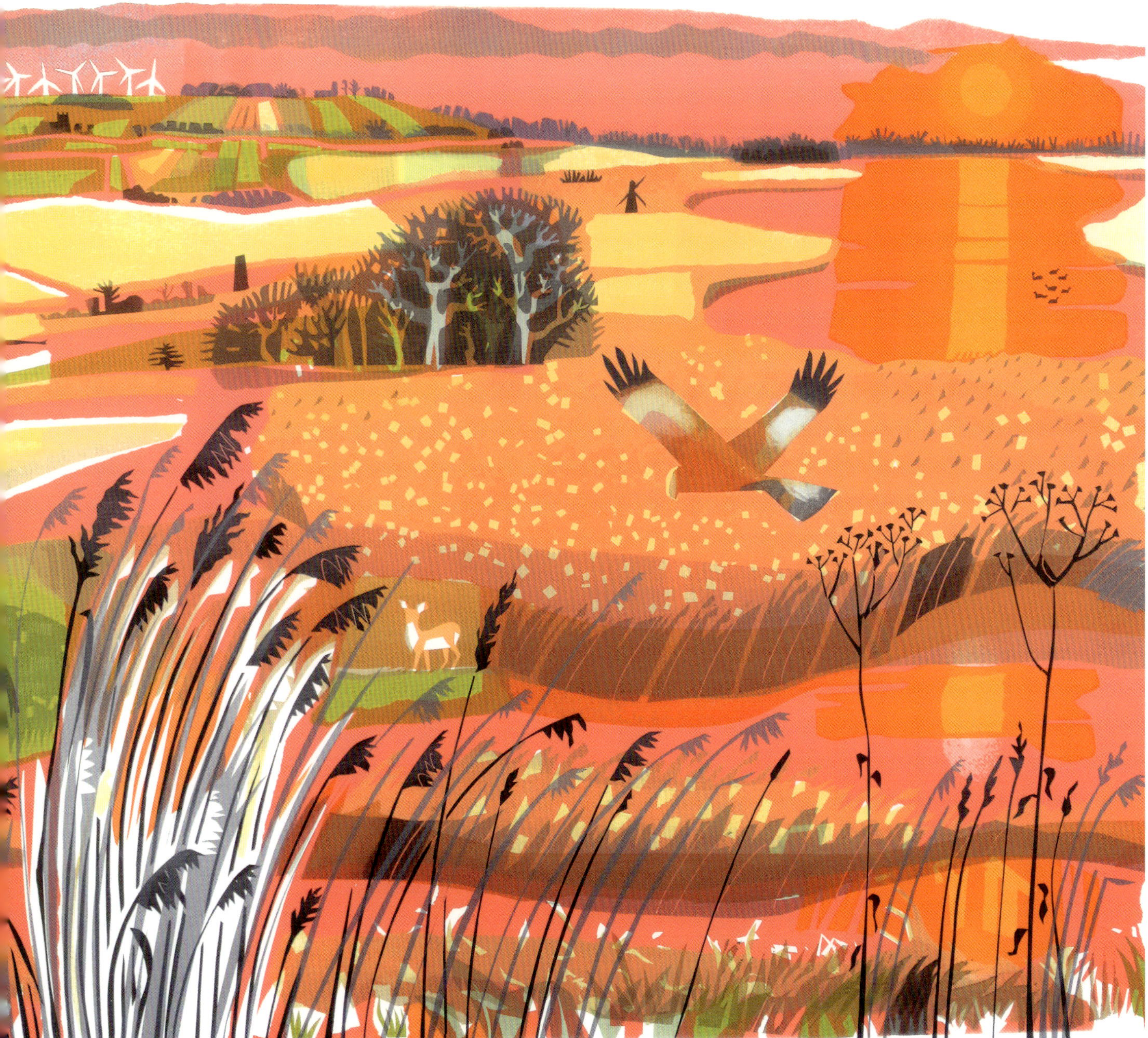

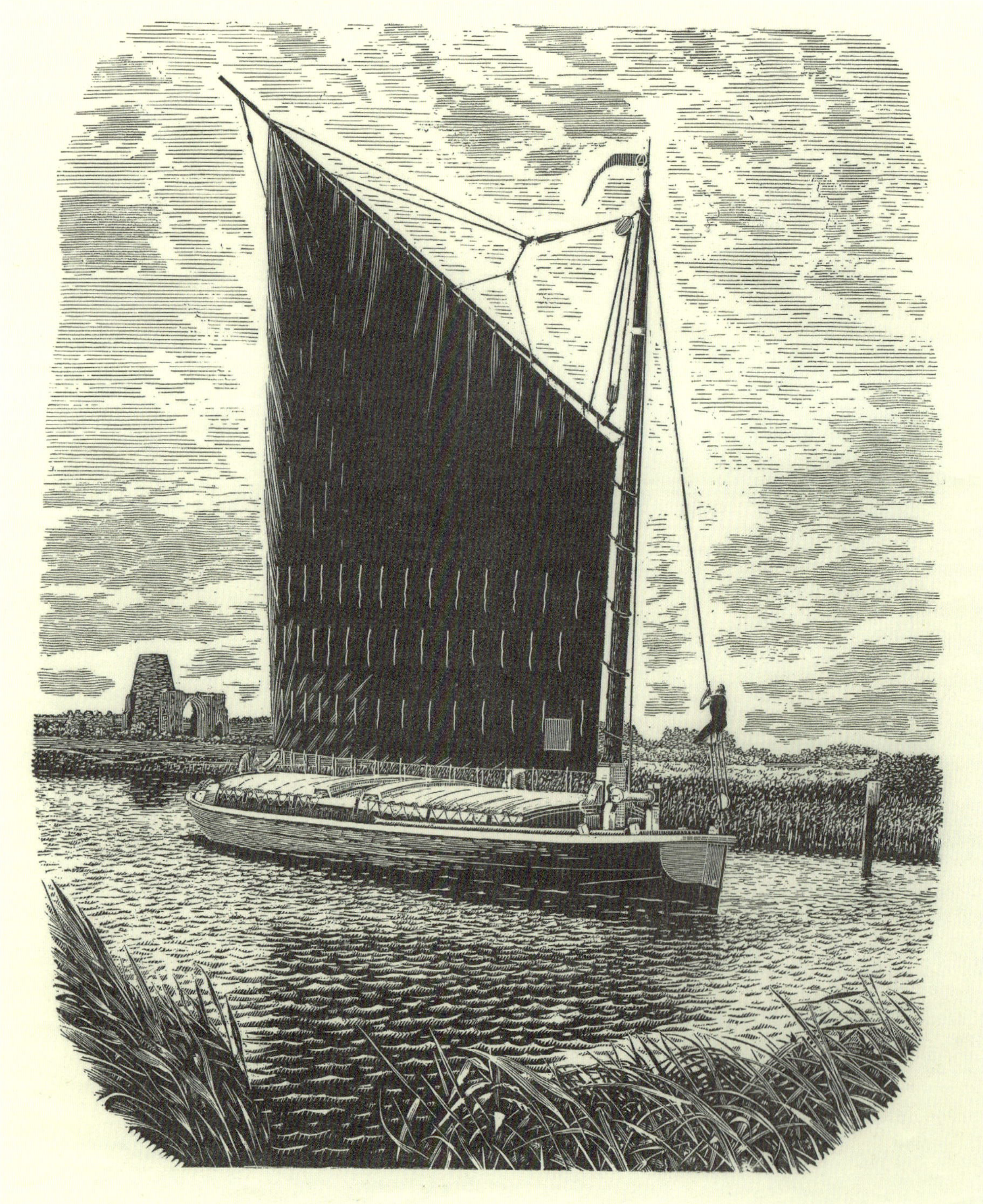

Left: *Anthony Dunigan – A Norfolk Wherry (St Benet's Abbey), 38cm x 32cm, 2002 edition of 40 on engraver's plastic.*
Right: *Amelia Bowman – St Benet's Abbey (Daisy, Daisy), 2014 collagraph print, 38cm x 27cm, edition of 10.*

In spite of large numbers of tourists, the Norfolk Broads still represent a secret wetland sanctuary for wildlife. Away from the holiday season, boat traffic is reduced greatly and peace returns to the 300 sq km of meadows, shallow lakes and winding rivers.

Perhaps because so much of the Broads remains beyond the reach of land-based artists, the body of work is surprisingly small and few printmakers have specialised in an environment that has changed visually very little in decades.

The Broads are located largely between Great Yarmouth and Norwich. The wide, shallow lakes that give the region its name are man-made and began as pits dug for peat to provide fuel during medieval times and filled over the centuries to become today's holiday playground and nature reserve.

Six rivers link the Broads: each of the river valleys has different characteristics, from woodland at the upper reaches of the Bure to the meandering waters of the Waveney. Around the Broads themselves visitors can find a variety of habitats including fen, carr woodland and grazing marshes.

This book's author and his wife number among only around 6,500 residents in The Broads. However, around eight million visitors arrive each year to share Britain's third-biggest inland waterway system and its surrounding villages. They have access to 200km of navigable waterway linked by the rivers Bure, Ant, Thurne, Yare and Chat – plus part of the River Wensum where it runs through the City of Norwich.

As well as 13 fixed scheduled ancient monuments, there are pieces of floating history in the form of the timber-built sailing wherries

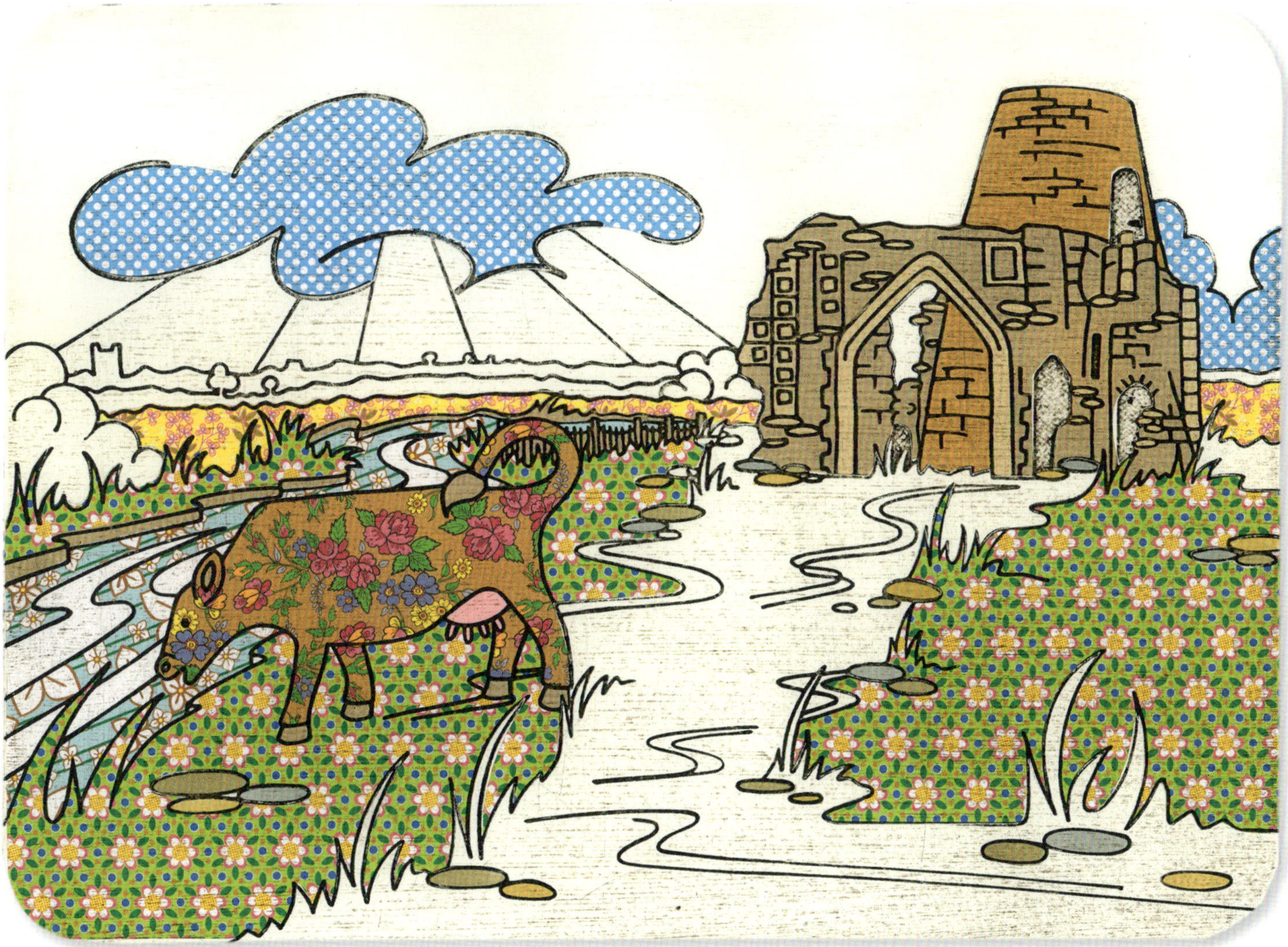

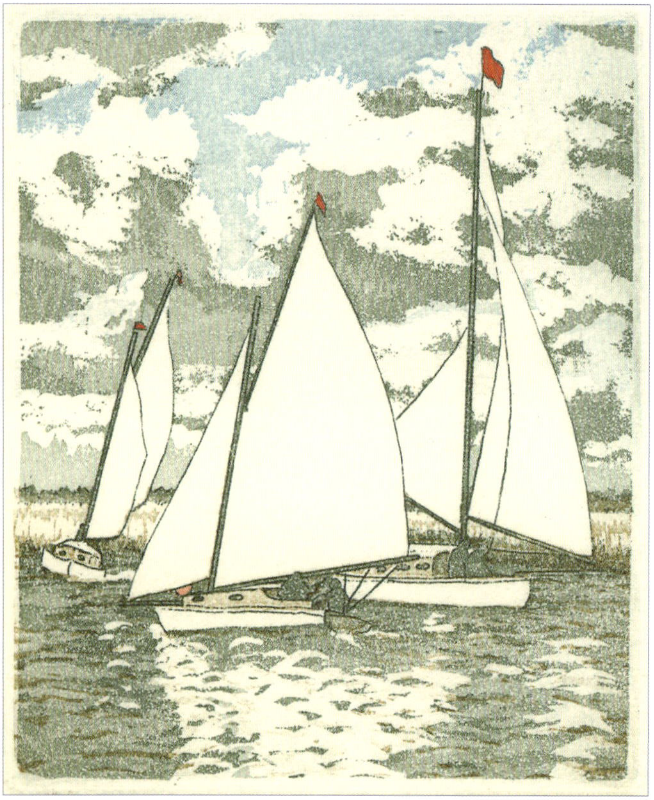

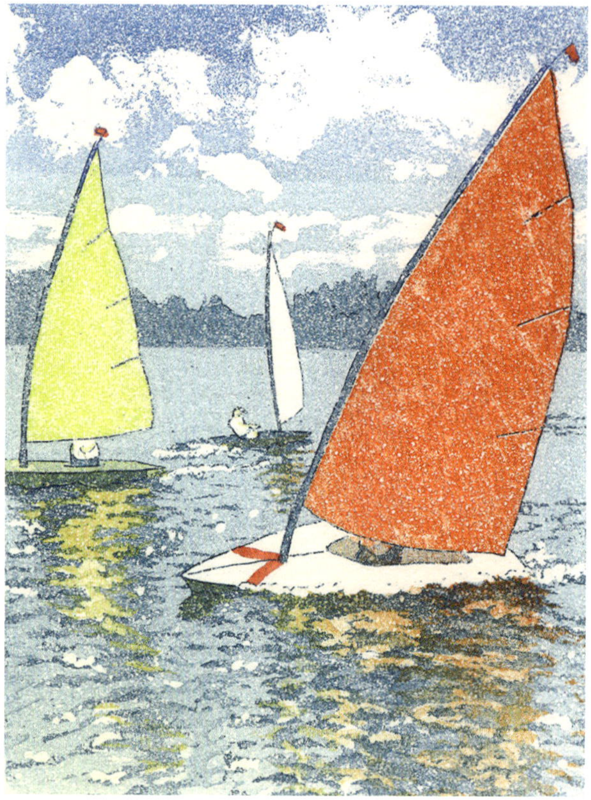

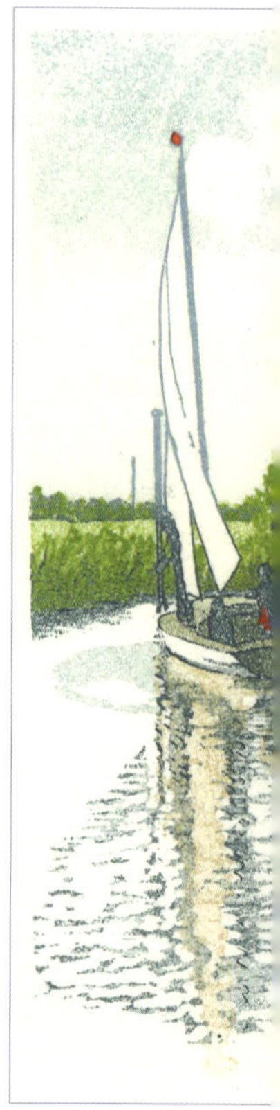

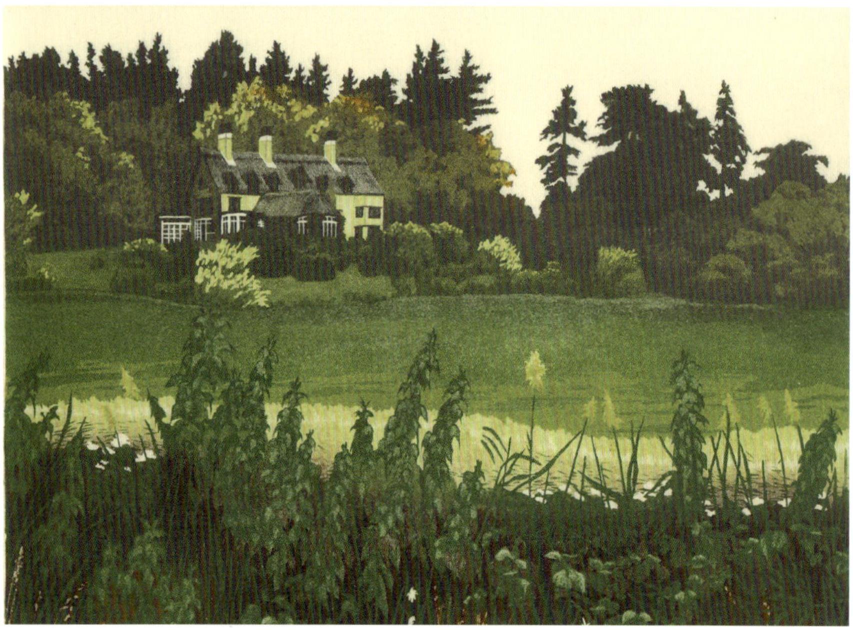

and other traditional non-motorised vessels. Page 42 features wood engraver Anthony Dunigan's portrayal of a black-sailed cargo wherry passing the ruins of St Benet's Abbey. The vessel is likely to be the *Albion*, which has been restored and still sails the northern Broads (see also Jan Dingle's etching on page 52).

Most of the familiar mills along the Broads waterways are, in fact, wind pumps. The sails turn not to grind grain into flour but, perhaps less romantically, to move water. Many are beautifully preserved, such as the National Trust's Horsey wind pump – another of Anthony's engravings seen on page 49.

Jan Dingle, based on the banks of the Thurne, is this book's sole Broads specialist. Her etchings are dominated by scenes of sail, but also depict the lush landscape and a number of the key landmarks. This section begins with her image on page 40 of sailing on the Bure. On this page, bottom left, is the field study centre at How Hill, near Ludham, while the Bure, South Walsham Broad and the River Ant feature in the sailing sequence above.

Ludham is the subject of HJ Jackson's linocut on the

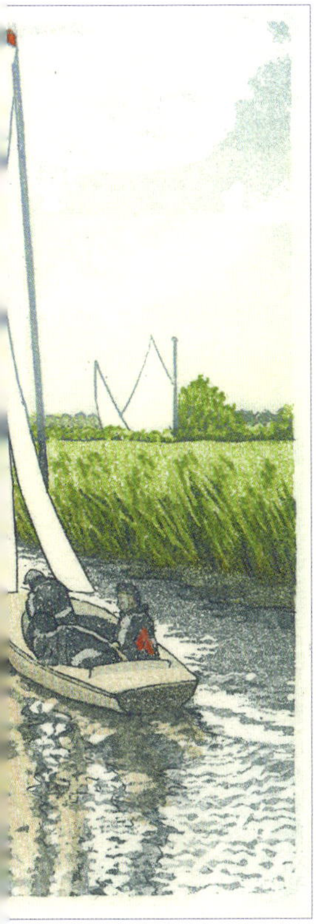

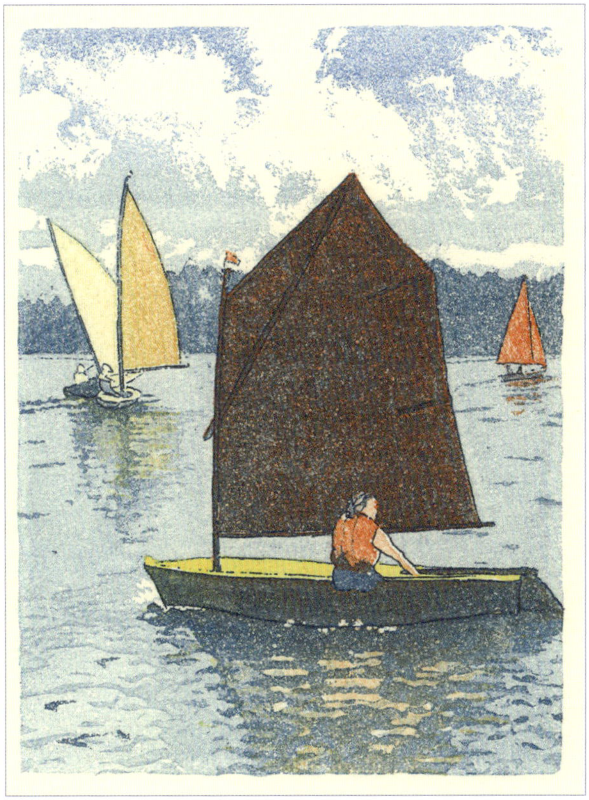

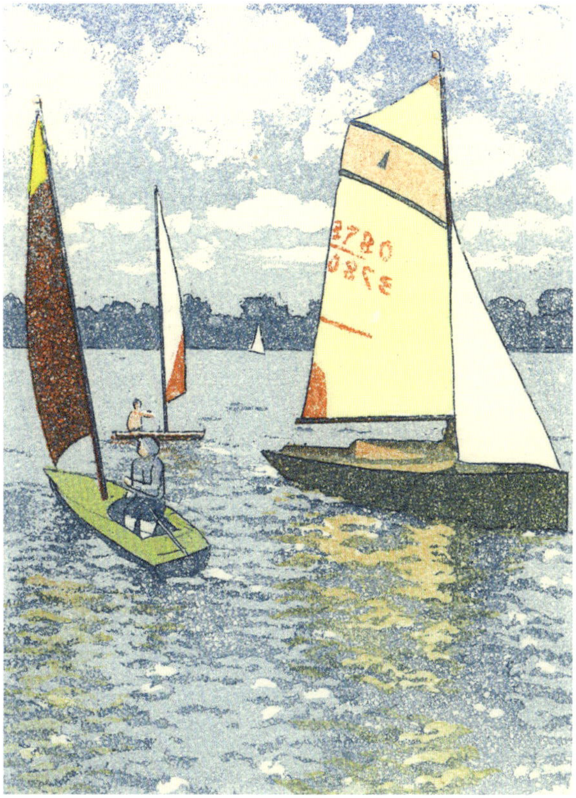

right, featuring majestic architectural gunnera seen in the gardens of local house The Moyle – which once opened to the public each year.

St Benet's Abbey, with the remains of a later windmill creating a familiar landmark, is represented on page 43 in Amelia Bowman's typical collagraph style. *St Benet's Abbey (Daisy, Daisy)* is a 2014 print, 38cm x 27cm, forming an edition of 10. Amelia adds extra colour to the printmaking process by way of an additional technique called 'Chine-collé', which involves the lamination of extra paper to the print as it is transferred.

Carry Akroyd's colourful print on the

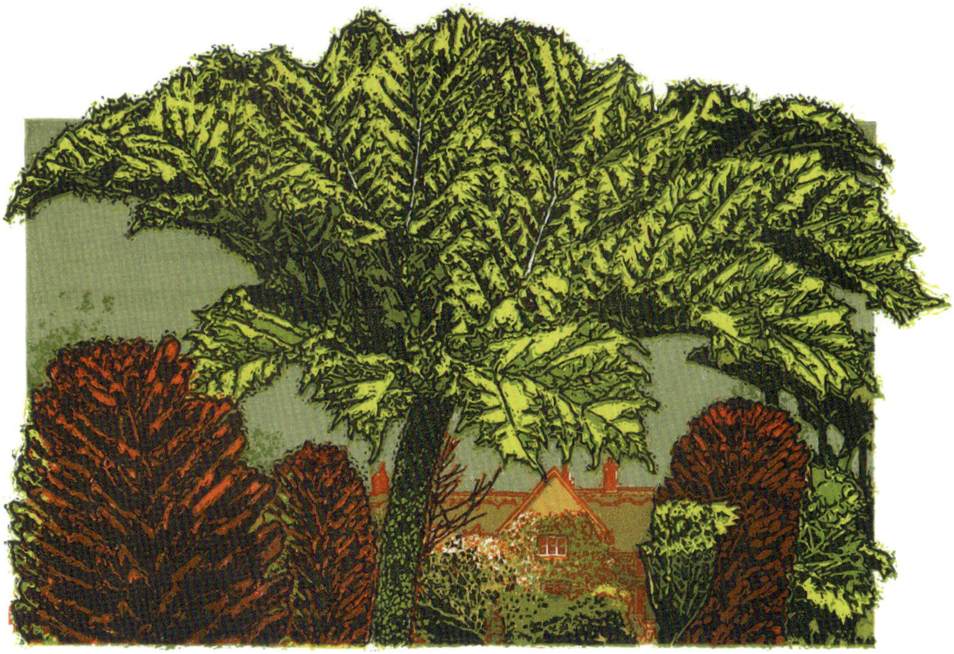

Clockwise from top left: *Jan Dingle – Still Turning (Bure), 8.5cm x 7.5cm; Free Board (South Walsham), 9cm x 7cm; Still Drift (Ant, Three Rivers Race), 9.5cm x 7cm; Free Time, Free Breeze (both South Walsham Broad), 9cm x 7cm (all etchings); HJ Jackson – Gunnera, Late Spring II, linocut; Jan Dingle – House on How Hill, etching, 23cm x 28cm*

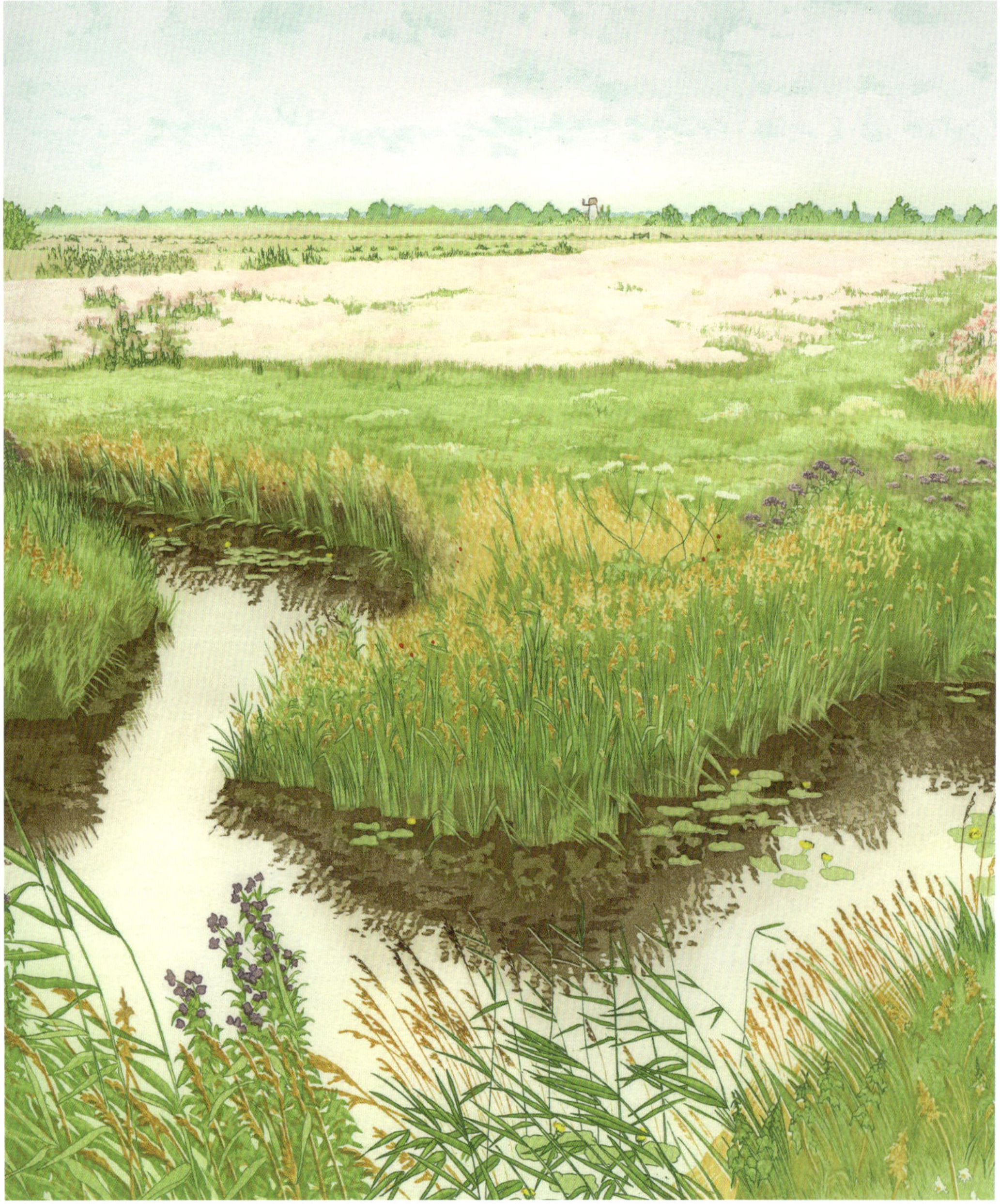

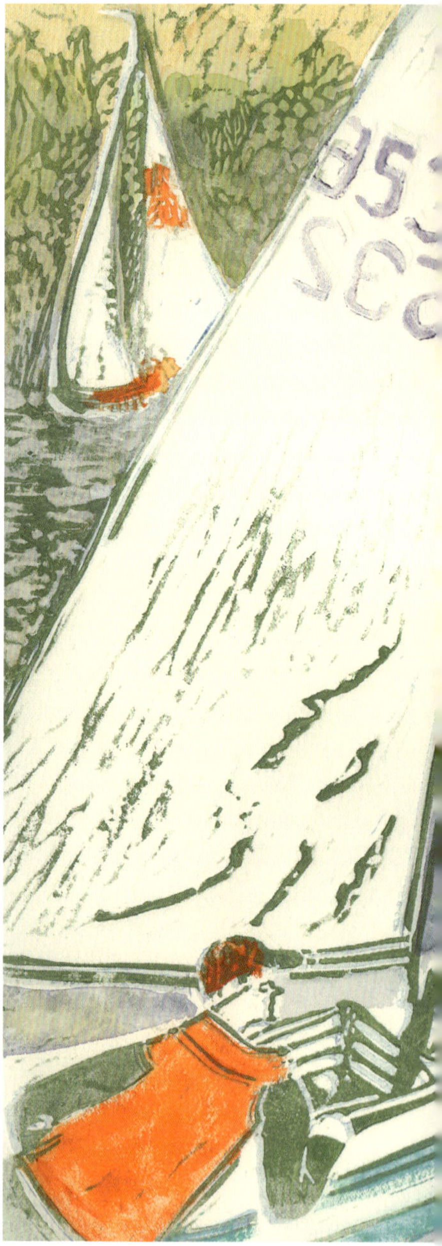

From left: *Jan Dingle – Summerlands (view from Neave's Mill, River Ant) etching, 38cm x 31cm. Moyra Byford – Morning Yacht Race, River Yare) linocut, 40cm x 30cm. Anthony Dunigan – Windpump at St Olaves, engraving on lemonwood, 33cm x 23cm.*

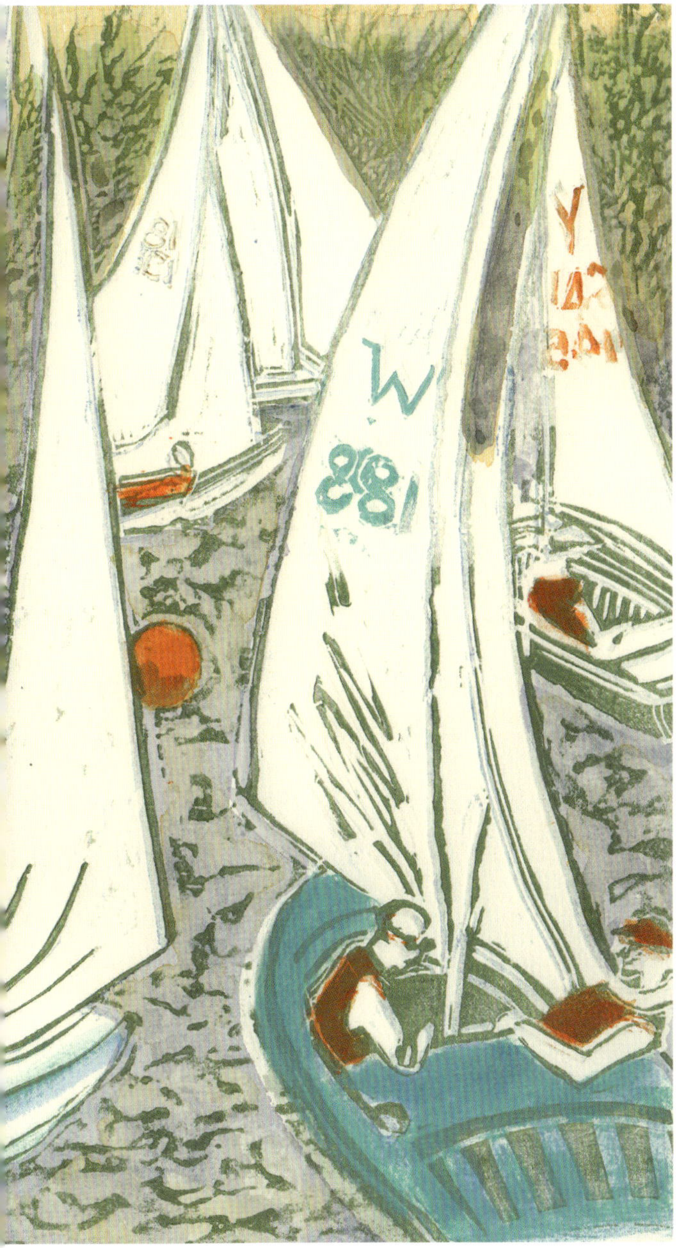

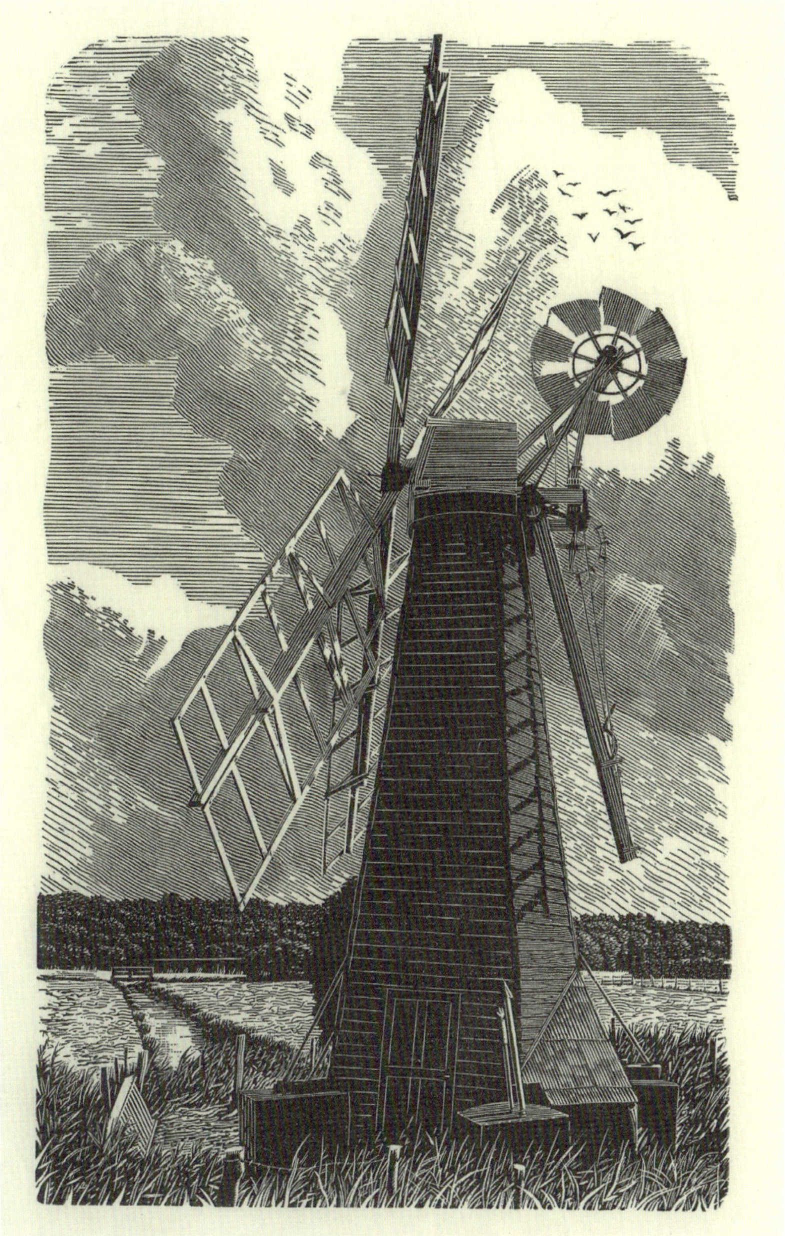

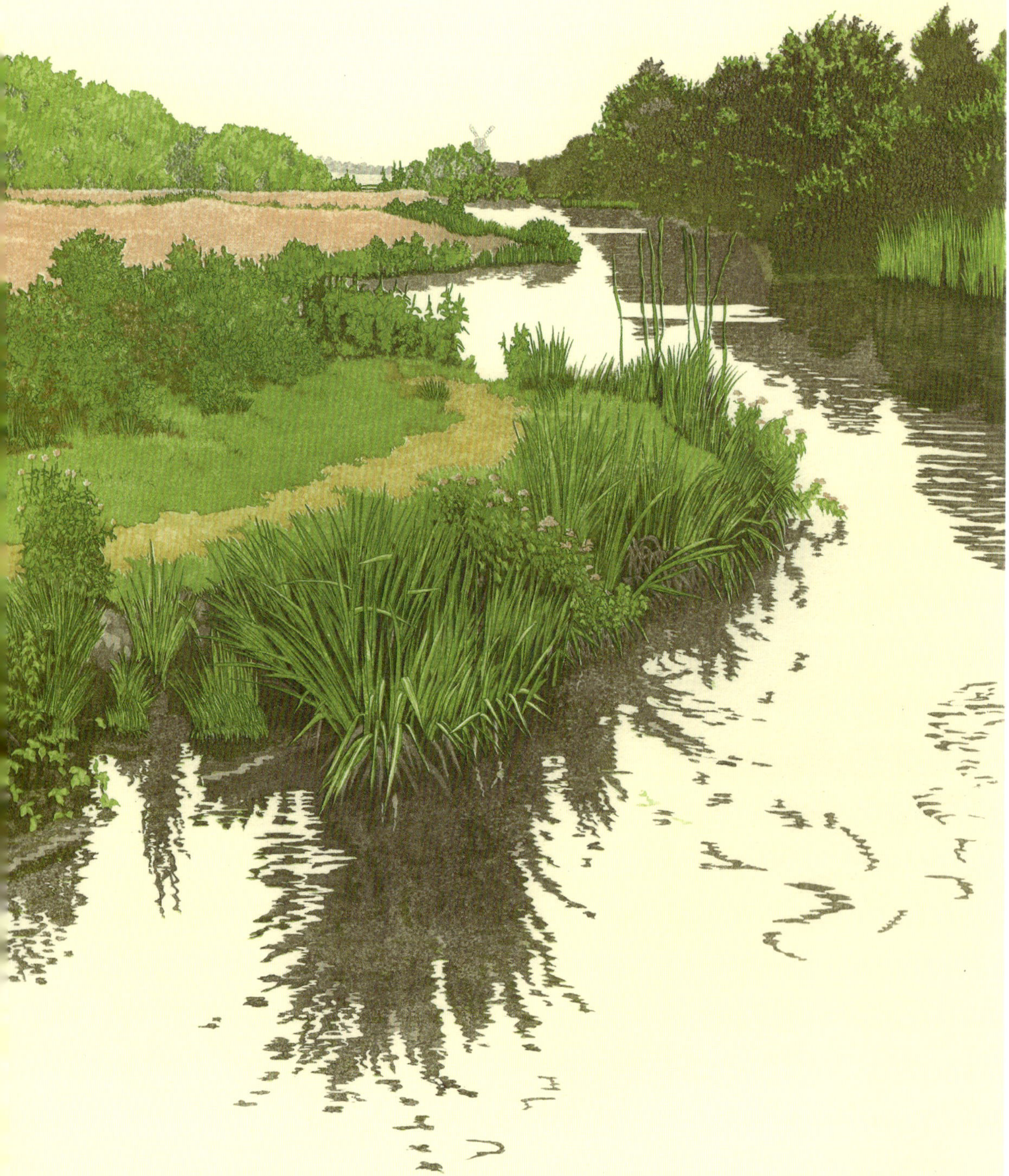

opening spread of this section is the serigraph *Broadland Winter Afternoon* (70cm x 100cm). The artist spent a short midwinter day wandering around Hickling Broad, "peering through reedbeds, standing on tiptoe on higher ground. Sunset came early and the most astonishing redness reflected everywhere."

On page 46 is Suffolk artist Moyra Byford's *Sunday Morning Yacht Racing* (River Yare), which is a linocut appearing alongside a Jan Dingle etching entitled *Summerlands* and Anthony Dunigan's wood engraving of St Olaves mill.

On this page is another large Jan Dingle print *Winding River* (etching, 37cm x 27cm) portraying the River Ant near Hunsett Mill. To the right is Anthony Dunigan's engraving on plastic of *Horsey Mill* (39cm x 32cm, edition of 40).

Page 50 features a linocut print from Norwich-based Vanessa Lubach entitled *Winkle Brig on the Broads*, which is set at Hickling Broad (36.5cm x 27cm, edition of 50). The image on page 51 is another Jan Dingle etching, this time *Abbey Pastures at St Benet's* (22cm x 27cm).

As well as the group of Jan Dingle etchings on pages 52 and 53, we have included a 1981 steel-plate etching by Robert Greenhalf. *Broadland* (23cm x 40cm) is inked in three colours, with yellow hand-colouring in watercolour. It is an imagined scene based on memories and sketches made while visiting the Broads. Robert has a colourful woodcut portraying Swallowtail butterflies at

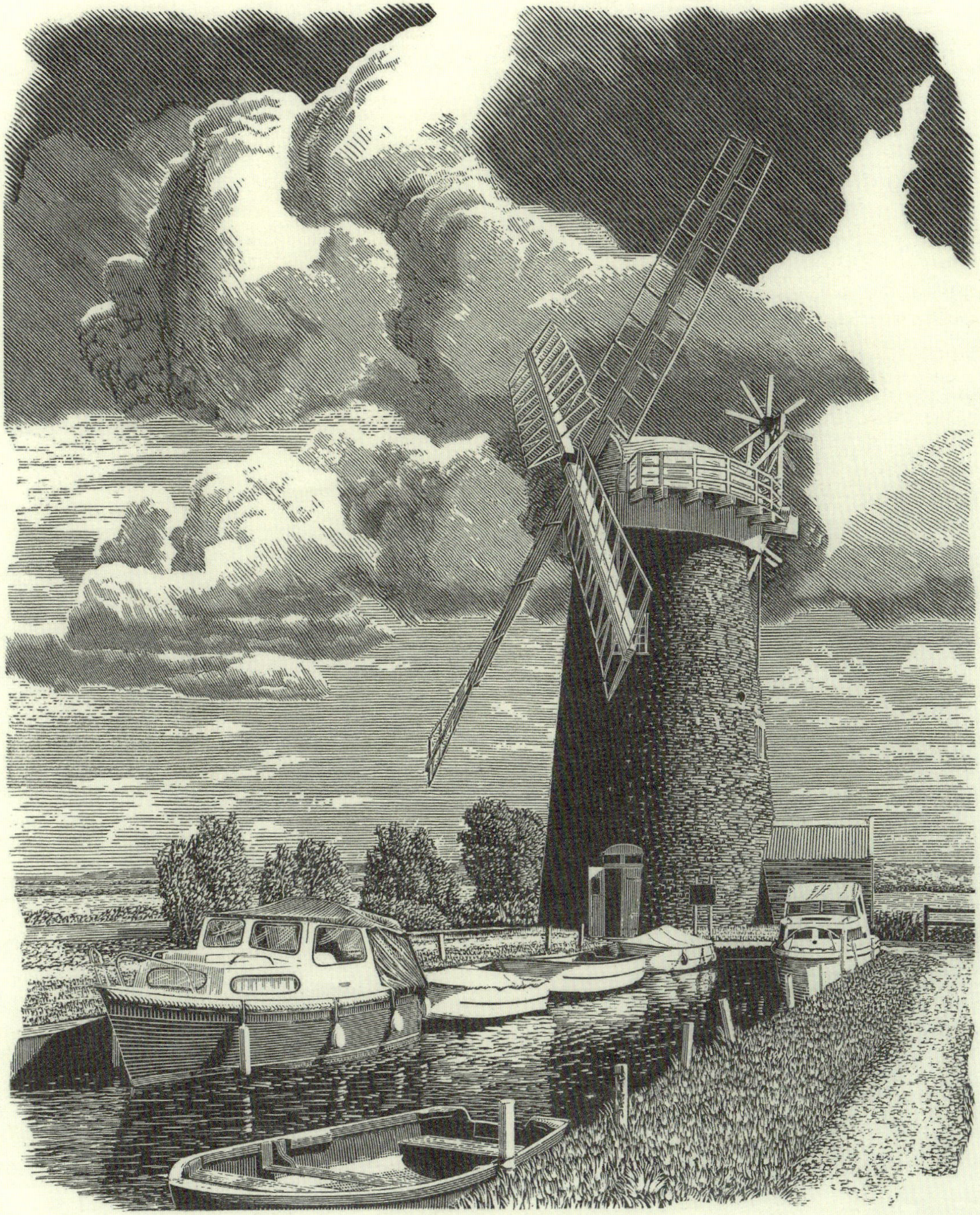

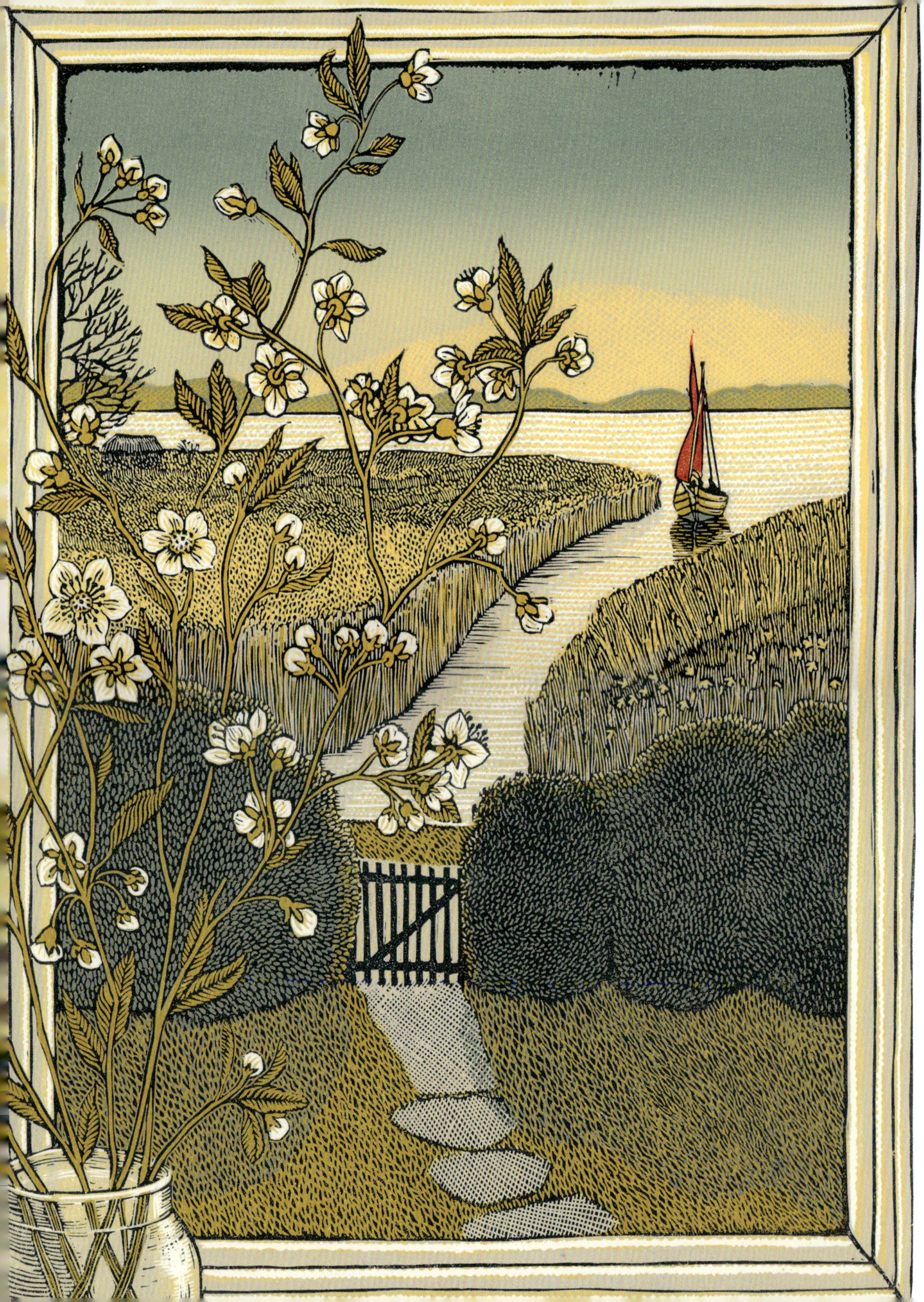

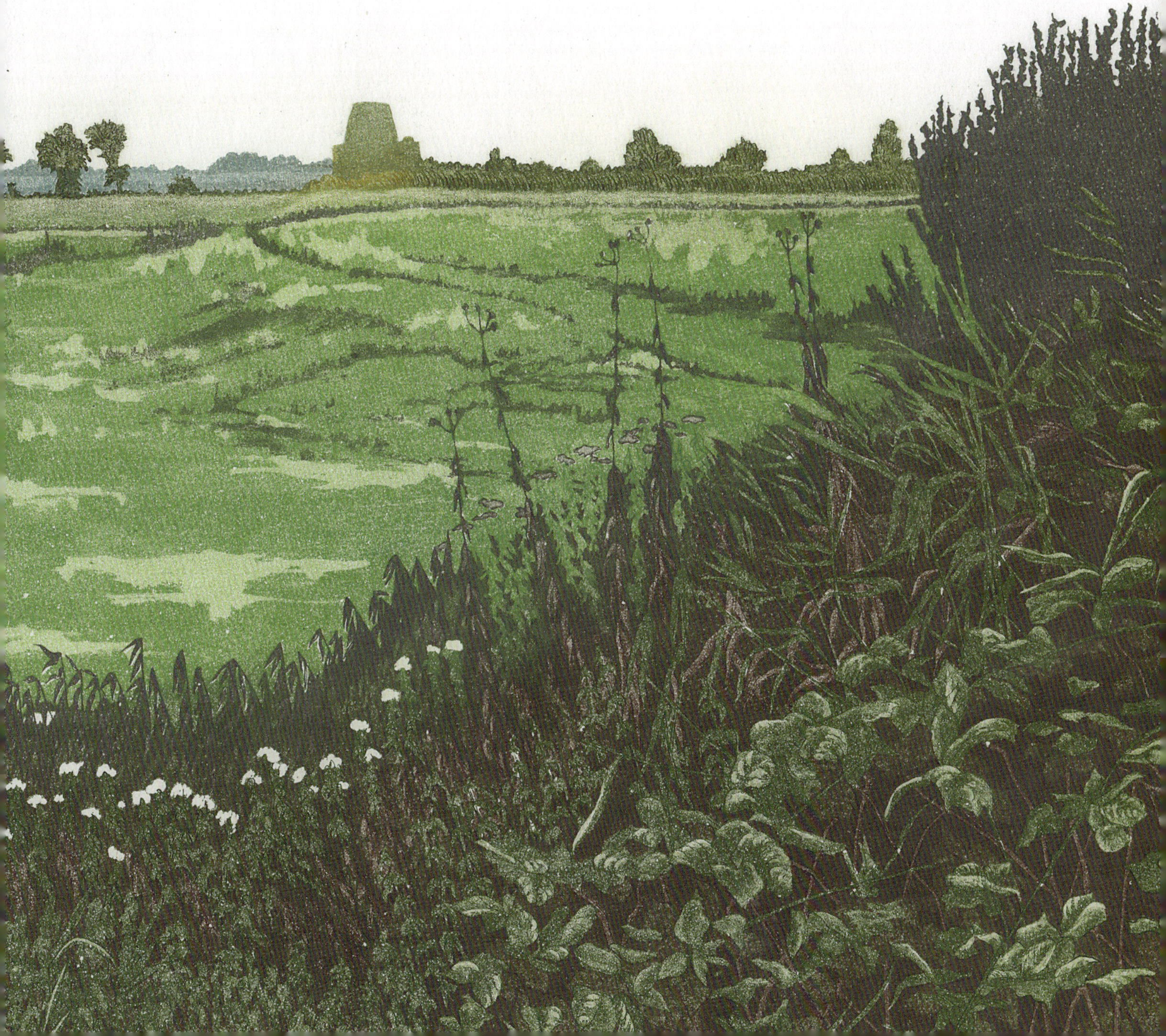

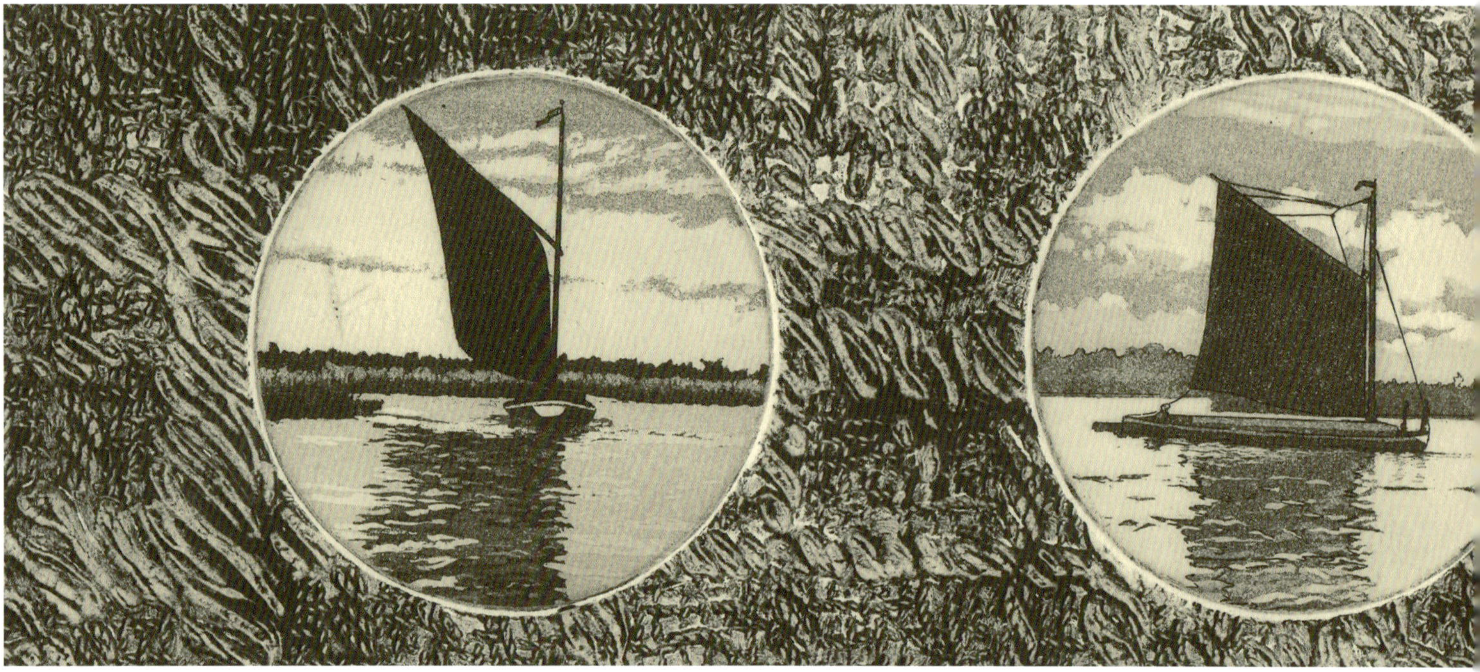

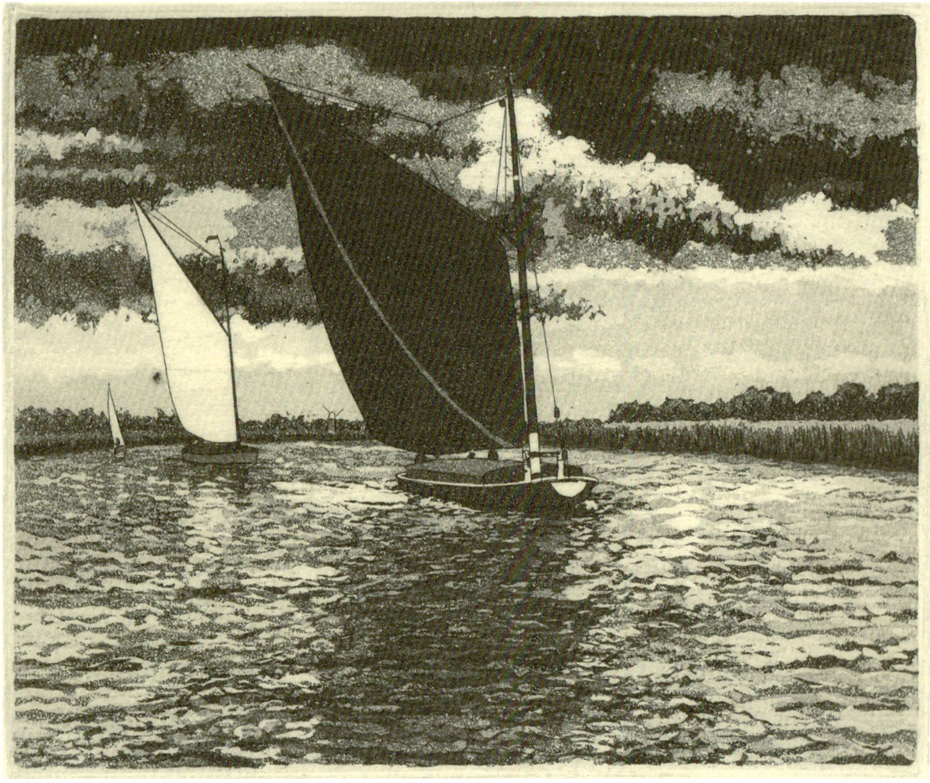

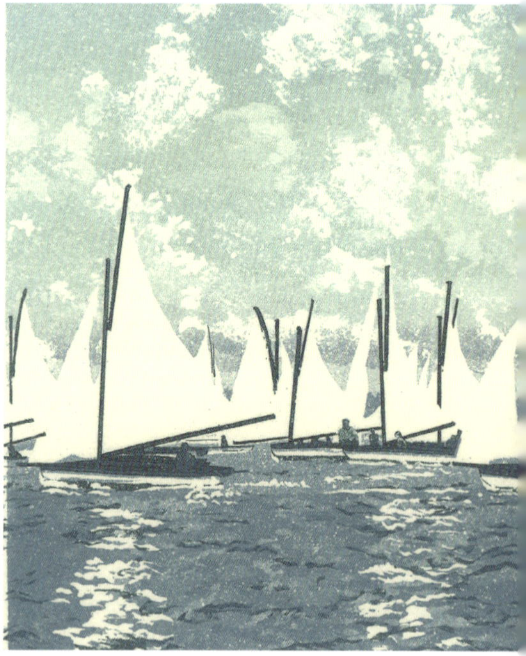

Clockwise from top left: *Jan Dingle – Wherry triptych; Thurne Mill (etchings); Robert Greenhalf – Broadland (etching); Jan Dingle – Whiteout on Barton Broad; Albion Approaching (etchings)*

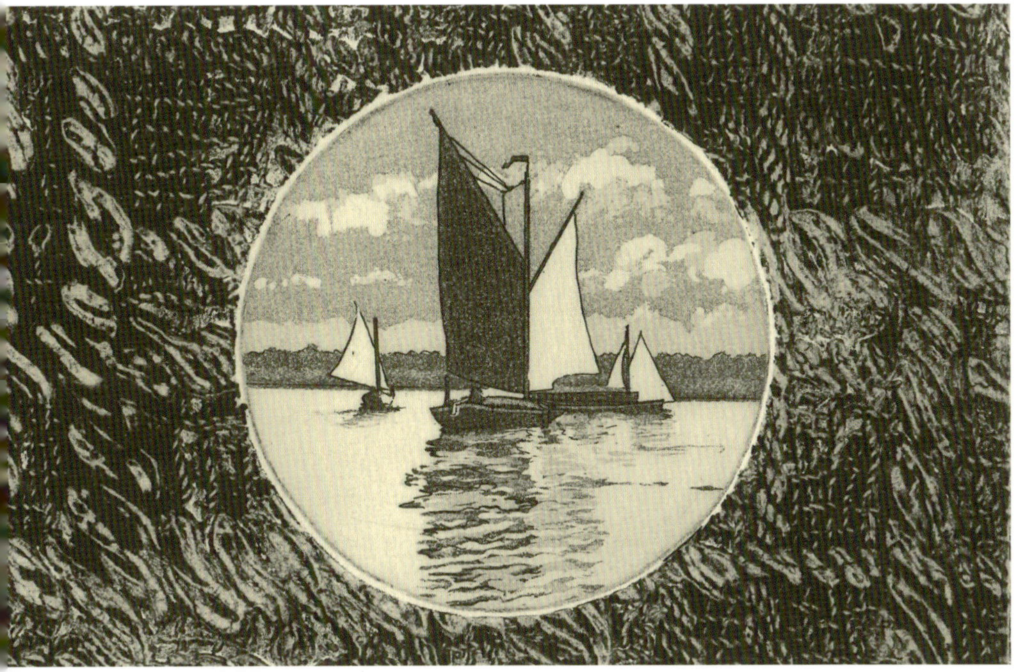
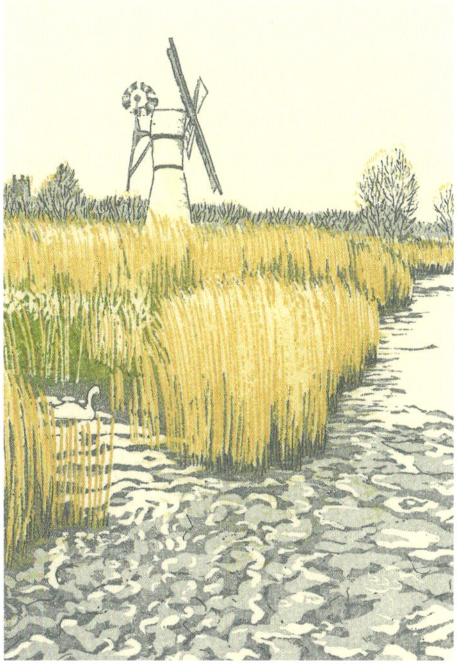
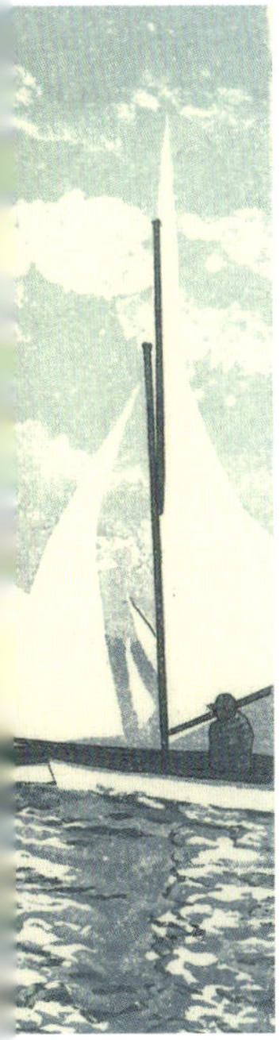
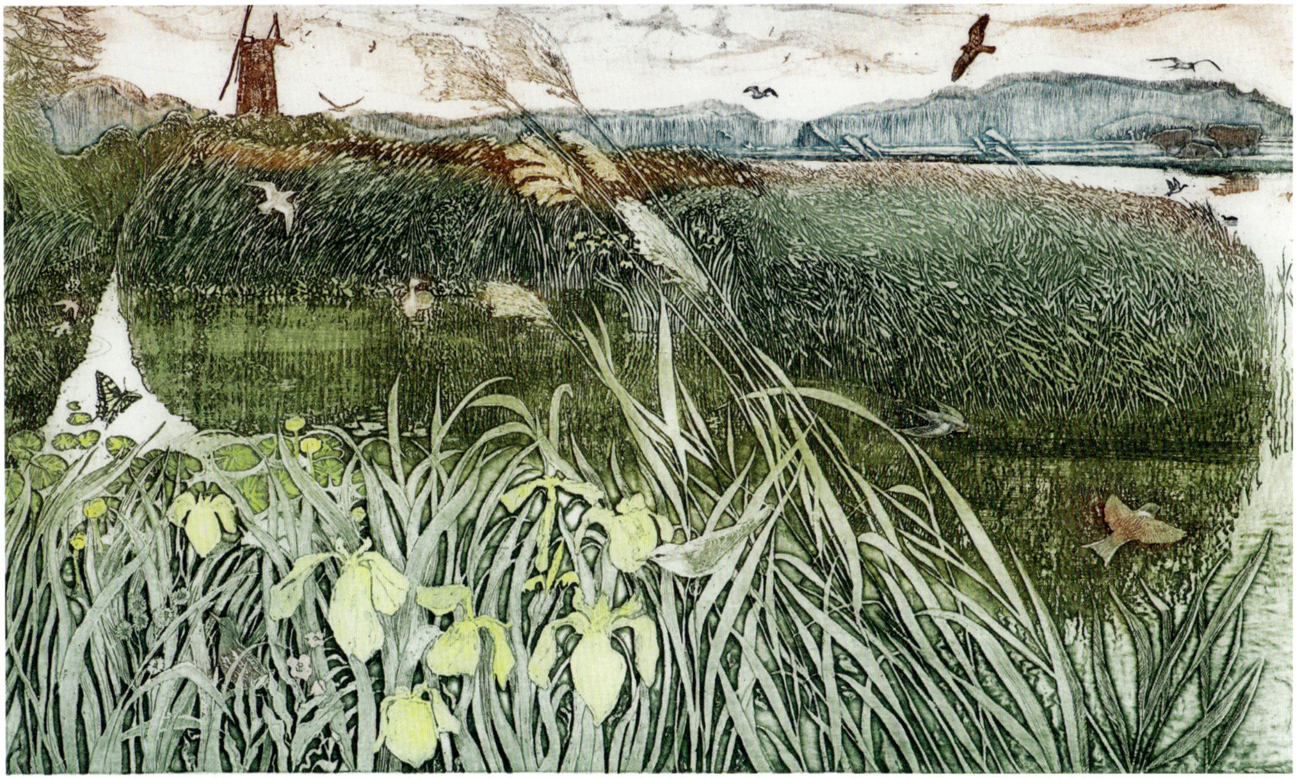

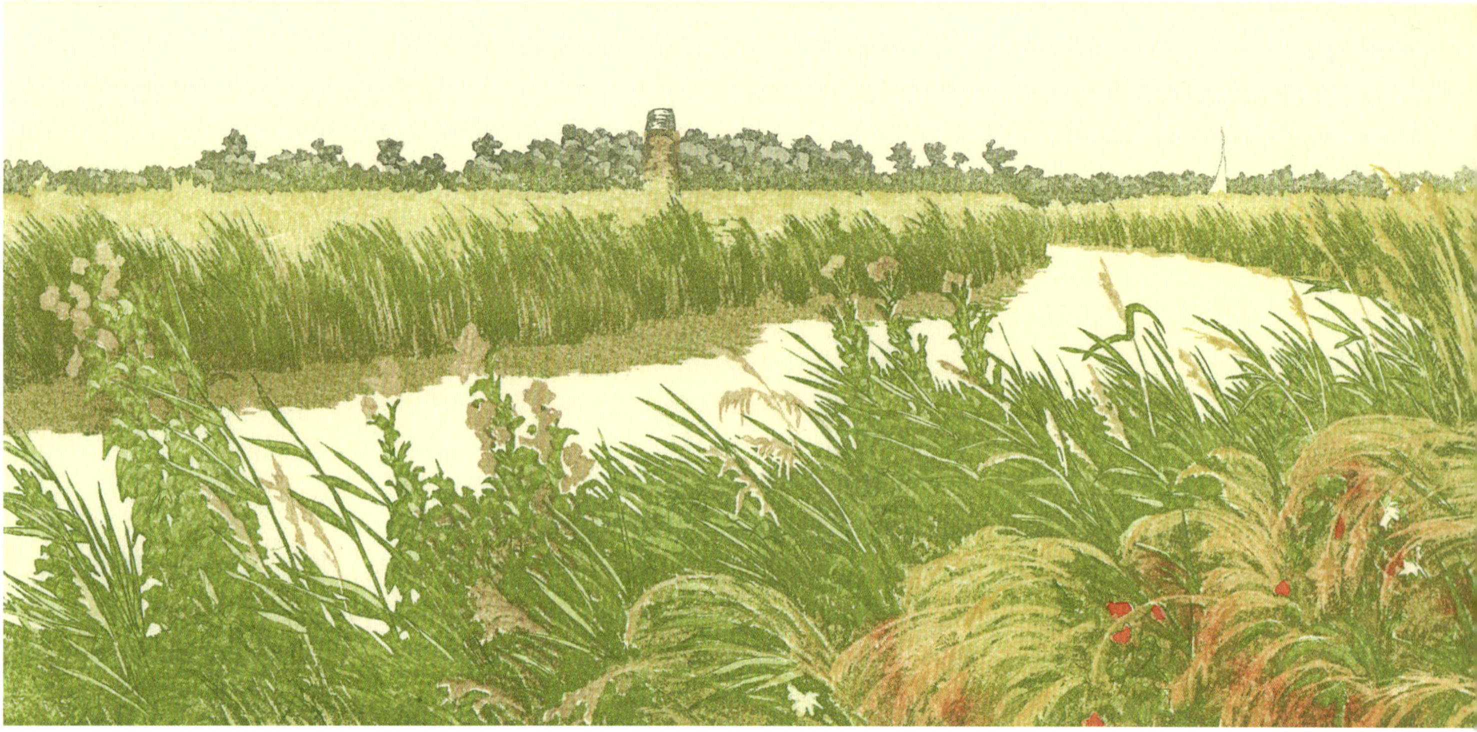

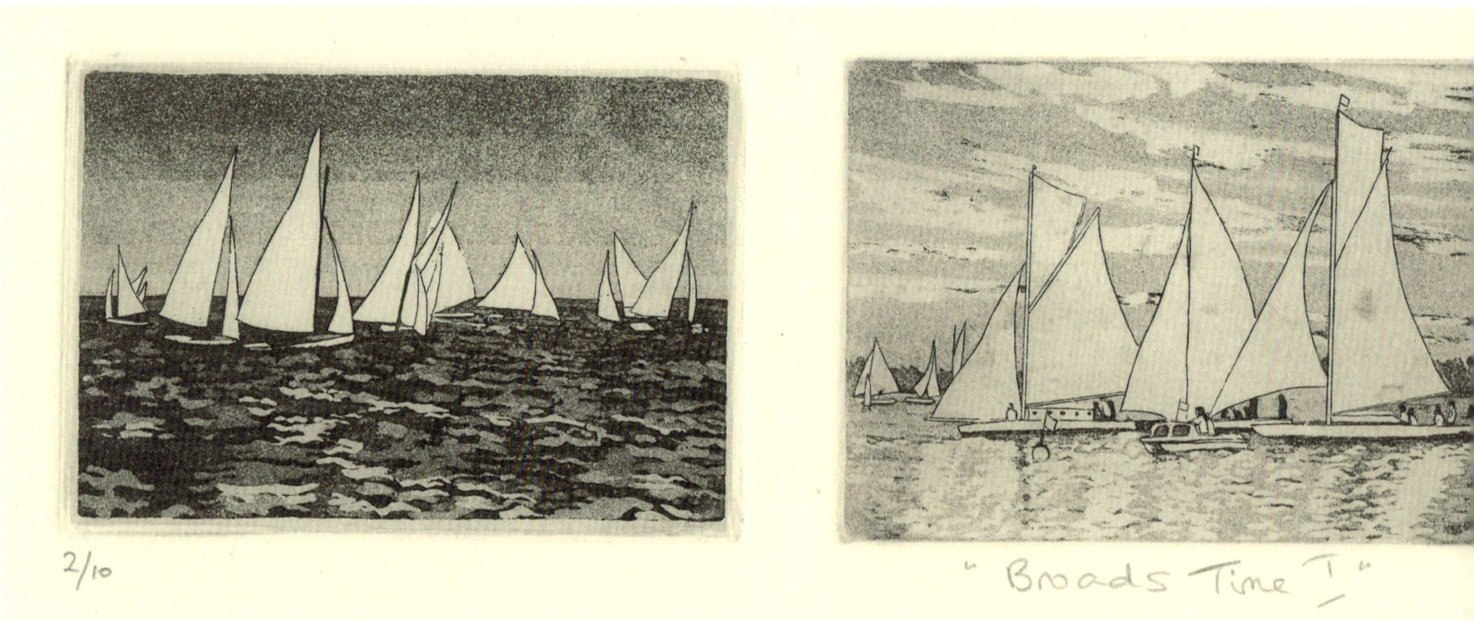
2/10
"Broads Time!"

Left: *Jan Dingle – Riverside Path (the Ant), etching, 9cm x 30cm.*
Below left: *Jan Dingle – Broads Time I (Wroxham Broad), etching, each 7cm x 10cm.* ***Below***: *Jeremy James – Great Crested Grebes, linocut.*
Bottom: *Jenny Portlock – Summertime, linocut.*

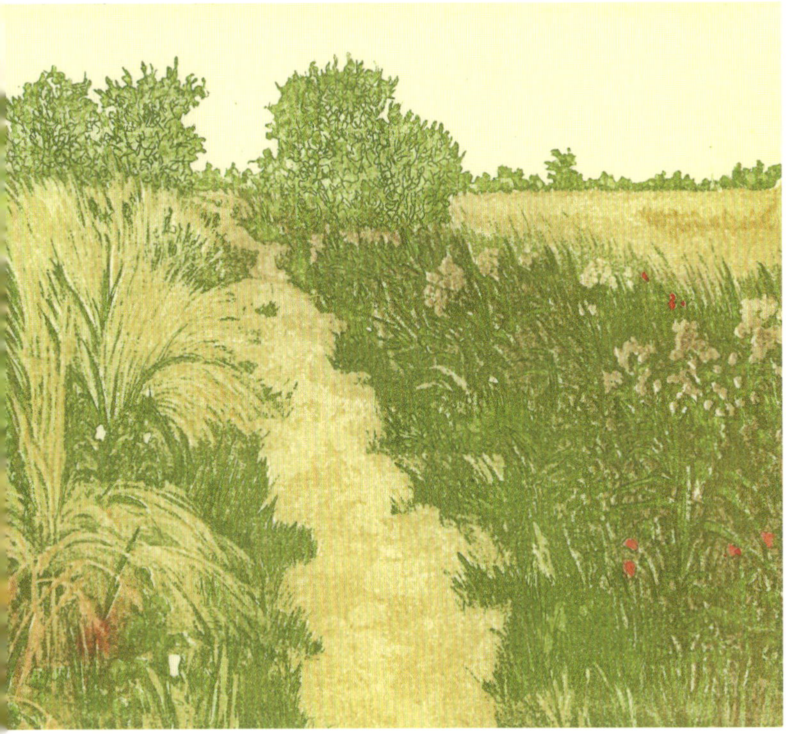

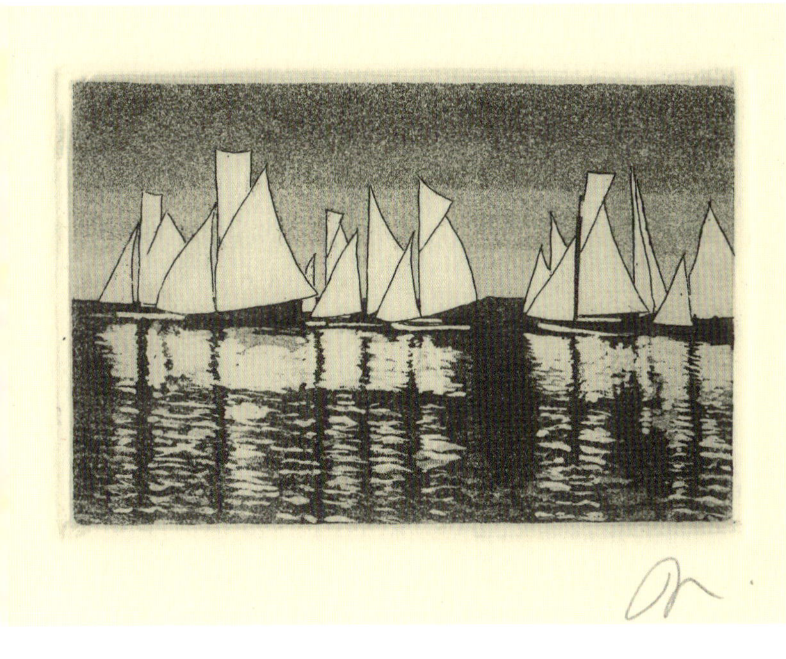

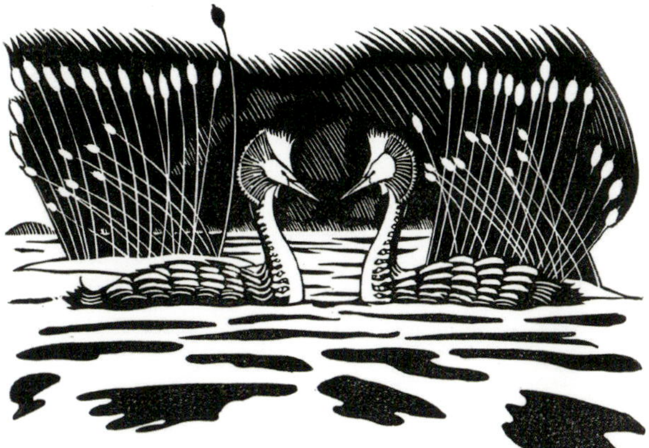

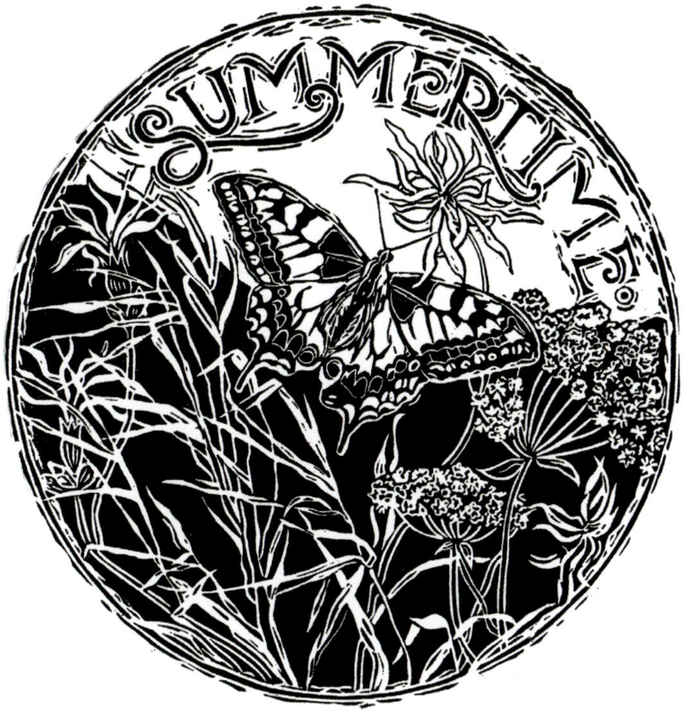

Hickling Broad, which appears below. *Swallowtails*, from 2009, is a five-block print featuring six colours. The small dots of red on the butterflies are hand-coloured with watercolour. Robert made the print based on pencil and watercolour sketches made at Hickling Broad.

Staying with a wildlife theme, ceramic artist and printmaker Jeremy James provides us with a small linocut of *Great Crested Grebes* on page 55, above Jenny Portlock's 15cm-diameter linocut *Summertime* featuring Broads butterfly speciality the Swallowtail.

Fiona Carver's *Sailing on the Broads* (far right, top) is one of the Suffolk artist's earlier prints, dated 2009. The composition was put together from a series of sketches she produced on a trip to the Norfolk Broads on August bank holiday. "The traditional gaff-rigged sailing boats have a very 1920s feel to them, and this is reflected in the print."

Jan Dingle captures a piece of history with her etching *The Reedcutter's Harvest* (far right, bottom), as it shows famed reedman Eric Edward's last harvest at How Hill. He died in 2012.

Norwich-based Sarah Bays tends to work with drypoint and monotype. Her image of Repps with Bastwick (right) is a Broadlands scene near the River Thurne. The 2012 drypoint *Across the Marsh* was inspired by a day of sketching on the Thurne. "I turned my back (to the river) and was struck by the panoramic view across the marsh towards Repps with Bastwick with the distinctive round tower of the church in the distance."

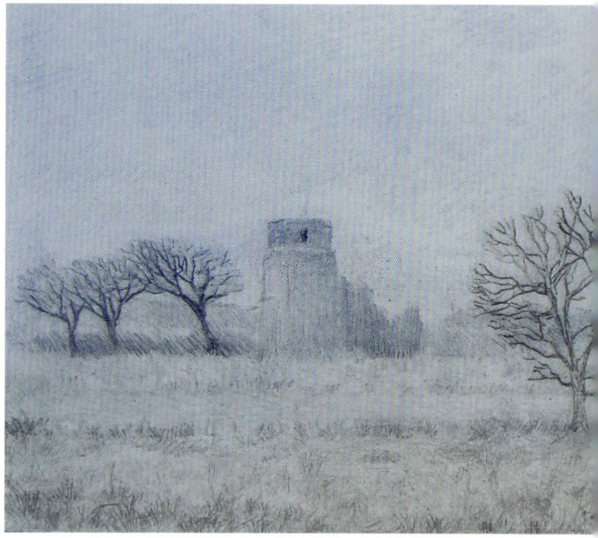

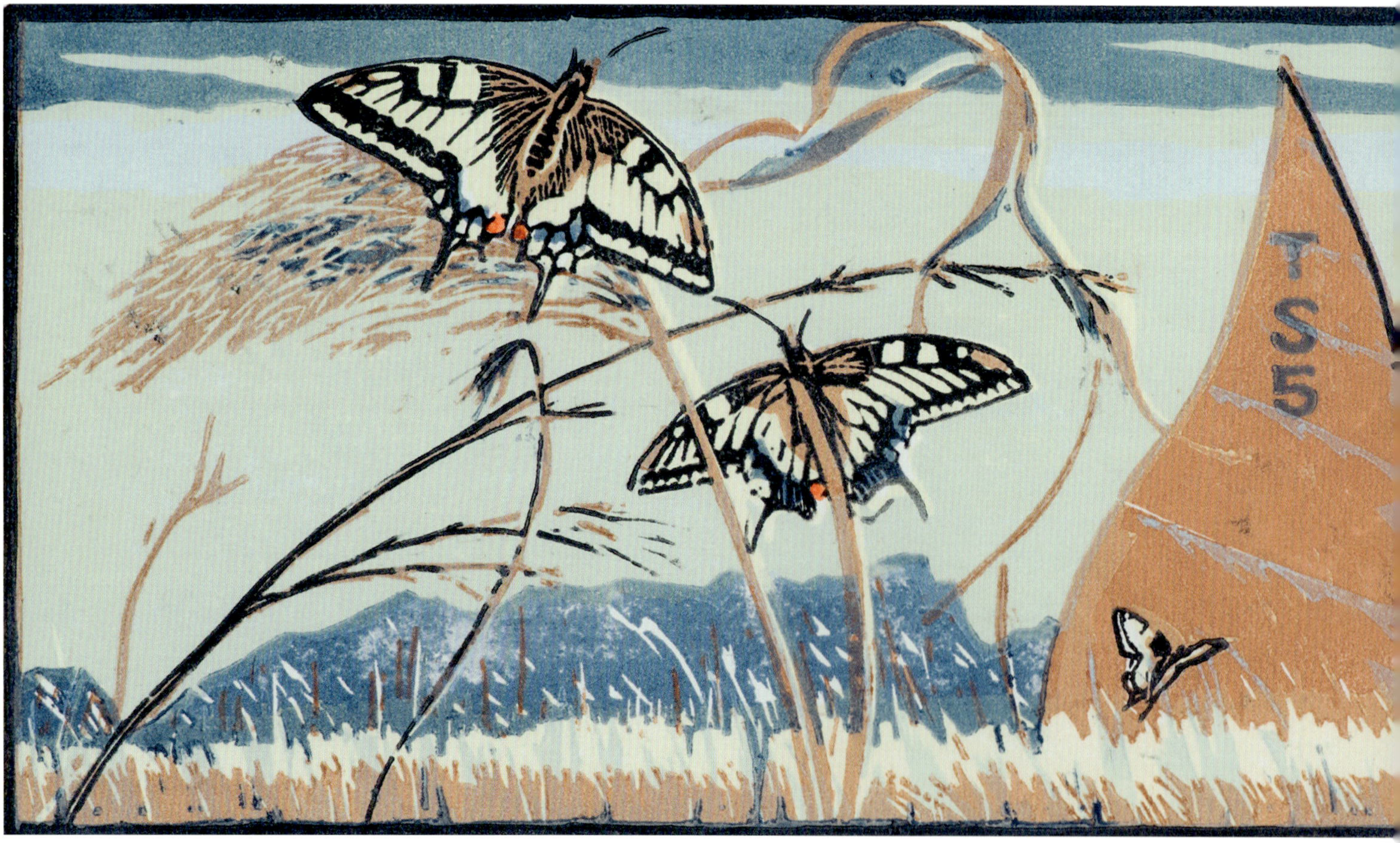

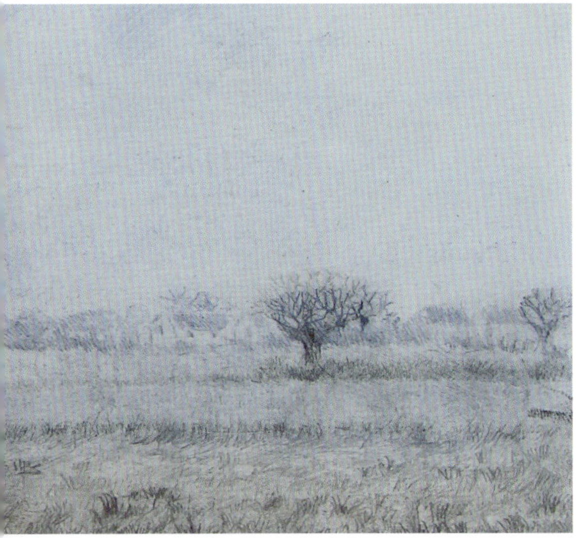

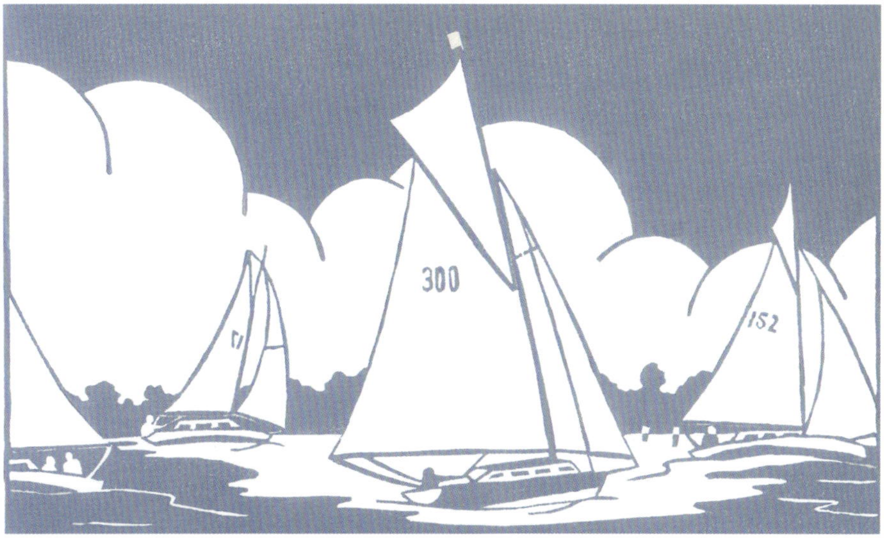

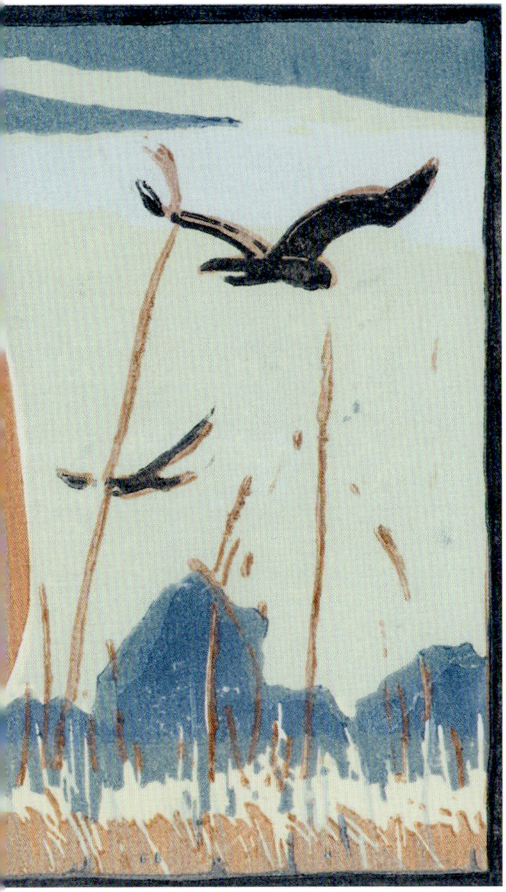

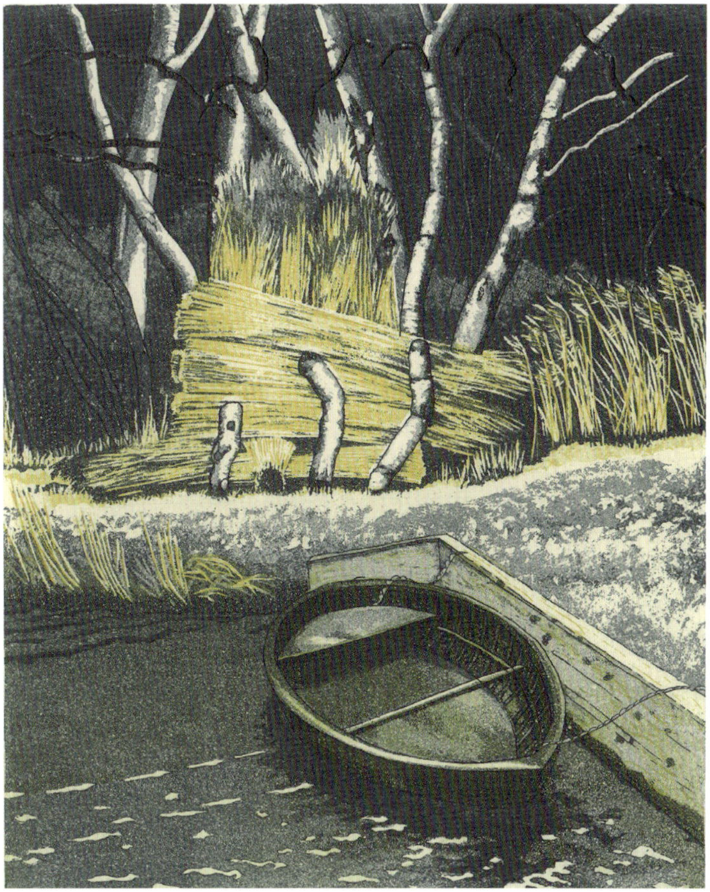

Left: *Jan Dingle – The Reedcutters' Harvest (How Hill), etching, 17cm x 14cm.*
Far left: *Robert Greenhalf – Swallowtails (Hickling Broad), woodcut, 16cm x 39cm.*
Above: *Fiona Carver – Sailing on the Broads, linocut, 18cm x 29cm.*
Top left: *Sarah Bays – Across the Marsh (Repps with Bastwick), drypoint, 7.5cm x 17cm.*

Burnham Overy Staithe

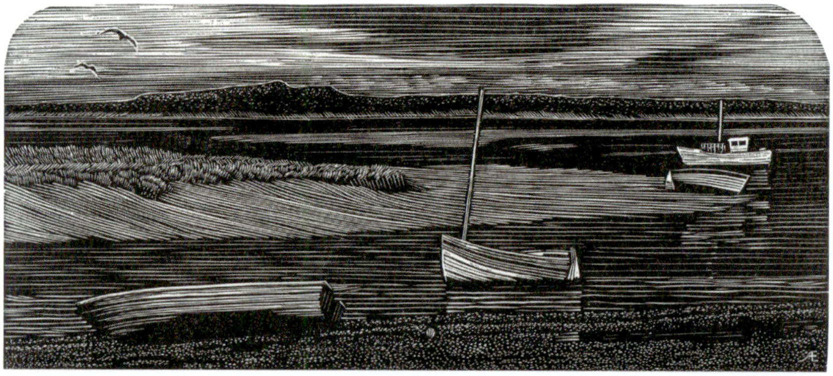

***Left**: Andy English – Low Tide (wood engraving), 5cm x 12.9cm. **Below**: Burnham Overy Staithe – Colin Moore (linocut), 23.5cm x 35cm sheet size. **Opposite**: Glynn Thomas – Burnham Overy Staithe (etching), 29cm x 20cm.*

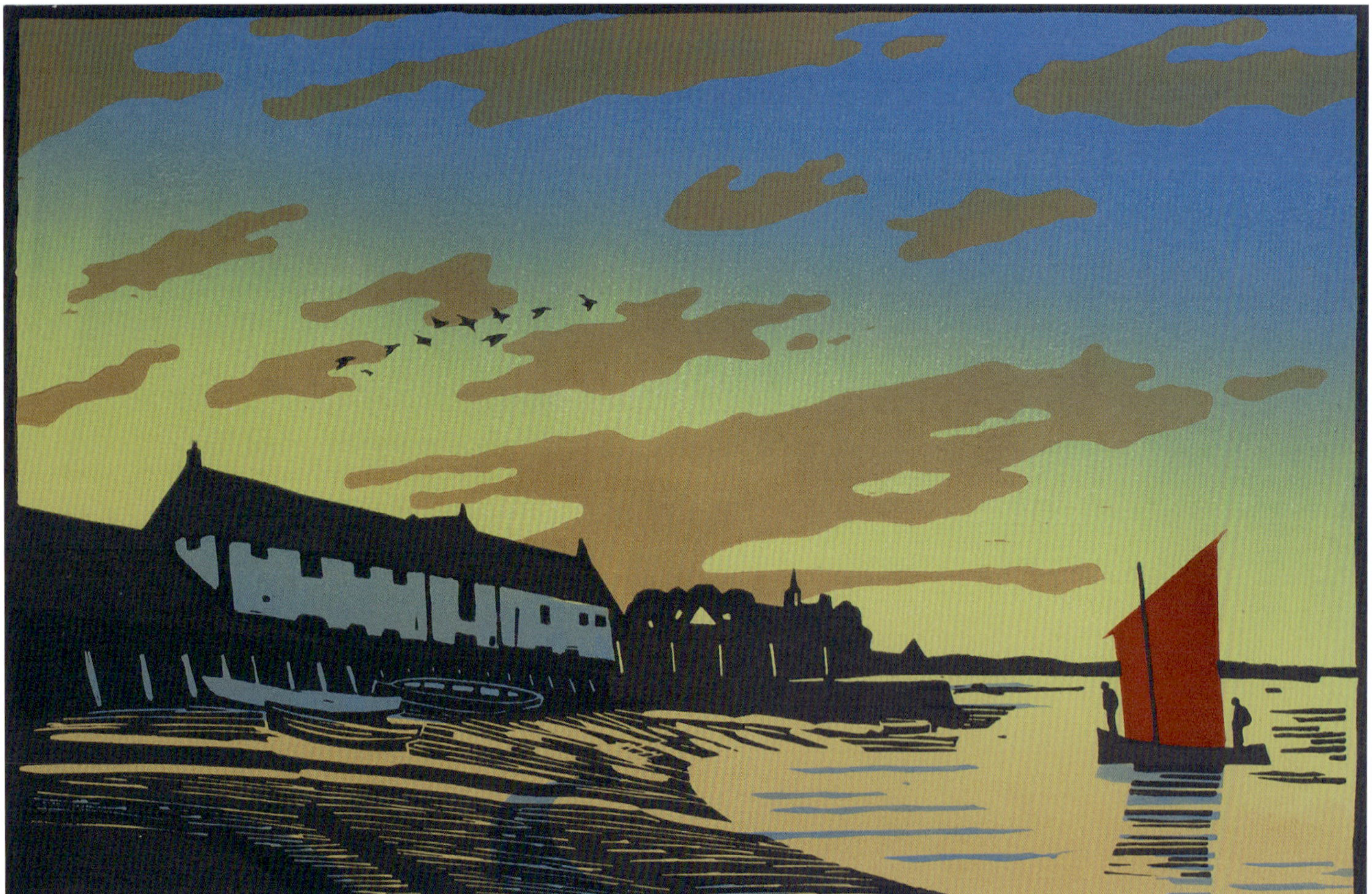

A mill, mud, birds and boats are the main features of Glynn Thomas's 2009 etching on the right, and reflect pretty much the scene at this attractive North Norfolk hamlet. Forming one of many 'Burnhams' in the area, this is Nelson country, home of Britain's greatest naval hero. Burnham Overy lies between the larger village of Burnham Market to the west, and Holkham to the east. Burnham Thorpe, the birthplace of Horatio Nelson, lies one mile to the south-east.

According to various letters and documents, Nelson at the age of 10 learnt to row and sail a dinghy at Burnham Overy Staithe, two years before joining the Navy. Between Burnham Overy Staithe and the sea, the river spreads out into numerous tidal creeks cutting through the salt marshes, and finally reaches the sea by passing though the fronting sand dunes at a gap known as Burnham Harbour. Small boats can reach Burnham Overy Staithe through this gap and creek. Today, Burnham Overy Staithe and the associated harbour is a major recreational sailing centre.

Colin Moore's 2013 three-block linocut on the left shows two weekend sailors tiding in on the last of the breeze. According to the artist, their eyes are fixed on the pub...

Norfolk-born but Ely-based wood engraver Andy English contributed the print *Low Tide* originally for the 2015 Front Street Press edition of *Destination Norfolk*, a childhood journey to North Norfolk written (in prose) by former Poet Laureate Sir Andrew Motion.

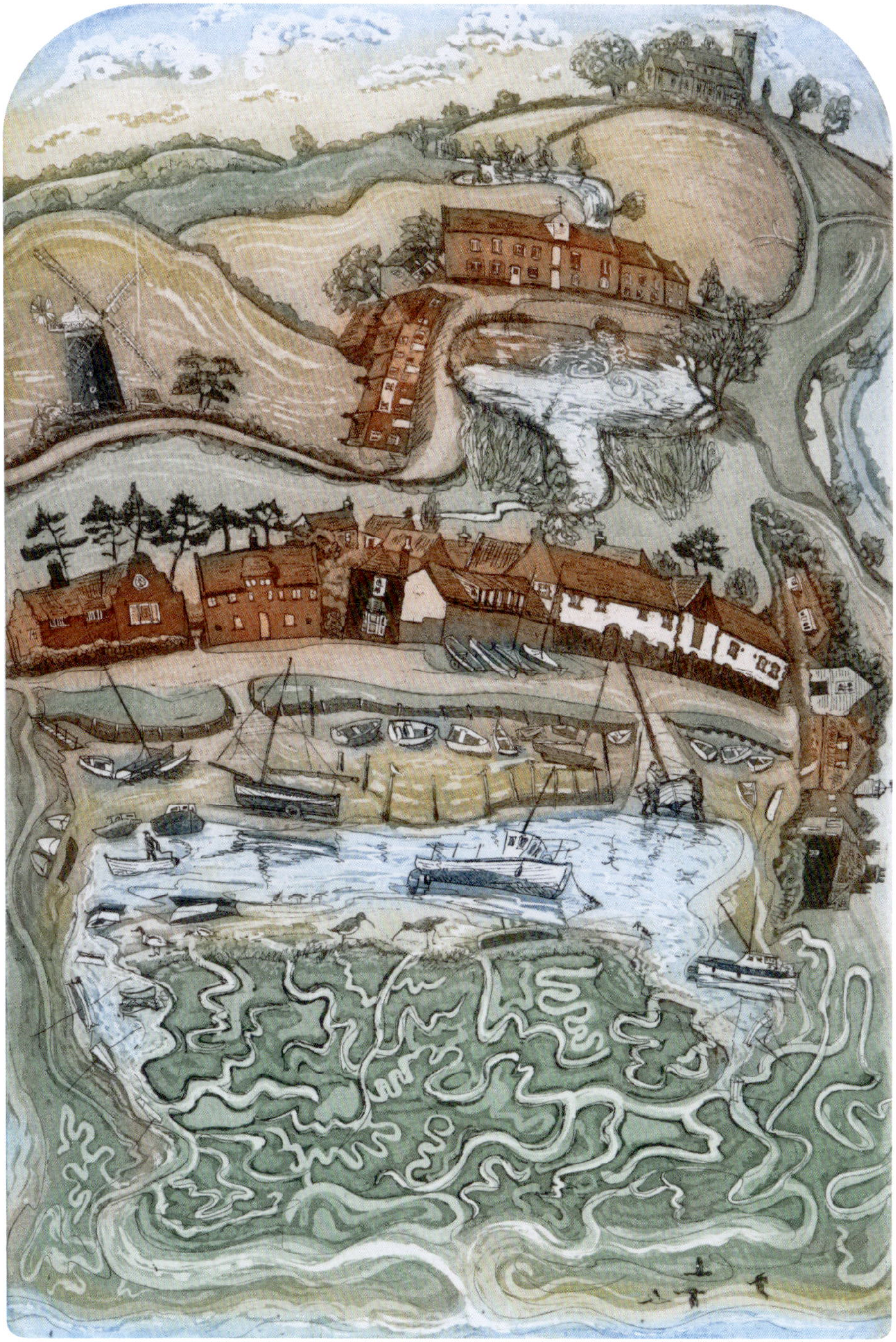

Cley-next-the-Sea

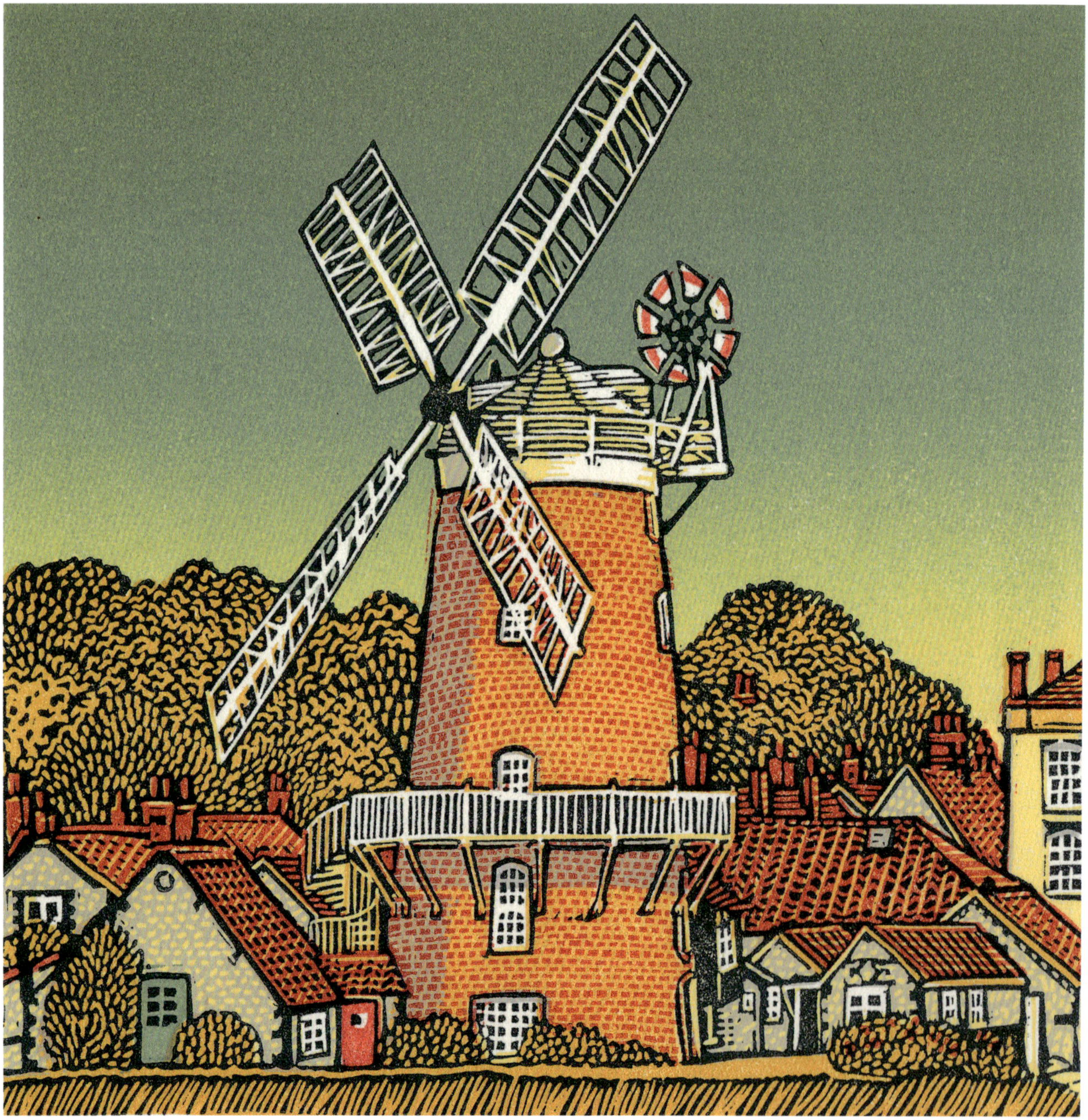

Nowadays a mile from open water, Cley was once a major port, importing and exporting a variety of goods. The main trade today is tourism, with the village a magnet for bird-lovers and artists. The 18th-century windmill (shown on the left in a linocut by Vanessa Lubach) is beautifully preserved and provides B&B accommodation, with rooms looking out on to the marshes and shingle beach beyond. The area between the village and the sea is an Area of Outstanding Natural Beauty. Vanessa's *Cley Windmill* print measures 14cm x 14cm and forms part of an edition of 50.

The atmospheric linocut below is by wildlife artist Max Angus, who spends plenty of her spare time in North Norfolk and stalks the coastline in search of inspiration for the next printmaking idea.

Just a week after the December 2013 sea surge that flooded large parts of coastal Norfolk, Max returned to the area. "The

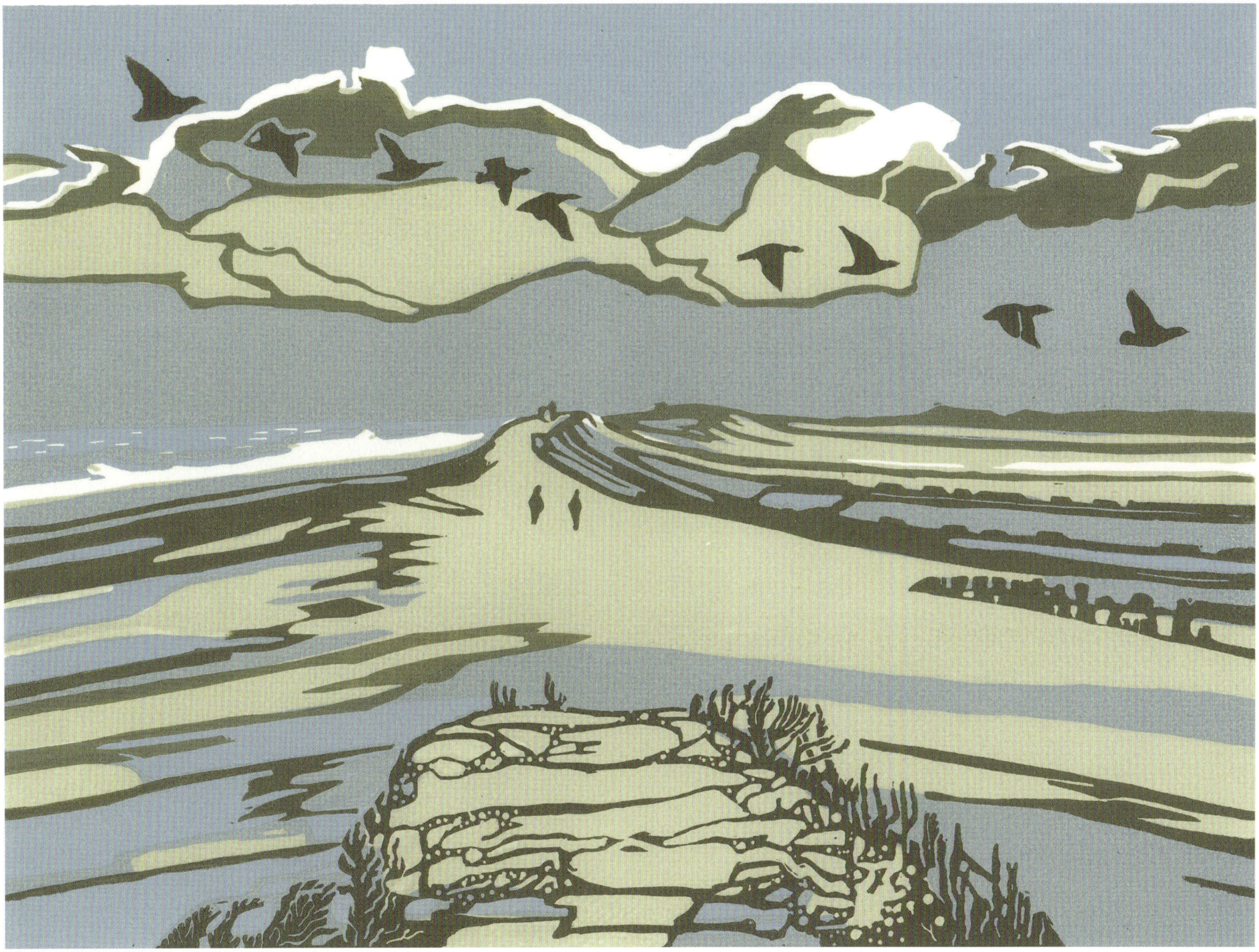

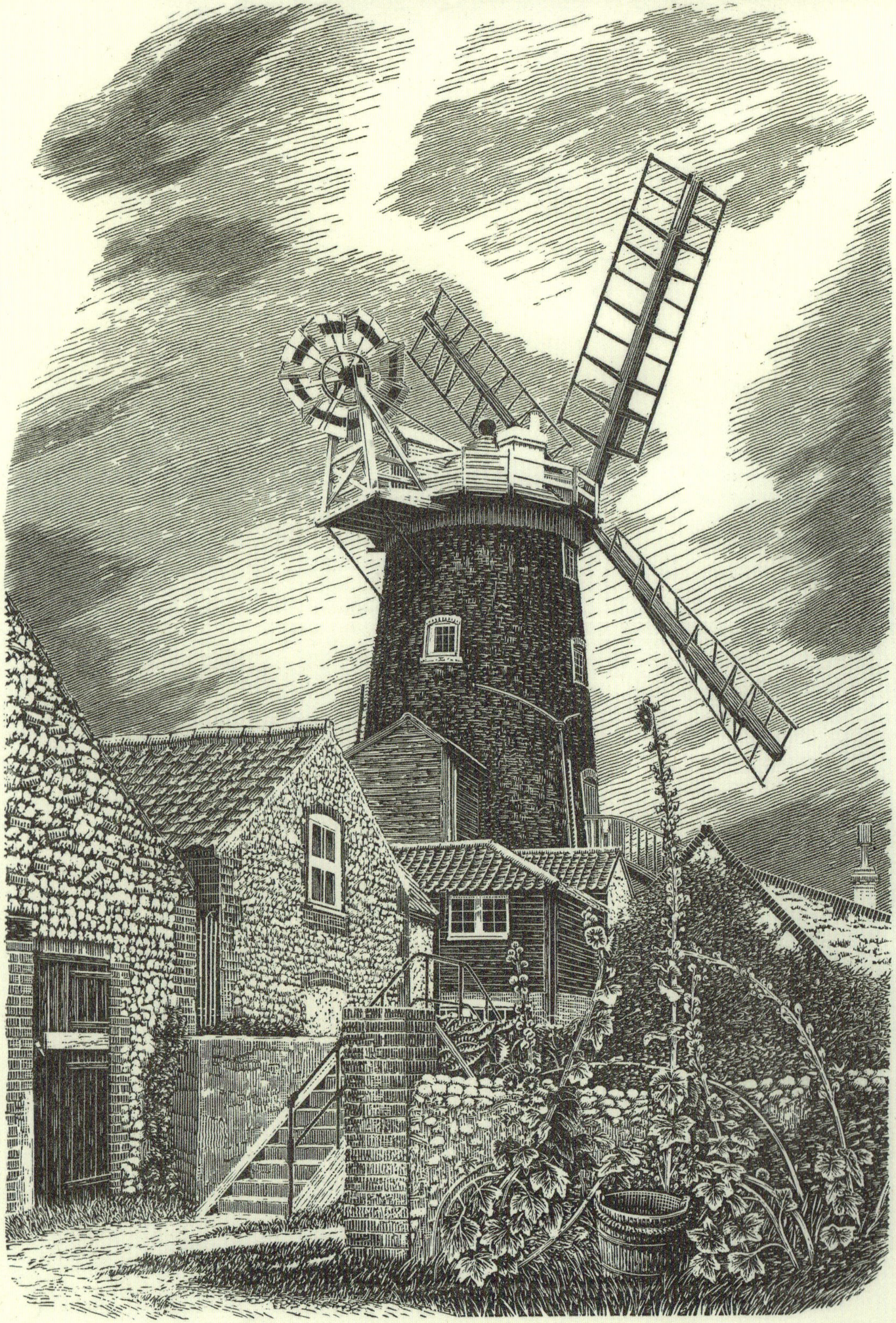

car park at Salthouse beach was impassable and completely filled with shingle," she remembers. Max also noted that the high shingle bank that protected the land from Salthouse to Cley had all but gone. "Streams of water running off the land travelled under the shingle beach and bubbled up from unexpected places. Where the shingle bank had been completely flattened, a stream poured out into the sea dividing the villages of Salthouse and Cley. Everyone walking the path looked bewildered at the changes."

Already developing in the artist's mind was the print *Cley Shingle Bank*, shown on page 61. "The Brent geese circled the saltmarshes as if they were also unsettled by the changes to the coastline. The changes to the terrain were dramatic. A gentle mist just rested on everything as a blanket of calm. The colours of the sky reflected on the now quiet sea." Max's resulting print with its simplicity of colour came together in only a few weeks using just three blocks.

In the Glynn Thomas etching opposite (*Cley-next-the-Sea*, 19cm x 33cm), the mill is being circled by swifts, which also mob the village every summer. Glynn cleverly avoids showing the snake of slow-moving traffic that clogs the main road throughout the tourist season.

Anthony Dunigan captures the mill in his 2010 engraving (*Behind the Mill,* 36cm x 26cm), left, and the landmark appears again overleaf in a colourful interpretation by Norfolk artist Amelia Bowman. Her 2016 print *Cley Windmill (Mayweed)* shows a building that has also become one of her favourite collagraph plates. "I love the fact that the surface area of the mill itself is big enough to really showcase one of my pattern designs. In recent times I have added a setting sun into the design which, although

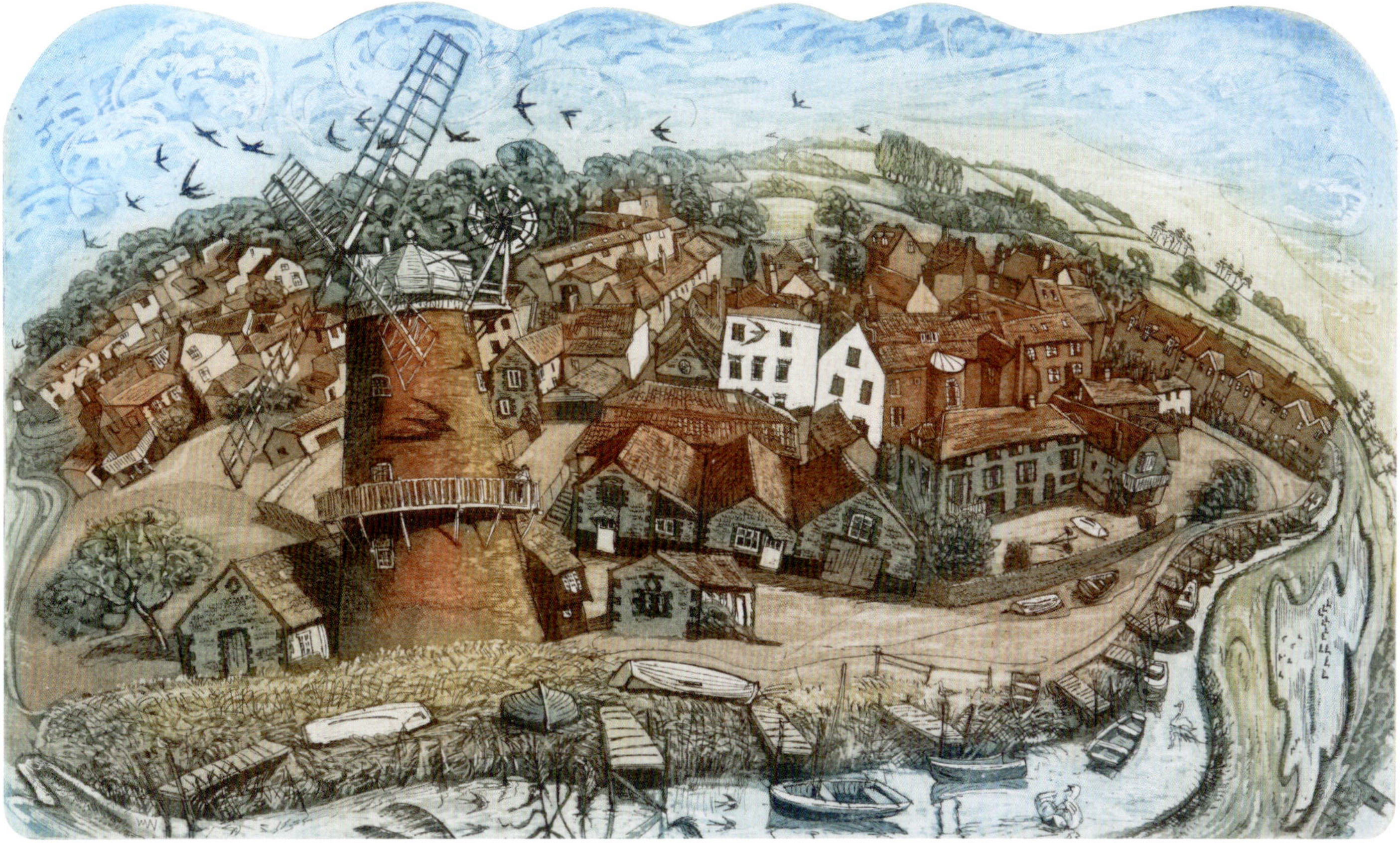

Left: Anthony Dunigan – *Behind the Mill* (wood engraving), 36cm x 26cm. **Above**: Glynn Thomas – *Cley-next-the-Sea* (etching), 19cm x 33cm. **Right**: Thelma Sykes – *Cley: Sleeping Partners* (woodcut and linocut), 16cm x 28cm.

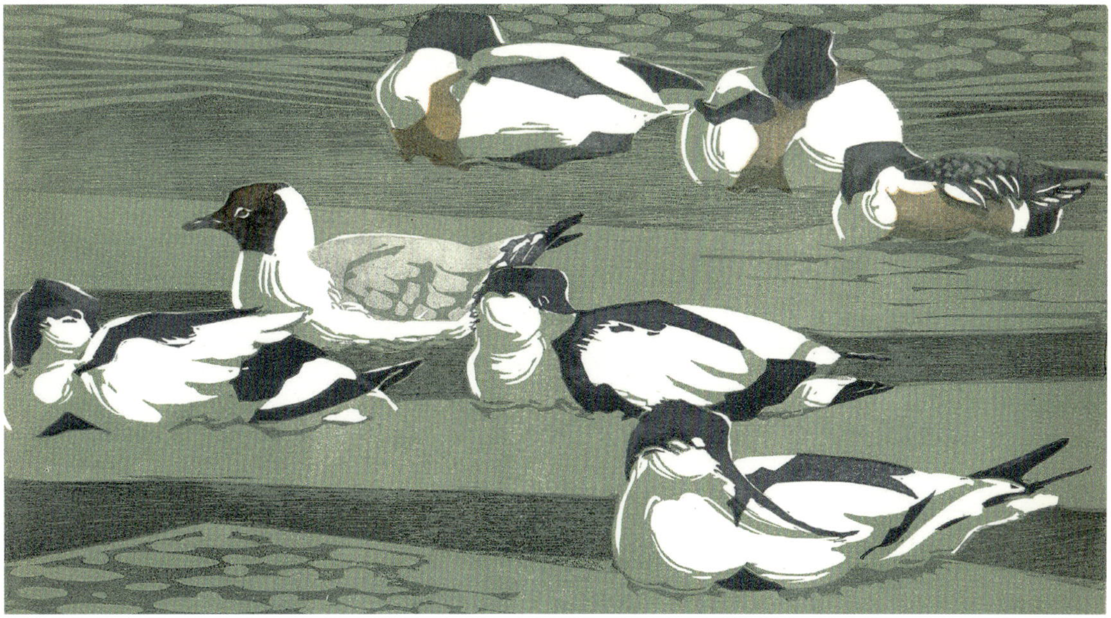

not outlined on the plate itself, really seems to add something worthwhile to the image."

The restful bird image on page 63 is by Thelma Sykes. Titled *Cley: Sleeping Partners*, it represents Avocet, Shelduck, Shoveler and Black-headed Gull resting on the Norfolk Wildlife Trust reserve at Cley. This is a combination of woodcut and linocut (16cm x 28cm) created in 2002.

"Cley Marshes is famed for turning up rarities, but for me its attraction lies in the variety," says Thelma. This group was observed and sketched from Bishop's hide on a sweltering day. "The hazy atmosphere leaches out strong colour. The rusty flanks of the Shoveler and the Shelduck's breast-bands are the only warm accents in a muted scene. I'm drawn to the repeating patterns of plumage and shadow and to the change where a hush of breeze ruffles parts of the water."

Cley is a popular haunt for Barn Owls. As well as Robert Gillmor's 2002 linocut (41cm x 31cm) *The Cley Church Owl* (opposite page, top centre) and another (25.4cm x 17.5cm) linocut entitled *Cley Owl* by Jeremy James (opposite page, top right), we reproduce below centre an etching from 1980 by Robert Greenhalf named *Norfolk Barn Owl* (26cm x 28cm). Only one plate was used, but inked up in four or five colours. The view is from just outside Cley on the road to Wiveton, looking towards Blakeney Church.

Norwich printmaker HJ Jackson provided the 1983 Cley windmill linocuts below (*Mill/2*) and right (*The Windmill*, 1994). Fellow Norfolk artist Colin Bygrave's aquatint etching *Big Trees, Cley* (38cm x 26cm) appears bottom right.

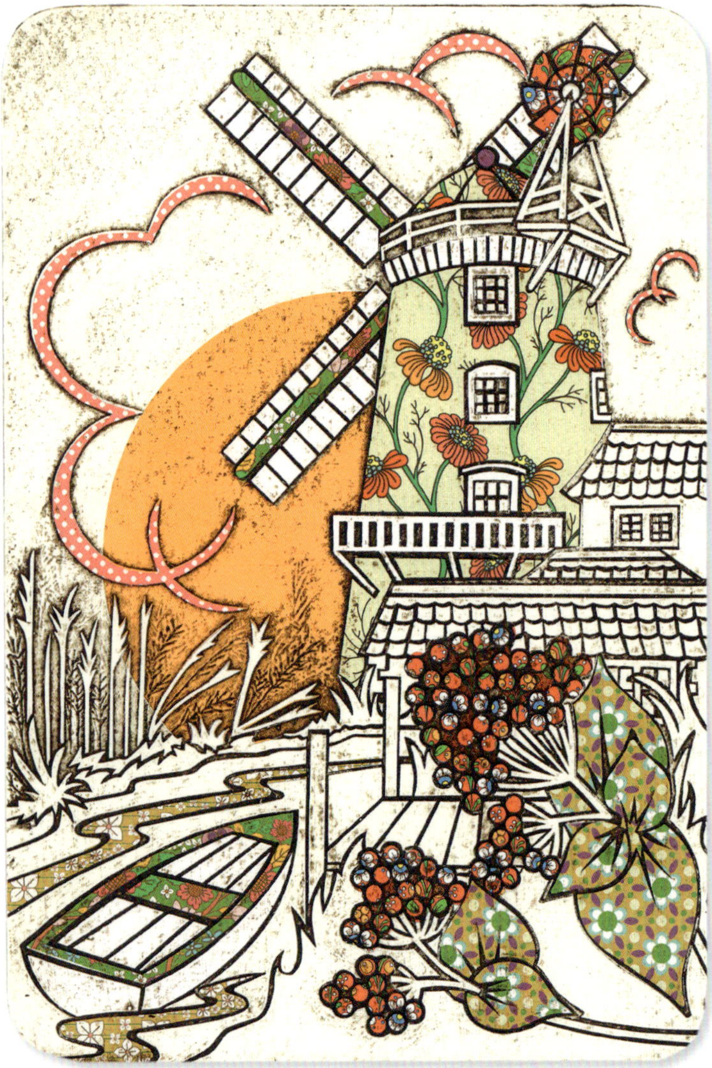

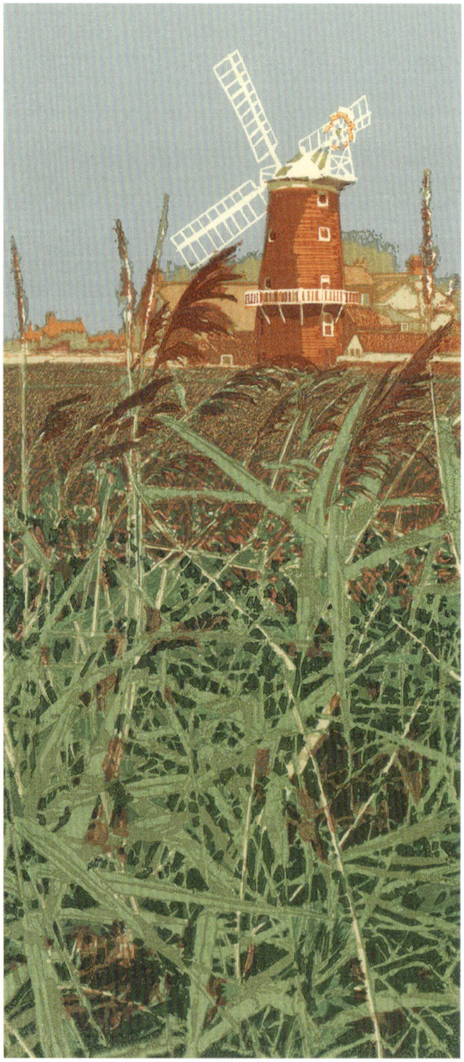

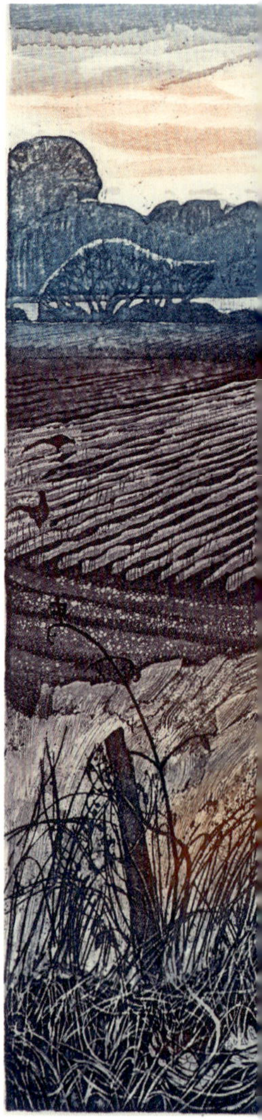

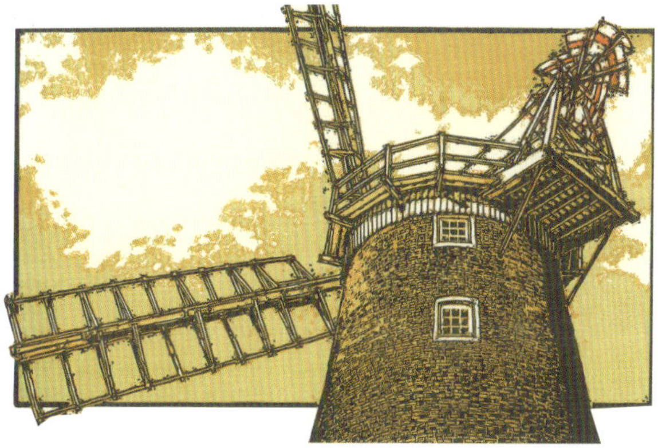

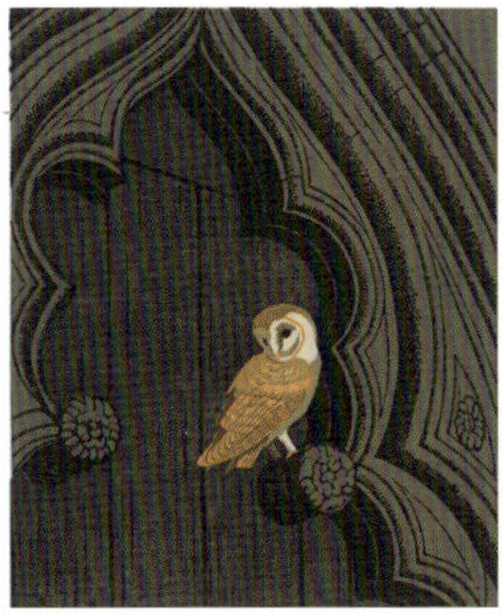

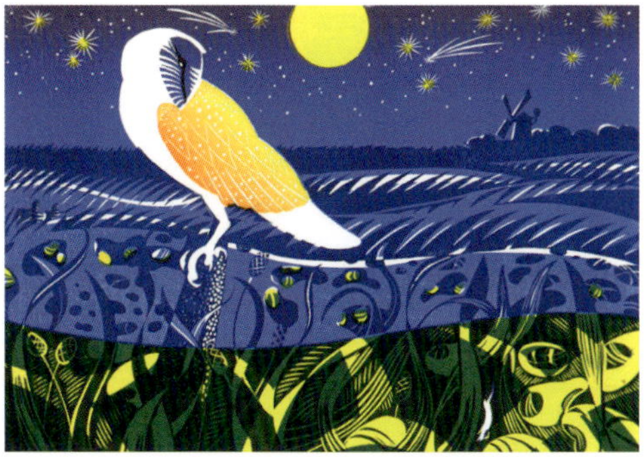

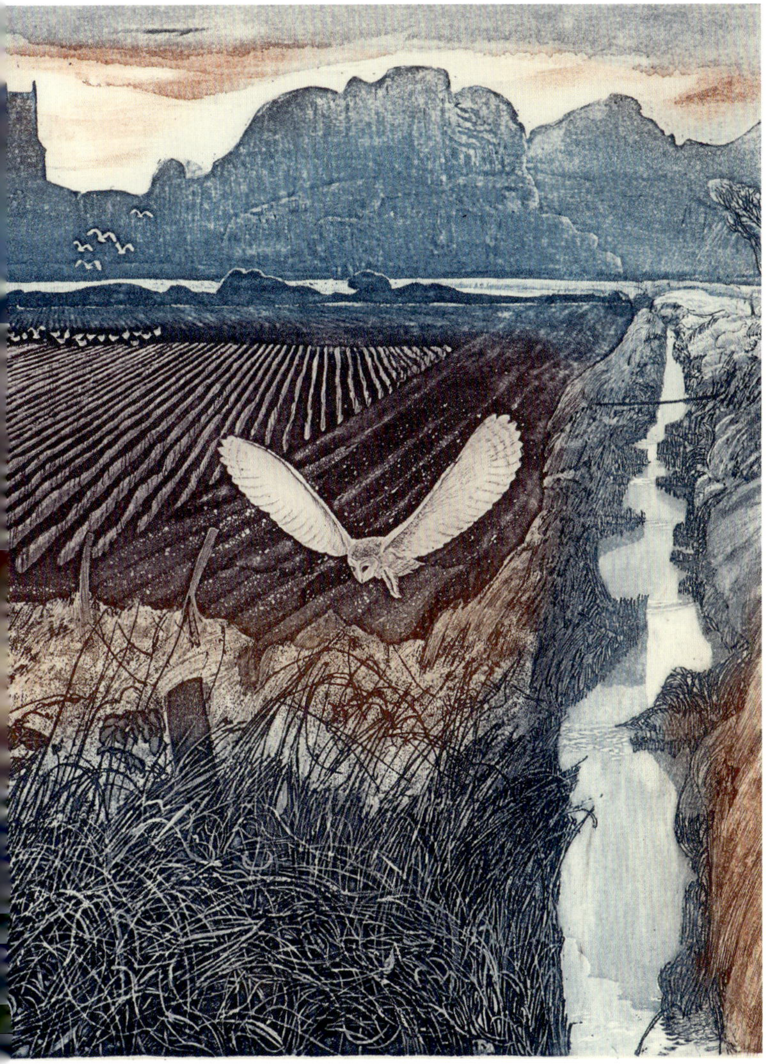

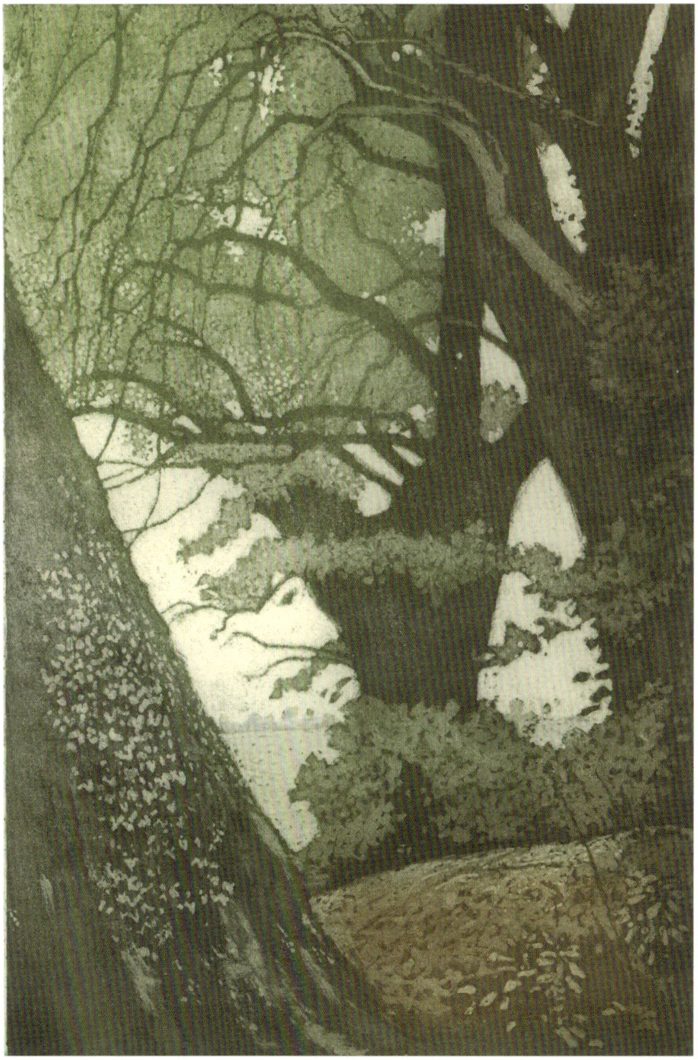

Cromer

Not surprisingly, the pier looms large in many of the prints reproduced here. Cromer is a visually striking seaside town that has resulted in a large number of printmaking interpretations. Below is Amelia Bowman's take on the pier – typically colourful.

"I think piers are wonderfully quirky, and they represent all the things I try to include in my coastal work – sea, fun and a little bit of vintage throwback! Cromer beach has plenty going on, and I really wanted to get a tractor into this design – as seen from the east side of the pier."

Norfolk artist Leanda Jaine Hughes recently had to relocate temporarily from Norwich to her parents' home in Cromer. While best known for the alphabet of Norwich locations seen later

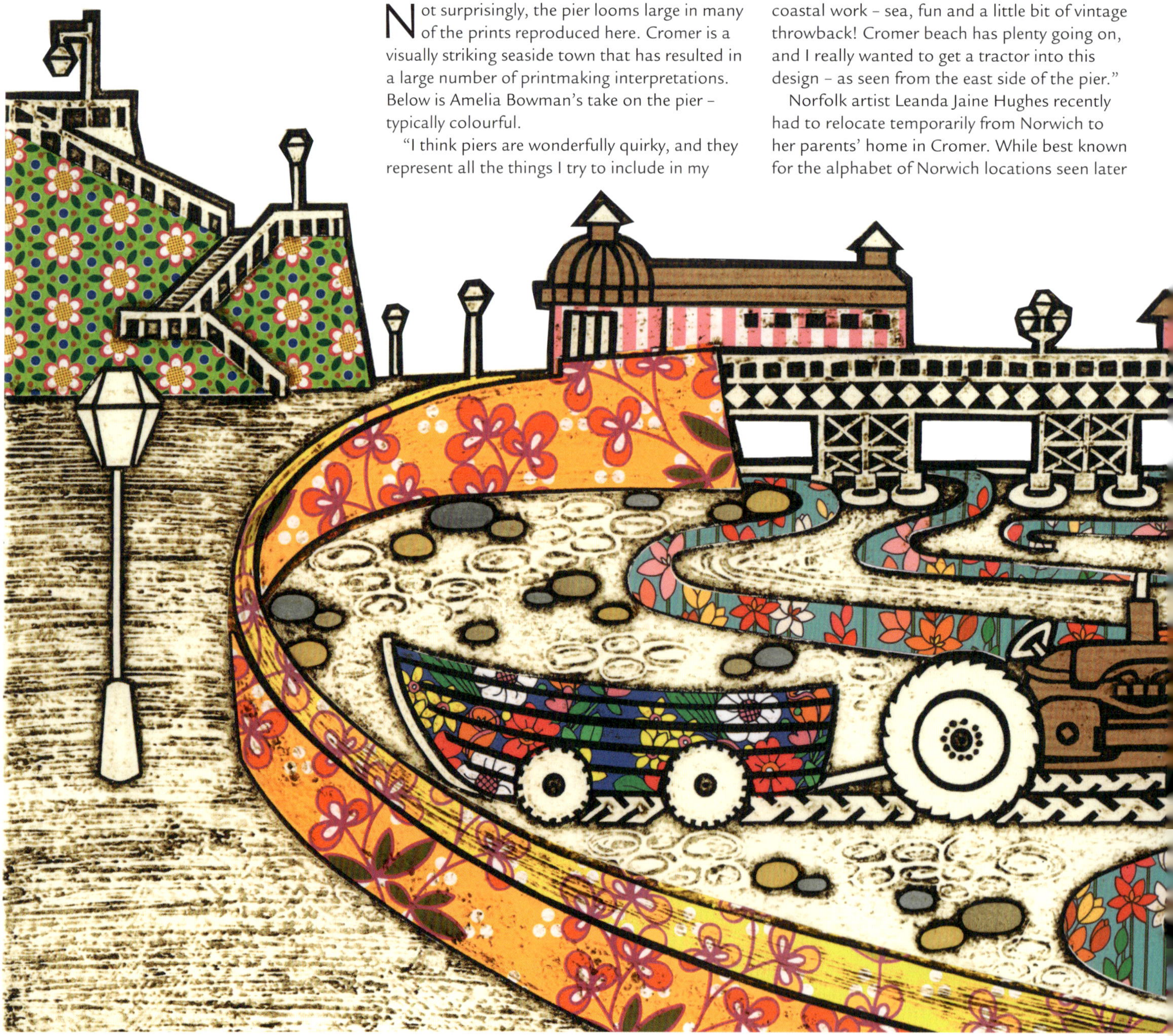

Left: Amelia Bowman – Cromer Pier (Clover), 2015 collagraph, 26.5cm x 37.5cm, from an edition of 10.
Right: Leanda Jaine Hughes – Ahh! Cromer, 2017 embossed screenprint from an edition of 50.

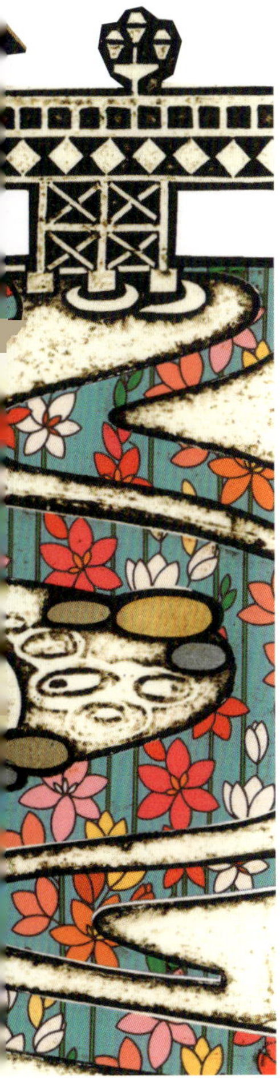

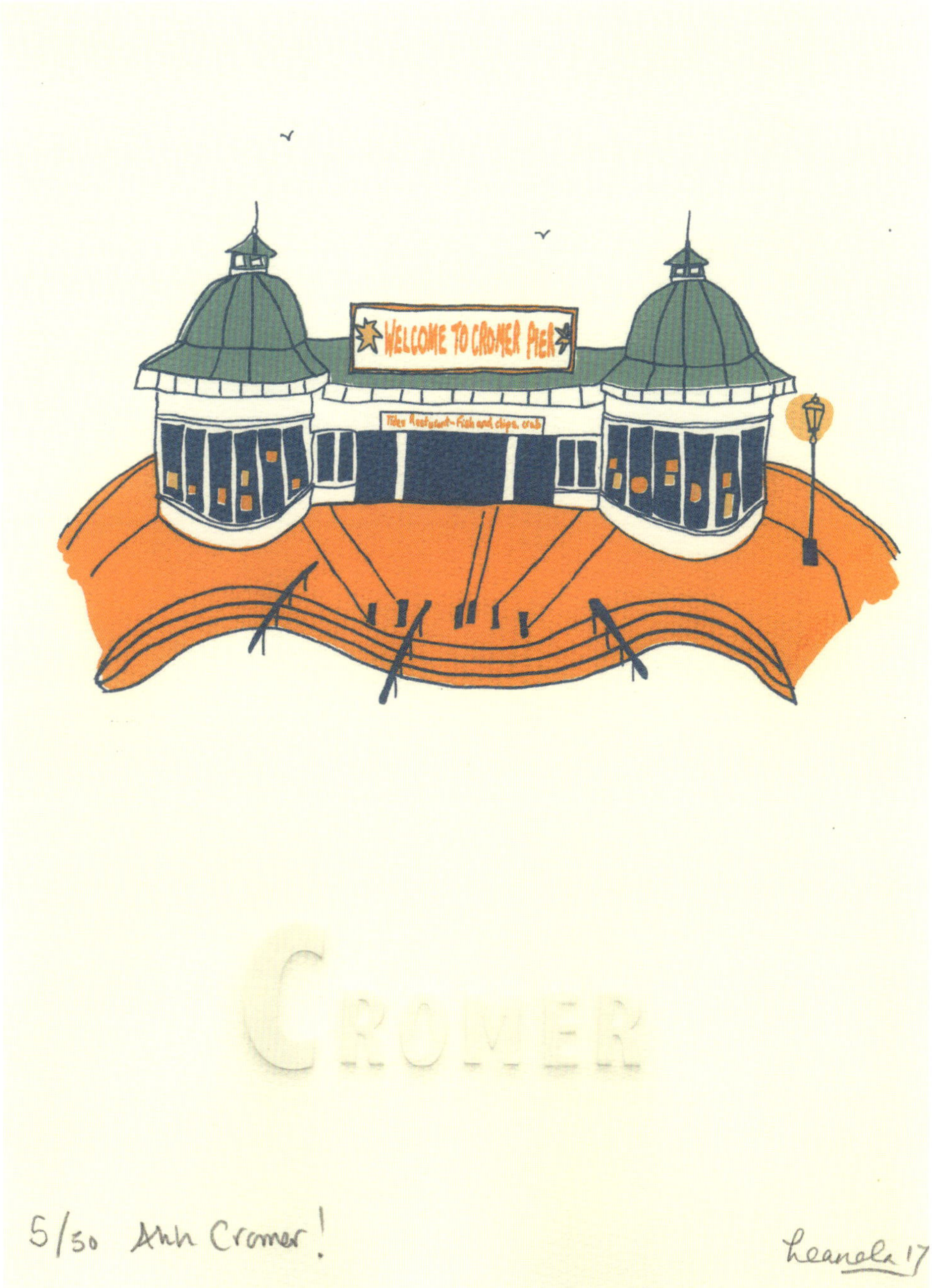

in this book, she took the opportunity to tackle Cromer pier in the prints shown on pages 67 and 77.

In addition to the pier, crabs, tractors and the church are perhaps the most memorable features of this Norfolk coastal town. All play a part in the Glynn Thomas etching below.

Cromer was 'discovered' in the 18th century by well-to-do travellers as a watering place, growing only slowly at first due to its remote location, but gathering pace when the railway arrived in 1877 to connect the town with London. By the 1890s, Cromer was fashionable and many fine residences were built. In 1900, a new pier was erected and the promenade was lengthened and enhanced.

The town's reputation for crab fishing is unrivalled, in spite of many setbacks for the small fleet, and you can still watch the crab boats arrive every morning with their catch, landed on the beach as there is no harbour.

Glynn's picture hints at just how traditional the crab fishing fleet is, hauled from the sea by ancient tractors to deliver the famous Cromer crab to locals, town shops and restaurants. At the end of the 19th century, the beaches to the east and west of the pier were crowded with fishing boats. Now, only around a dozen ply their trade from the foot of The Gangway on the east beach.

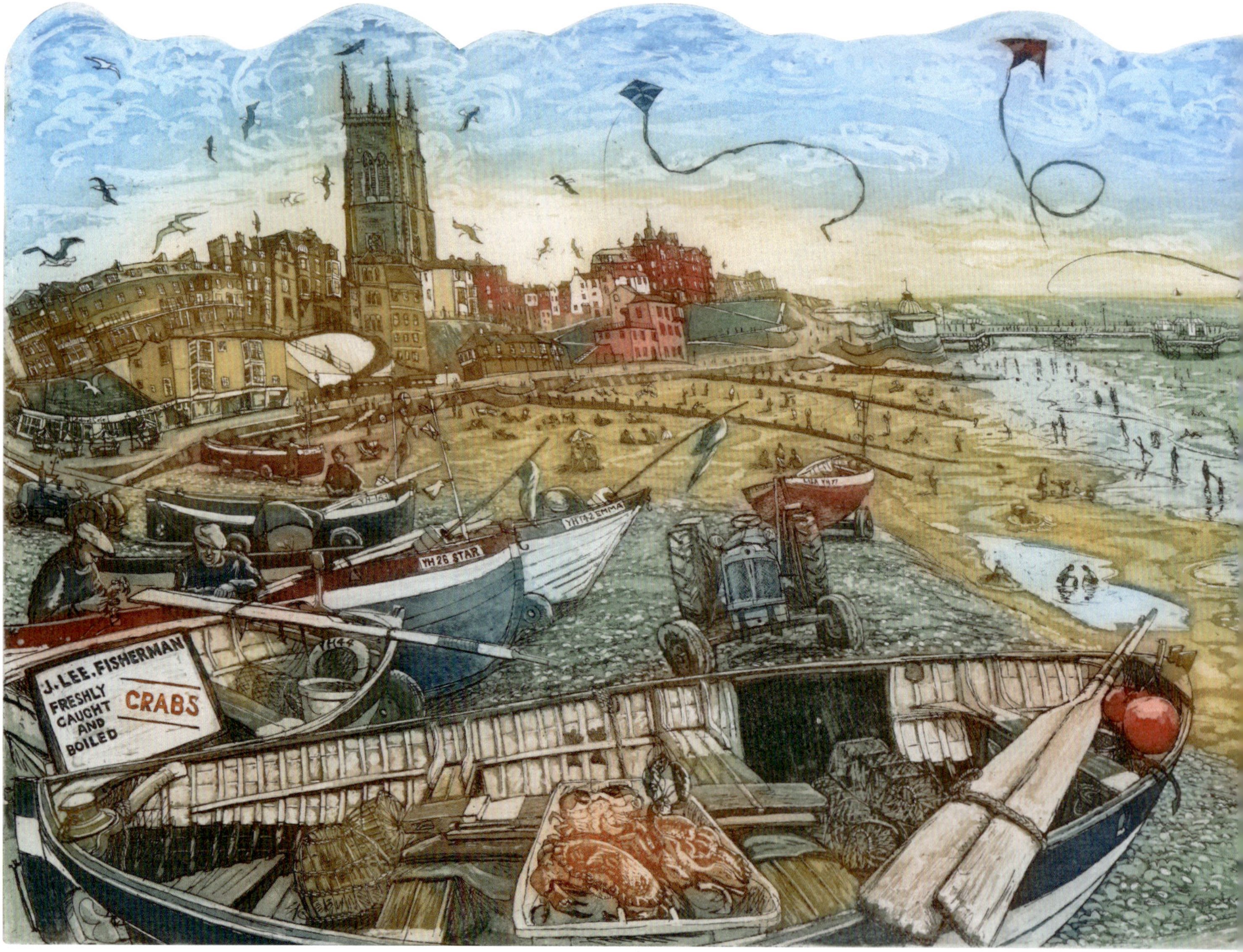

London-based Gail Brodholt spends some of her holidays in north Norfolk, staying within a few miles of Cromer. Her portfolio of bold linocut prints focuses on London and transport themes, but she has indulged herself with the three prints of Cromer that appear in this section. Below is *Indian Summer*. The town's beach huts may not be as desirable (or as expensive) as those farther along the coast in Wells-next-the-Sea or in the Suffolk hotspot of Southwold, but still make for a welcome splash of colour. On page 77 (*Washed Away*, 13cm x 13cm, linocut with carborundum), Northamptonshire-based Annette Sykes also depicts Cromer's beach huts, but in a sadly battered state in the wake of the December 2013 storm surge.

Overleaf, Gail turns her attention to the pier with her linocut *Wishful Thinking* (33cm x 34cm), and uses it again as a subject on page 73 with

Left: *Glynn Thomas – Cromer (etching), 2003, 26cm x 44cm.* ***Below***: *Gail Brodholt – Indian Summer (linocut), 33cm x 34cm.*

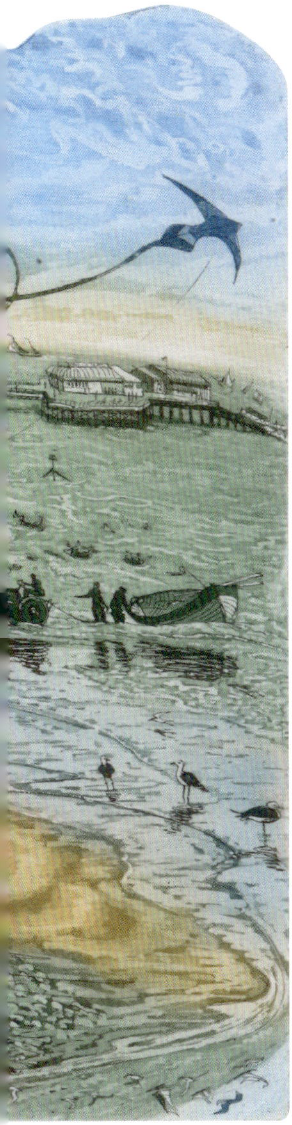

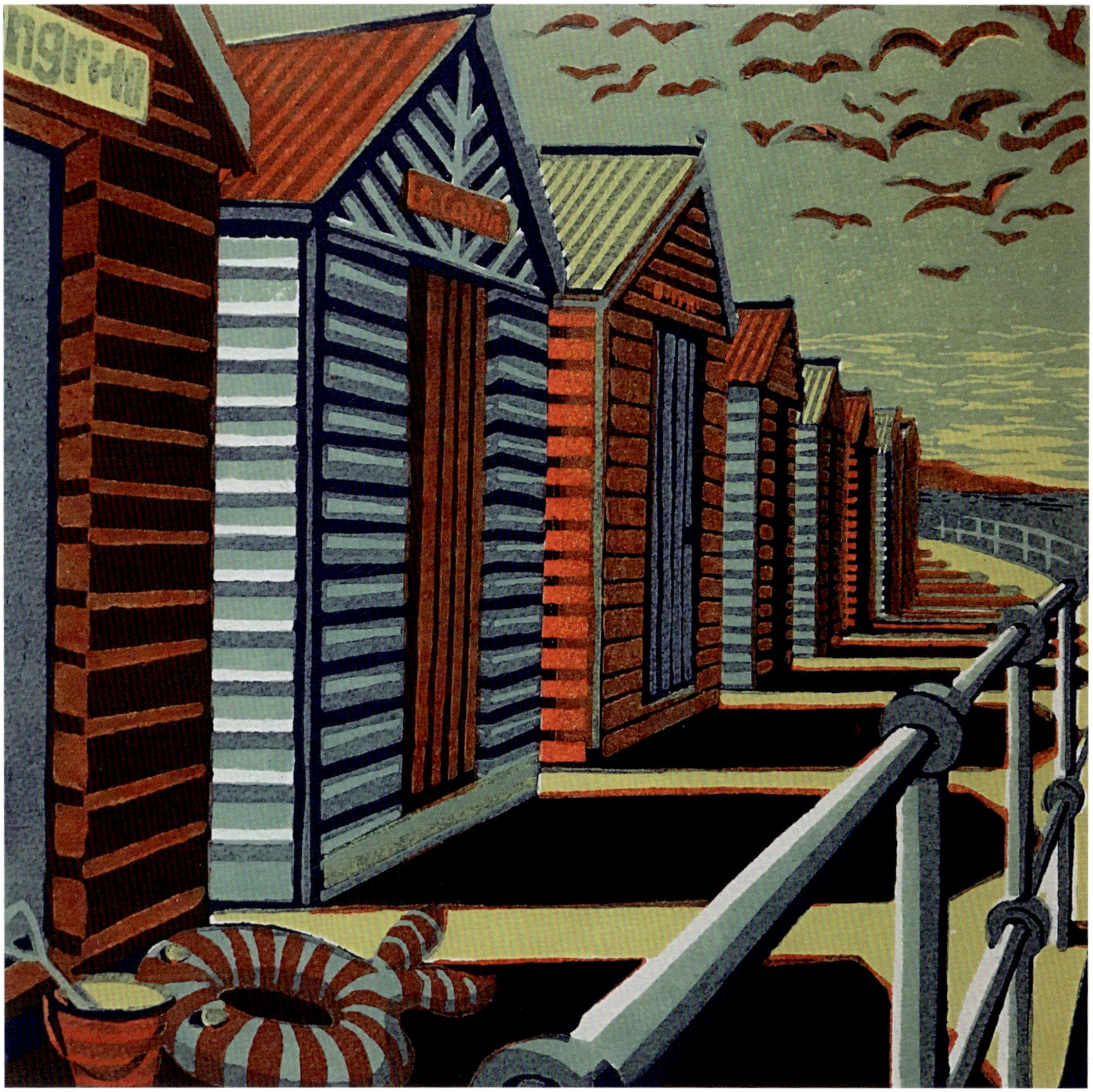

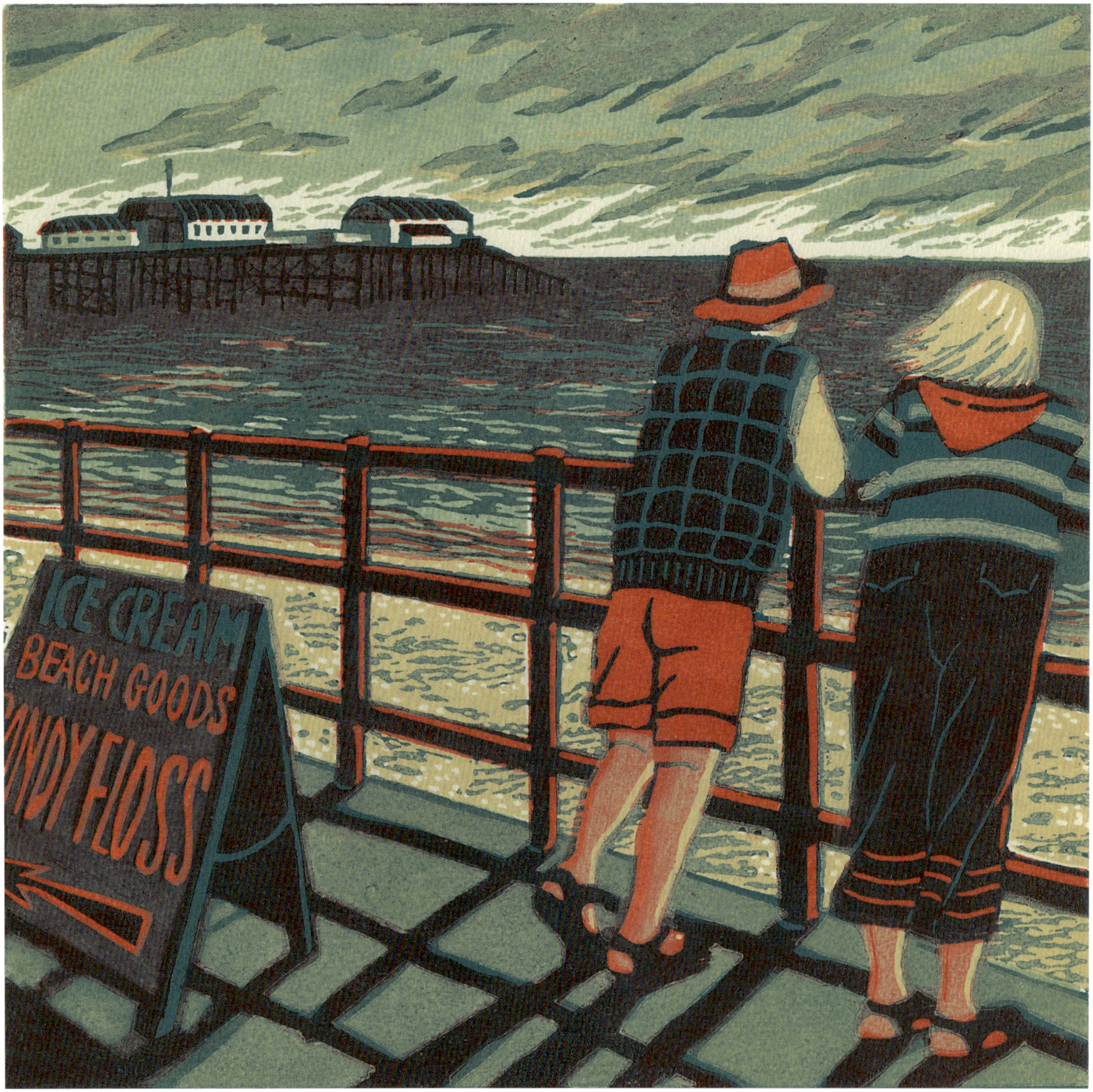
ICE CREAM
BEACH GOODS
NDY FLOSS

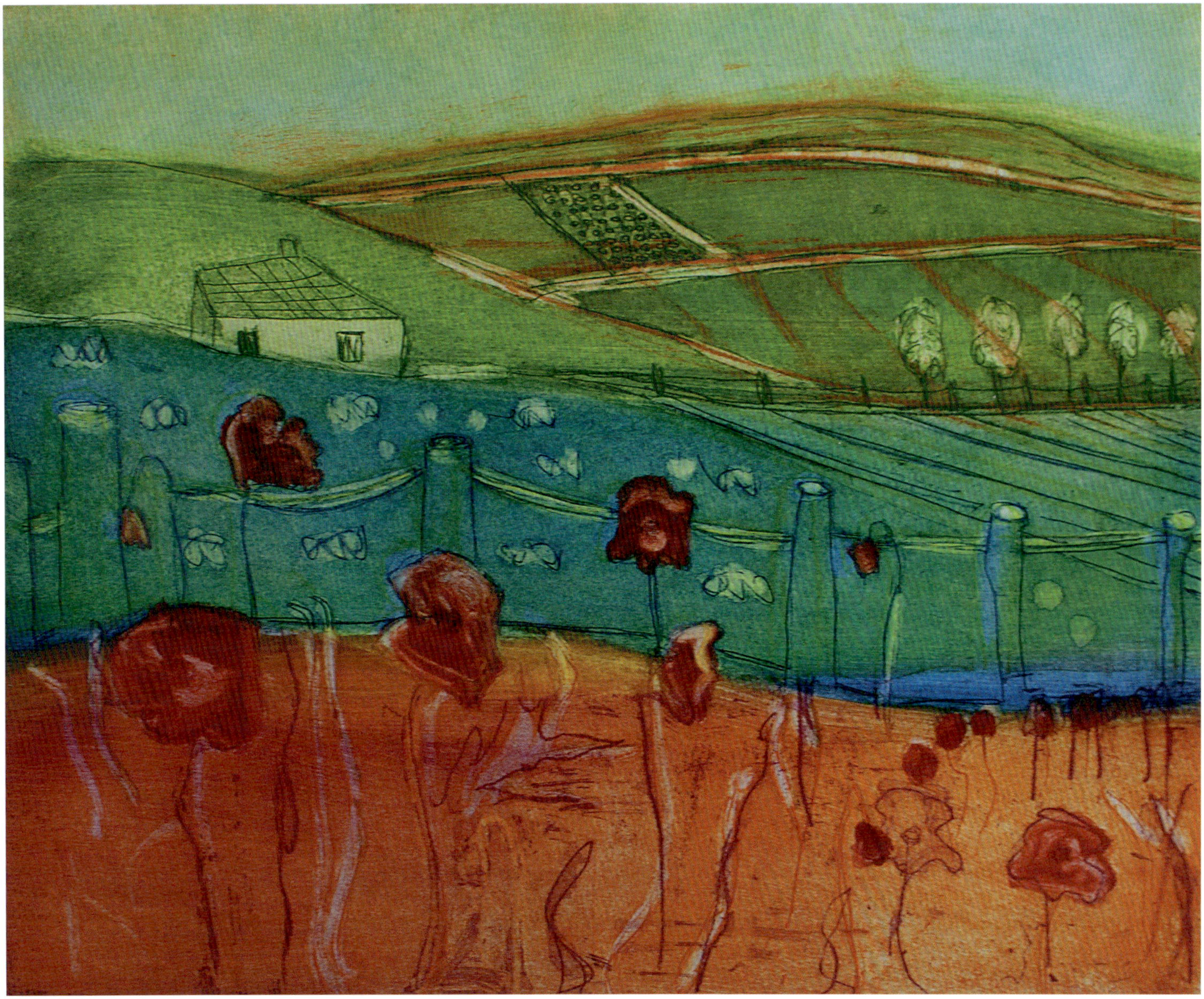

The Last One to Leave (linocut, 33cm x 34cm). Her studio companion in London, Louise Davies, is a printmaker with a more abstract approach, producing colourful etchings such as *Red Meadows*, above. "This is a recent print from the summer when I visited Norfolk between Cromer and Overstrand, and was so excited by the poppies in the foreground of the fields. I felt their strong colour would have great impact in a print."

James Green is another long-distance visitor to Cromer. Based in Yorkshire, he has developed a fondness for the north Norfolk town – and particularly its pier, depicted on page 74 in linocut form. "I first decided to try and capture the view from the pier, including the town's grand architecture, the curved walkways and the glistening sea. After this,

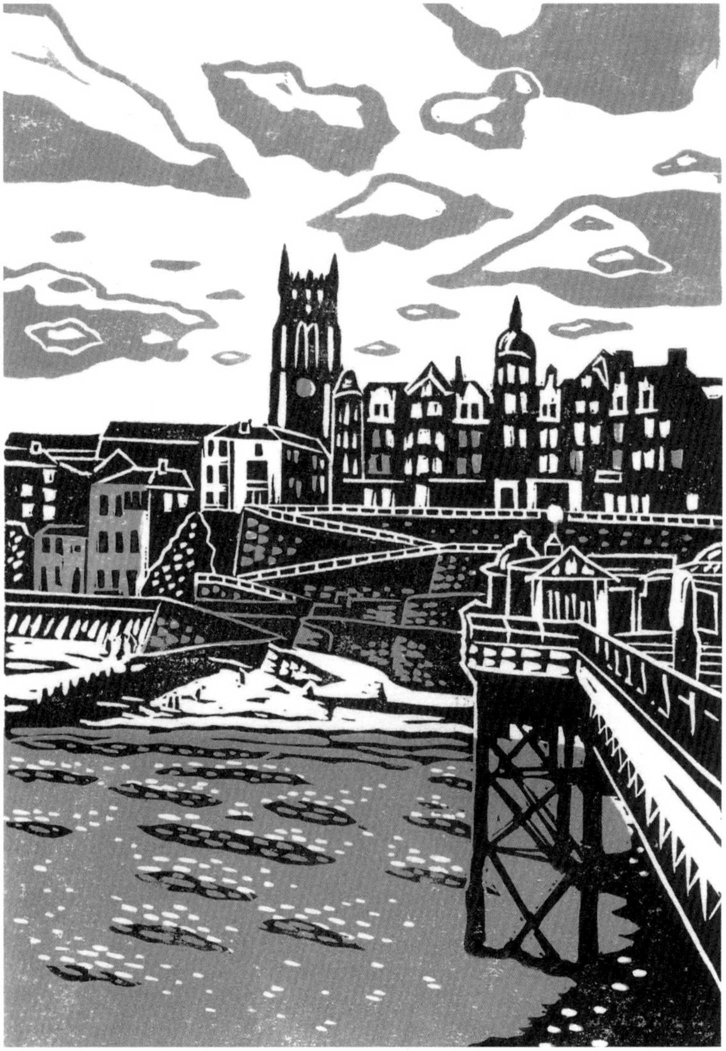

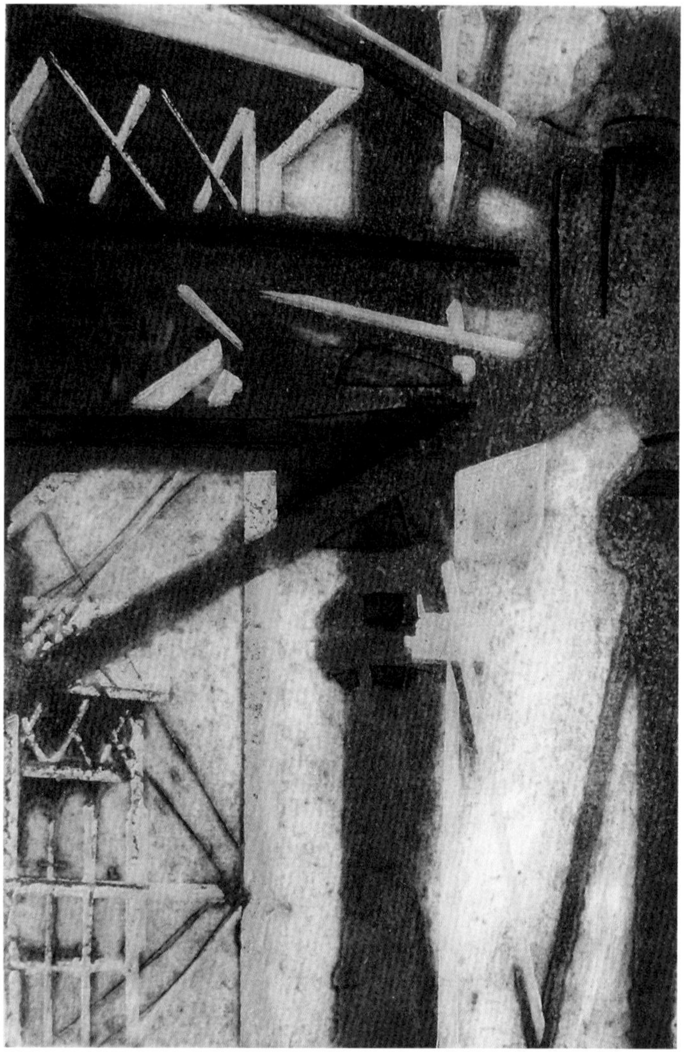

***Above left**: James Green – Cromer no. 1 (linocut).*
***Above right**: Sally Hirst – Under the Pier (collagraph and carborundum), 18cm x 25cm,*

***Facing page**: Gail Brodholt – The Last to Leave (linocut), 33cm x 34cm.*

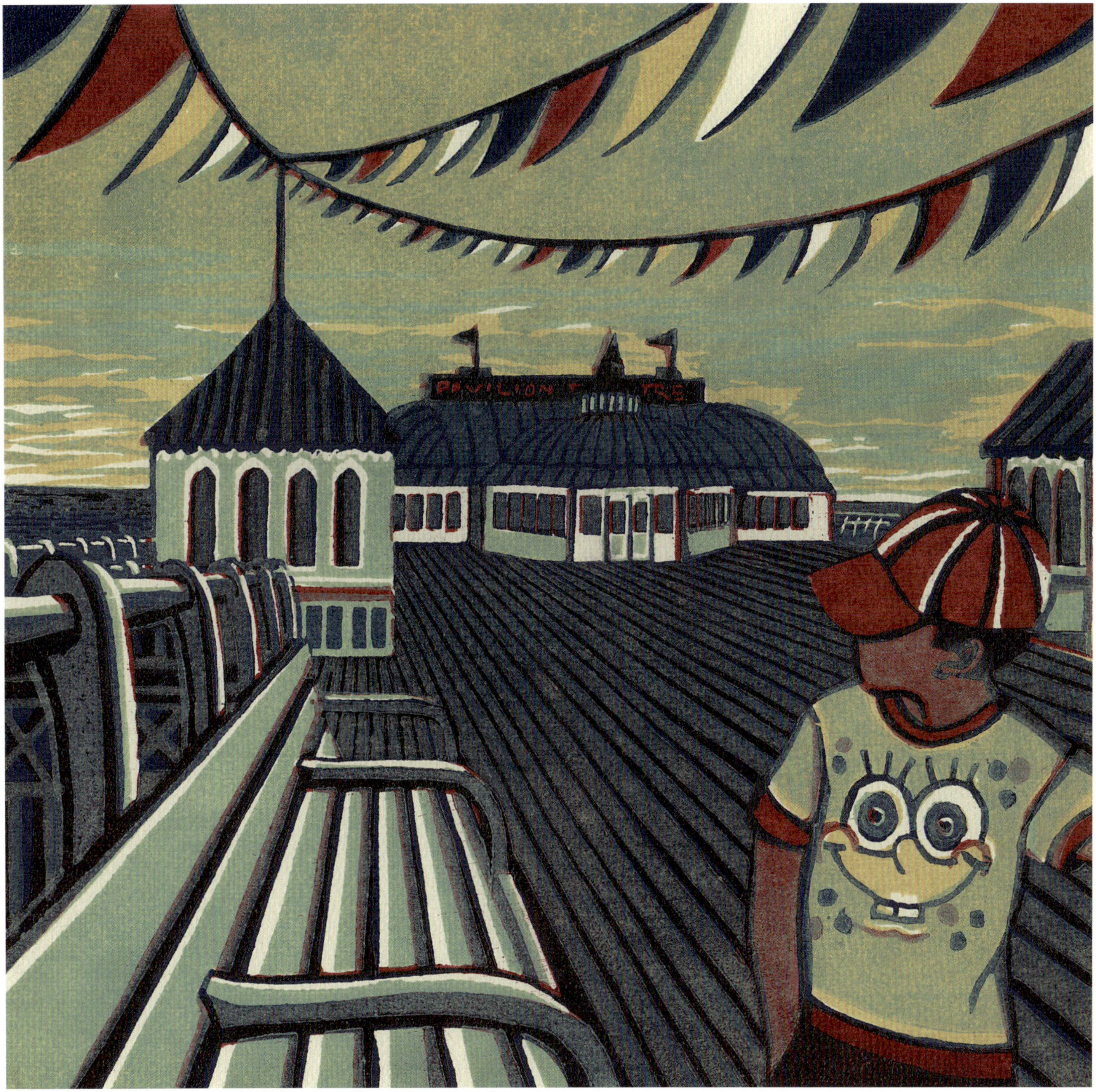

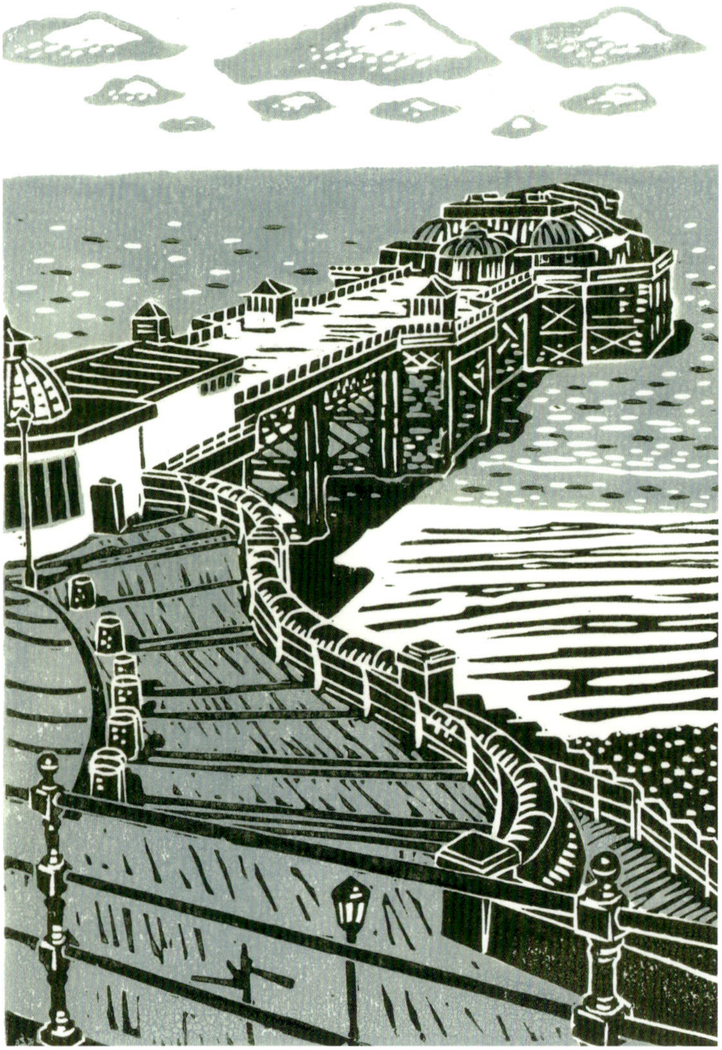

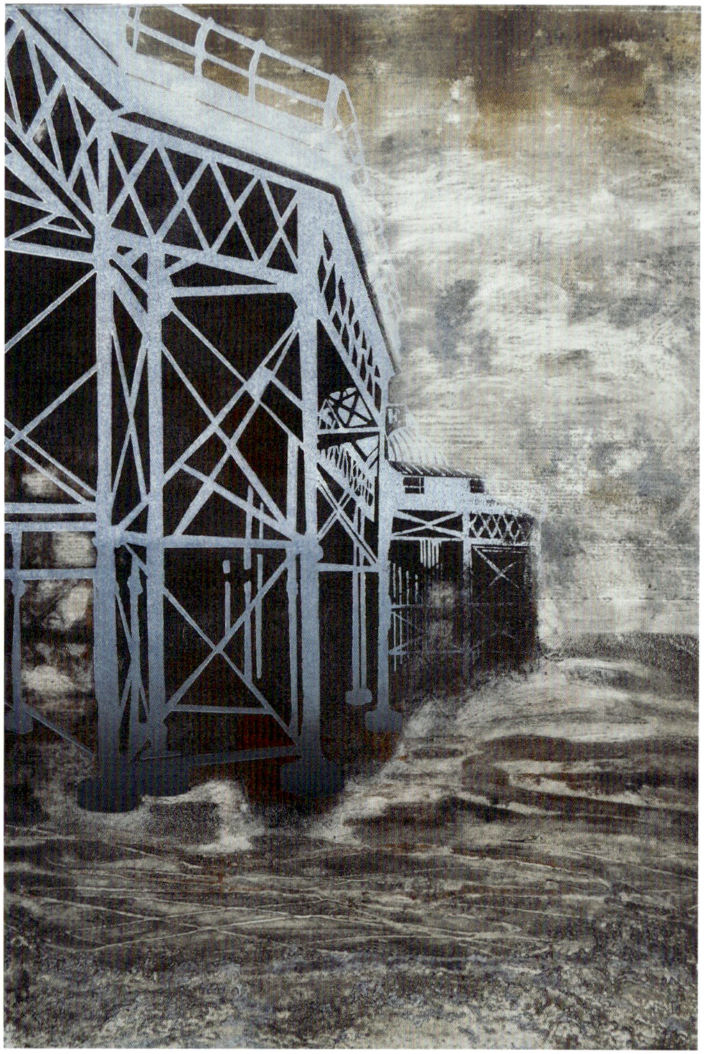

and perhaps more of a challenge, I attempted the pier itself [page 72], with all its crossing ironwork, renovated grand entrance and the beach/sea. I have had to simplify details in both, but this is just part of what I do with my landscapes. I found them both as much of a puzzle to solve as my Northern cityscapes, and just as rewarding."

Norwich-based Sally Hirst's prints of Cromer pier capture a very different perspective. Her prints are the result of a year spent living by the coast, and are inspired by the ravages of time and tide on man-made structures: piers, bridges, abandoned gas towers, old fishing huts and boats. *Under the Pier* (page 72) and *Cromer Pier* (above right) are both collagraph prints with carborundum.

HJ Jackson finds much to enjoy when making prints of Cromer. He appreciates not only the elderly and decaying fishing boats, but also the

Above left: James Green – Cromer no. 2 (linocut).
Above right: Sally Hirst – Cromer Pier (collagraph and carborundum, 40cm x 30cm).
Facing page: HJ Jackson – Boats and Tractors (linocut, 2002).

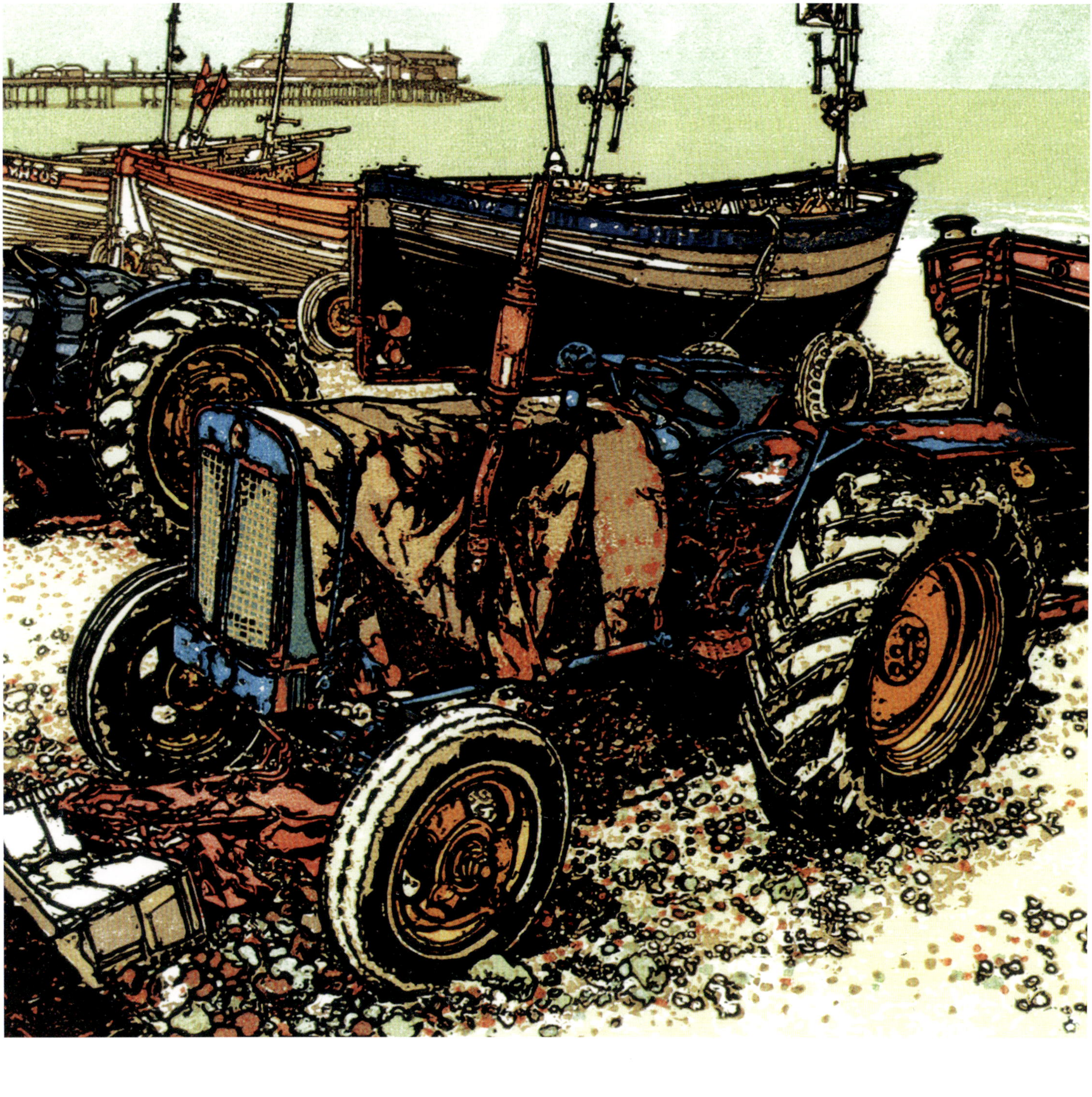

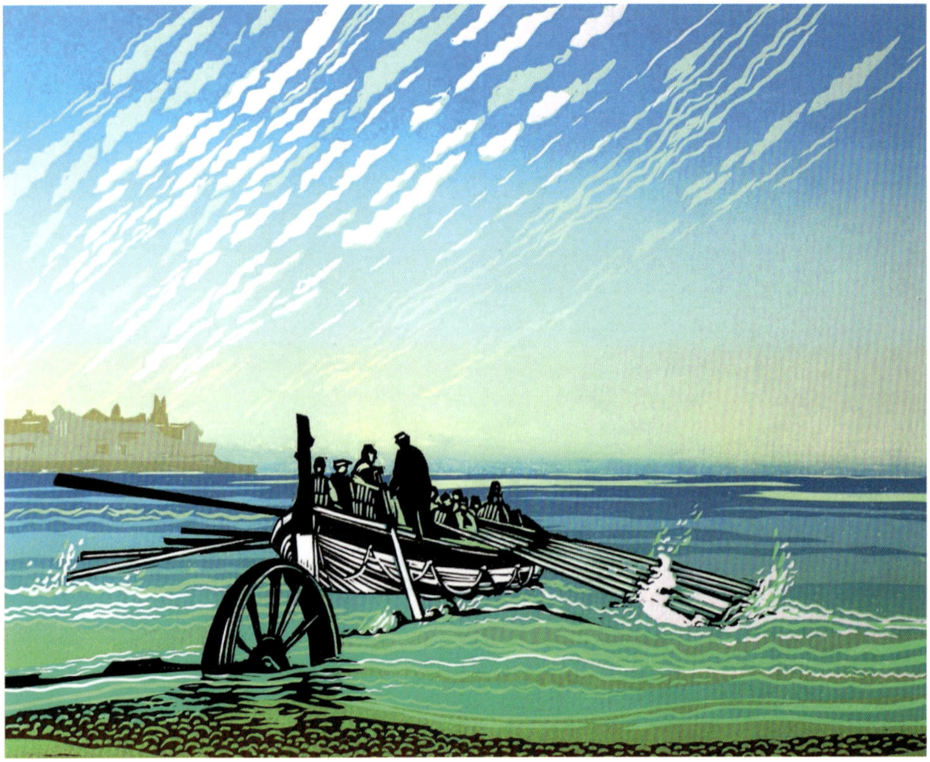

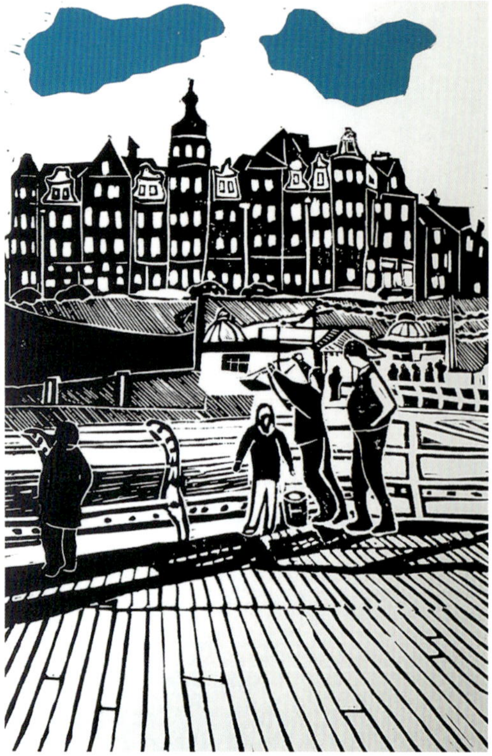

battle-scarred tractors found on the beach and the backdrop of the pier. On page 75 is a 2002 linocut named *Boats and Tractors*, while the impressive print *The Gangway*, from 1996, appears on pages 78 and 79.

Fellow Norfolk artist Rob Barnes portrays an early lifeboat training exercise with his linocut print entitled *Cromer Life (*above left). This appears alongside *Crab Fishers in Cromer*, a linocut by Suffolk-based printmaker and bookbinder Janet Watson.

Shadow Line (opposite page, top left) is the HJ Jackson linocut of a tractor ready to haul a crab boat at Cromer; while the print on the far right is *Washed Away* by Annette Sykes, which recalls the aftermath of the December 2013 tidal surge that badly damaged Cromer's seafront, pier and beach huts.

The embossed screenprint, *Cromer Pier*, on the bottom of the facing page is the second by Leanda Jaine Hughes from her unplanned but very welcome Cromer portfolio.

Above left: *Rob Barnes – Cromer Life (linocut).* **Above right**: *Janet Watson – Crab Fishers in Cromer (linocut).* **Facing page, top left**: *HJ Jackson – Shadow Line (linocut);* **top right**: *Annette Sykes – Washed Away (linocut with carborundum);* **bottom**: *Leanda Jaine Hughes – Cromer Pier (embossed screenprint).* **Overleaf**: *HJ Jackson – The Gangway (linocut).*

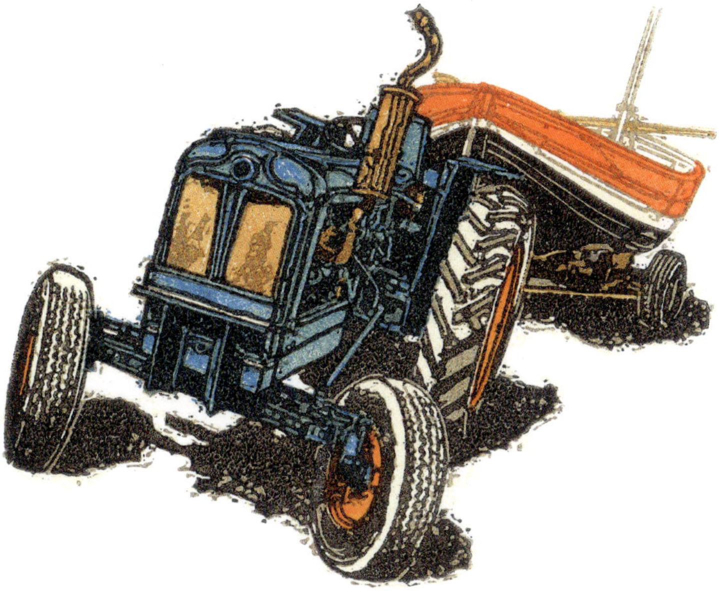

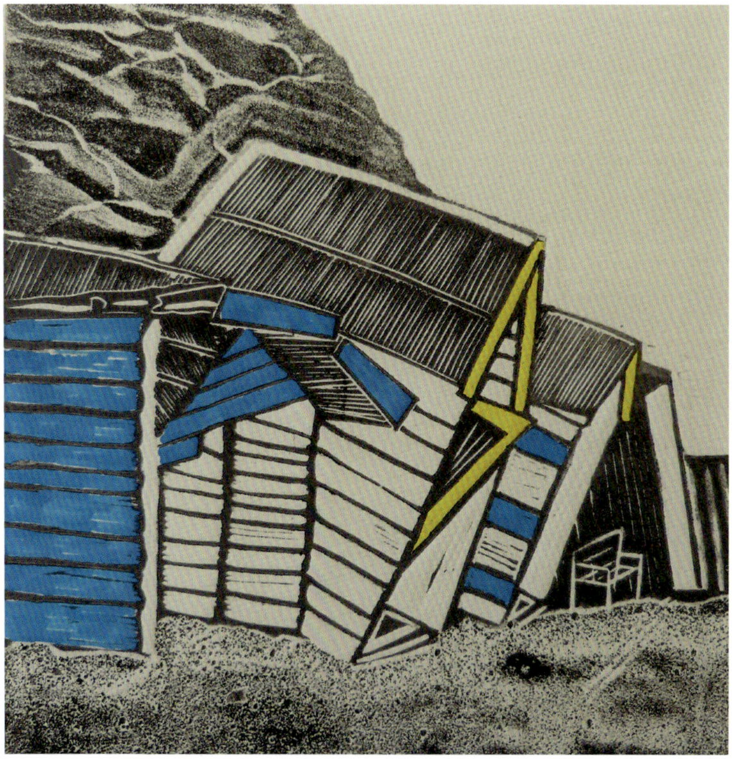

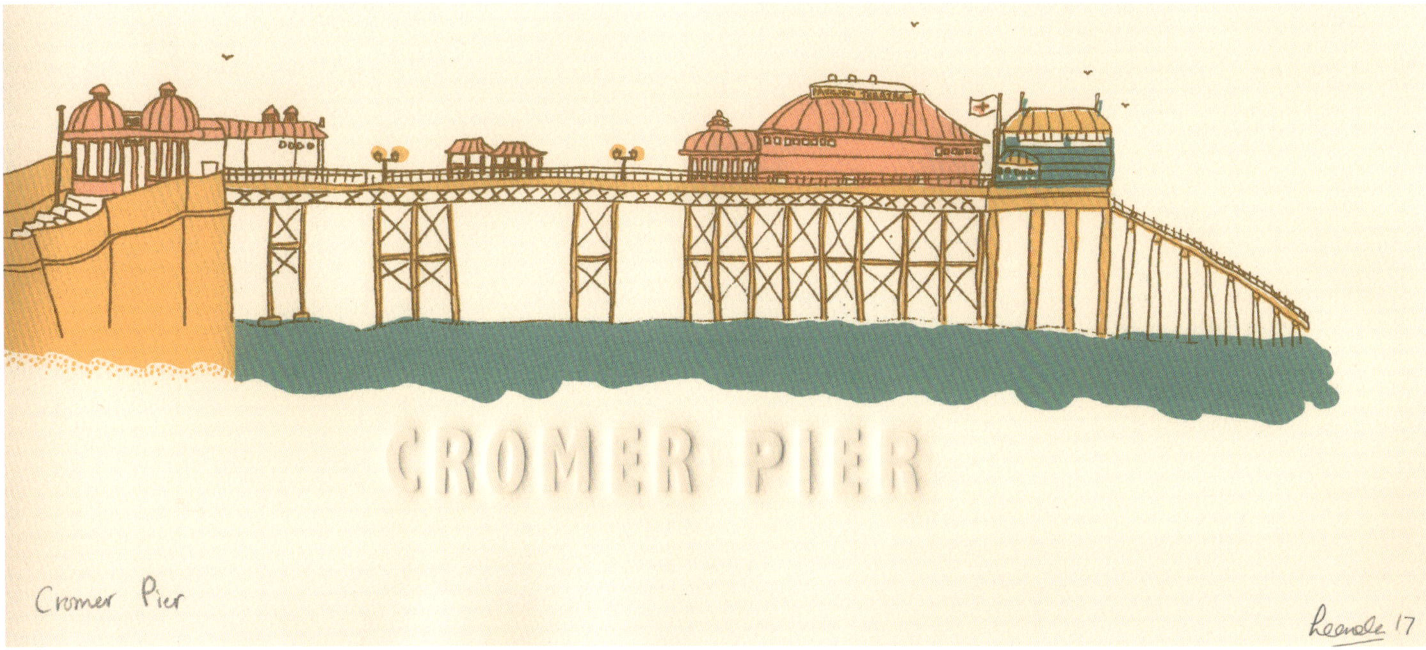
CROMER PIER
Cromer Pier
Leende 17

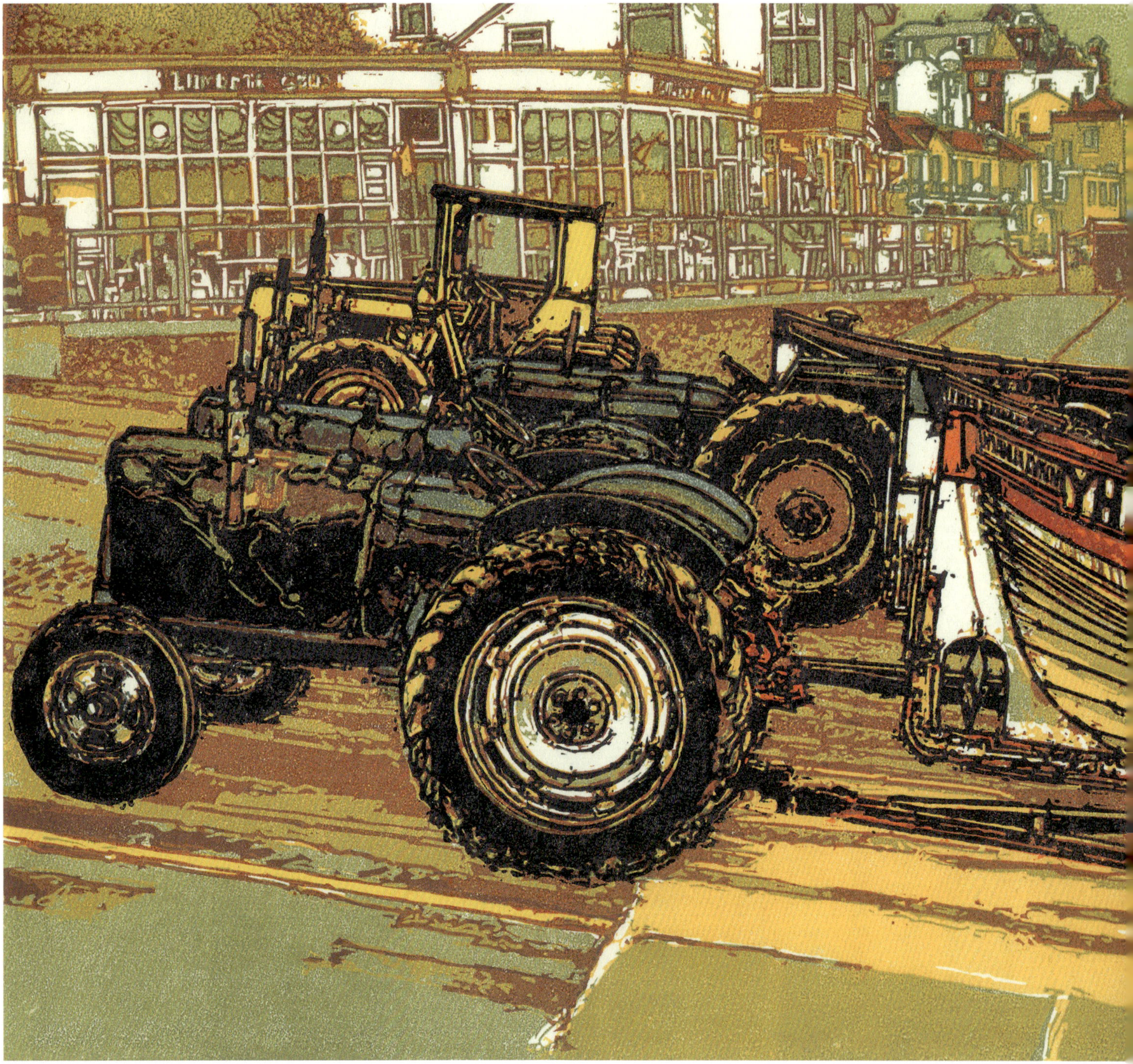

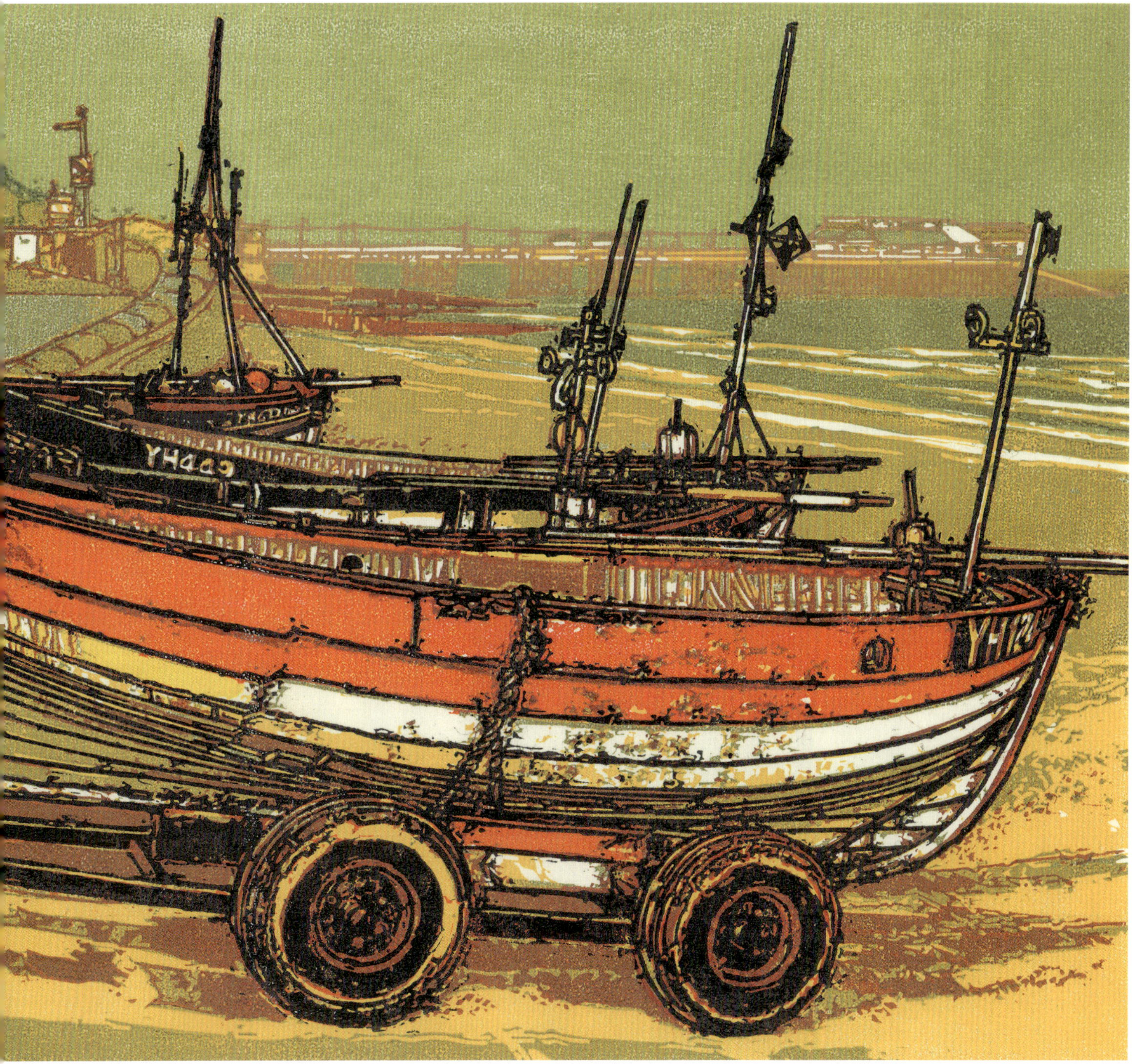

Diss

The market town of Diss lies in the valley of the River Waveney, close to the border with Suffolk. Its six-acre mere is a popular duck-feeding location, but is up to six metres deep. The town takes its name from an Anglo-Saxon word meaning either ditch or embankment.

Suffolk-based printmaker Chris Evans lives nearby and finds the mere to be an attractive mixture of water, surrounding buildings and trees. His etching, *The Mere, Diss*, measuring 10cm x 24.5cm, was produced in 2012.

Chris attended St Martin's School of Art in London, where he studied illustration and fabric design. As an illustrator the majority of his work was figurative; now, by contrast, he

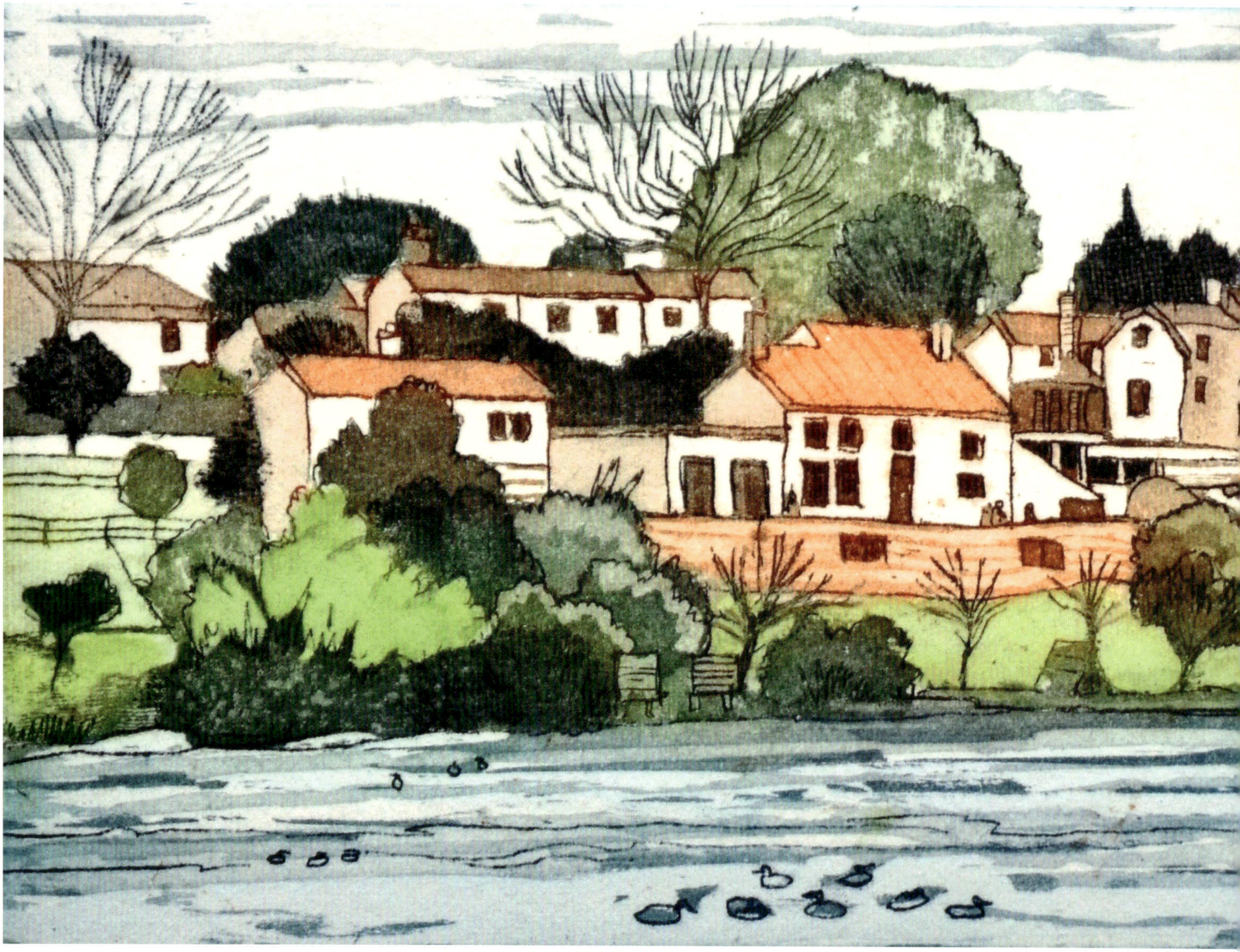

tends to explore landscape and architecture in his prints – the majority of which are etchings produced on zinc plates using soft ground for line/texture and aquatint techniques for different tones.

"I usually ink up plates with several colours, blending them as I wipe the plate. I also make drypoint prints on perspex using a sharply pointed tool to engrave the plate and cardboard templates to add colours. I only edition 20 prints for etchings, and 15 for drypoints on perspex."

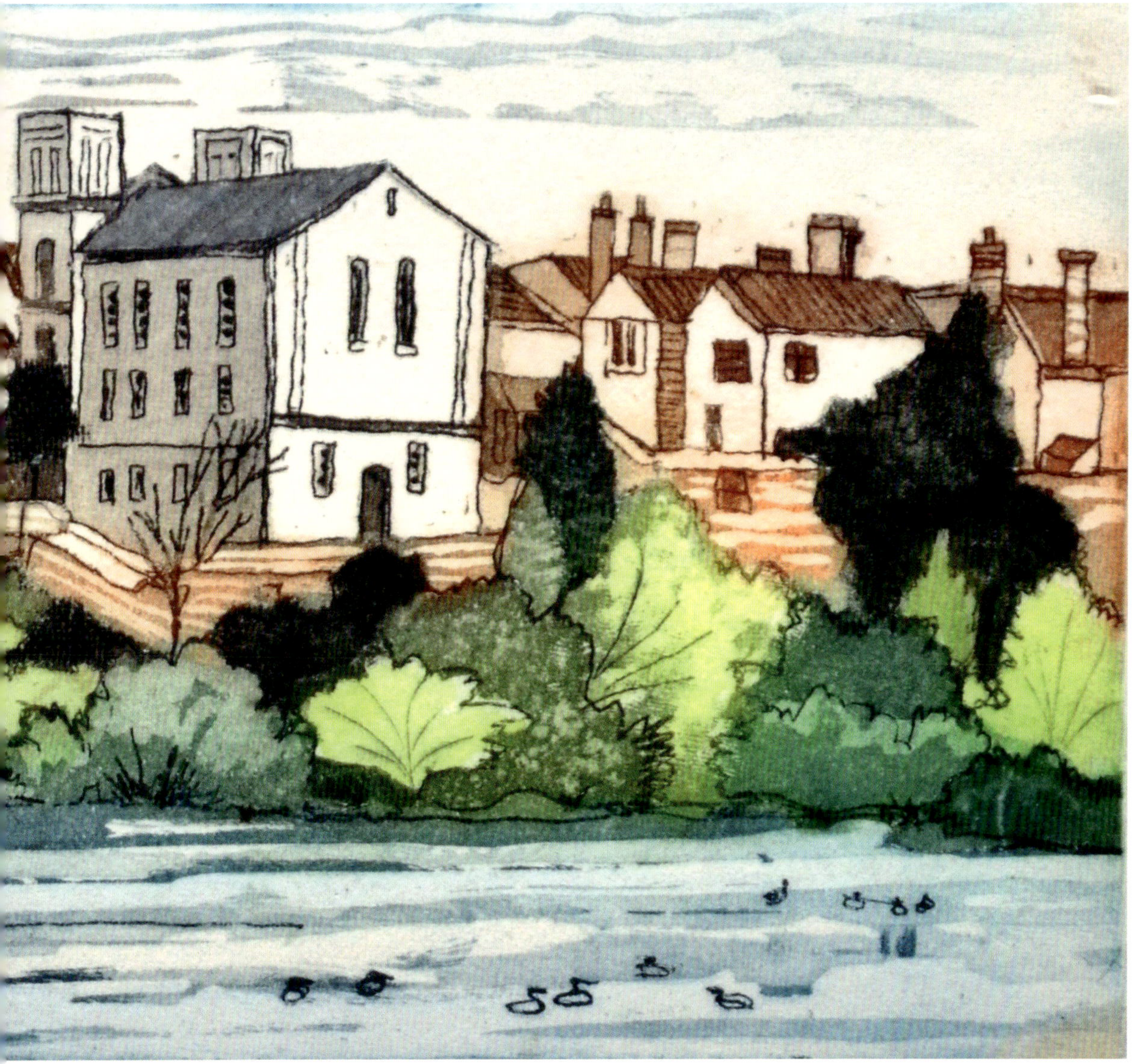

Eccles-on-Sea

This wood engraving by Norfolk artist Neil Bousfield is entitled *On Eccles Beach* (12cm x 19.5cm; edition of 40) and provides a glimpse of the sea defences on the north-east coast of the county. Eccles-on-Sea is an ancient coastal fishing village which the sea has largely reclaimed through centuries of storms and tidal surges pounding the low-lying land.

The place name Eccles is believed to derive from the Latin word *ecclesia*, meaning church, which often indicates an early Christian site. By the time of the Domesday Book, Eccles-on-Sea was a thriving community of some 8 sq km. By the early 1600s it was not much more than a tenth of this size, remaining largely unchanged until the late 19th century, when there were just 17 inhabitants on two farms.

Occupants of the pre-war bungalows built in the village are nowadays afforded post-1953 protection courtesy of concrete and stone sea defences. Neil, a member of the Society of Wood Engravers, has a fascination for the landscape around his home and the uneasy relationship it has with nature.

"Temporality, loss, fragility, the process of coastal erosion, storms, sea surges and rising sea levels impact directly on the settlements of Norfolk's east coast," says Neil. The exploration of the concepts of transformation and change, and their 'over-writing' of the landscape, drives Neil's printmaking practice.

His most recent engravings are a continuation and development of this approach, and are developed from drawings made on location in the Broads National Park and on the North Norfolk coast.

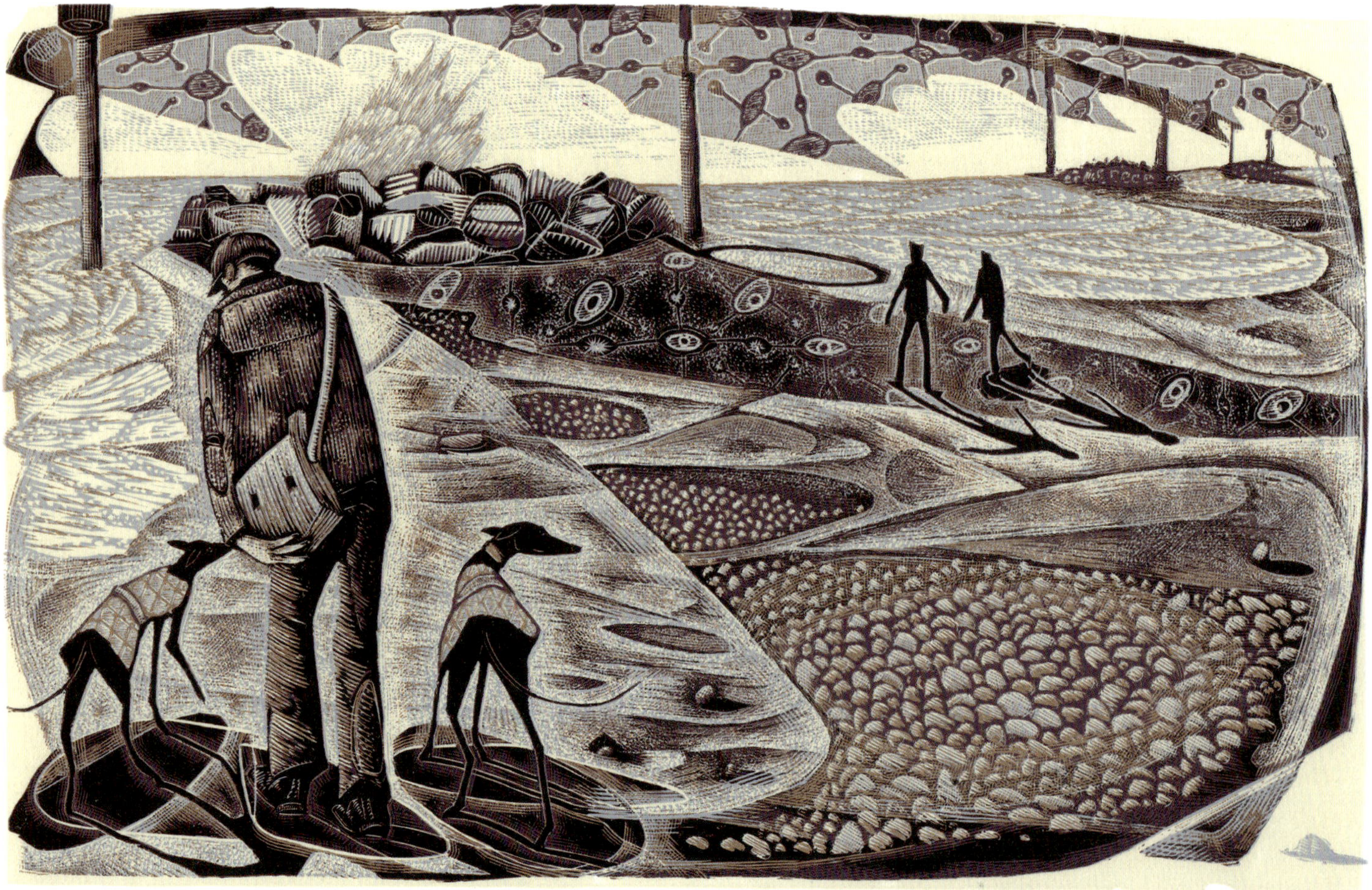

Edgefield

Colin Bygrave specialises in aquatint etchings, which he loves for their subtle colour range. *Road to Edgefield* (32cm x 43cm) shown here reflects his interest in landscape, trees and country lanes.

Based in north Norfolk, just a few miles from Edgefield, Colin describes himself as having a "strong sense of place; therefore, most of my subjects suggest some sort of enclosed spaces.

"I am always intrigued by depth, by subjects that invite this, such as paths, lanes, tracks – even, occasionally, roads. With roads, there are always questions posed by these: what is around the corner, where does it lead, who made these tracks, with what instrument, how long has it existed?

"Inevitably, this is a private preoccupation of mine, like that of most visual artists, but to me it carries with it ideas of loneliness and privacy, so very few of my prints are inhabited."

Edgefield itself has a population of fewer than 400, spread over a large area with the centre concentrated around the village pond. The settlement has an entry in the Domesday Book, recorded under the name of Edisfelda, and is described as having a mill and two beehives! The landholder is listed as Peter de Valognes, and his main tenant 'Humphrey from Ranulf brothers of Ilger'.

Colin's etchings are printed using a beautiful Hunter Penrose No 8 press.

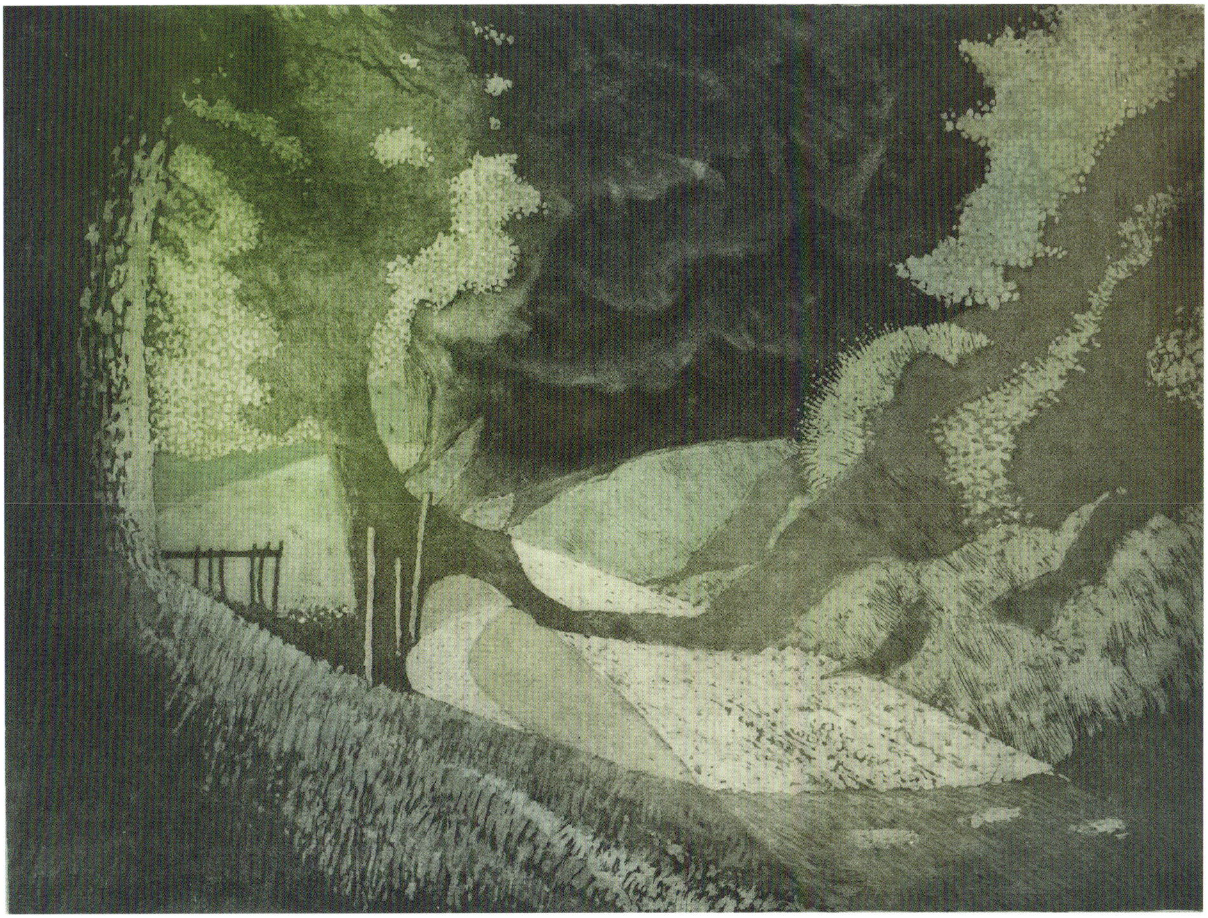

Felbrigg Hall

This hand-coloured linocut print, *Felbrigg Hall*, illustrates artist Vanessa Burroughes' love of fashion and furnishing fabrics (she studied printed textiles at Middlesex University). She also produces collaged screenprints with richly patterned backgrounds.

Now based in Norfolk, Vanessa has found inspiration in one of the county's great houses. The estate at Felbrigg was developed before the Norman Conquest and enlarged by the Felbrigg family between the late 11th century and the mid 15th century, when it became the property of the Windhams. The south front was formed out of the carcass of an early Tudor building in the 1620s, while William Windham I built the west wing in the 1680s with the architect William Samwell. William Windham II later employed James Paine to make improvements to Felbrigg including the existing staircase.

William Windham III was born in 1750 and went on to become Secretary of State for War. Having no direct descendants, he left the estate to William Lukin, the eldest son of his half-brother George Lukin, then rector of Felbrigg. William became a Vice Admiral before leaving the Navy in 1814.

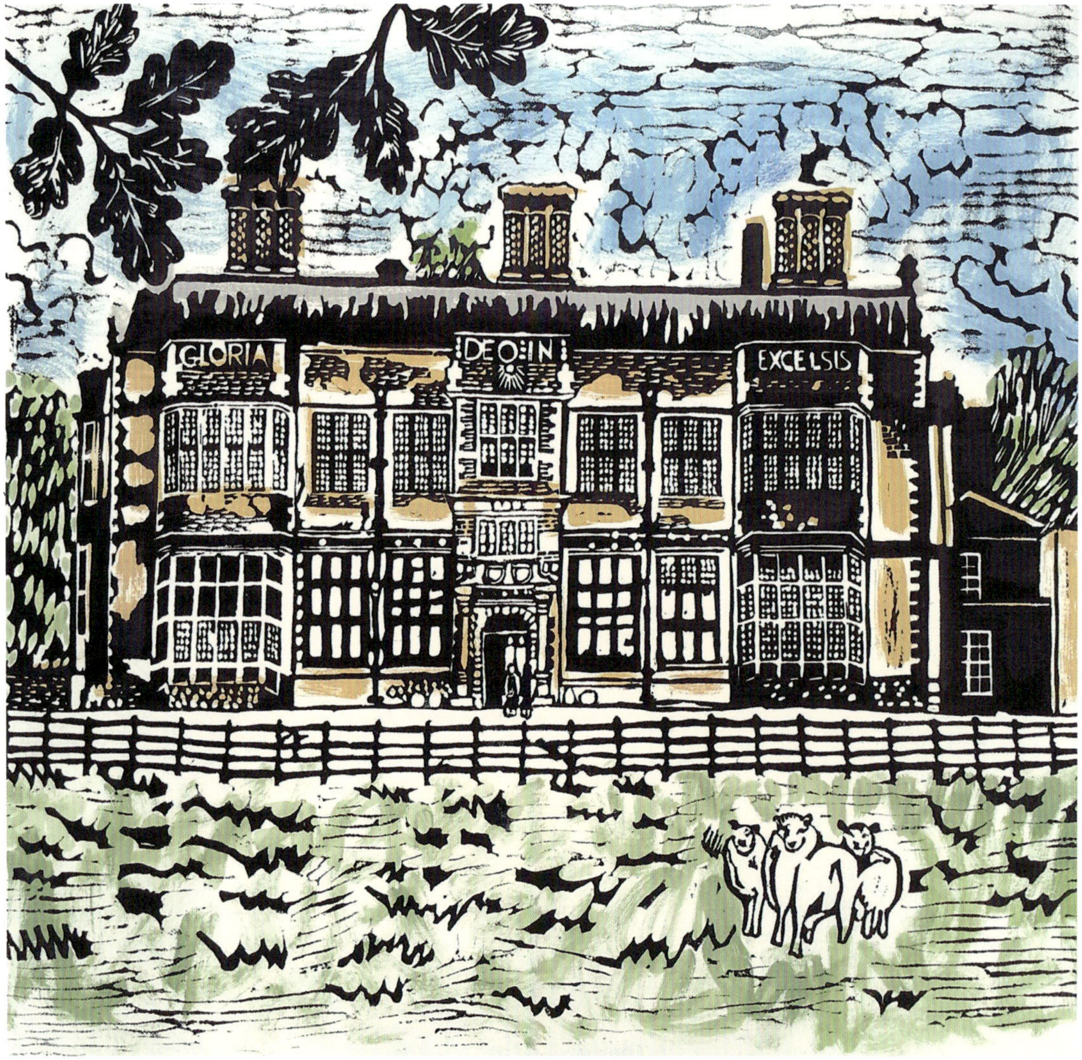

Admiral Lukin's son, William Howe Windham, was born in 1802, and became a model landlord, investing heavily in the farms. He was responsible for the re-modelling of the great hall with neo-Jacobean details, and introduced the stained-glass windows. His son, 'mad' William Frederick Windham, was a notorious figure, bringing little to the estate but scandal and losing control of Felbrigg in 1863.

It was bought by Norwich merchant John Ketton, who eventually disinherited his elder son – the estate was left to his younger son Robert in 1872. Robert lived there with his two younger sisters, who kept house for him. When they died prematurely in the 1890s, Felbrigg fell into a state of decay.

In 1924 Robert gave up Felbrigg, making it over to his nephew Windham Ketton-Cremer. His elder son Robert, a historian, became Felbrigg's last and most learned squire. A High Sheriff of Norfolk and a justice of the peace, he was actively involved in founding the University of East Anglia, to which he bequeathed his library of books on Norfolk history.

Robert never married, and on his death in December 1969 Felbrigg passed to the National Trust.

Gorleston-on-Sea

Gorleston may to some extent live in the shadow of adjoining Great Yarmouth, but has plenty of seaside appeal for visitors and retains some quasi-industrial interest for artists such as Chris Evans.

The 2014 etching *October Evening* (15 x 19.5cm) shows some of Yarmouth's infrastructure in the background. "I was delighted by the subtle colours of the scene, the timber constructions, the fishing boat and the reflections in the water," says Suffolk-based Chris, who formerly worked in advertising and as an illustrator.

Situated at the mouth of the River Yare, Gorleston was a port town at the time of the Domesday Book, later becoming a centre of herring fishing; its salt pans were used for the production of salt to preserve the fish. Gorleston was merged with Yarmouth in 1835, having once been part of the county of Suffolk.

Like Yarmouth and nearby Lowestoft, the town suffered badly from the decline of the commercial fishing industry. Its main attractions nowadays are its sandy beach, an elegant promenade, seaside gardens and pier.

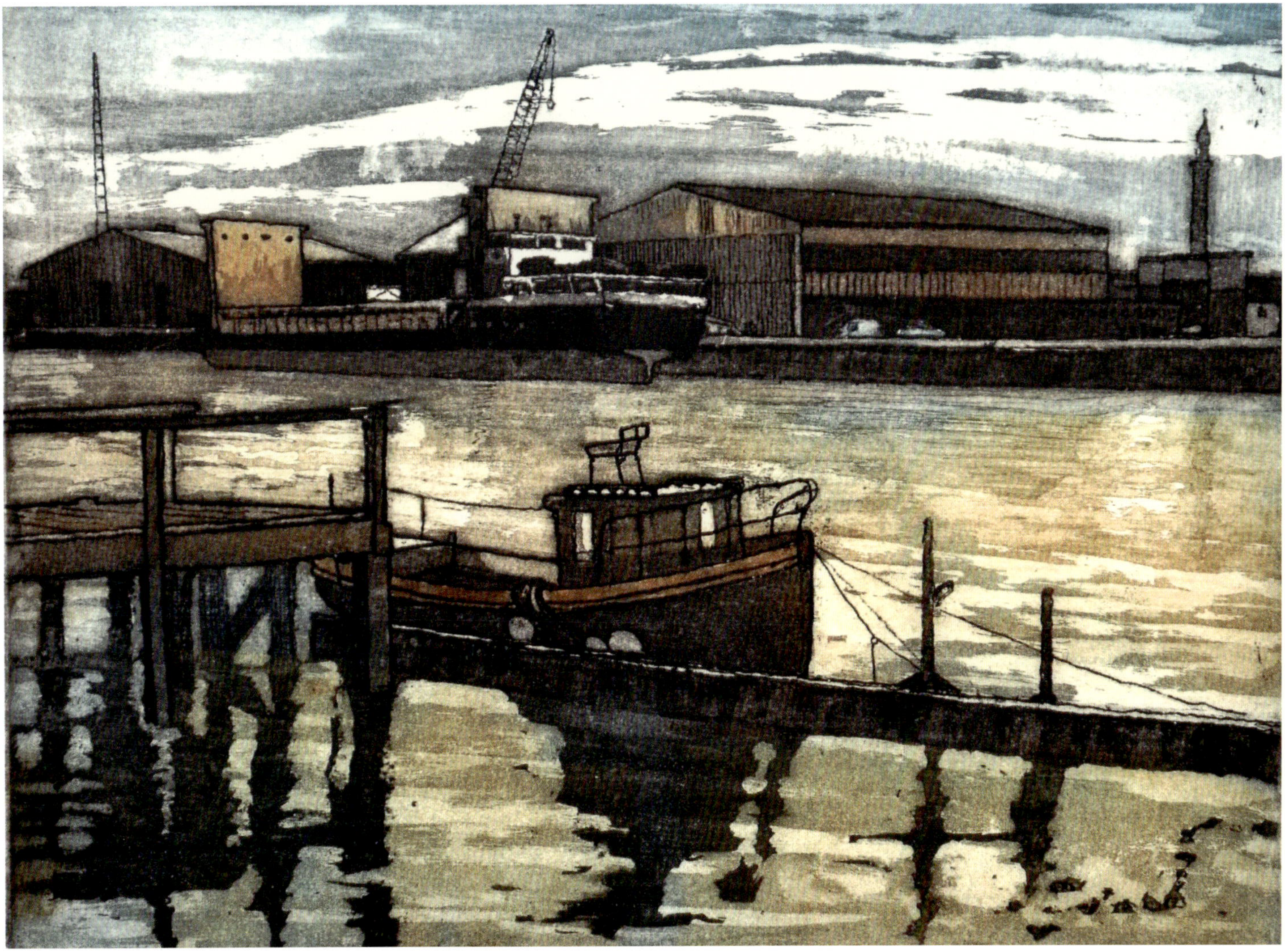

Great Yarmouth

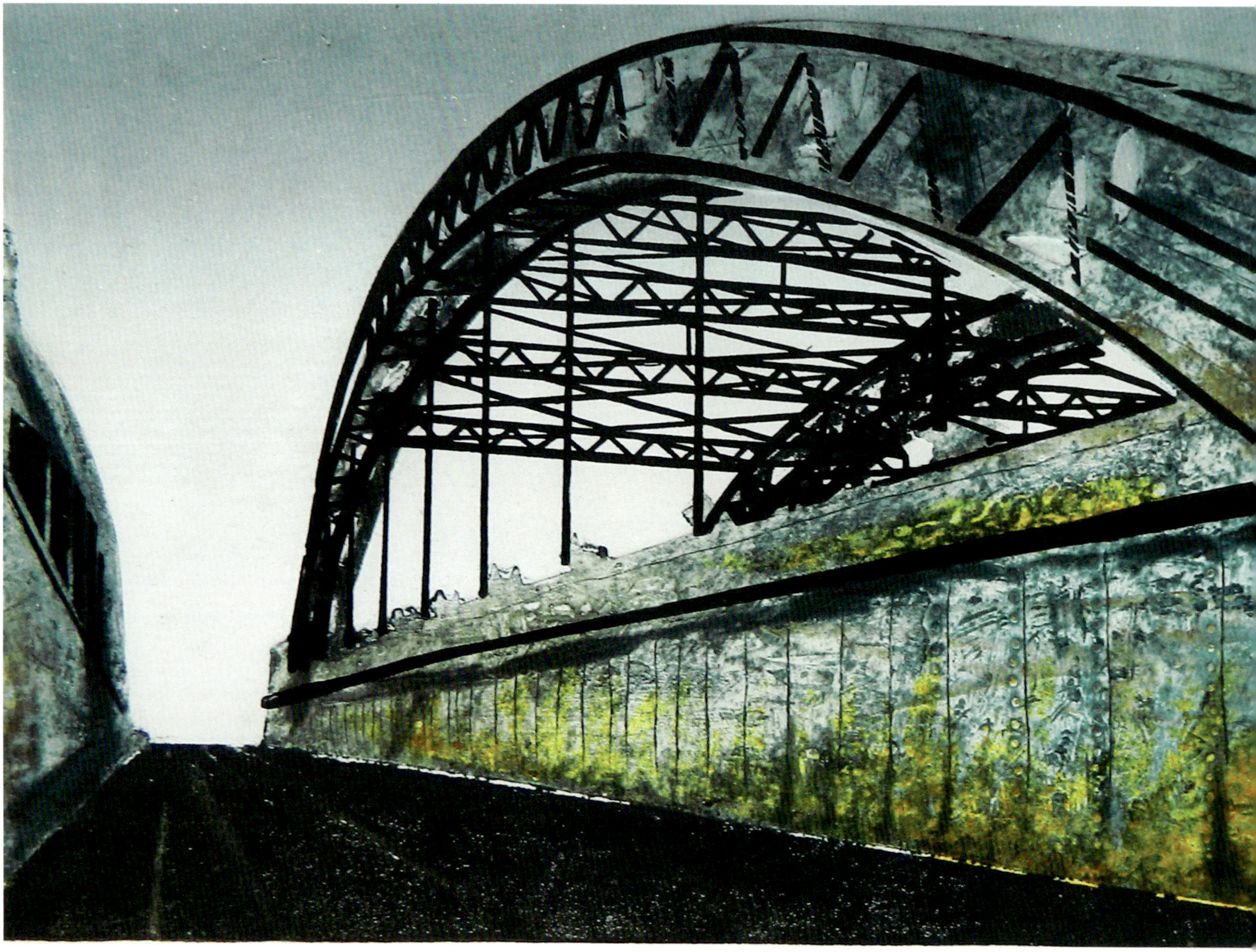

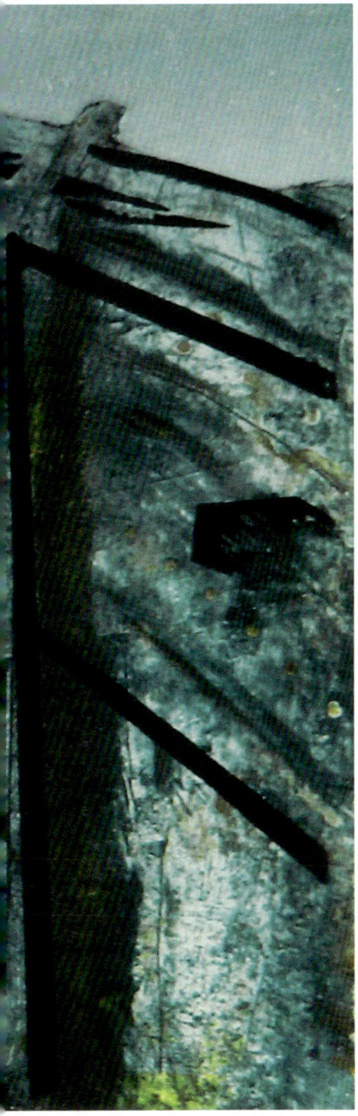

Reproduced below is an evocative 1968 linocut print by Norwich-based HJ Jackson of *Darby's Hard*, the area on Gorleston riverside across the river Yare from Great Yarmouth. One of the elder statesmen of Norfolk printmaking, John has a long association with the local fishing trade, having produced a large number of highly detailed linocuts of the boats and associated paraphernalia over the past six decades.

Even he illustrated only the tail end of what was once Yarmouth's dominant industry. By the time his first commercial fishery prints were made in the early 1960s, the trade was virtually finished. Just 50 years earlier, there were 740 visiting Scottish fishing boats crammed in Yarmouth, along with around 260 English vessels. In 1913, boats from Yarmouth and Lowestoft caught more than 238,000 tonnes of herring.

Today, Great Yarmouth is a mixture of tourist attractions, historic buildings, the decaying

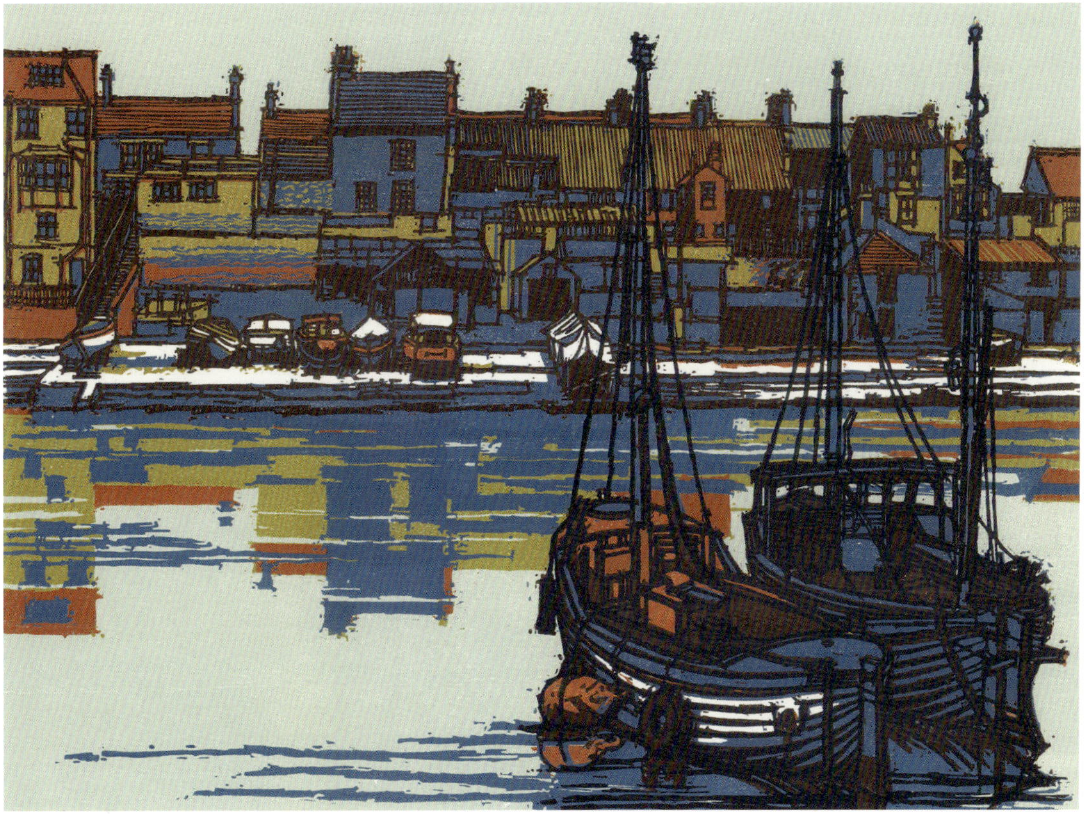

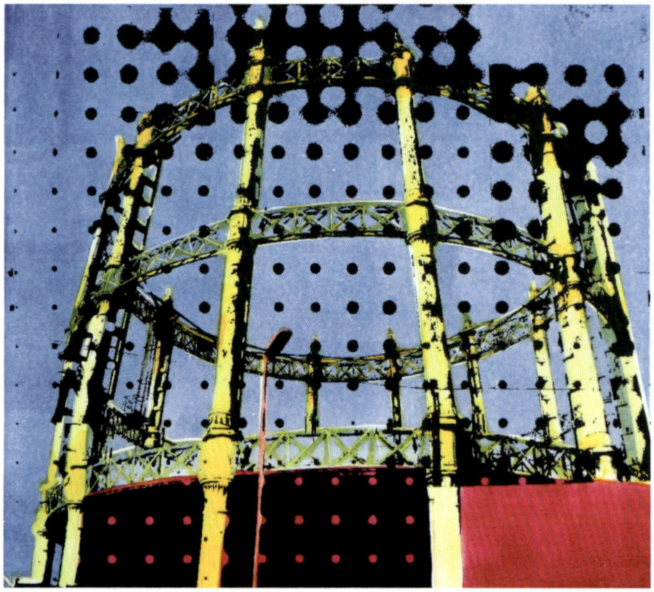

remnants of industry past and the infrastructure of industry present. Charles Dickens used Yarmouth as a key location in his novel *David Copperfield*, and described the town as "the finest place in the universe". Opinions today are perhaps a little more divided...

The town itself is on a 5km spit sandwiched between the North Sea and the river Yare. During World War I it was on the receiving end of the first aerial bombardment in Britain, by *Zeppelin L3* on 19 January 1915. The town was also shelled by the German navy on 24 April 1916. During WWII, Luftwaffe bombing did significant damage as returning bombers would dump unused ordnance on the town as they crossed the east coast.

In spite of all this, much remains of the old town. Two-thirds of the original protective medieval wall survives, while the South Quay boasts the 17th-century Merchant's House, as well as Tudor, Georgian and Victorian buildings. Behind South Quay is the maze of alleys and lanes known as 'The Rows'. Originally 145 in number, and linking Yarmouth's three main thoroughfares, a few are still intact.

Sally Hirst's print of Vauxhall Bridge on page 86, which begins this section, is an example of decay followed by renewal. The bridge was opened in 1852, spanning the river Bure, and continued in its original guise throughout the boom times created by the Scottish fishing fleet.

Norfolk-based Sally wanted to

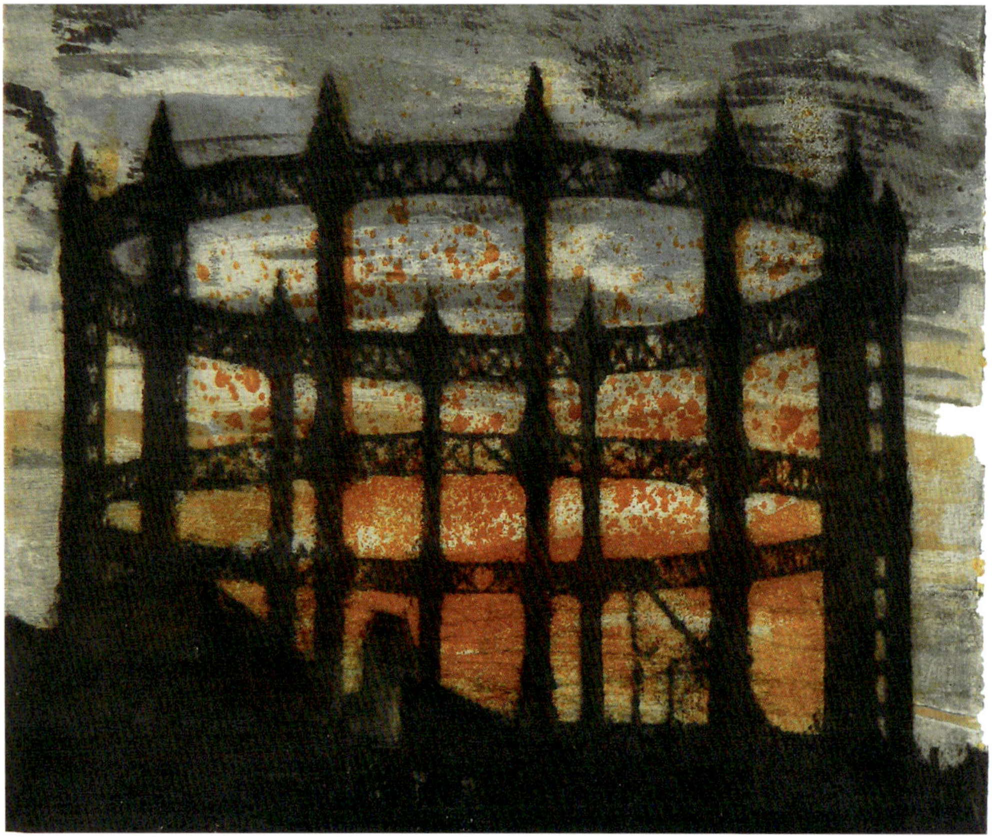

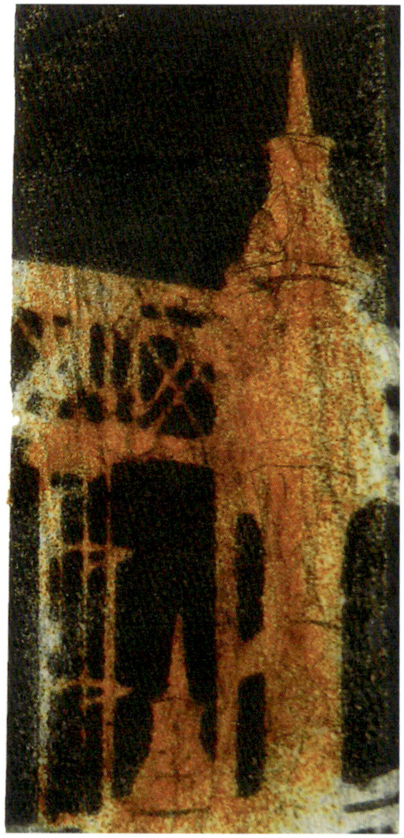

depict the bridge in all of its faded glory before its renovation in 2013. "After first using monoprinting to depict the sky, I then built up layers using a collagraph plate for the textures and a relief plate for the bridge ironwork."

On the facing page are images of Yarmouth's Victorian gas holder, used formerly for storing the town's gas supply and helping meet peak demand. Clare Johnson's print on the top left is entitled *Crown of South Quay.* Clare lives and works in the very urban environment of the North Quay of Lowestoft dock, surrounded by cranes, forklifts and lorries and with views of the grain tower, railway tracks and dock. She searches maps for shapes and symbols signifying gas holders or water towers plus other loved or loathed structures. Photographs are transformed into screened black-and-white images, tinted with a number of colour monotypes.

Sally Hirst was also drawn to the 1884-built gas holder with her 2013 print *Gasholder #1* (below far left). Shortly after she created it, National Grid announced plans to demolish a total of 76 gas holders across England, and Southern and Scottish Gas networks followed suit with their proposals to get rid of 111 over a 16-year period.

"I rusted the paper using iron filings before

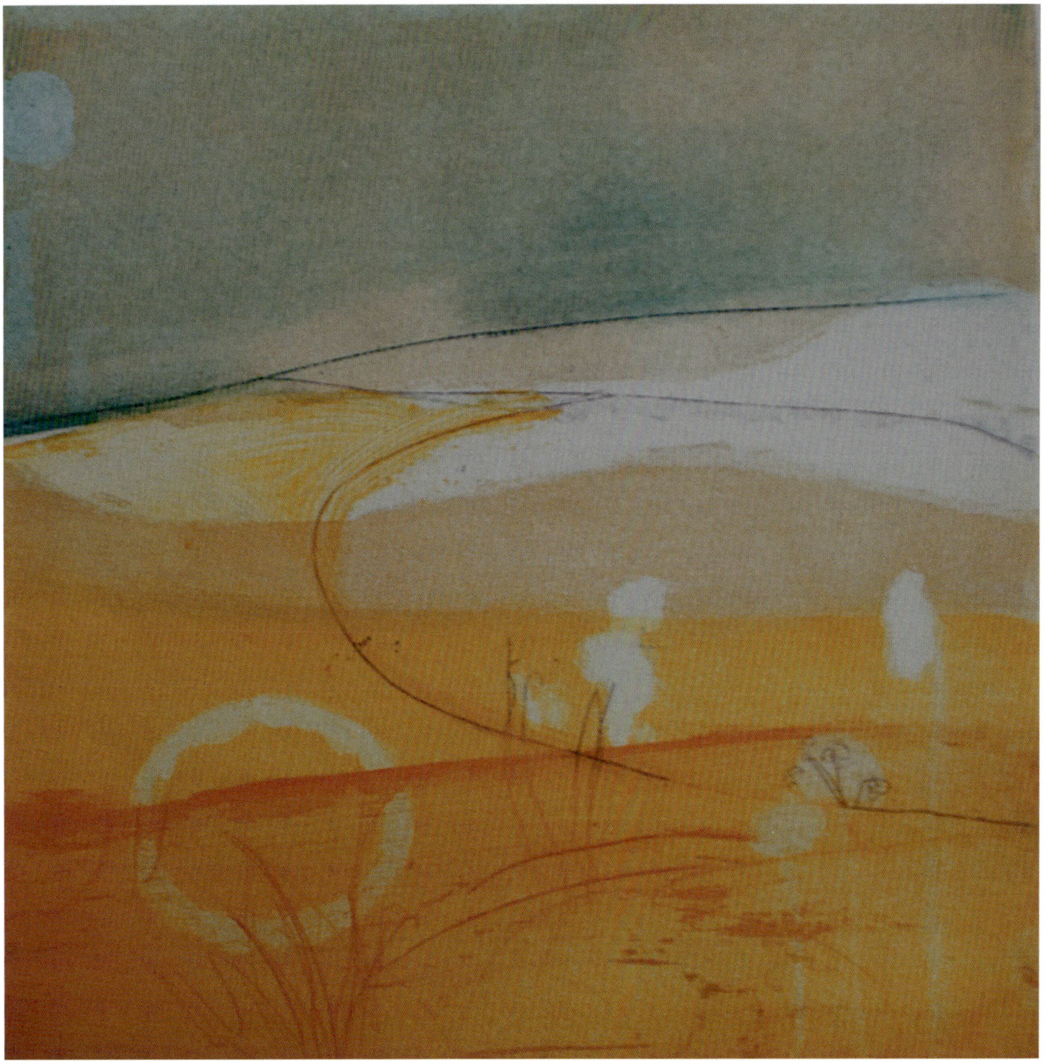

***Above left**: Clare Johnson – Crown of South Quay (photo-monotype, 39cm x 43cm); **Below far left**: Sally Hirst – Gasholder #1 (collagraph with carborundum, 25cm x 40cm); **Below left**: Sally Hirst – Decaying Spires (collagraph with carborundum, 43cm x 32cm); **Right**: Louise Davies – Golden Sands (etching, 16cm x 16cm, edition of 75).*

printing on it with two plates," explains Sally. "The first collagraph plate gives the light grey tones of the sky; the second plate is a carborundum plate depicting the tower."

With the adjoining 2014 print *Decaying Spires*, Sally explores in more detail the cast-iron construction of the gasholder. "In typical Victorian fashion, even a structure used for industrial purposes is highly ornate, celebrating both the Industrial Revolution and the skill of the maker." This print was made using three plates: the first collagraph plate gives the textures of the structure, the second carborundum plate gives the velvet-like texture of the sky, and the third is a relief plate to define details and add lighter tones.

In stark contrast to the town's industry, London printmaker Louise Davies was inspired by the golden sands of Yarmouth's famous beach for her 2012 etching *Golden Sands*, reproduced on page 89. "I wanted to recreate the golden softness of the beach at Great Yarmouth and the colour of the chalk of the cliffs in the background," she explains.

The 1970 linocut print reproduced below is another piece of Yarmouth history. HJ Jackson created the image as part of a series of nostalgic prints showing a Sunday at Yarmouth when the fishing community was attending church. *Fish Wharf Sunday/2* celebrates an attempt in 1970 by a handful of Scottish fishing boats to revive a trade that was virtually at an end.

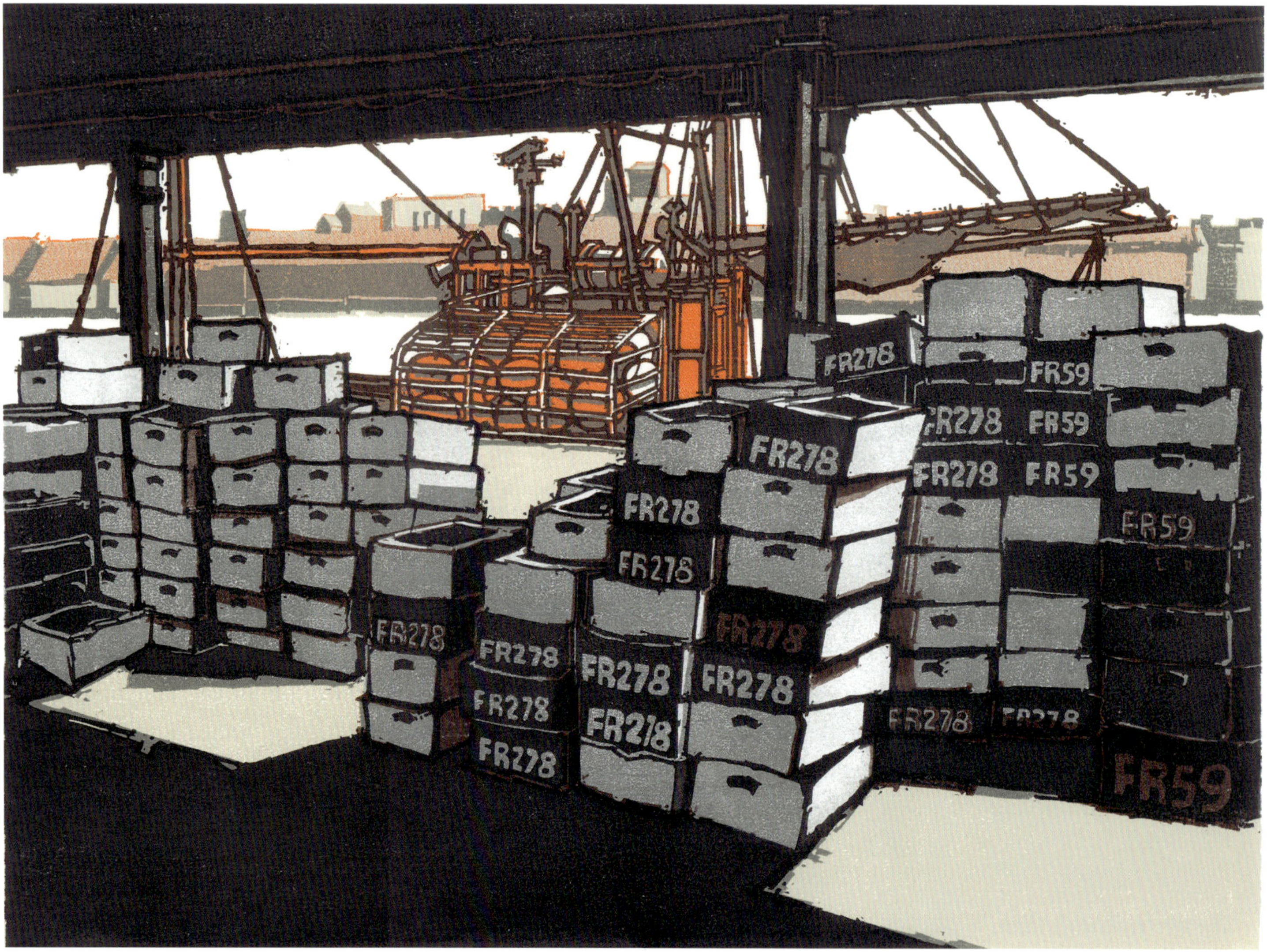

Happisburgh

Famous as a disappearing Norfolk village, due to coastal erosion, the candy-striped lighthouse remains the dominant feature of Happisburgh, sited midway between Cromer and Great Yarmouth. The wooden sea defences built in the late 1950s have been failing for many years, and large chunks of the sandy cliffs fall regularly into the sea, with the loss of footpaths and even buildings.

Happisburgh Lighthouse is the oldest working light in East Anglia, and the only independently run lighthouse in Britain. Built in 1790, originally one of a pair, the tower is 85 feet high and the lantern is 134 feet above sea level. Saved as a working light by the local community, it is maintained and operated entirely by voluntary contributions.

Equally prominent in the 1991 print *Happisburgh* by Glynn Thomas (top right) is the nearby 15th-century church of St Mary. In 1940, a German bomber released a trapped bomb during its return to Germany, and the shrapnel can still be seen embedded in the aisle pillars of the church.

In May 2013, a series of early human footprints was discovered on the beach at Happisburgh, providing direct evidence of early human activity at the location. Visitors still come in large numbers, drawn by the eroding cliffs and disappearing properties, as well as by the remote charm of this part of the Norfolk coastline.

Stuart Brocklehurst, a printmaker based in Yorkshire, is only an occasional visitor to Norfolk but was captivated by the candy-striped lighthouse tower and the fields in the foreground. His linocut print appears on the right.

Wildlife artist Max Angus also chose

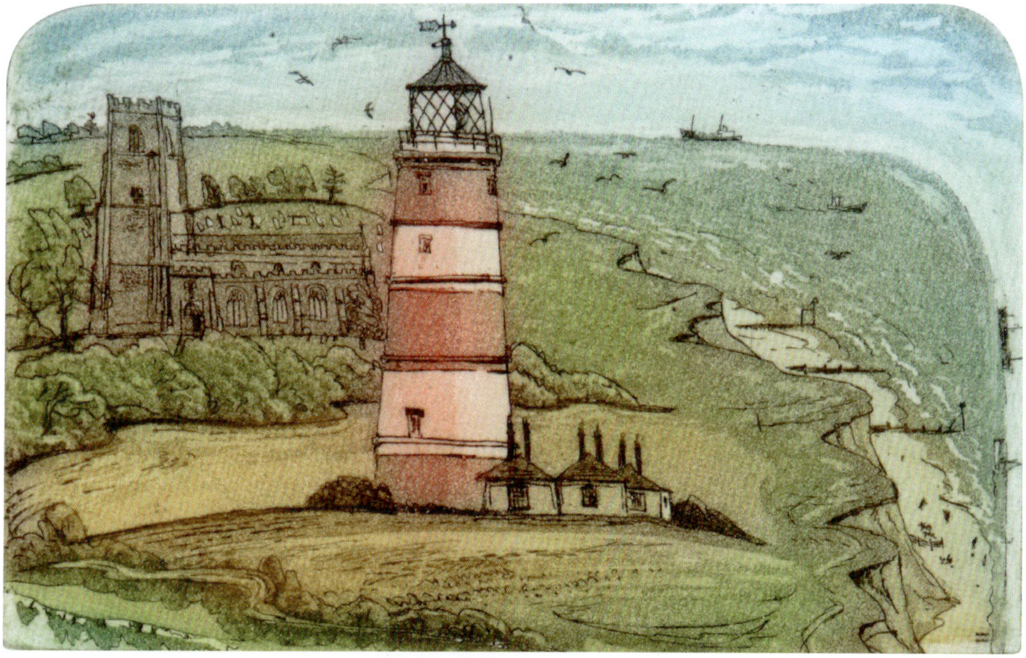

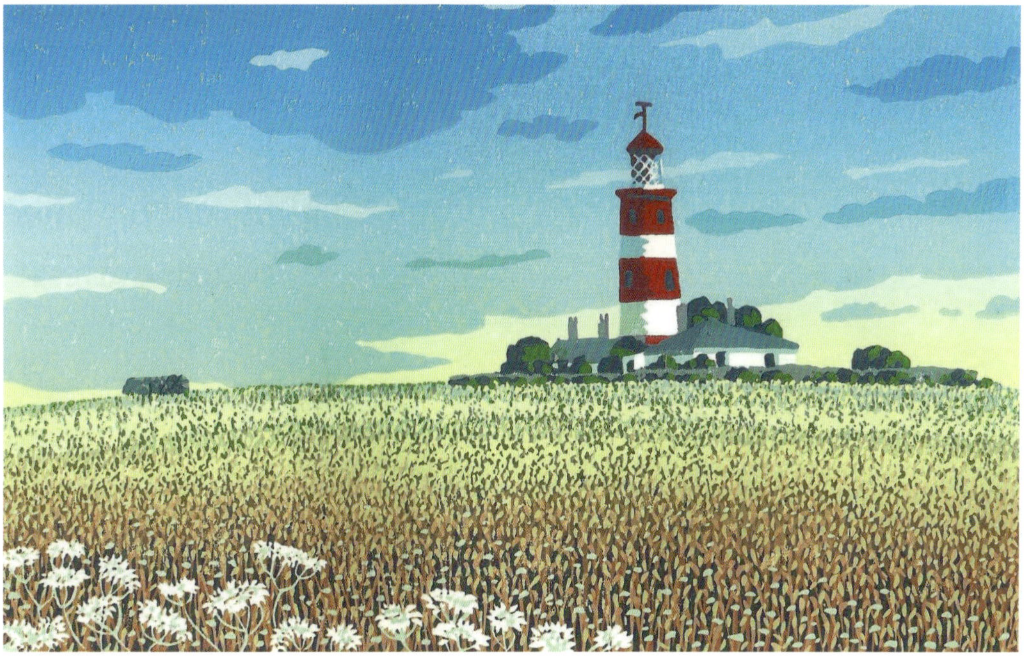

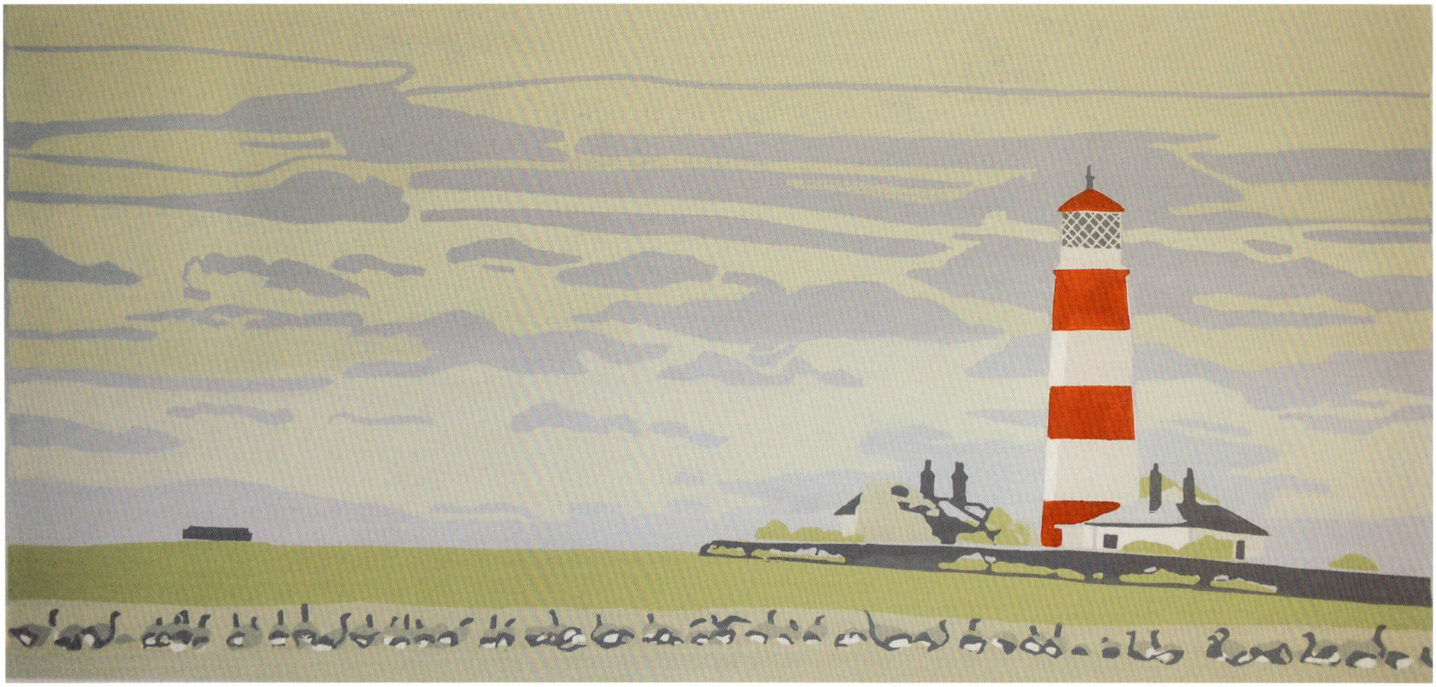

the lighthouse as a subject, but adorns her foreground with geese in the linocut *Disappearing Landscapes* (above).

"Happisburgh and many of the villages around that area have suffered dramatic coastal erosion in the last few years. The sandy cliffs protecting the coastline are reduced at every storm and extreme high tide. The viewpoint of the pastel sketch of the lighthouse at Happisburgh [right] was drawn from the car park. In the picture the lighthouse is on the far right. On the left edge of the image is where the land drops away to the sea.

"I intend to return to the same viewpoint in five years and then again possibly in ten years. Each time I hope to be able to create the same size image from standing in the same place. If the coastline has not receded, then I will be most happy. If the coastline has receded, the lighthouse will move to its new position in any subsequent picture."

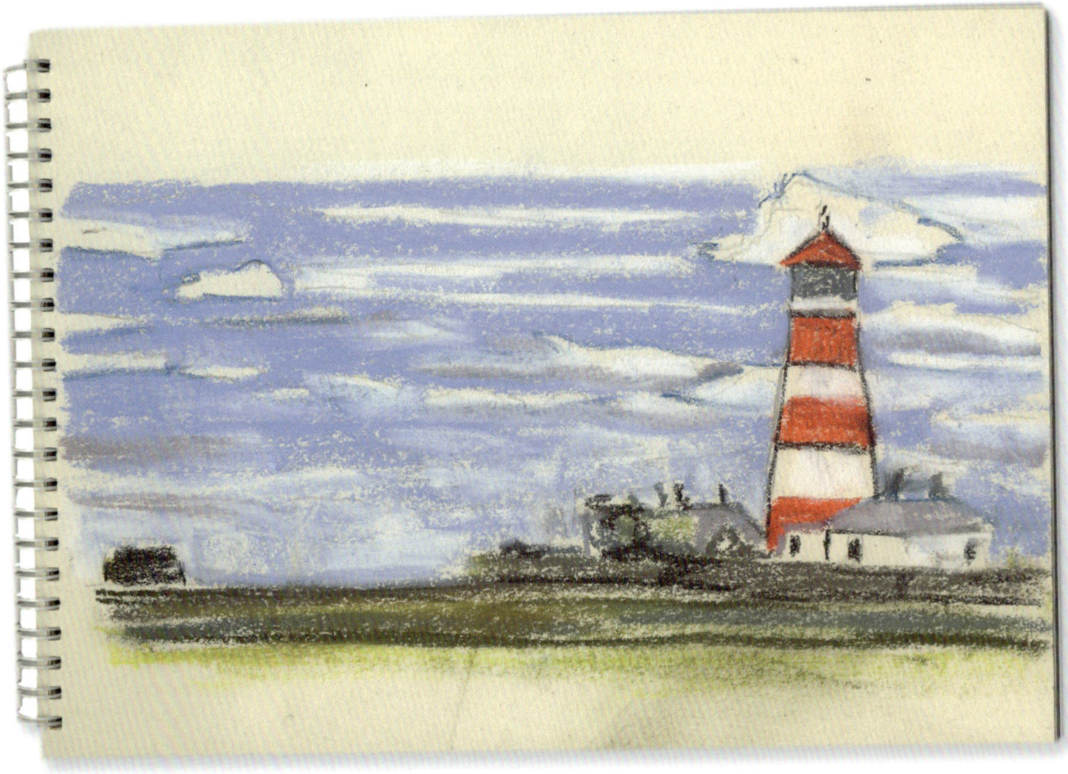

Heacham

London-based artist Louise Davies has an eye for the colours of Norfolk and a taste for more abstract interpretations of landscape. Here, a scene of the lavender fields near the village of Heacham in north-west Norfolk fired her imagination and resulted in this 2017 etching (16cm x 16cm).

Louise studied Fine Art at St Martin's School of Art and then gained an MA in Printmaking at Camberwell. She is a Fellow of the Royal Society of Painter-Printmakers (RE). Her work is very much based on the landscape and the response that she has to it, trying to evoke the seasons and atmosphere of a place.

Norfolk Lavender was founded in 1932. Francis Dusgate of Fring Hall provided the land, and the first lavender field was planted on Dusgate's land at Fring. In 1936, Dusgate acquired Caley Mill on the River Heacham and the ground around it. Lavender has been grown there ever since.

Heacham started to become popular with the Victorians as a seaside resort due to the opening of the railway between King's Lynn and Hunstanton in the early 1860s. It remains a family favourite. Both North Beach (Jubilee) Road and South Beach Road are lined with caravan parks. The beaches at Heacham are situated on the east banks of The Wash; this means it is one of the few places in eastern England (like nearby Hunstanton) where the sun sets over the sea instead of over the land.

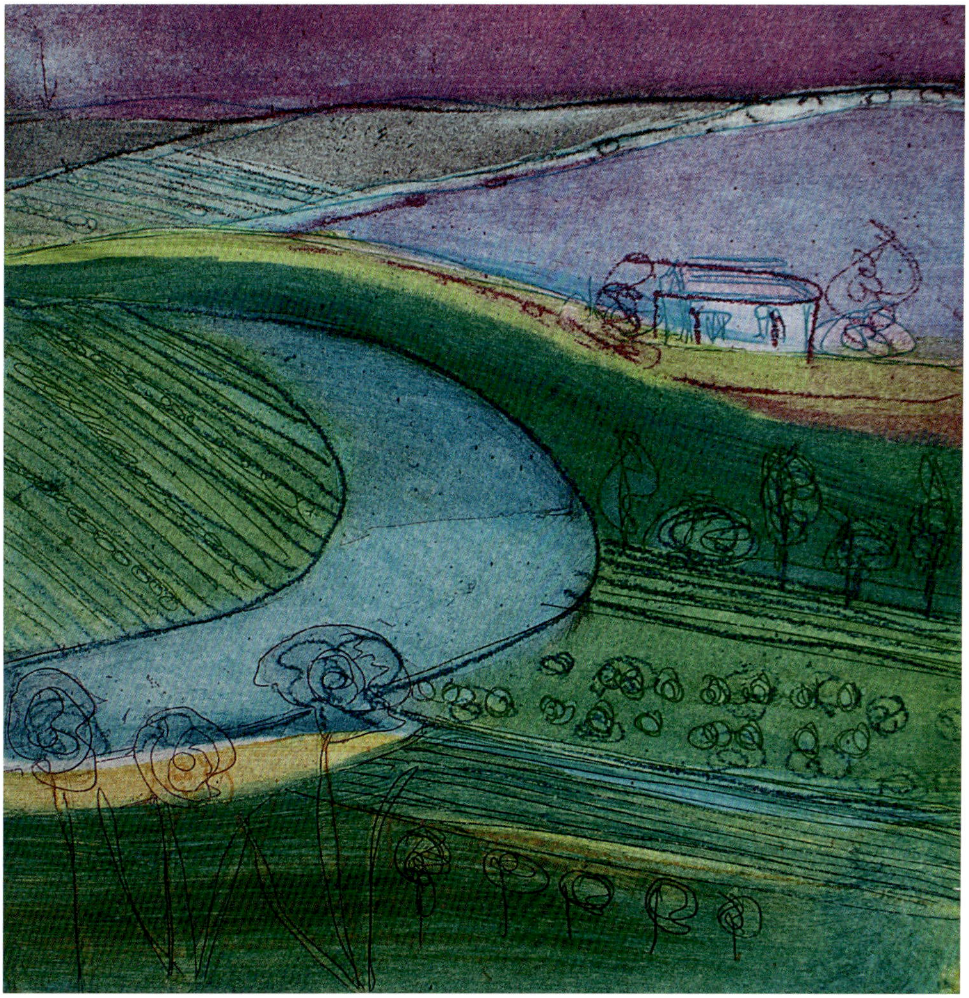

Holkham

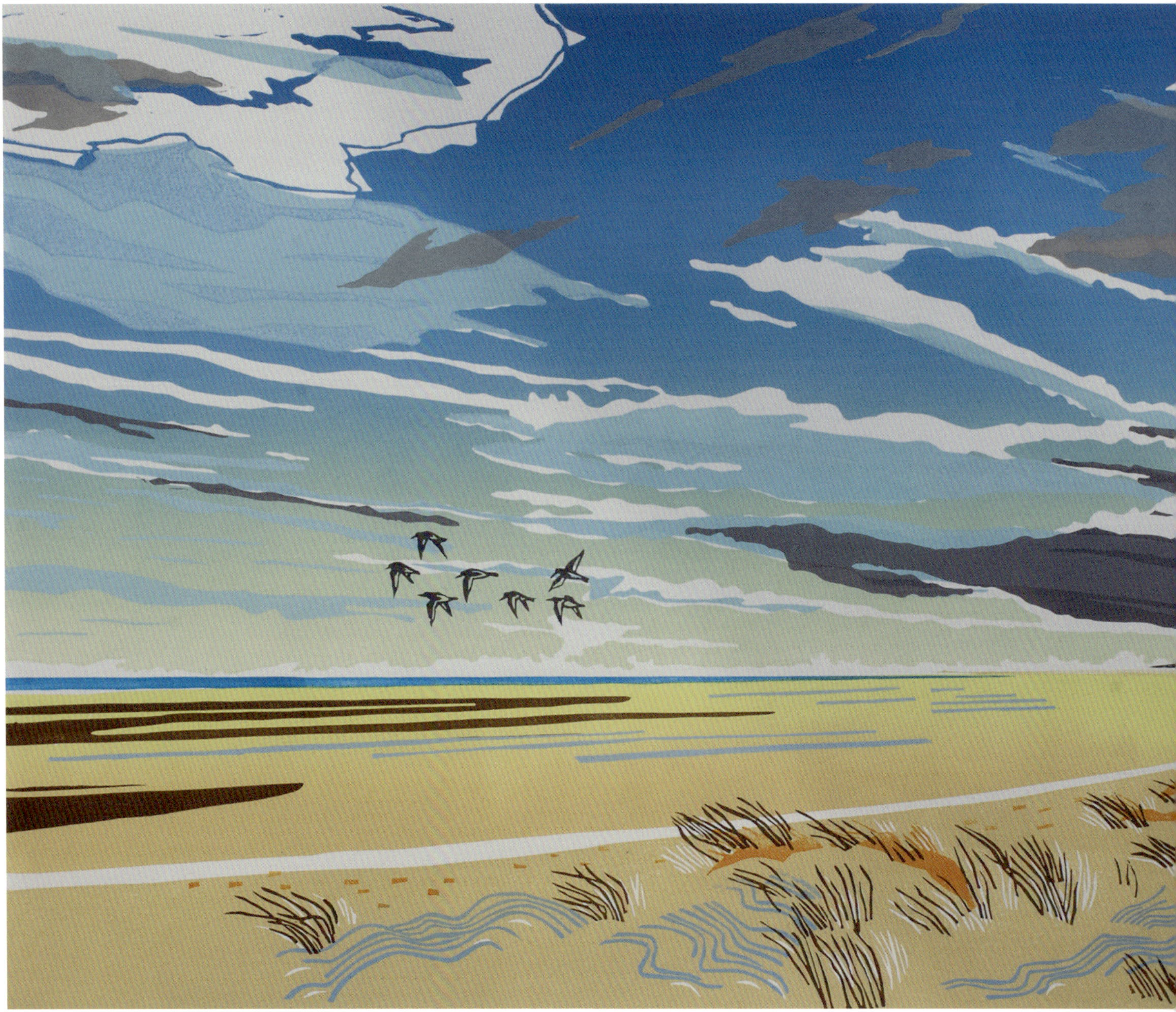

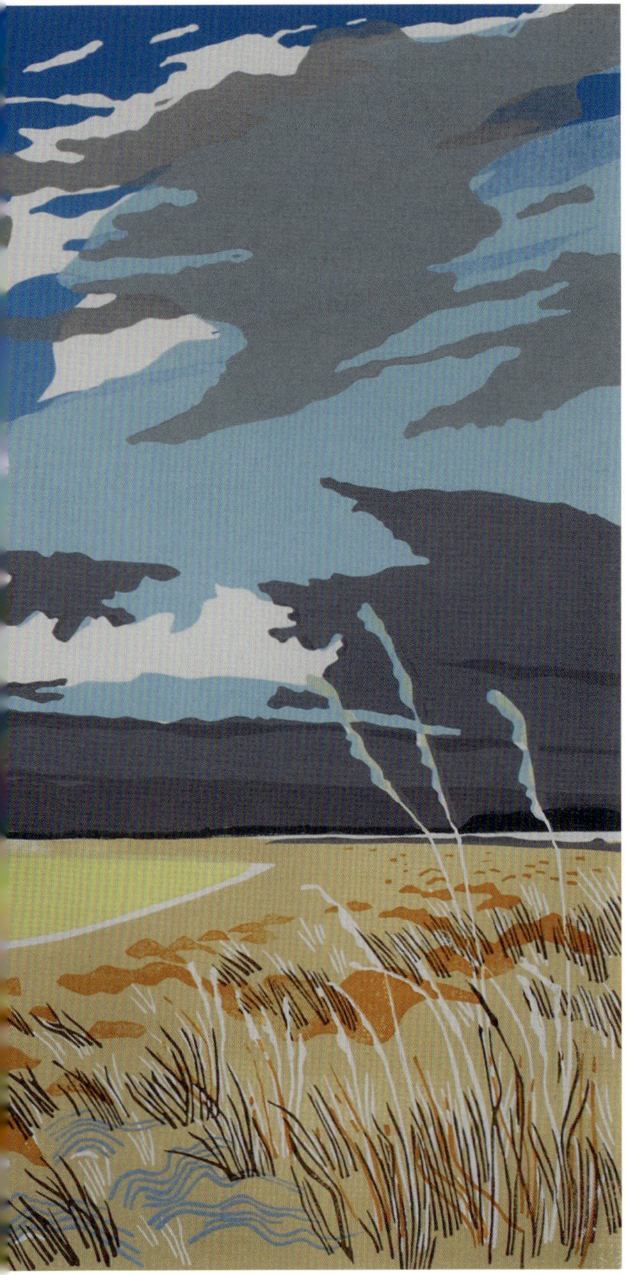

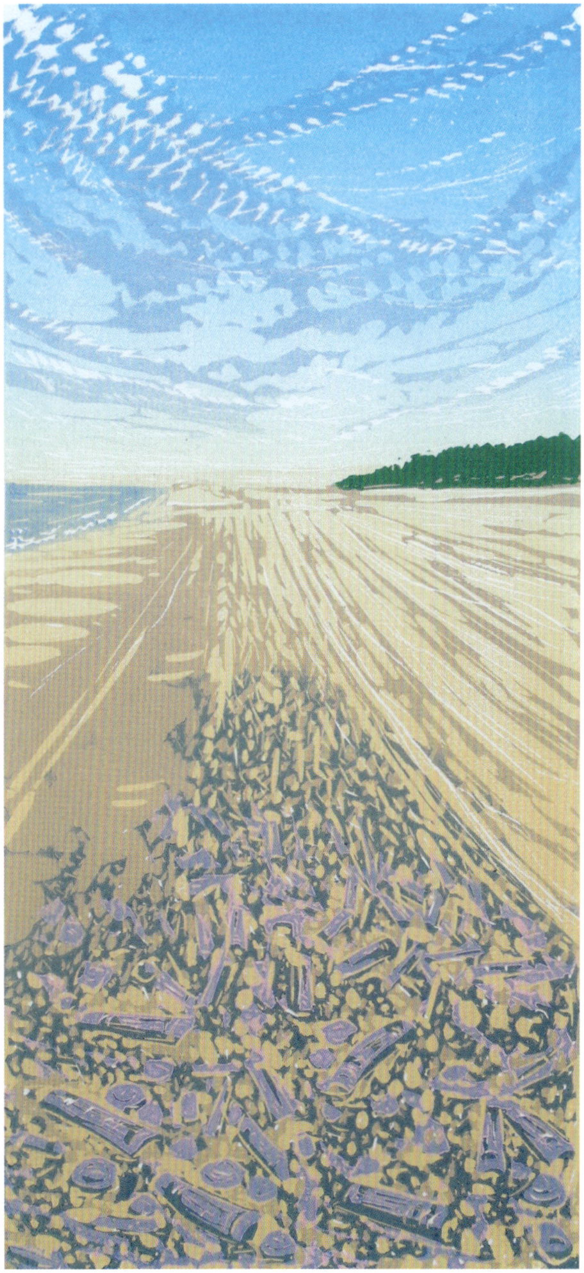

***Far left:** Colin Moore – Holkham (sheet size 53.5cm x 77.5cm), 3-block linocut from 2017, edition of 100.*

***Left:** Louise Stebbing – Razor Shells (39.5cm x 18.5cm), reduction linocut from 2016, edition of 16.*

***Page 96, top left:** Kate Heiss – Holkham Walk (30cm x 30cm), linocut and screenprint from 2013, variable edition of 30.*

***Page 96, top right:** Valerie Sims – Pinkfoots (18cm x 18cm), woodcut from 2016, edition of 20.*

***Page 96, bottom:** Lisa Hooper – Holkham Great Barn (21cm x 49cm), etching from 2003, edition of 25.*

***Page 97, top right:** Sarah Bays – Holkham Memory (19cm x 24cm), monotype from 2015.*

***Page 97, bottom right:** Fiona Carver – The Long Beach, Holkham (23cm x 29cm), 5-block linocut from 2014, edition of 50.*

***Page 97, bottom left:** Robert Gillmor – Shorelarks (20.5cm x 28cm), linocut from 2016, edition of 75.*

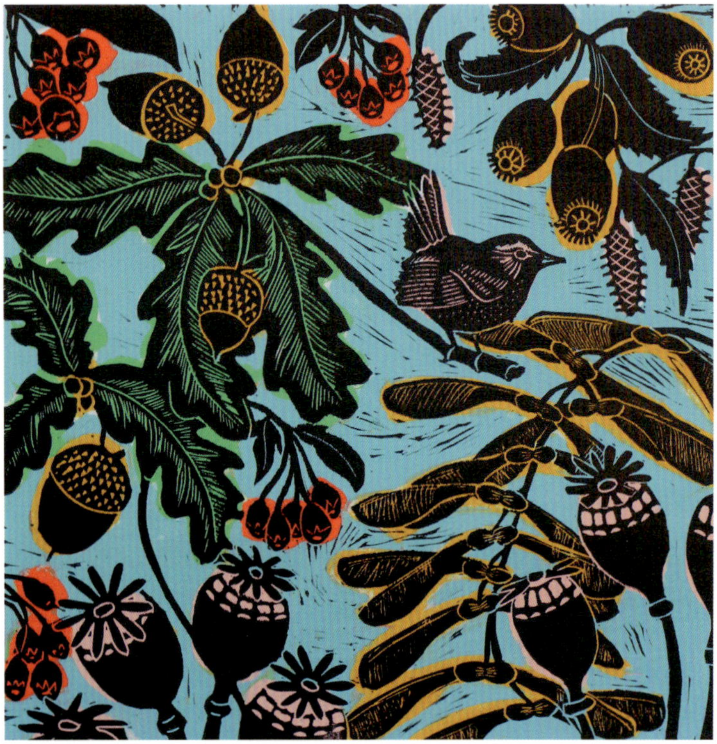

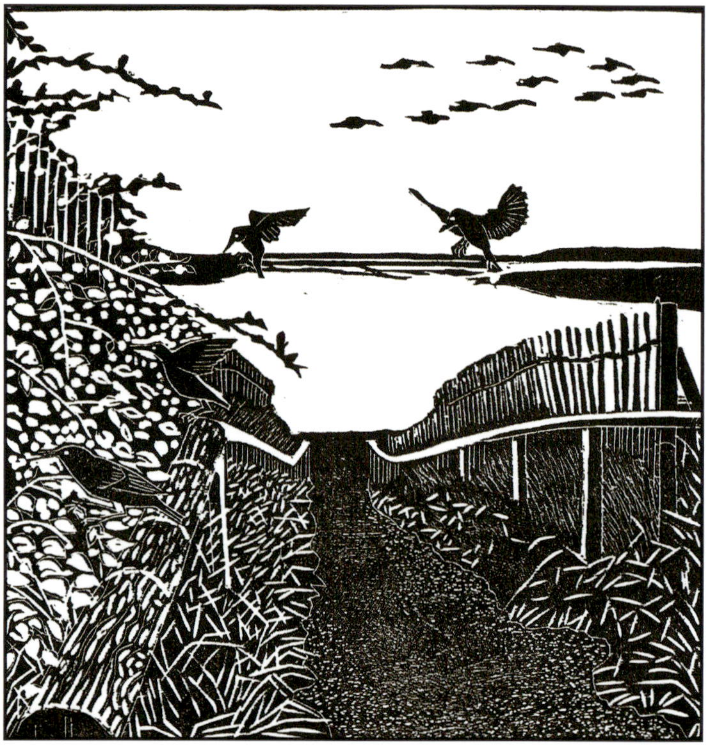

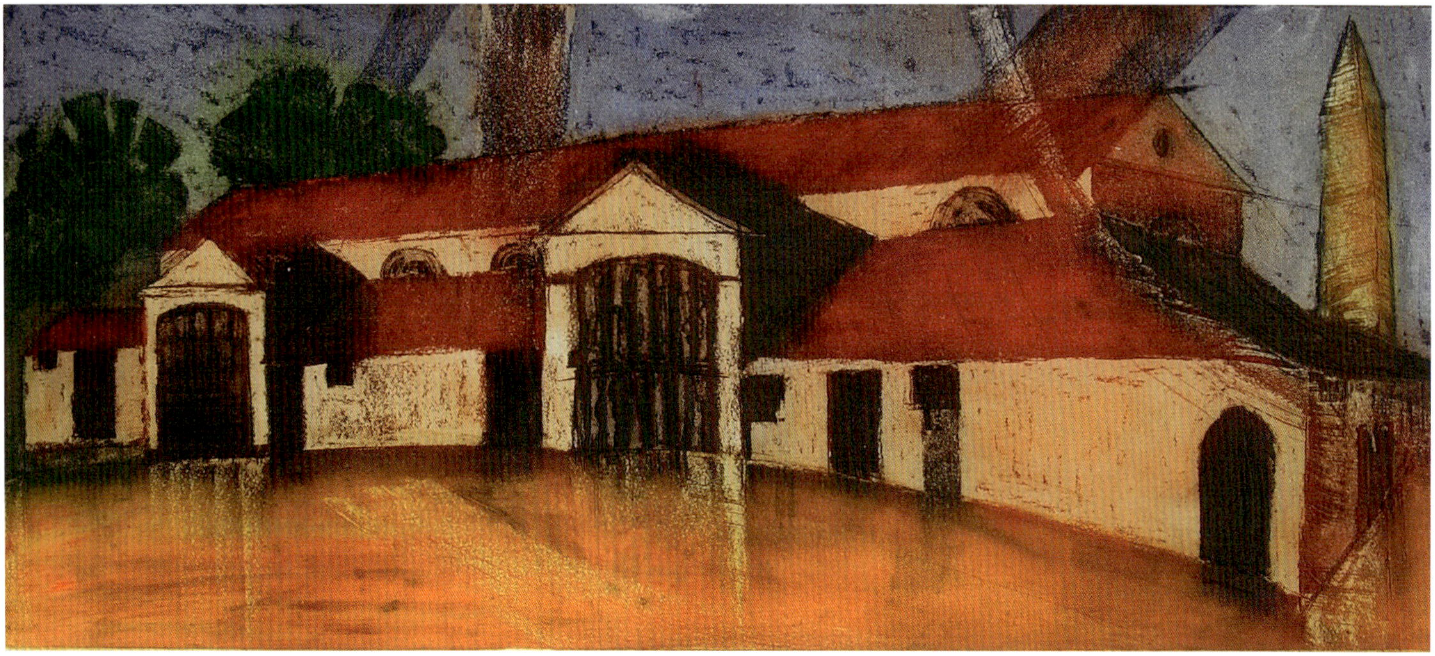

Colin Moore's biggest print to date appears on page 94, and the large linocut is a fitting tribute to the vast expanse of sand at Holkham Beach. "It isn't always as dramatic as this, but the air is fresh and there is always something to see." The neighbouring linocut by Louise Stebbing was the result of a commissioned acrylic painting. "I love the expanse of Holkham, and followed up the painting with this print."

Kate Heiss provided the linocut/screenprint *Holkham Walk* on the far left. "An autumn walk along the coastal path between Holkham and Wells inspired this print. The path here follows the edge of the fields at the back of the pine trees. The Wren was keeping me company dashing between the branches as I walked."

Valerie Sims in her woodcut (left) captures the path down to Holkham Beach, with seasonal visitors Pinkfoot Geese passing overhead, while Dumfries and Galloway-based artist Lisa Hooper provides this magnificent etching of *Holkham Great Barn* (below left). The print was one of a number of barns undertaken in 2002/3 for an AA2A (Artists' Access to Art Colleges) award.

According to Fiona Carver, "when the tide is out Holkham Beach seems to go on forever". For her print *The Long Beach, Holkham* (bottom right), she wanted "to capture the great expanse of sand and sky and the feeling of emptiness and space. I also wanted to show the contrast between the light sand and dark trees, which is why this is my only print where you can't actually see the sea."

Holkham Memory is a monotype by Sarah Bays (top right). "The wide open space of the beach at Holkham and Wells, which seems to stretch on forever, often inspires my monotypes."

The birds in Robert Gillmor's *Shorelarks* (below) are a relatively common sight at Holkham Beach, providing an unexpected splash of yellow as they forage in the shingle.

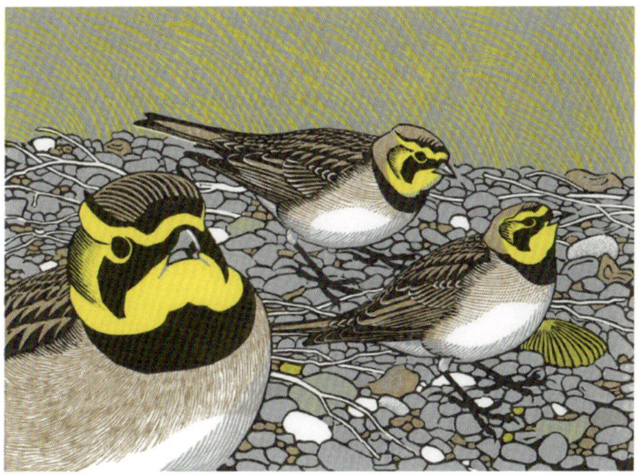

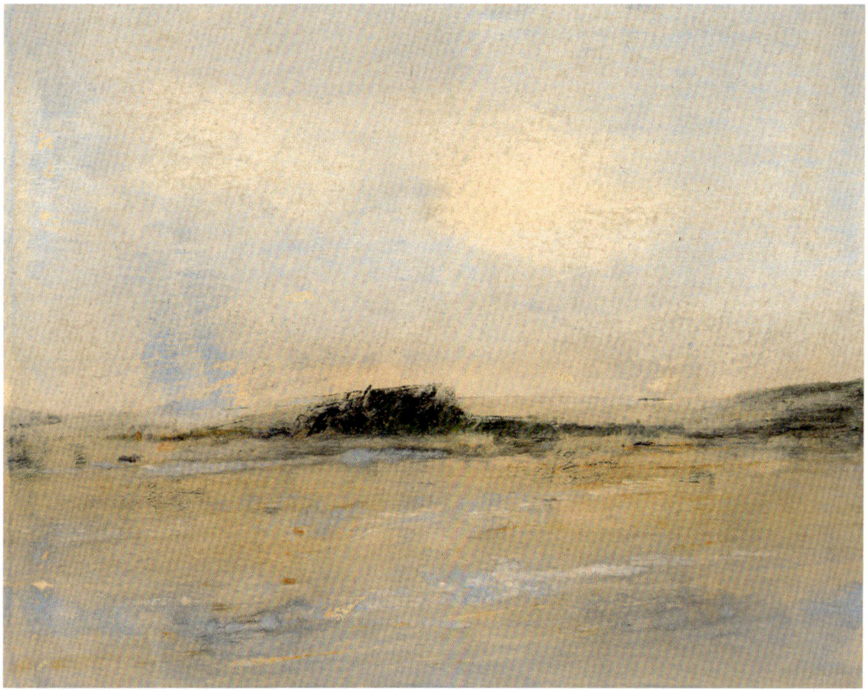

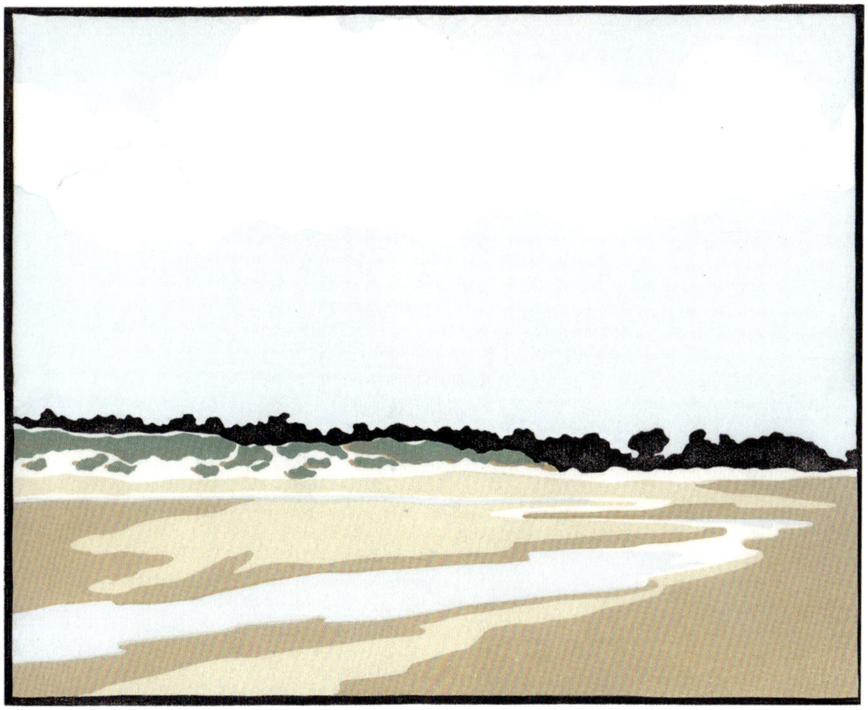

Holme-next-the-Sea

Holme Nature Reserve was the inspiration for Hertfordshire artist Kate Heiss's print *Holme Dunes*. "I love how the Corsican pine trees hug the beach here," she says. "The reserve has such a diverse range of wild flowers and wildlife that every view you take shows a different habitat."

Kate's 2013 linocut and screenprint (30cm x 30cm, from an edition of 30) shows a Chiffchaff perched on a pine tree nestled between sea buckthorn, evening primrose and ragwort. The print features colours hand-painted directly on to the screen and printed. The details of the image are cut in lino and then printed over the top.

Max Angus, a Kent wildlife artist with strong ties to Norfolk, is responsible for the linocut *Winter Dunes* (below right) featuring Snow Buntings at Holme. She visited the north coast in November 2013 hoping to see the elusive birds. Having failed to spot any between Salthouse and Cley, the following day she got lucky at Holme Nature Reserve.

"The temperature was perishing with a lazy wind that would blow through everything rather than go round it. There in the lea of the silver sand dunes, a pair of exhausted Snow Buntings were sheltering in the marram grass and seablites. Due to the direction of the wind, I was able to sit about six yards away in the dunes. I sketched the outlines of the various movements of the pair while I was being sandblasted. I was soon so cold that I could no longer hold the sketchbook or the pencil. Once back in my studio, the most successful sketches were used to create the positioning of the birds in *Winter Dunes*."

Max didn't have enough detail for the foliage to be incorporated into the image, so returned to Norfolk in the immediate wake of the December 2013 storm surge. "I arrived at Holme beach expecting to sketch the dunes and some foliage. The dunes and all the vegetation had been stolen by the storm. Walking along the edge of the sea ran a thin line of tangled flotsam. I found a few small broken pieces of lichen that I could take back to the studio. The original seablites in

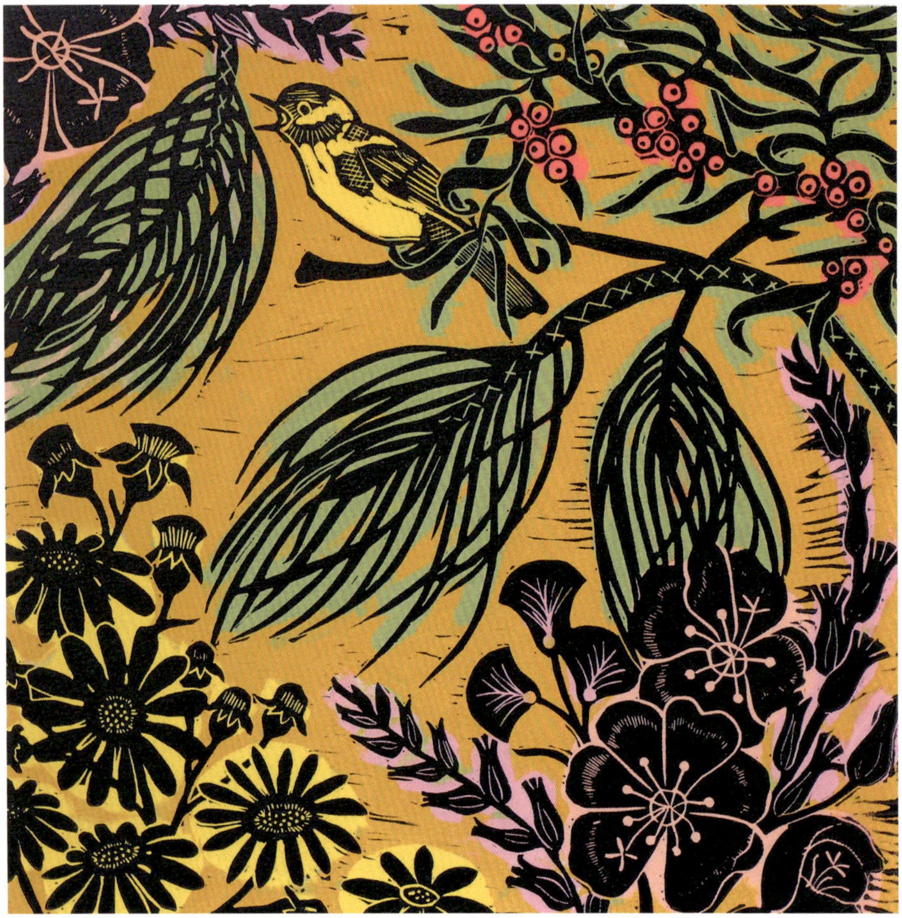

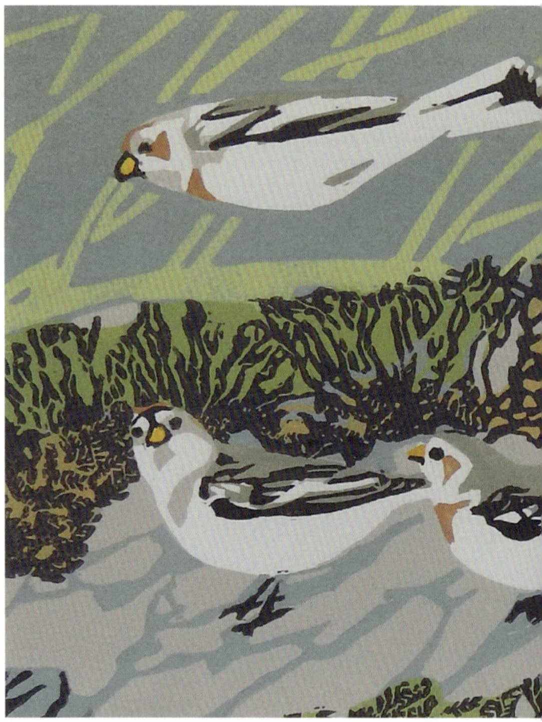

the sketches were replaced by lichen, but it enabled the development of the background of the print.

"The linocut was made up of four blocks. From the original drawing to sourcing the background, it took around two months to develop before starting the printing of the edition."

To the right is a reduction linocut named *An Evening at Holme* (16cm x 14cm) from 2001 by Thelma Sykes, featuring Black-winged Stilts. "I'm an artist whose eye focuses on birds in their landscape, yet whose hand folds more happily round the gouge than the brush," she says. "I'm comfortably at home with the relief print – linocut, woodcut, and sometimes a combination of the two."

She was at Holme Dunes Reserve in May, the day on which two Black-winged Stilts arrived. These were the first she had ever seen. "Though the light was poor, it was atmospheric, and the pair clearly felt at home here, too, because they subsequently laid three eggs and raised two chicks to flying stage.

"Black-and-white birds are a gift for a printmaker, and I wanted to celebrate this day – but the work came 14 years later. Such distance between the experience and its expression is not unusual for me, but by then I had observed other Black-winged Stilts including one that ultimately stayed at Titchwell RSPB Reserve for 12 years and became known as Sammy.

"The day I saw the stilts at Holme was a bad-weather day, and I brought that low light into my linocut by choosing an evening setting. I wanted to describe the pair only by a calligraphic line of light; and the habitat by sparkles from the bubbles that rise around the reed stems. I cut the block with this minimum, and took a black proof. It felt nearly right, but to give the birds scale within their surroundings I included the reeds and their reflections."

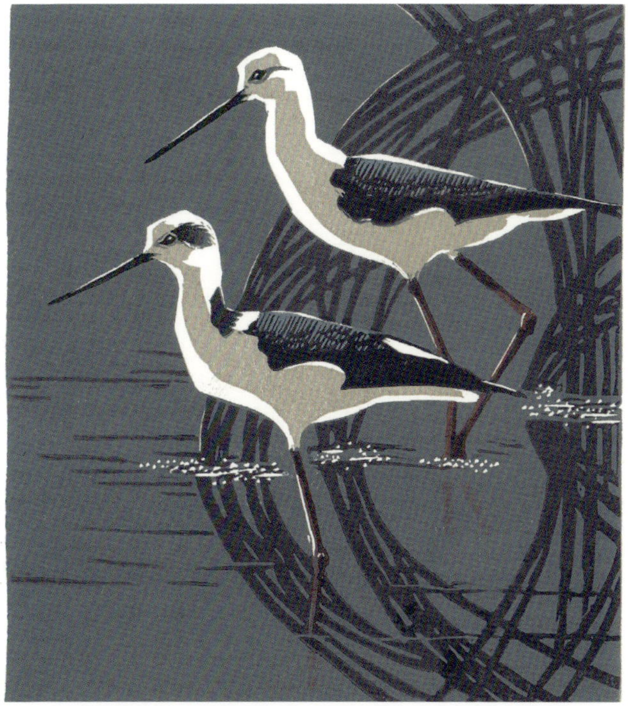

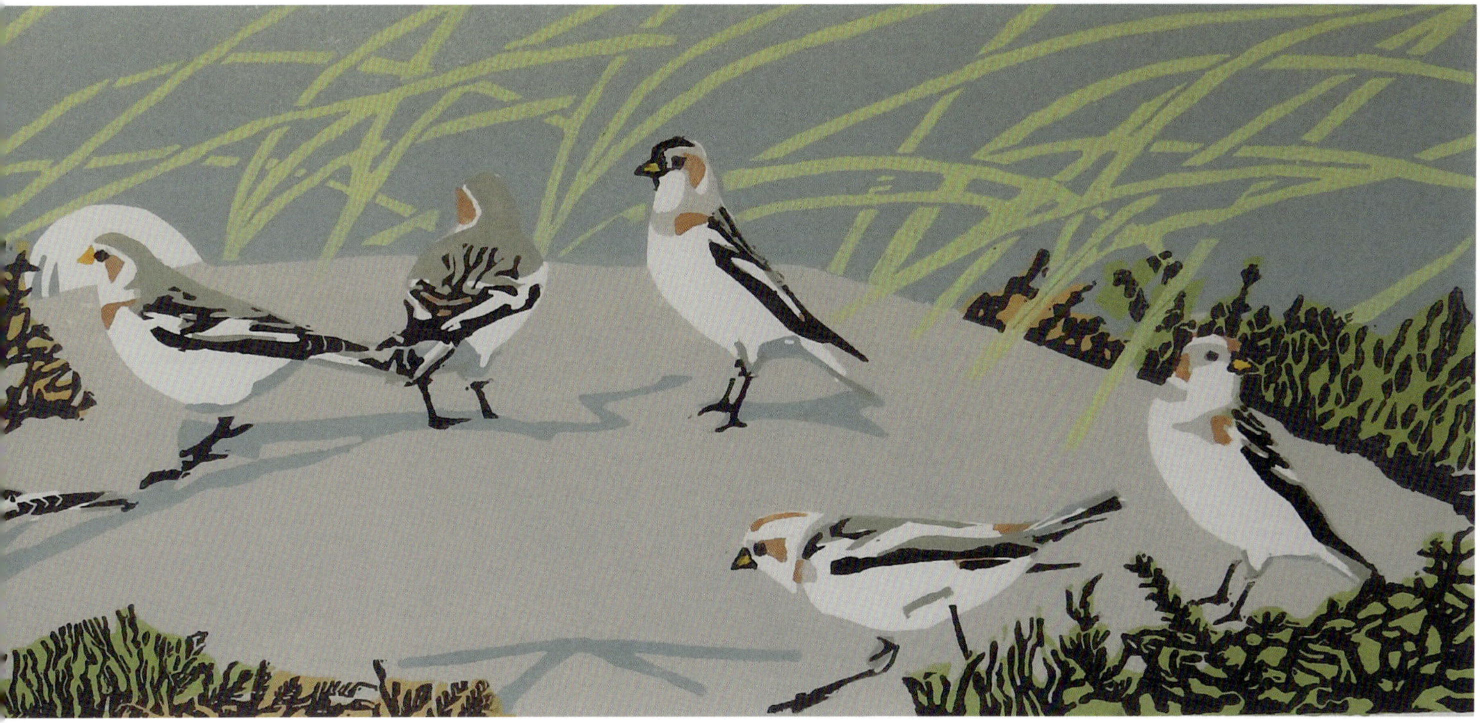

Holt

The market town, civil parish and electoral ward of Holt lies 15km west of Cromer and just inland from the north Norfolk coast. It has a railway station on the outskirts that represents the end of the preserved North Norfolk Railway which runs steam services from Sheringham.

The name Holt is thought to derive from the Anglo-Saxon word for woodland, and the town is located on wooded high ground of the Cromer-Holt ridge at the crossing point of two ancient byways. As such, it was a natural place for a growing settlement, with Holt mentioned in the Domesday Book, when it could still claim a port at nearby Cley.

On 1 May 1708 the town was devastated by a fire that destroyed most of the medieval buildings, spreading quickly from its source at Shirehall Plain. After the conflagration, the town received many donations from all over the country and the task of reconstruction began. The rebuilding process made Holt notable for its abundance of Georgian architecture, although it retains its Norman parish church, dedicated to St Andrew.

Below left is a linocut print entitled *Good to See You*, by regular Holt visitor Max Angus. Her work is sold by the gallery in the centre of the picture. Max recalls that the sadly missed Neville from Baron Art said quietly one morning, "Come and look at this". Outside the gallery in the small courtyard, they both peered into the hedge between the shops. Neville pointed at a tiny bright ring of saffron yellow-orange. A blackbird's eye was staring out from the hedge. The bird was hunkered down on the nest as people jostled by.

As described by Max, "ornamental olive trees in large pots stood at the entrance to the courtyard. There, on one of the trees, the

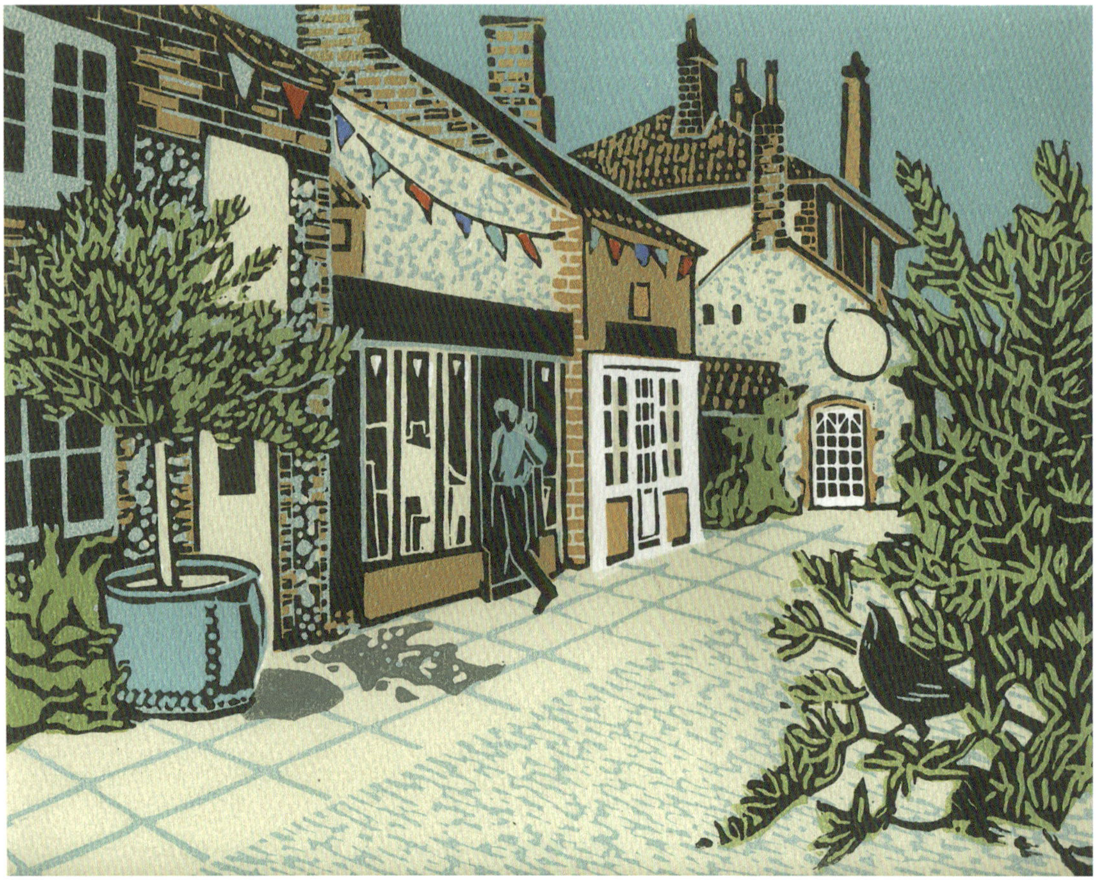

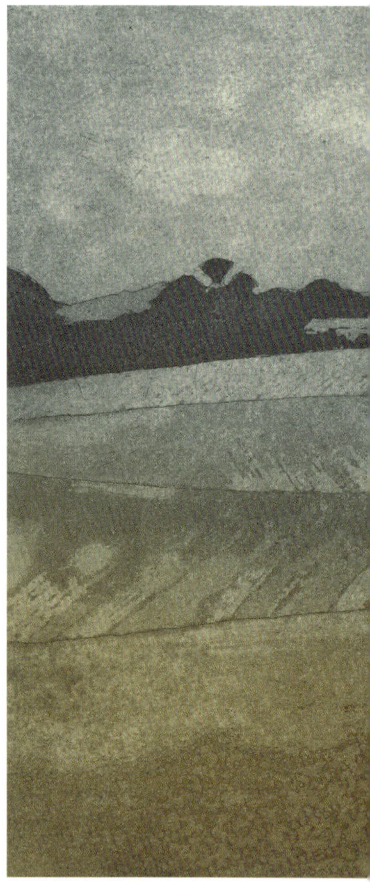

female waited like a centurion – appearing to look everywhere except at the nest. The lookout blackbird dived into the nearest end of the hedge while its mate flapped distractingly as it departed from the opposite end of the hedge to complete the illusion of being the same bird."

Neville observed that all of Holt's spare ground had been built on or used for parking. "The first bit of green the birds find, they take advantage of."

On the far right is a very different scene recreated by Max. The wooded area of Spout Hills lies within a short walk of the centre of Holt. A small brook runs through the area and spills over to create a water meadow. Spout Hills is surrounded by mature woods, and in the spring a great number of bird species – including cuckoos – may be heard.

"To create the linocut *Cuckoo and the Water Meadow*, I sat near the small bridge and sketched parts of the meadow. I have to admit that, as the woods were so dense, even though I could hear the cuckoo I had not even seen a glimpse of the bird at that time. The cuckoo image used in the linocut was taken from one of my sketchbooks."

In the centre is an aquatint etching by local artist Colin Bygrave. *Lawn Farm Lane II* (20cm x 27cm) is a typical Colin print, capturing a combination of trees, narrow lane and farmland. He has a particular fascination for the winding rural roads, in this case on the outskirts of Holt. Based just a few miles away at Briston, Colin has mapped out much of his local landscape in the form of etchings printed in his garden studio.

"I like the subtle colour range that comes with etching – it is a tonal rather than a colour medium."

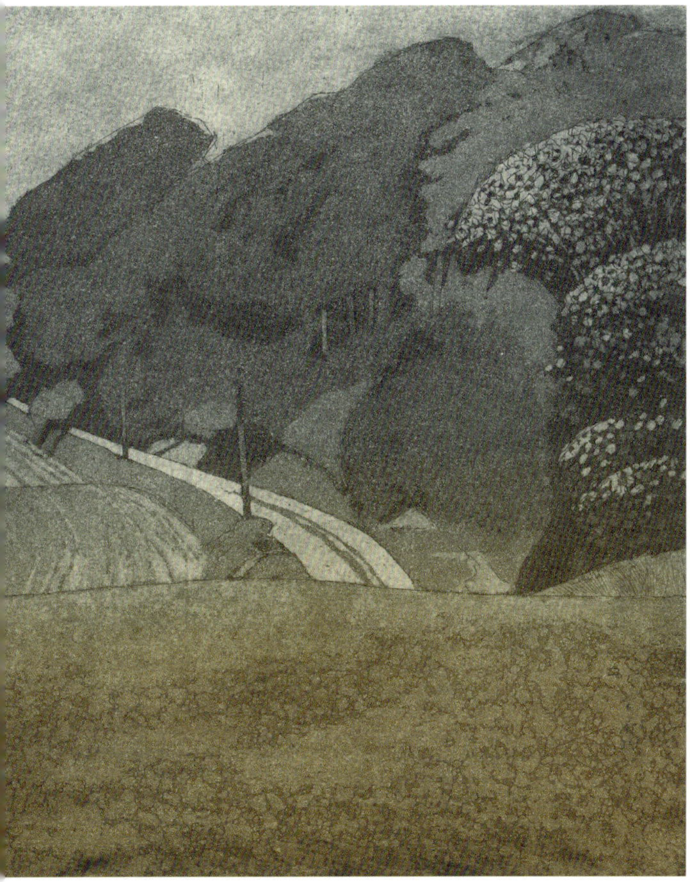

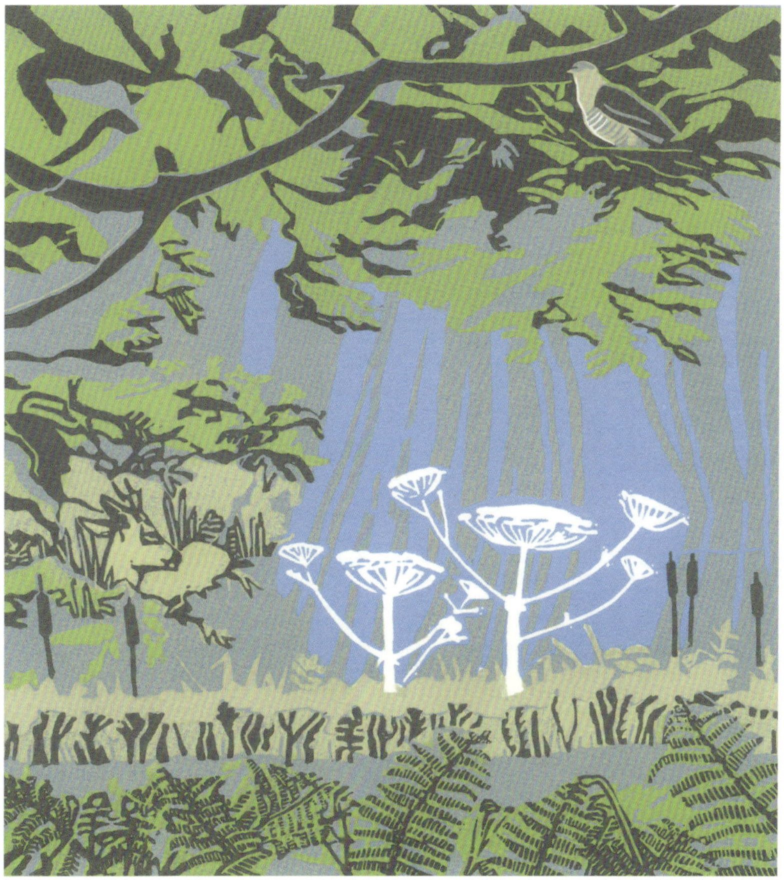

Hunstanton

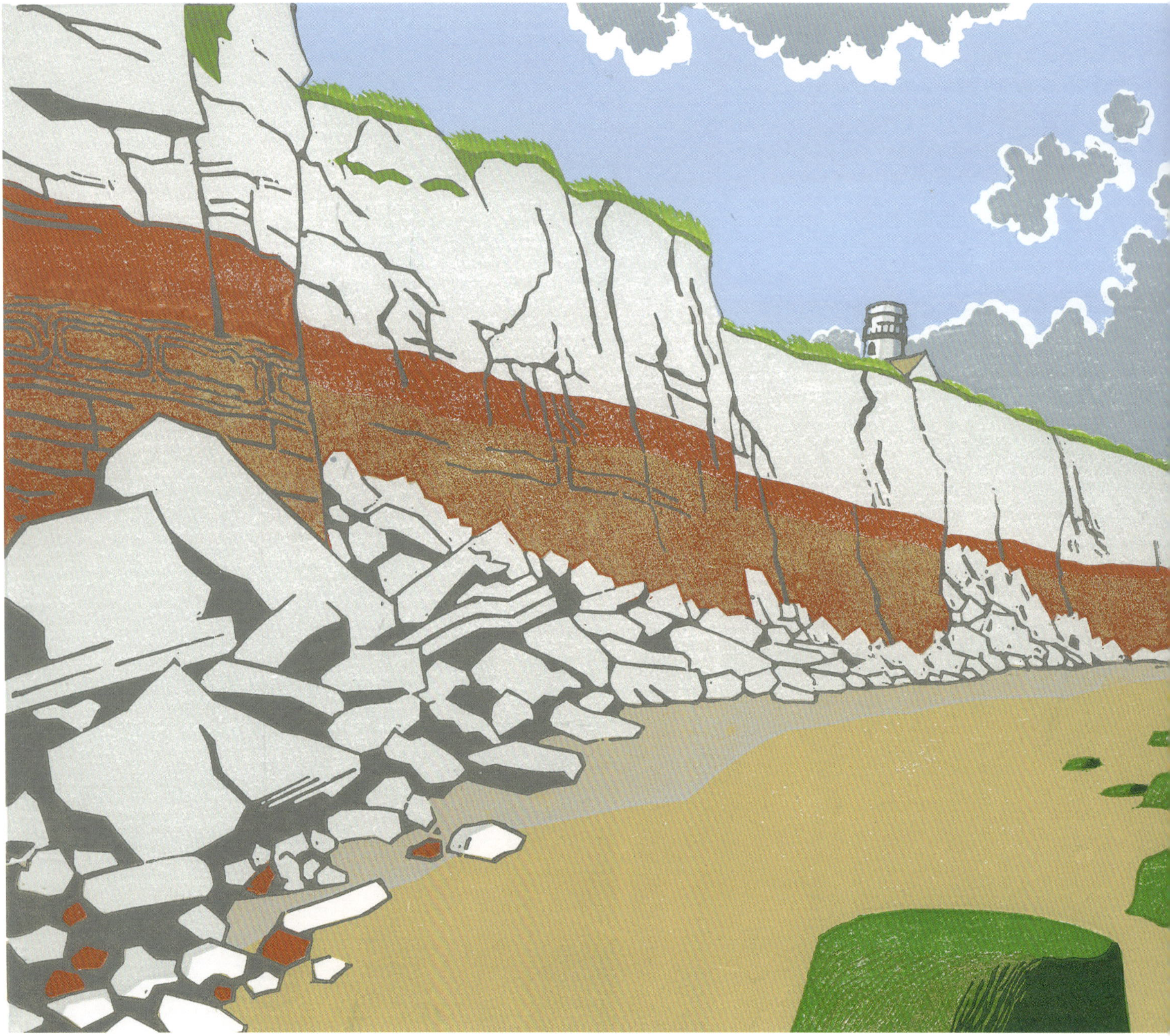

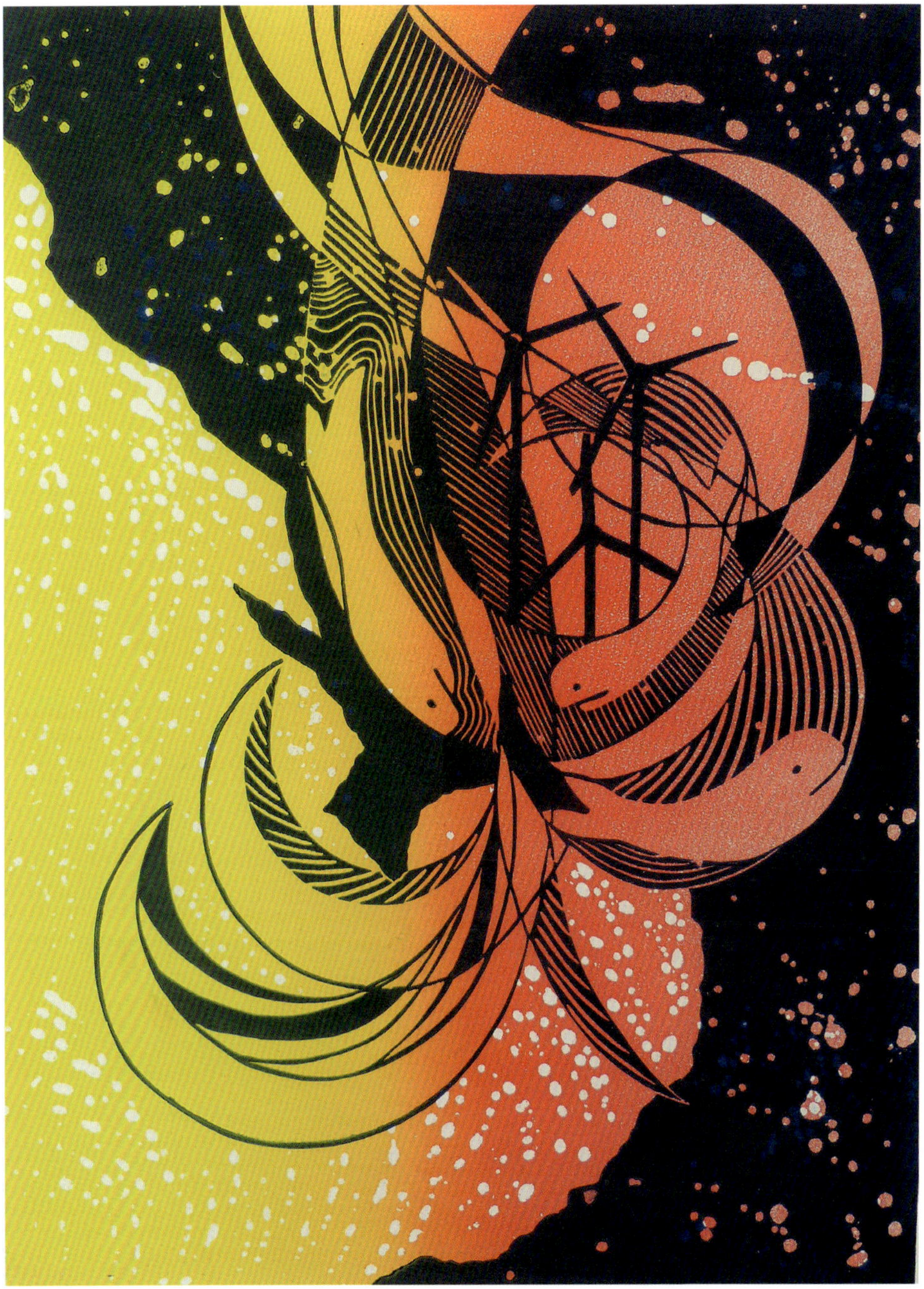

Known fondly as 'Sunny Hunny', the town of Hunstanton is one of very few on the north Norfolk coast that is actually west facing (it sits on the east bank of The Wash).

Reproduced on the far left is a piece of artwork used for the cover of *Southern England* in the 'New Naturalist' series. It was created as a linocut by Cley-based artist Robert Gillmor, and is notable for its lack of wildlife. Robert is primarily a wildlife printmaker, but was many years ago commissioned to produce the 'New Naturalist' covers and will therefore encounter situations that simply do not require his beloved birds and beasts. This, of the spectacular banded Hunstanton cliffs, could easily have been adorned by perched or passing Fulmars, as there were plenty present when Robert made his sketching expedition. The publisher felt, however, that the inclusion of the birds would perhaps give the cover too much of a wildlife feel, when the content was dedicated to landscapes.

A similar scene appears overleaf, albeit from farther along the coast at Old Hunstanton, in the form of a Louise Stebbing reduction linocut print entitled *Evening Beach* (38cm x 51cm) from 2016. "Since I was a child, Hunstanton has been our closest seaside town so has always been a place dear to me."

Swept Ashore (40cm x 30cm) on the left is a linocut/etching hybrid print that recalls the awful sight of whales washed up on Old Hunstanton beach. Annette Sykes said her heart "absolutely broke" when she saw the mammals stranded on the Norfolk shoreline, "confused perhaps by the weird vibrations from the forest of new wind turbines".

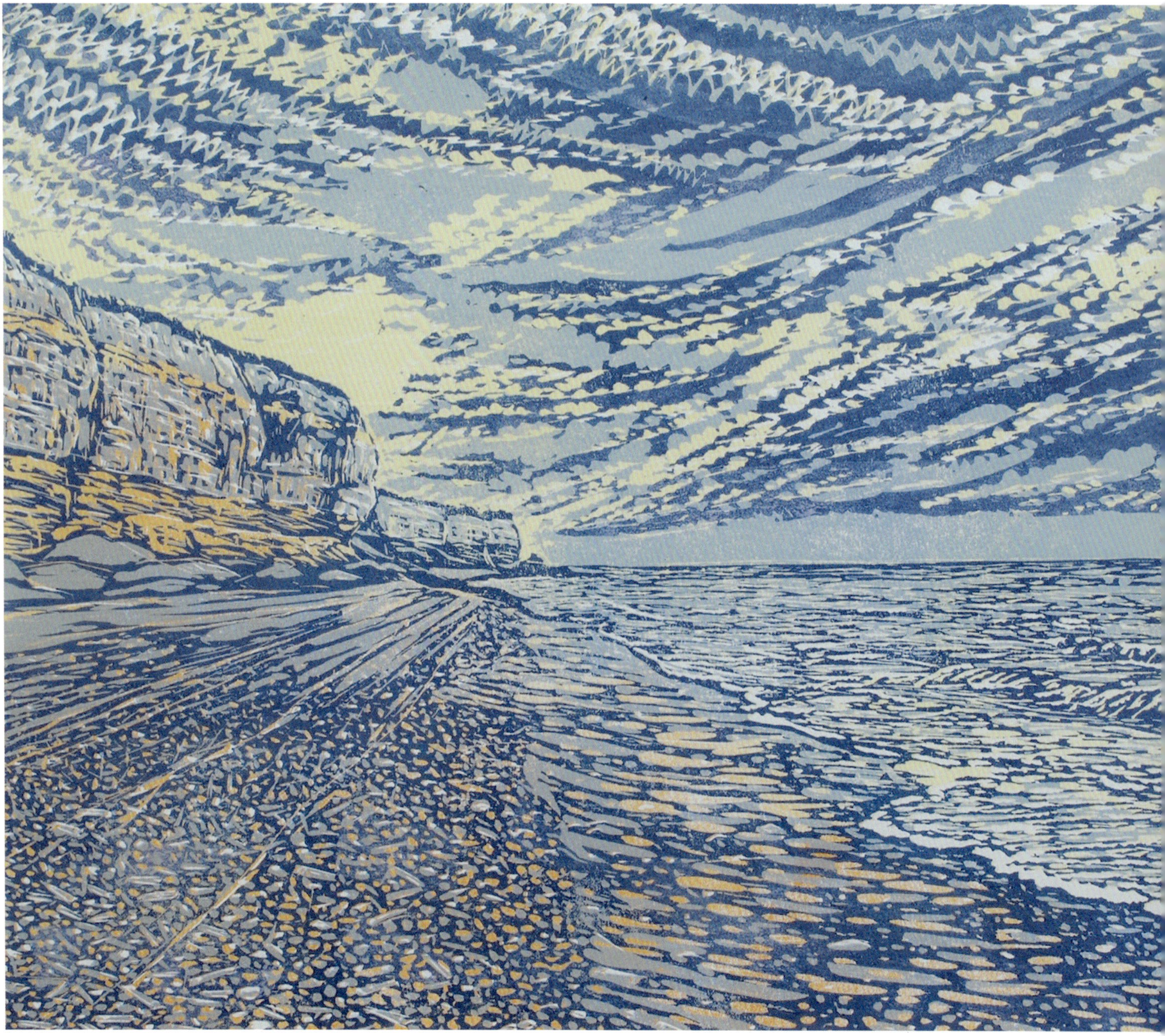

Hunworth

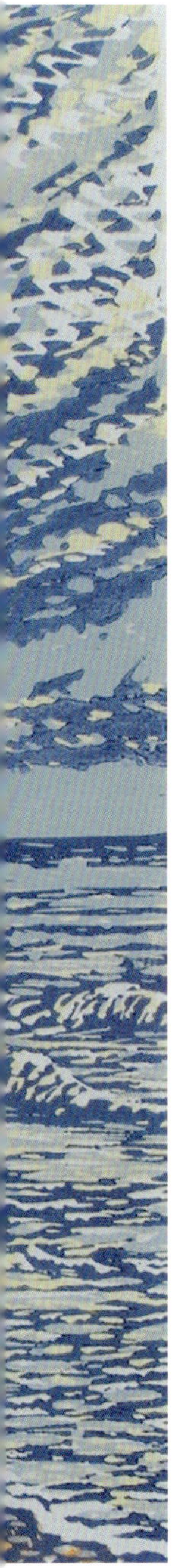

On the right is an aquatint etching by Norfolk artist Colin Bygrave named *Evening Lane, Hunworth* (38cm x 27cm), produced in his nearby Briston studio. Hunworth is a village in the parish of Stody and represents a happy hunting ground for Colin, thanks to the area's quiet country lanes, pockets of deciduous woodland and rolling farmland.

The ancient village, mentioned in the Domesday Book, is 18.5km east-north-east of Fakenham on the road between Holt and Briston. On the north-east edge of the village there are the remains of medieval ringworks situated on the spur of a hill overlooking Hunworth and strategically commanding two crossing points on the River Glaven. During excavations carried out in 1965, traces of a possible Norman timber castle were found. The earthworks are a scheduled monument protected by law.

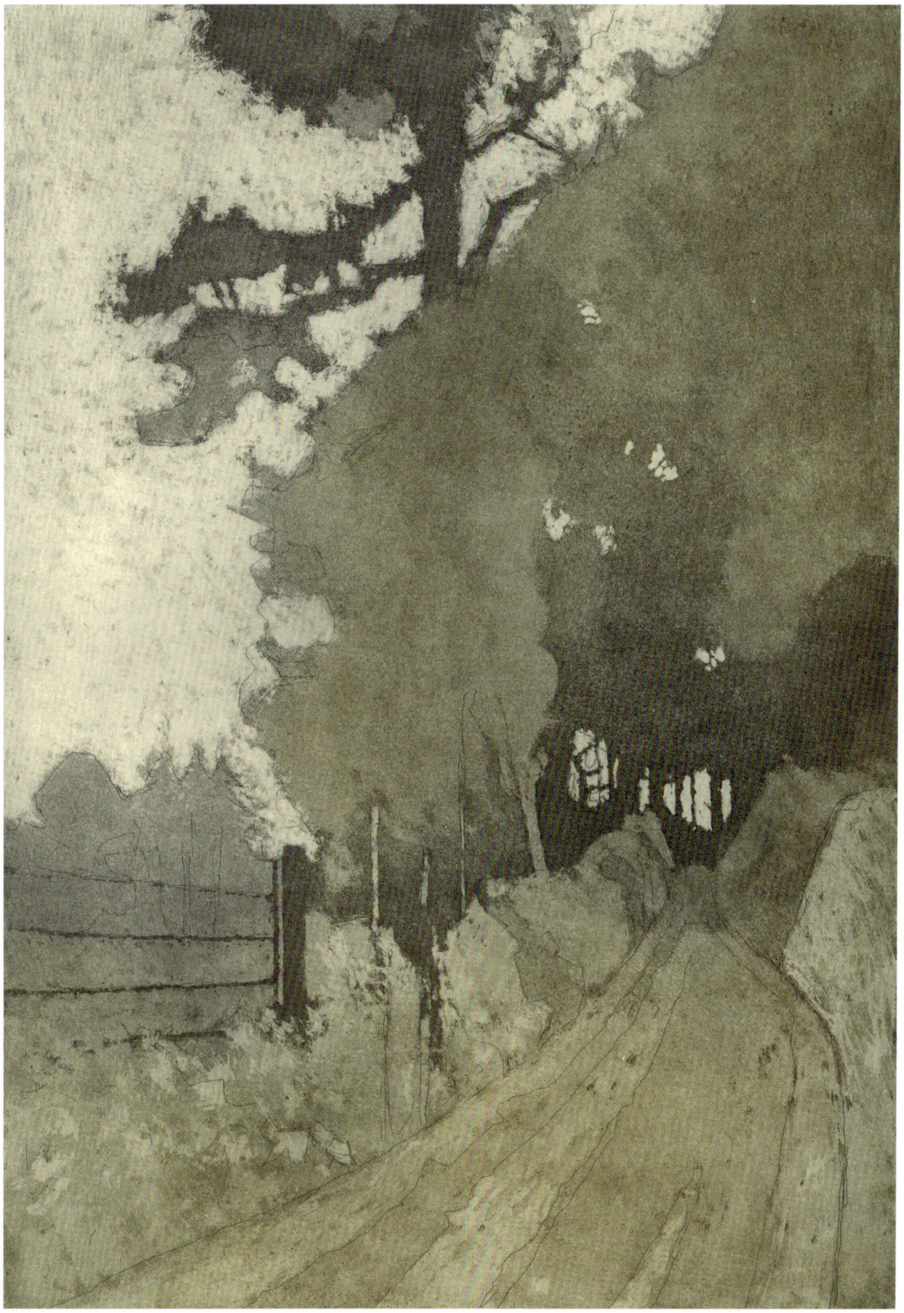

King's Lynn

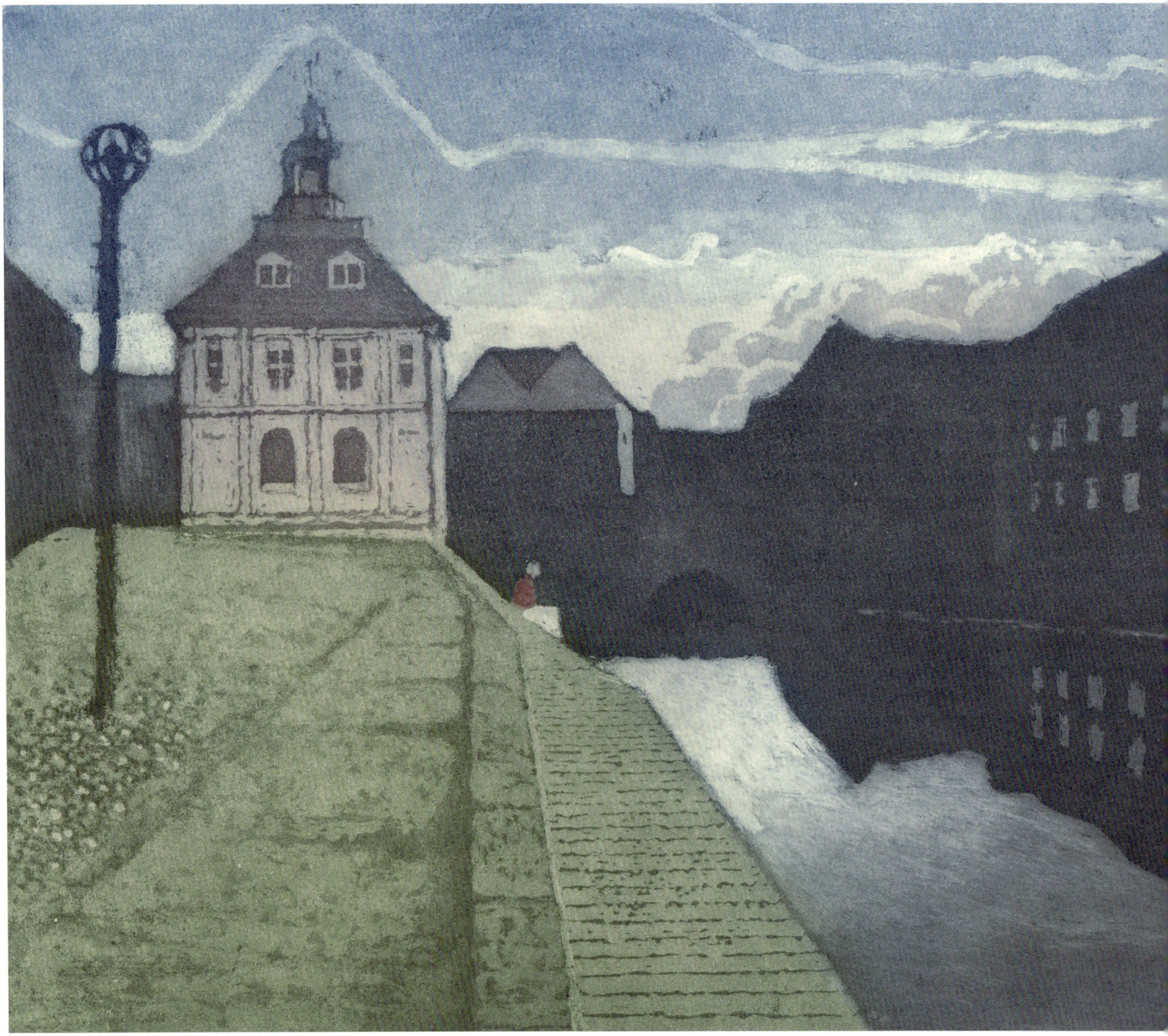

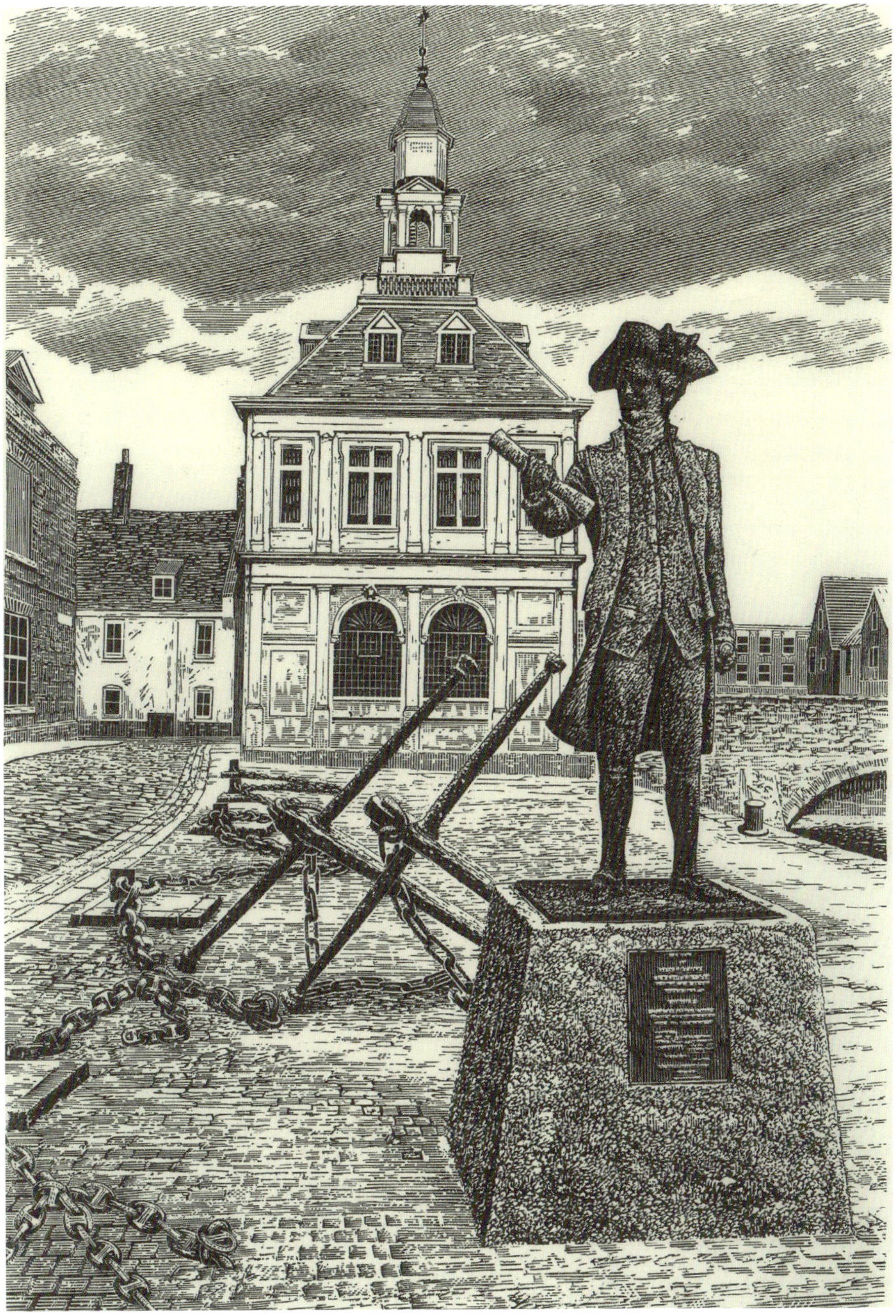

Wood engraver Anthony Dunigan describes the King's Lynn Custom House as one of Norfolk's loveliest buildings. He recalls that his print of the same name (left) took an extraordinarily long time to complete as there were so many different textures to decide upon and produce. "It was a particular challenge to portray the little statue of Captain George Vancouver in the foreground." Anthony's print is on engraver's plastic, was created in 2013 (39cm x 28cm) and is from an edition of just 10. "All of my printing is hand-burnished; and. since a good deal of careful masking-out of certain areas is required, I had to limit the number of prints made."

Architect Henry Bell was responsible for the design of the Custom House in 1683. He also designed the Duke's Head Inn, the North Runcton Church and Stanhoe Hall. His artistic inspiration was the result of extensive travels in Europe and exposure to Continental building styles and practices.

Norfolk artist Colin Bygrave also chose the Custom House for his aquatint etching *Lonely in King's Lynn* (far left) while, overleaf, Norwich-based HJ Jackson was taken by the colour, size and shape of these light floats. King's Lynn once had a lightship guarding the Roaring Middle shoal. Cost savings meant that a

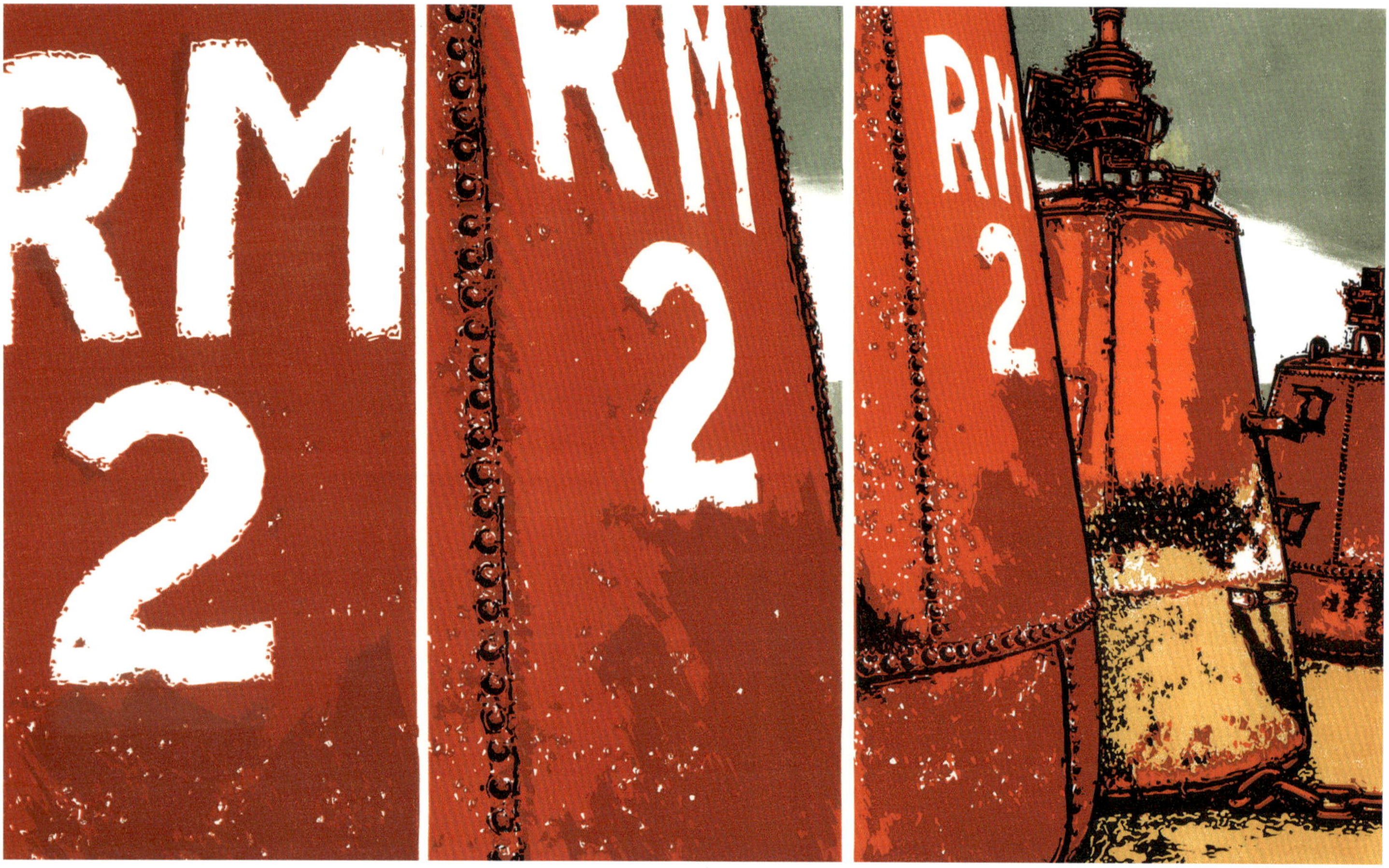

smaller, unmanned float was later used to mark the location of the shipping hazard. The linocut *Roaring Middle 2* dates from 1998.

During the 14th century, Lynn ranked as England's most important port. Sea trade with Europe was dominated by the Hanseatic League of ports – the transatlantic trade and the rise of England's western ports did not begin until the discovery of the Americas. Walls entered by the South Gate and East Gate were erected to protect the town, which retains two former Hanseatic League warehouses: Hanse House built in 1475 and Marriott's Warehouse, in use between the 15th and 17th centuries. They are the only buildings from the Hanseatic League left in England.

In the 16th and 17th centuries, the town's main export was grain. Lynn was no longer a major international port, although iron and timber were imported. In the late 17th century, imports of wine from Spain, Portugal and France boomed, and there was still an important coastal trade. Large quantities of coal arrived from the north-east of England.

The Fens began to be drained in the mid-17th century, and the land turned to agriculture, allowing vast amounts of produce to be sent to the growing market in London. Meanwhile, King's Lynn was still an important fishing port.

In the early 18th century, Daniel Defoe called the town "beautiful, well built and well situated". Shipbuilding continued to thrive, as did associated industries such as sail-making and rope-making. Glass-making was prosperous, and brewing was another important industry.

By the late 17th century, the town had begun to decline. This was only reversed by the arrival of railway services in 1847, provided mainly by the Great Eastern Railway – subsequently the London and North Eastern Railway, running to Hunstanton, Dereham and Cambridge. The town was also served by the Midland and Great Northern Joint Railway, which had offices in the town, and an important station at South Lynn. The former M&GN lines across Norfolk were closed to passengers in February 1959.

In 1962, King's Lynn was designated an overflow town for London and its population began to increase. The town centre was redeveloped in the 1960s, with many old buildings destroyed. Also in the 1960s, the council tried to encourage development by building a new industrial estate at Hardwick. The new industries that arrived included light engineering, clothes and chemicals.

Morston

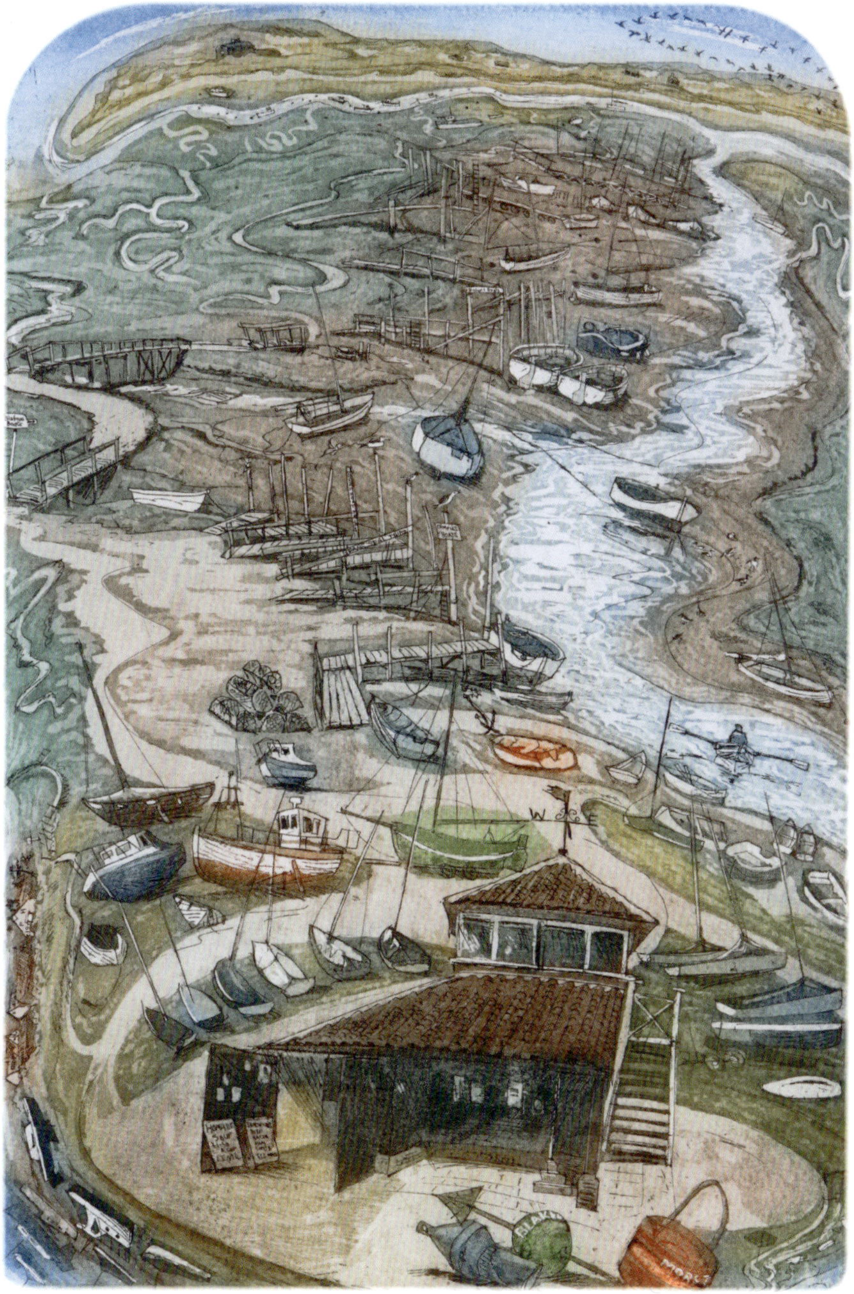

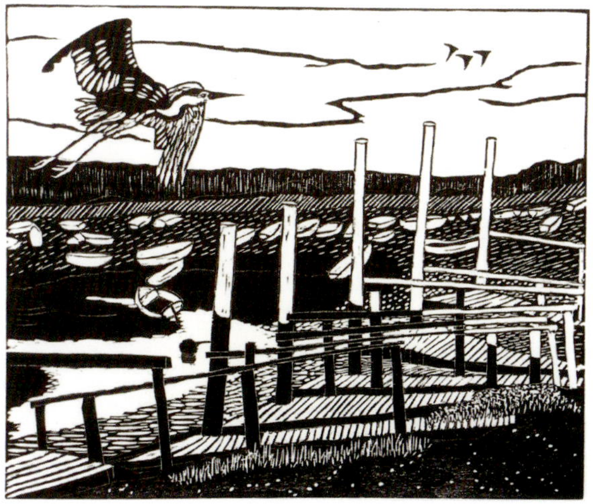

In the height of summer, the myriad small boats in the 2009 Glynn Thomas etching on the left (*Morston Quay*, 29cm x 20cm) are joined by long, snaking queues of tourists waiting their turn to board trips out to the seal colony at Blakeney Point.

Fleets of locally operated open boats haul visitors out to the sand banks and shingle spits to view the basking seals and colonies of terns. The National Trust visitor centre dominates Glynn's etching. It is the official centre for the Blakeney National Nature Reserve, and a good staging point for walkers on the Norfolk Coast Path that provides wonderful access to the vast acres of saltmarsh and the thousands of birds that feed there.

Cambridgeshire artist Valerie Sims contributed the woodcut above, entitled *Creek*, which portrays one of many narrow wooden jetties, boats pulled up on the mud and a disturbed heron taking to the air.

Morston, like neighbouring Blakeney, used to be a major port four centuries ago, but is now used only by a small-scale fish, mussel, crab and lobster fishing fleet, plus leisure craft and the seal-watching trips.

Norwich

By far the biggest collection of Norfolk prints is reserved for the 'fine' city of Norwich, with 14 artists lending their widely varying interpretations to this book. Leanda Jaine Hughes chose to produce an alphabet of Norwich that continues to grow with replacement 'letters' as the popular prints reach the end of their editions. We have reproduced one entire set of the images on pages 118-122.

The Norwich section kicks off with two very popular linocut prints by local artist David Jones, another printmaker keen to capture as many of the city's locations on lino and paper as possible. His so-called *Norwich 12* portray iconic buildings in the city, and we have reproduced a selection of them, starting with *Norwich Castle II* and *Norwich Cathedral & Erpingham Gate*.

Elsewhere in this section readers will find *Sir Thomas Browne & St Peter Mancroft* (page 114), *The Forum* (page 122), *St Giles* (page 128), *Wingnut Tree, Tombland Alley* (page 128), *The Halls (St Andrew's & Blackfriars' Halls)* also on page 128, *St John's Roman Catholic Cathedral* (page 129) and *The Assembly House* (page 129).

"My prints in particular often have prominent contemporary features, but they are still mindful of history since, once recorded, such scenes soon become history," says David.

Fellow Norfolk artist Sally Hirst is another prolific producer of Norwich prints, but her style is very different. "My work has always reflected where I live, places I visit and journeys I embark upon. The texture, architecture and structures of

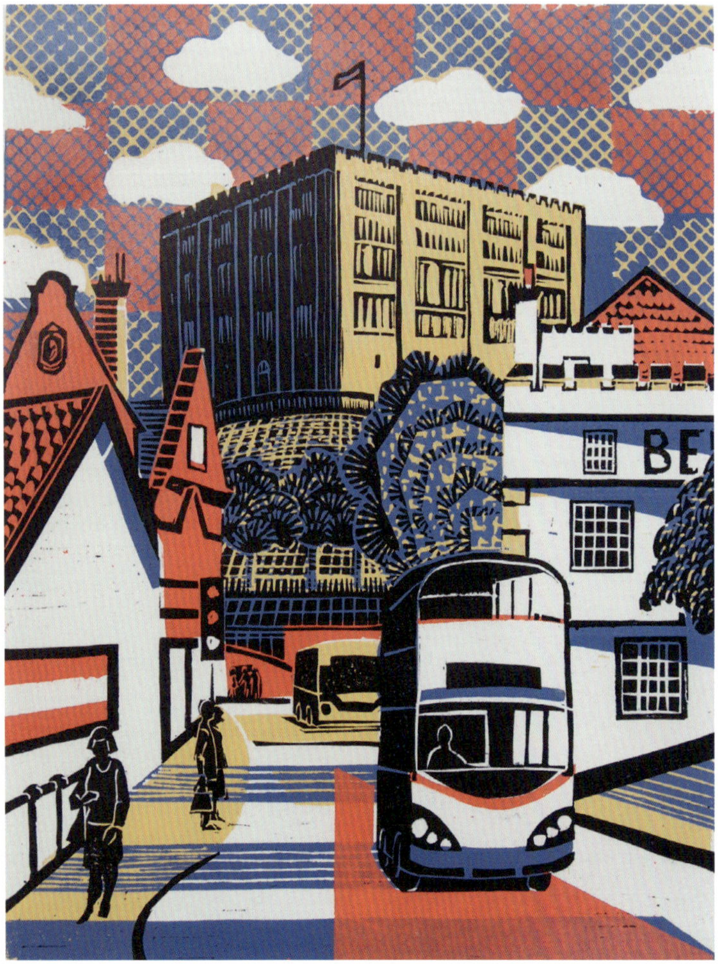

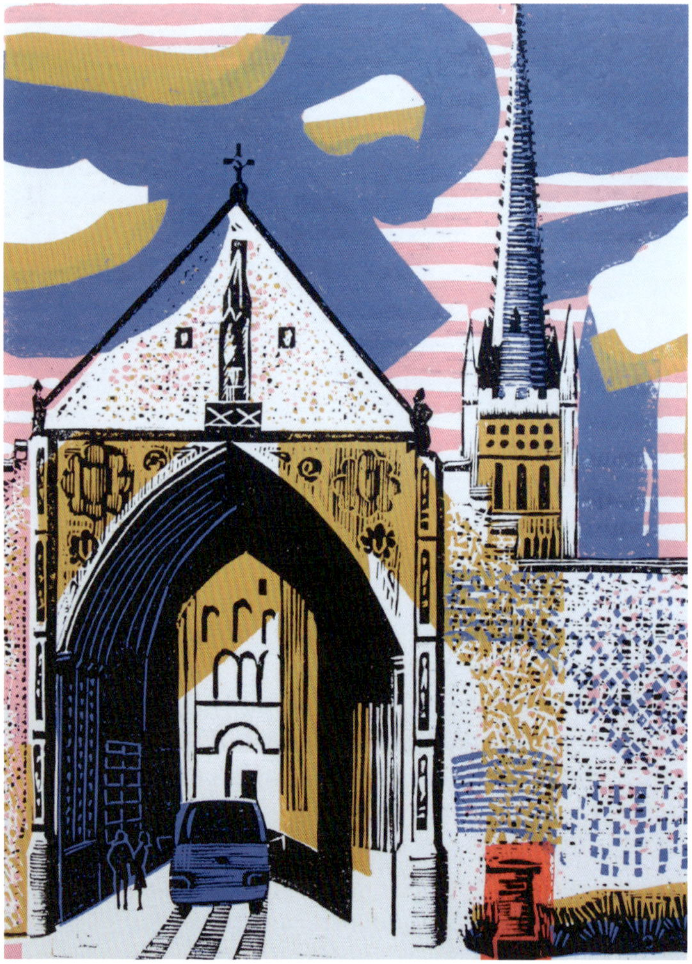

each new environment dictate the development of my artwork.

"While I employ printmaking techniques, my work does not easily fit into the traditional printmaking categories. I use a range of techniques that I have built up over many years that allow me the freedom to create unique pieces more akin to painting than printmaking. Each print incorporates a range of printing techniques including collagraphy, carborundum and relief printing."

The print on the far right comes from Sally's *St Stephen's Street Series*, and the one on the near right is from her *Exchange Street Series*. All were created in 2007 and are relief prints with collage.

On page 115 we feature the *Guildhall Series* and *Riverside*, a carborundum and relief print with iron oxide from 2013. "This is an iconic view in Norwich, much loved and regularly depicted by artists and photographers. The building was a warehouse built after the war on ABC wharf. The rusting exterior contrasts with the modern buildings that face it on Riverside.

"This was the first print in which I used my process of rusting the paper using iron filings. The print is made using two plates: a collagraph plate for the textures, and a relief plate for large areas of black and white. I find myself continually returning to this building, and what was the thriving port of Norwich."

On pages 126 and 127 are prints from Sally's *Forum Series* and her *Westlegate Series*, respectively – also forming part of the body of Norwich work produced in 2007.

Suffolk printmaker Glynn Thomas overleaf provides us with a mighty etching from 1980 entitled *Norwich* (64cm x 41cm). It captures the majesty of an elegant and ancient city, featuring the spire of the Anglican cathedral, the Art Deco lines of the City Hall and the historic Pull's Ferry and Bishop Bridge on the River Wensum.

Founded in 1096 and built using Normandy stone shipped over from Caen, the Anglican cathedral is one of the finest complete Romanesque buildings in Europe. Marked by a picturesque 15th-century water gate at

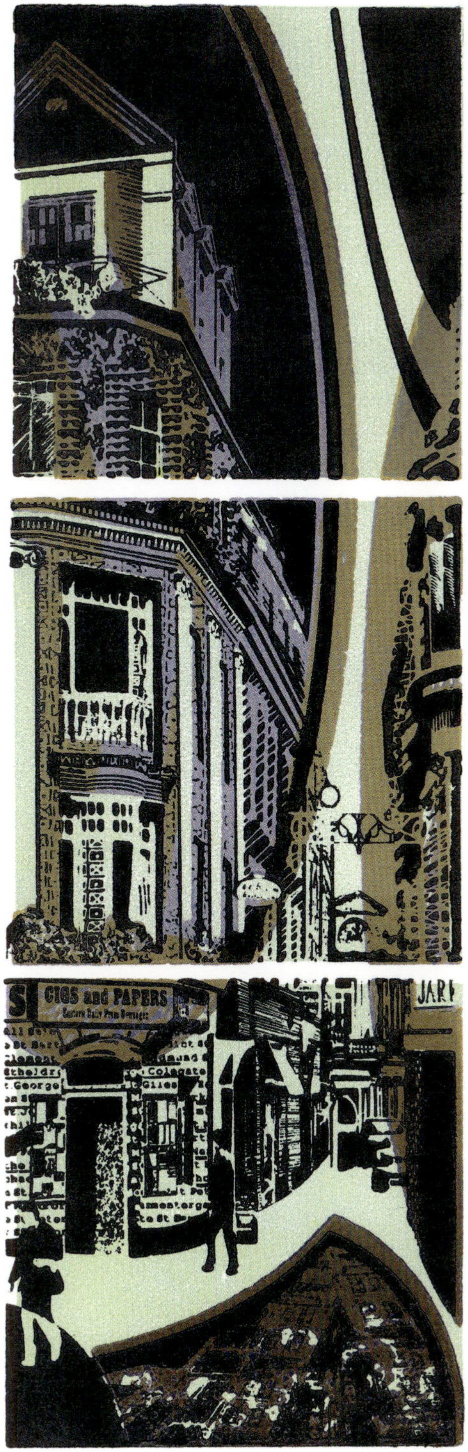

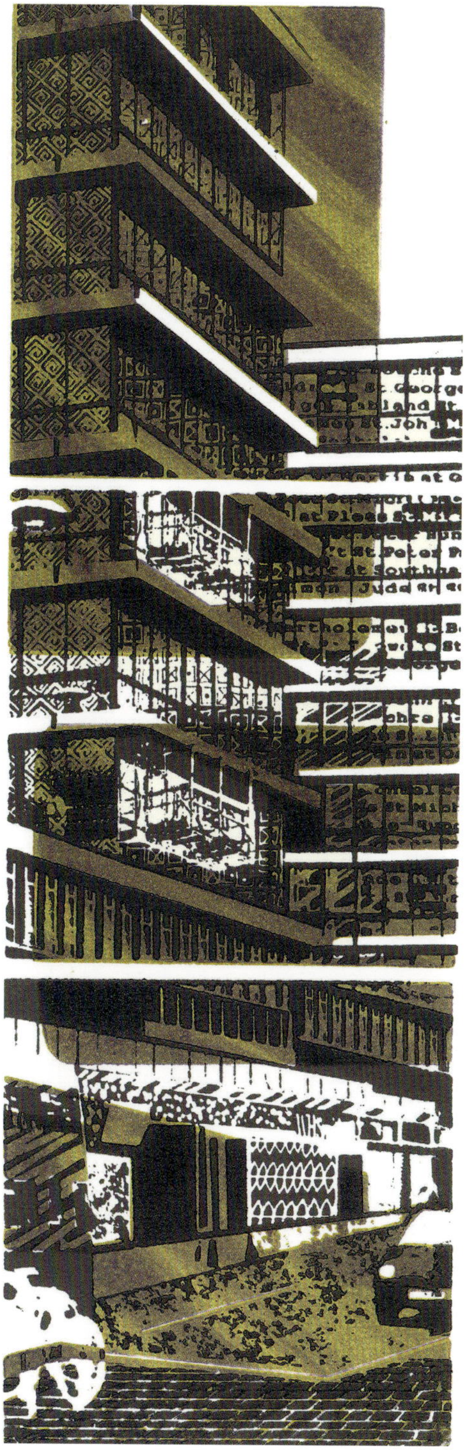

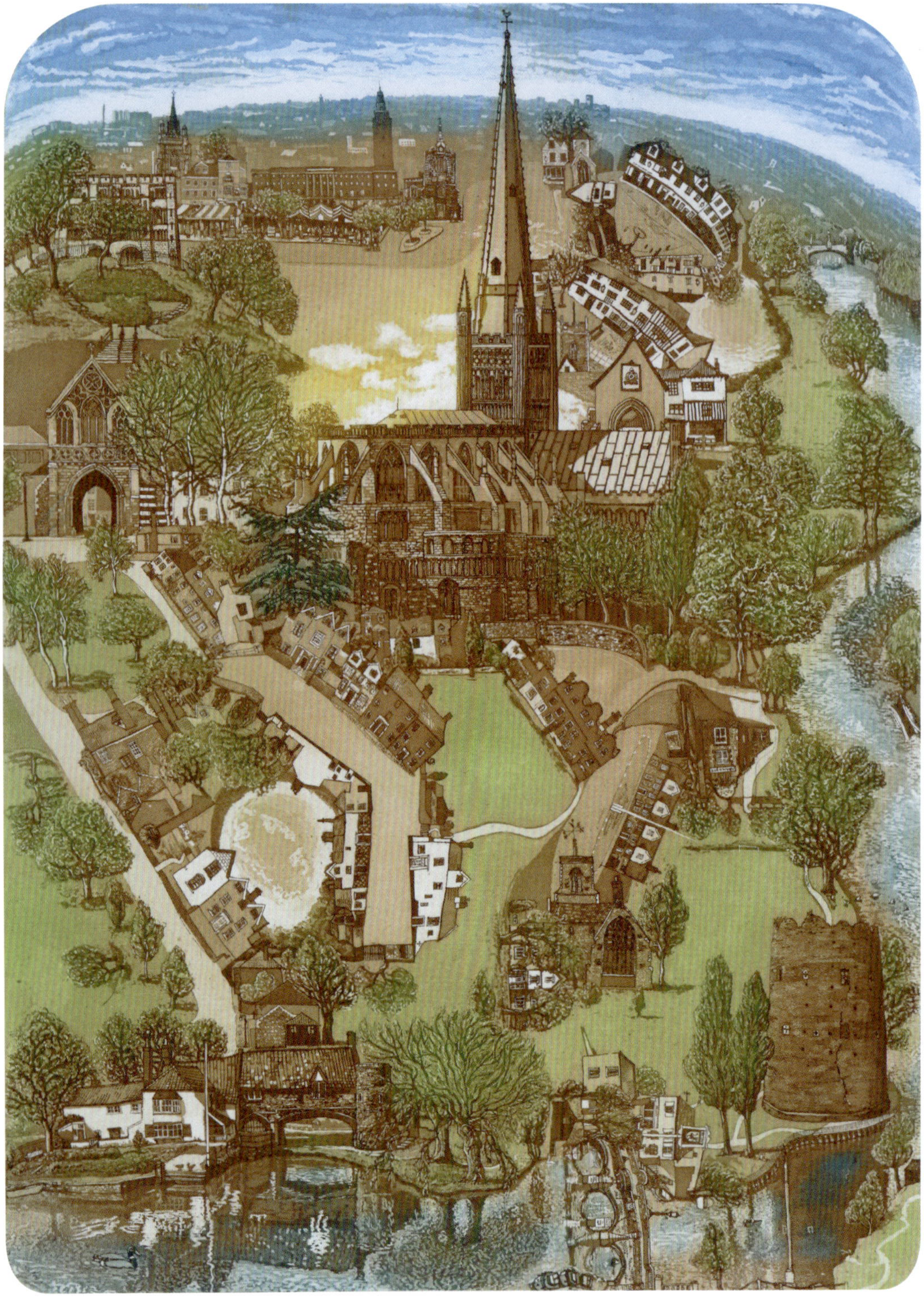

Pull's Ferry, a canal from the River Wensum was dug by the Normans to allow stone for the cathedral to be ferried as close to the construction site as possible.

The Caen stone was brought by sea from France and shipped up the river. Tombland, also featured in Glynn's print, is located in front of the cathedral and was once the Saxon marketplace in Norwich. From Tombland, two gateways lead to Norwich Cathedral: Erpingham Gate, built around 1420; and Ethelbert Gate, named after St Ethelbert, a young king of East Anglia who was killed in AD 794.

Norwich Cathedral Close, one of the largest in England, extends to more than 44 acres. It contains a mixture of 18th- and 19th-century terraces, plus more distinctive Dutch gables. The market, seen in the picture, is the largest Monday-to-Saturday open-air market in the country.

On the facing page is an image of Lord Wellington on a plinth. This statue, made by G G Adams in 1851, is located in Norwich Cathedral Close, near St Ethelbert's Gate. According to Suffolk artist Anthony Dunigan, the black figure on its light plinth inspired the engraving, created in 2017 using engraver's plastic.

"The sunlight on the sculpture had to be conveyed by cutting away all of the material on the brightest areas to leave pure white on the print. The scene is balanced by the birch tree on the left – a challenge to cut – and the cathedral tower and spire on the right." Anthony's print *The Iron Duke* measures 35cm x 27cm.

At the top of page 114 is a particularly striking print of an equally memorable structure. Clare Johnson, based in

Lowestoft, is arguably better known for her water towers and gas holders. The print here, *Ziggurat* (14cm x 41.5cm), is of the University of East Anglia, designed by Denys Lasdun.

Clare's basic approach is to create something new while being inspired by vintage, hand-tinted postcards. "Photographs are transformed into screened black and white (dotty) images, tinted with a number of colour monotypes. Prints are produced in series of up to 25 in larger sizes, and each is uniquely coloured – only the subject is repeated."

As well as the aforementioned David Jones linocut of Sir Thomas Browne and the two Sally Hirst prints referred to earlier, the spread overleaf features a Norwich print by HJ Jackson, from a series created to decorate rooms in a new Norwich hotel.

Then a budding young artist, in 1972 John was commissioned to create a series of six linocuts for the Hotel Norwich to hang on the walls of its 84 bedrooms. The blocks and resulting prints were made during the winter of 1972 into 1973, hence the bare trees that appear in some of them. Shown here is *Elm Hill*, from a new printing made in 2010. Another in the series, *The Market Place*, shows a scene from different times, when the Norwich Market had its striped awnings and earlier wooden stalls. A major redevelopment may have preserved the market's colours, but many believe its character has changed forever.

The full original Hotel Norwich series also included *Pull's Ferry*, *The Castle*, *The Cathedral from the Close* and

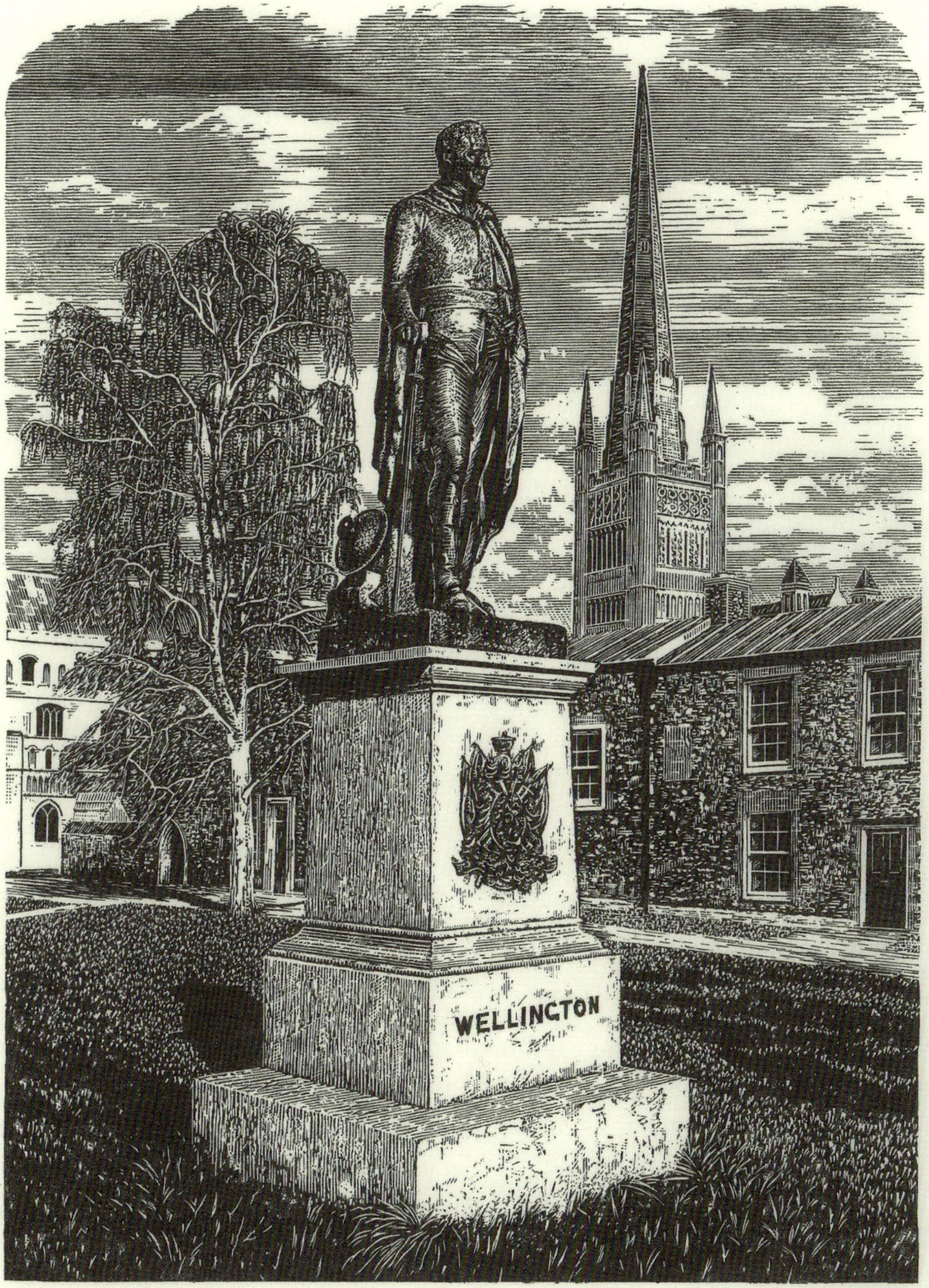

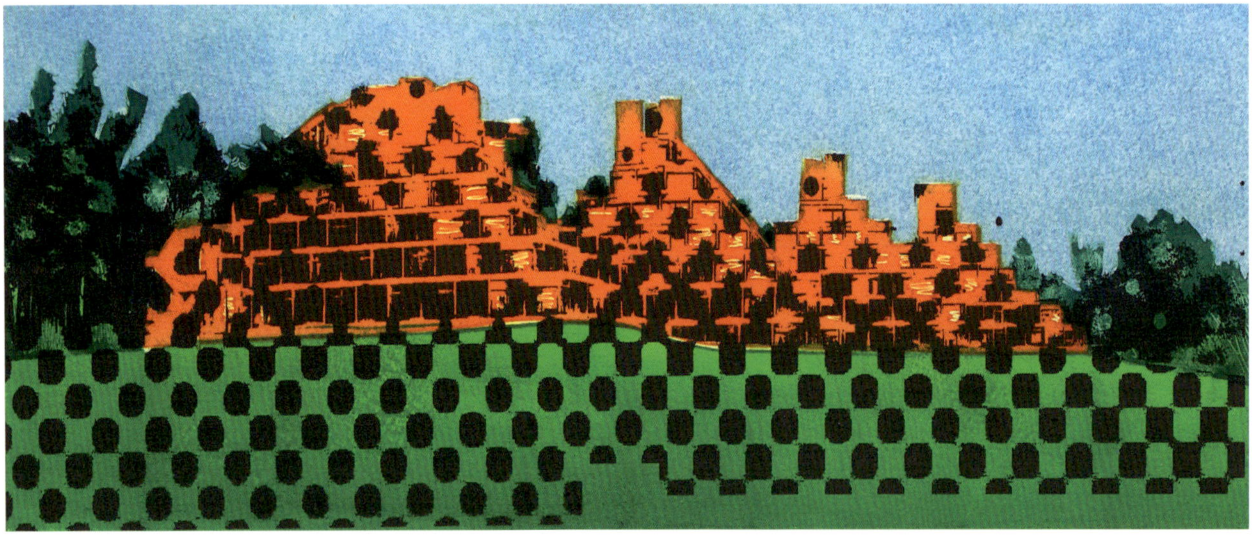

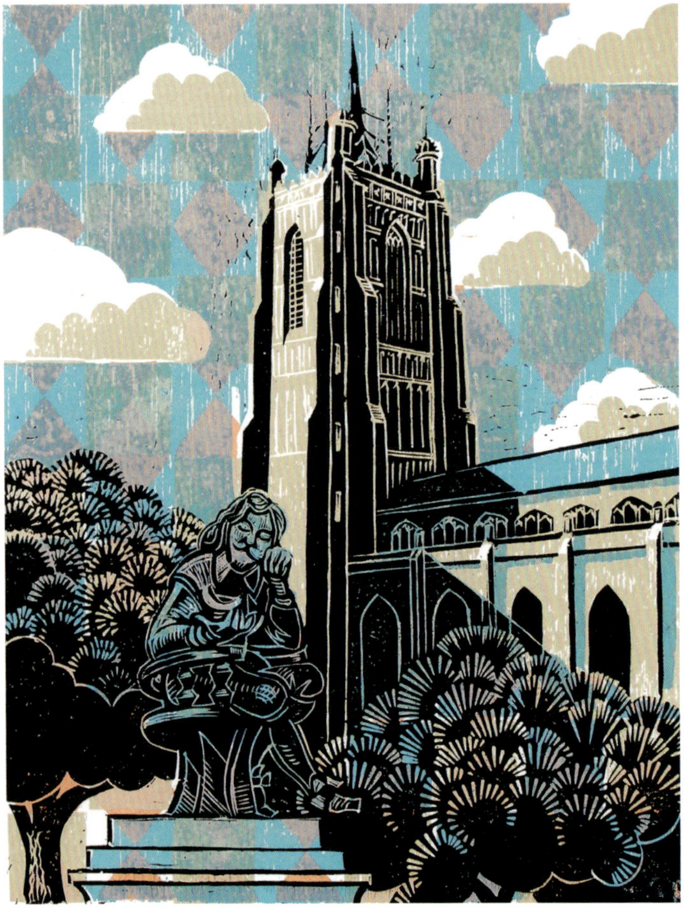

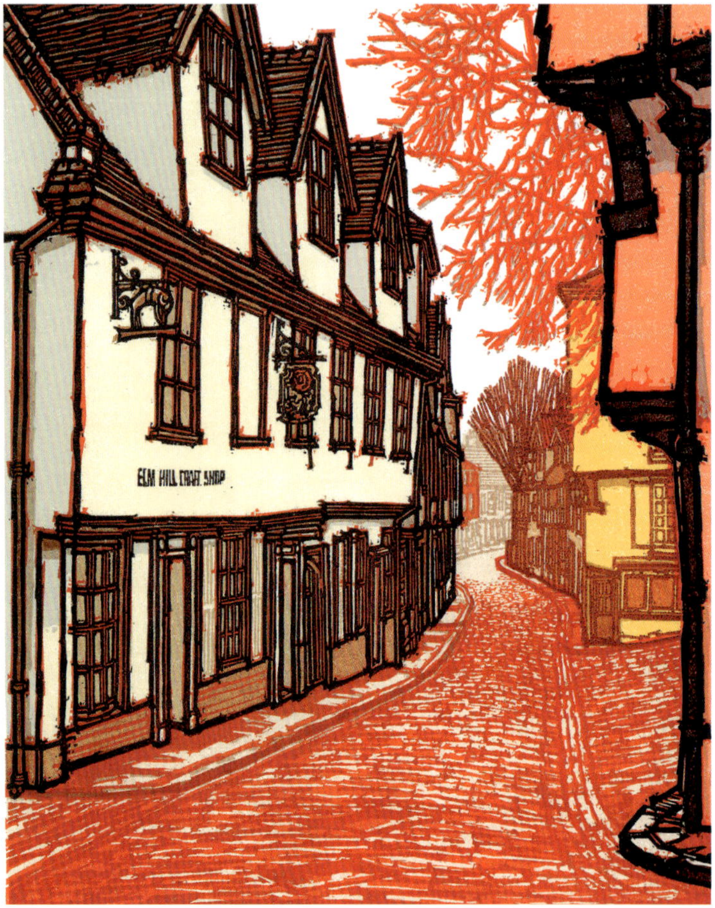
ELM HILL CRAFT SHOP

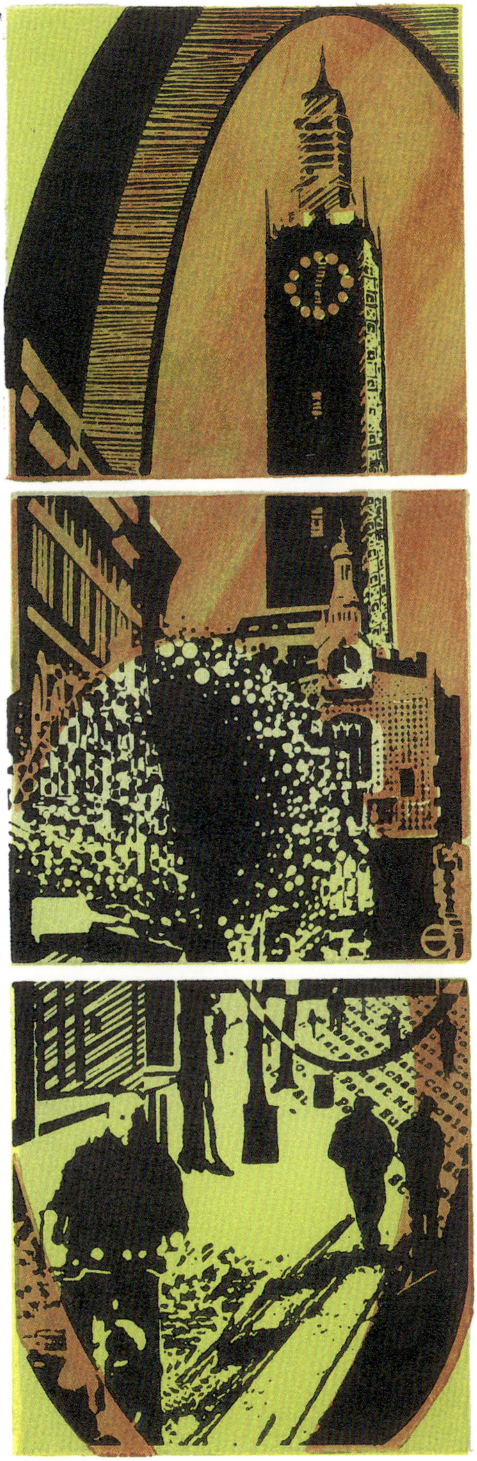

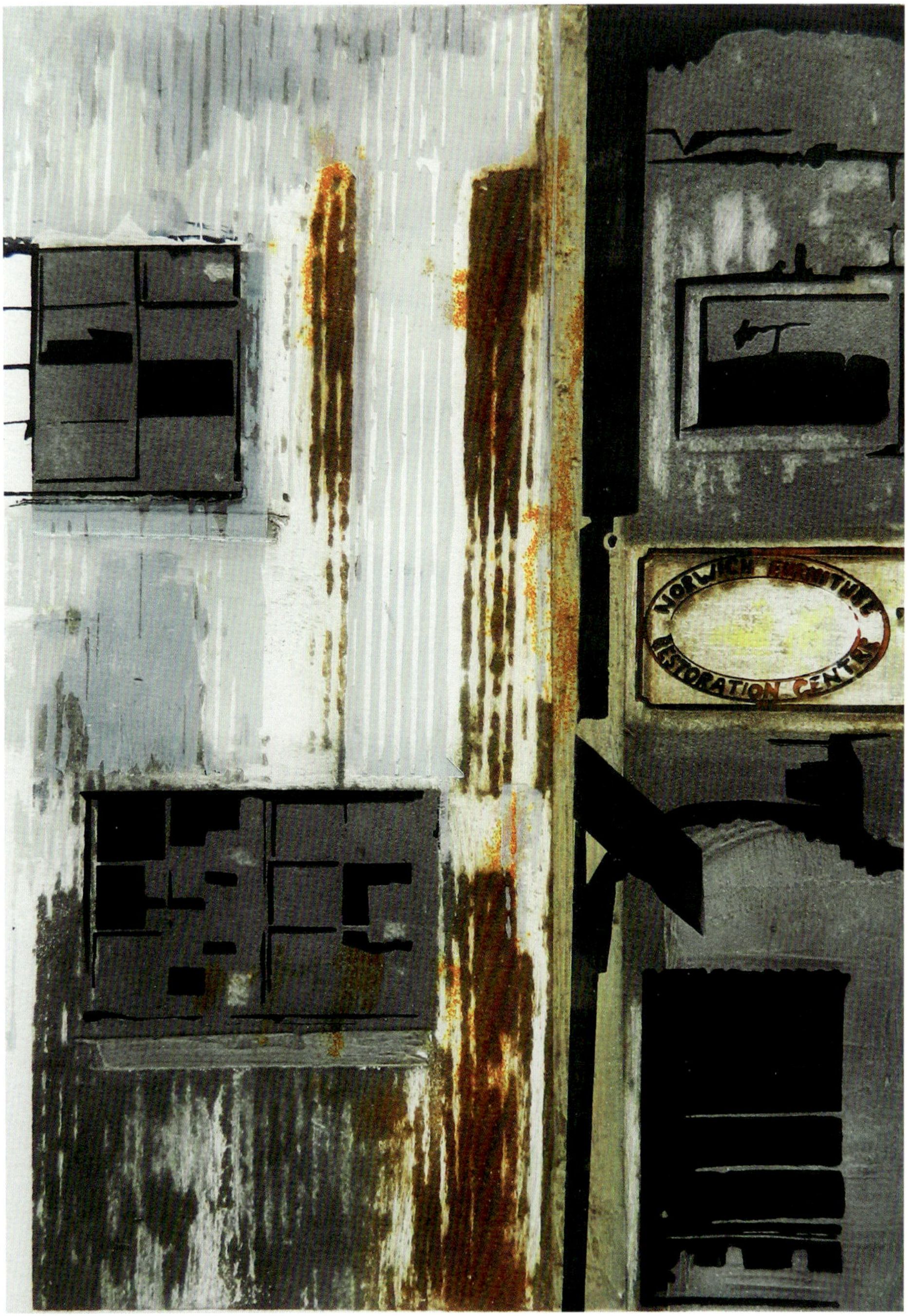
NORWICH FURNITURE
RESTORATION CENTRE

Tombland Alley. The artist wanted to reprint them all, but discovered that some of the original lino blocks had deteriorated too much over three decades, so prints from the first 1970s run are highly prized.

Below is an interpretation of Norwich Castle and the revamped market that bears the floral flourishes of Wymondham-based Amelia Bowman. *Norwich Castle (Hogweed)* is a collagraph print in an edition of 10 (26cm x 37cm) that was created in 2017 and updates an earlier design of the same subject. "Norwich is my nearest city and I am fond of it for a number of reasons, not least its impressive history which is immortalised by the castle and market, both of which date back more than 900 years and dominate the unmistakable landscape," says Amelia. "'Norwich Castle' was my first non-coastal collagraph design."

On the facing page is a large and colourful print by fellow Norfolk artist Vanessa Burroughes. It is a collaged screenprint created as part of a series of four covering the seasons. "The Plantation Garden is a hidden gem in the heart of Norwich," she explains. "It is a lovely place, preserved by volunteers, and provides space for reflection within a busy city." As Vanessa is often a visitor to the garden, where she will draw or paint, her print raises £100 per sale towards its upkeep.

The next few pages of the book are reserved for the Norwich alphabet created by Leanda Jaine Hughes and mentioned earlier. We didn't feel that a selection of letters would do, so borrowed the entire set for reproduction. The series continues to evolve, as editions

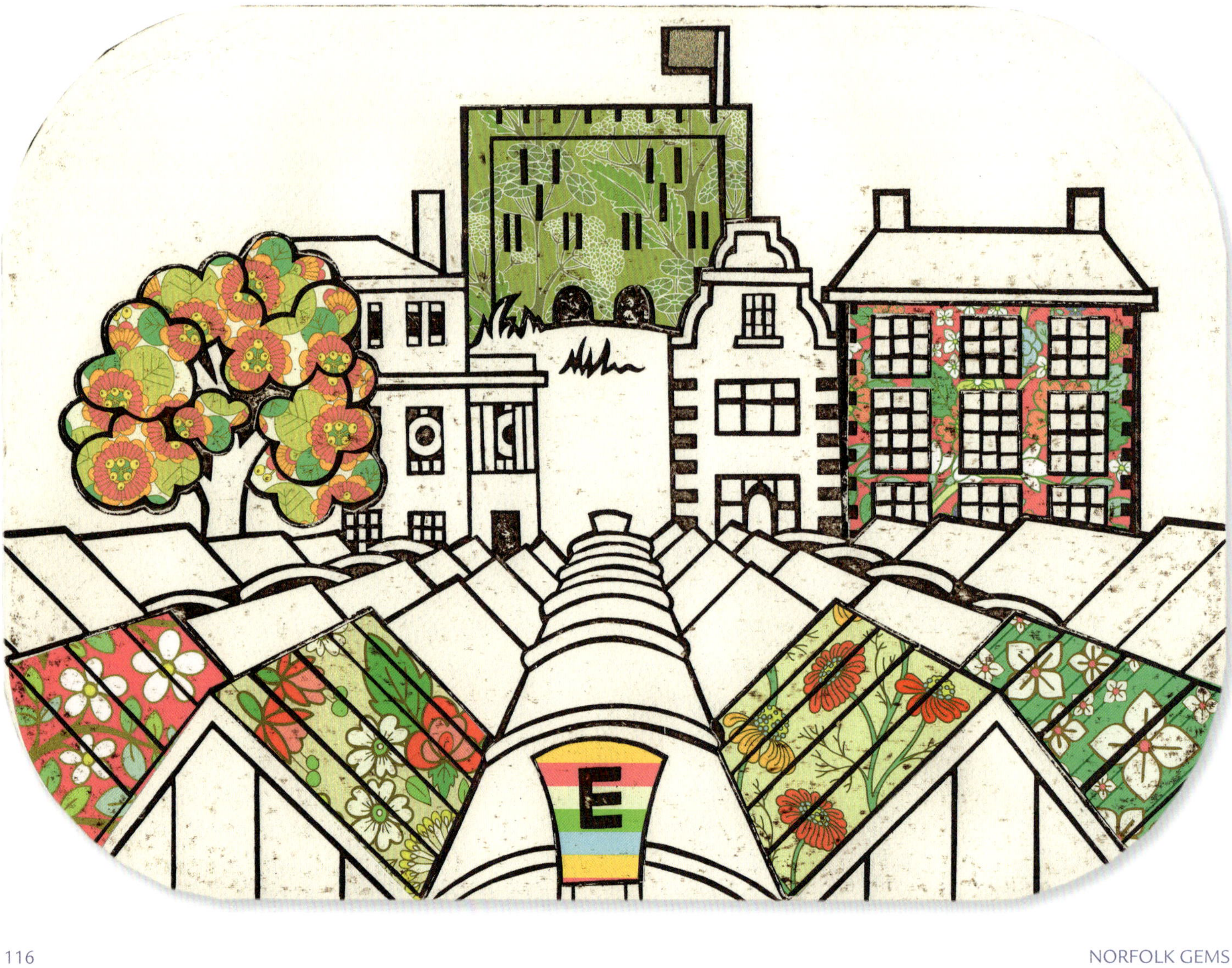

sell out and replacement letters are needed.

"The A to Z of Norwich is loosely based around my own 'psychogeographical' interpretation of Norwich, using landmarks and personal choices to navigate the audience in and around the city. My original drawings were screen-printed using a limited colour palette and embossed. They were then hung as a block, almost map-like, that encouraged the viewer to enjoy the journey with me."

Leanda's A-Z prints are each 38cm x 28cm on Somerset Velvet paper. The Norwich alphabet reproduced here begins overleaf with *Assembly House*, followed by *Book Hive*, *Colmans*, *Dipples*, *Eaton Park* and *Franks*. We then have *Grosvenor*, *Heigham* and *Imeldas*, together with *Jarrolds*, *Kofra* and *Lion*. On pages 120-121 we have reproduced *Magdalen*, *Norwich Castle*, *Opie*, *Playhouse*, *Quayside*, *Royal Arcade*, *Sainsbury*, *Thorns*, *Unthank*, *Vintage*, *Whitlingham* and *Ten (X) Bells*. Page 122 features *Yare* and *Ziggurats*. Leanda's prints of *Norwich Lanes* and the old *Norfolk and Norwich Hospital* are also included.

Leanda is a Norwich-based illustrator who graduated from Norwich University of the Arts with a first-class honours degree in Illustration. Inspired by the Norfolk and Norwich area, she uses screen printing, linocuts, etching and embossing to create her distinctive artwork.

Norwich Print Fair founder Martin Mitchell's work is firmly rooted in the traditional process of intaglio and relief printmaking, producing acclaimed atmospheric, tonal landscapes. His enduring interest is to comment without nostalgia or sentimentality on the physical changes in the countryside and society's attitude

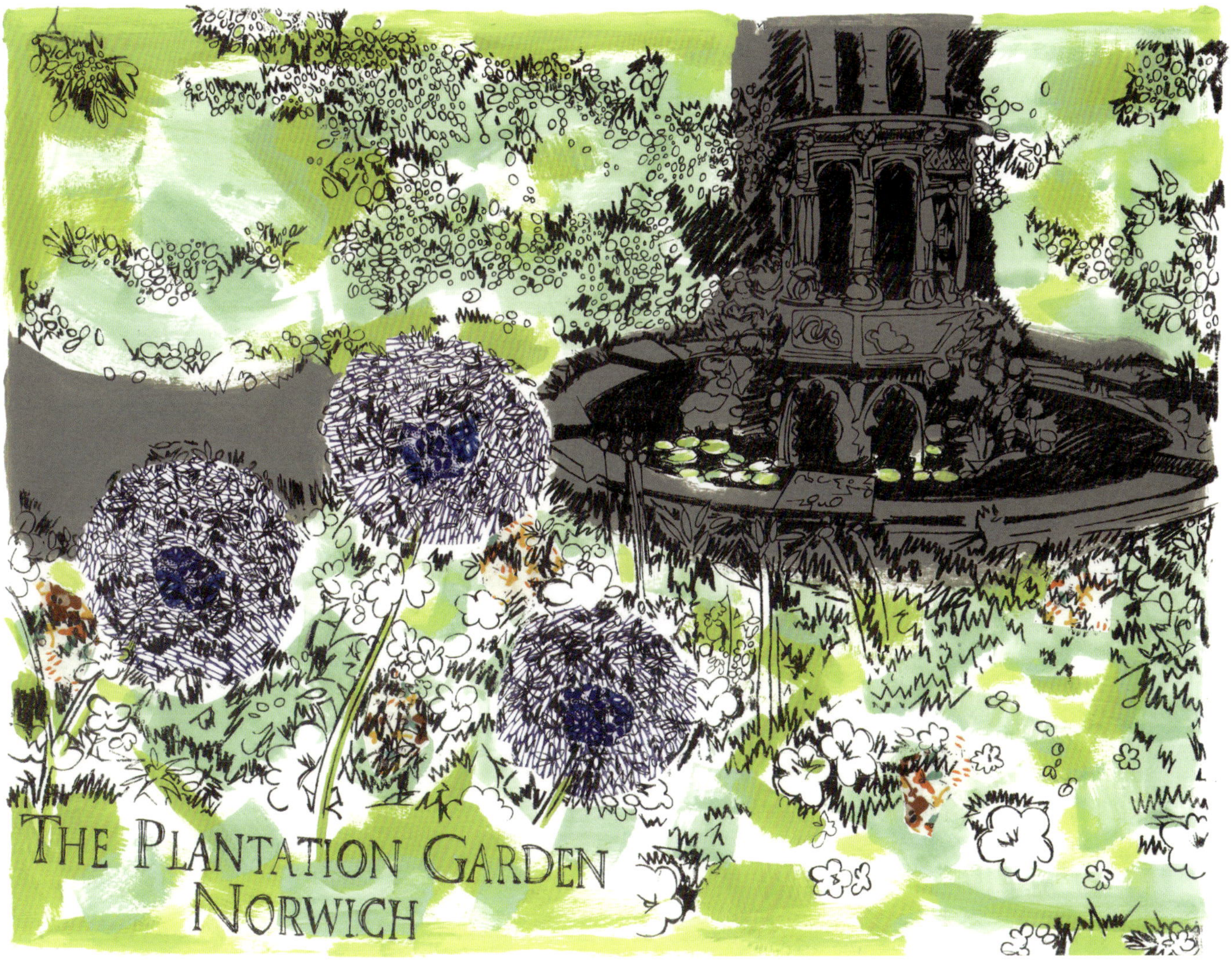

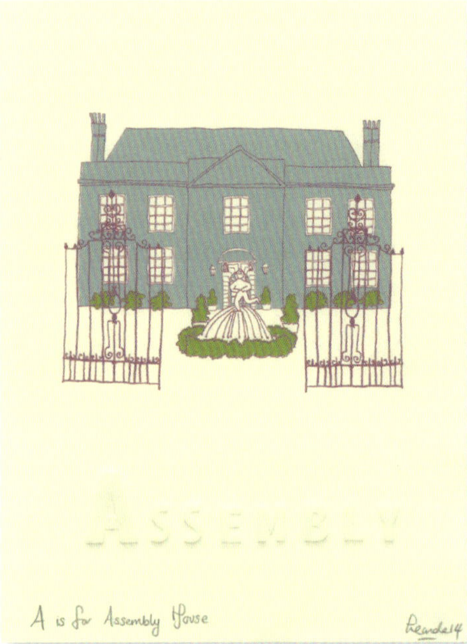

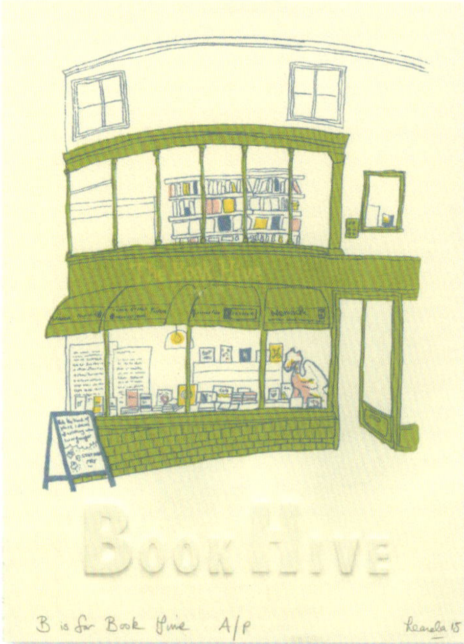

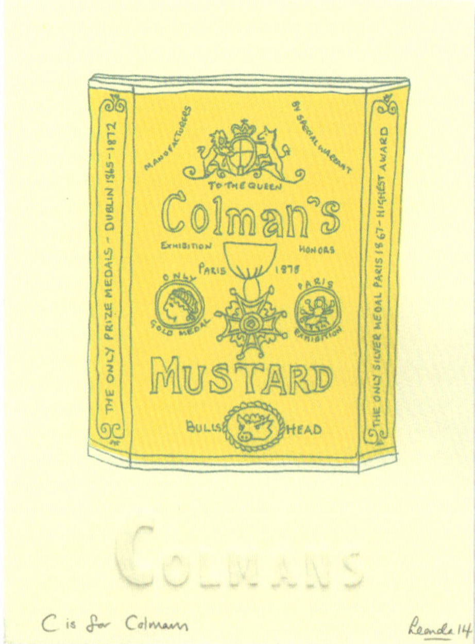

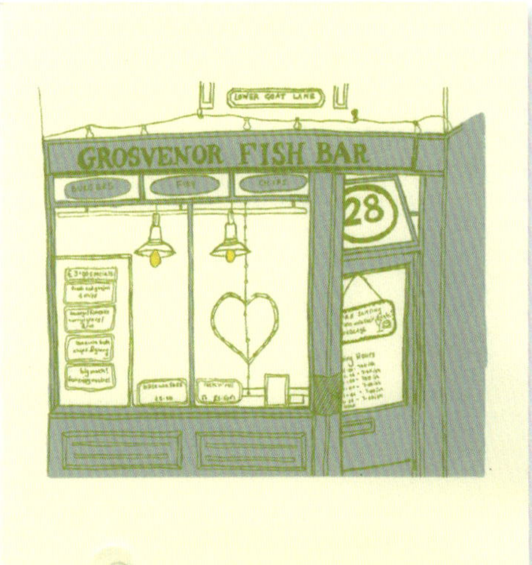

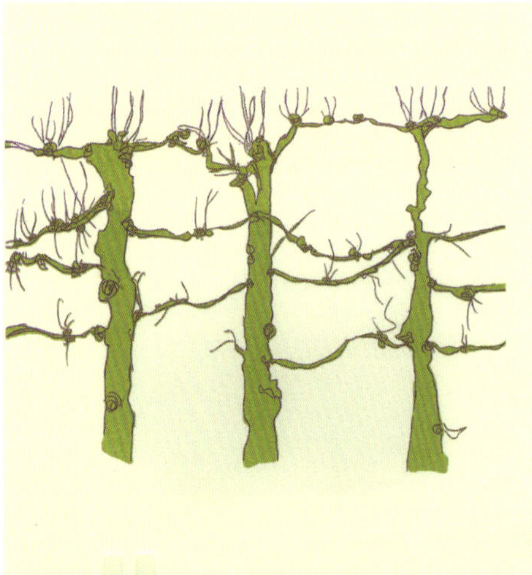

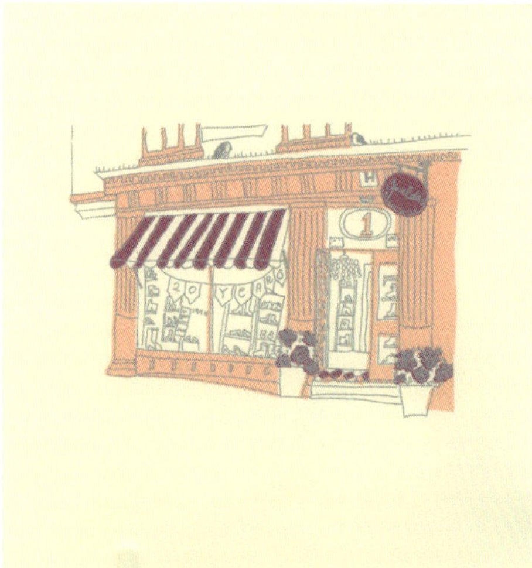

A is for **Assembly House**. **B** is for the **Book Hive** independent bookshop. **C** is for **Colmans Mustard** and a great Norwich institution. **D** is for **Dipples** the jewellers. **E** is for **Eaton Park** and **F** is for **Frank's Bar**. **G** is for the **Grosvenor Fish Bar**. **H** is for **Heigham** and **I** is for **Imelda's Shoe Boutique**. **J** is for Norwich department store **Jarrolds**. **K** is for coffee specialist **Kofra**. **L** is for **Lion**. **M** is for **Magdalen Street**. **N** is for the imposing **Norwich**

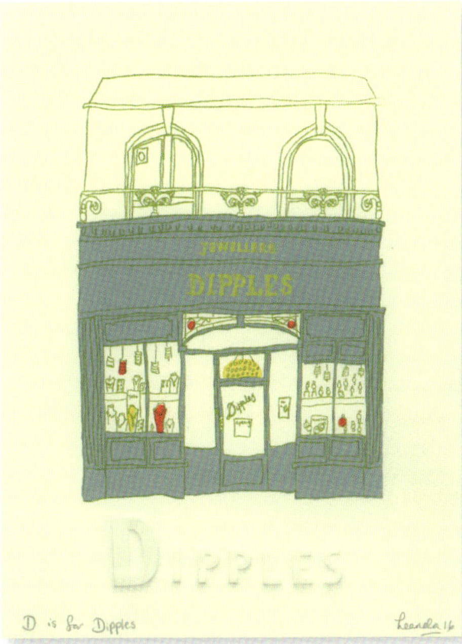

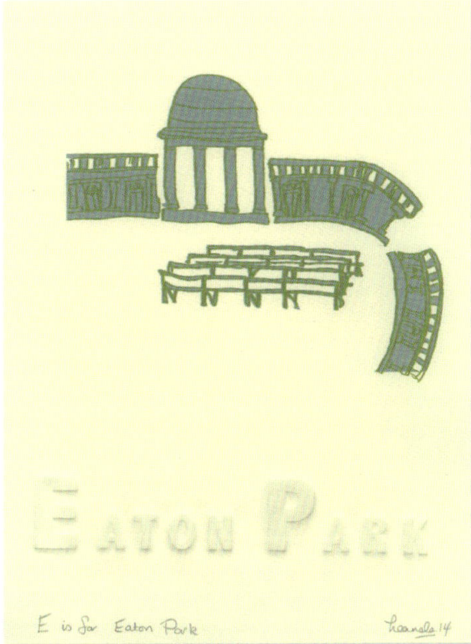

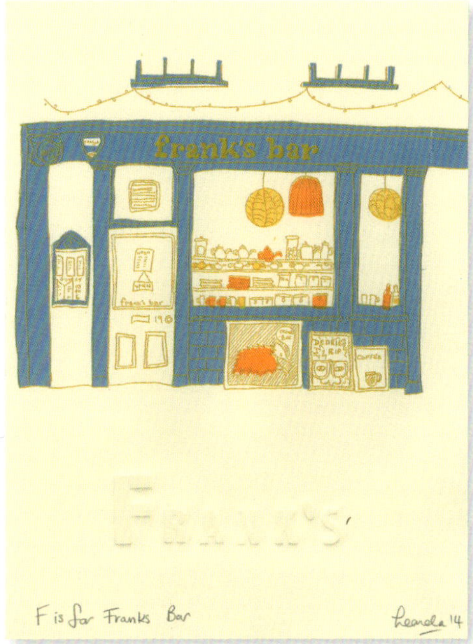

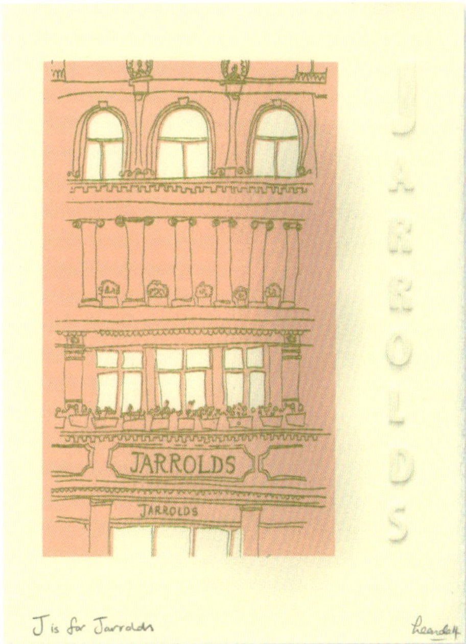

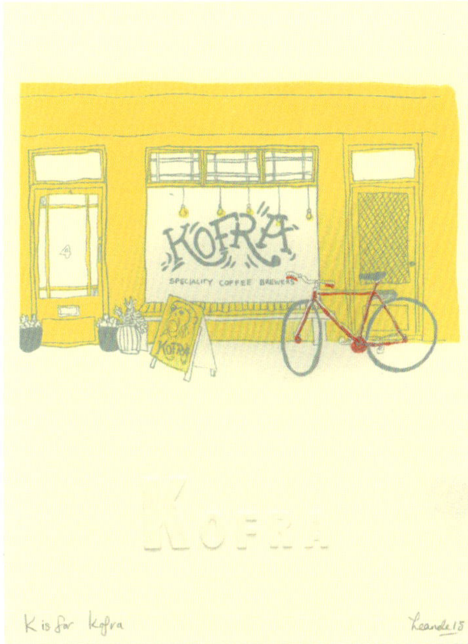

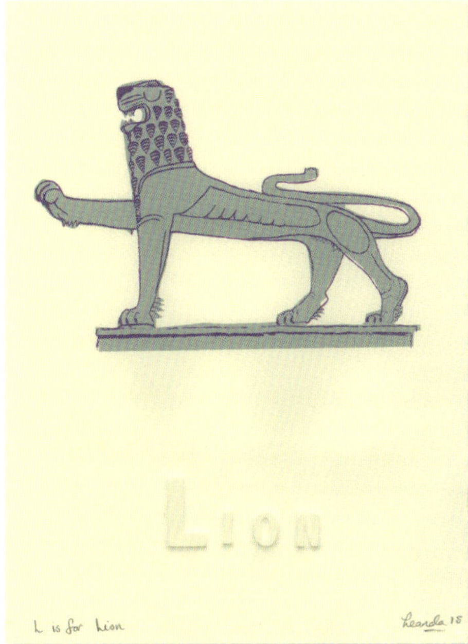

Castle. **O** is for **Opie Street** and **P** is for the **Norwich Playhouse**. **Q** represents **Quayside**, while **R** is for the Art Deco **Royal Arcade**. **S** is for the **Sainsbury Centre** and **T** for hardware store **Thorns**. **U** is for **The Unthank Arms**. **V** is for **Goldfinches Vintage Fashion**. **W** represents **Whitlingham Country Park** and **X** marks the spot for the **Ten (X) Bells** pub. **Y** is for the **River Yare** and **Z** can only be the university's **Ziggurats**.

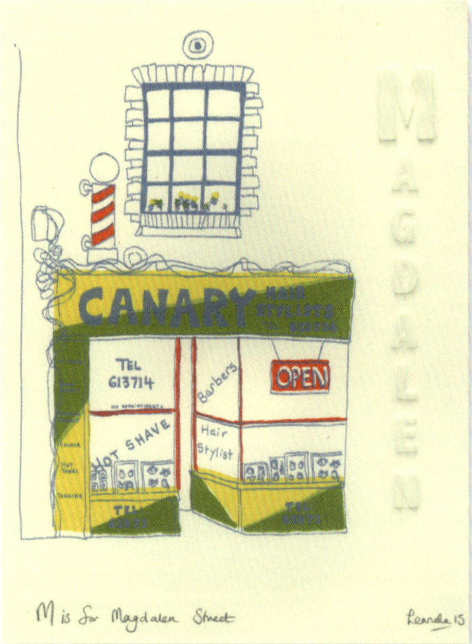
MAGDALEN
CANARY
HAIR STYLISTS
TEL 613714
OPEN
Barbers
HOT SHAVE
Hair Stylist
M is for Magdalen Street

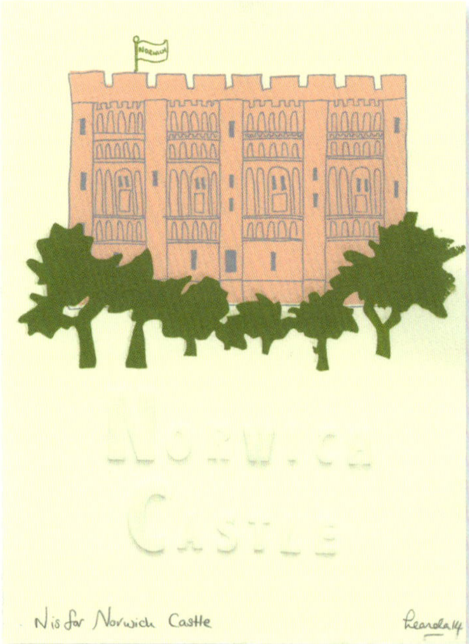
NORWICH CASTLE
N is for Norwich Castle

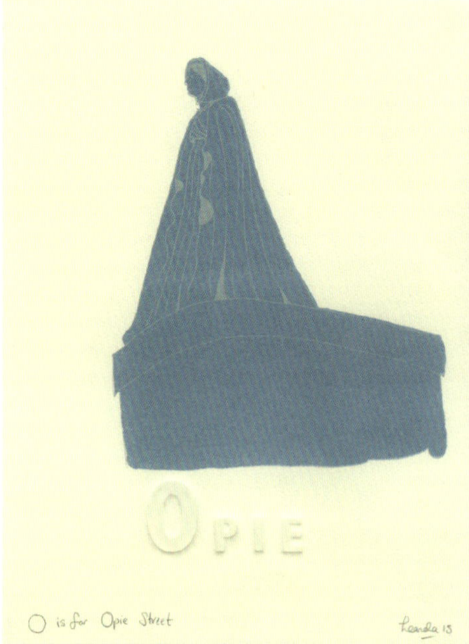
OPIE
O is for Opie Street

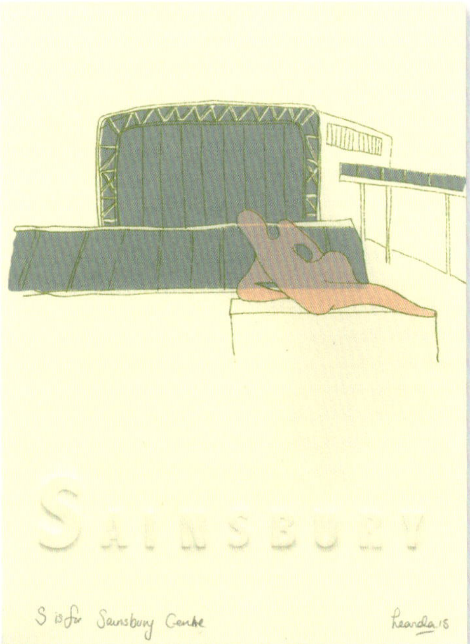
SAINSBURY
S is for Sainsbury Centre

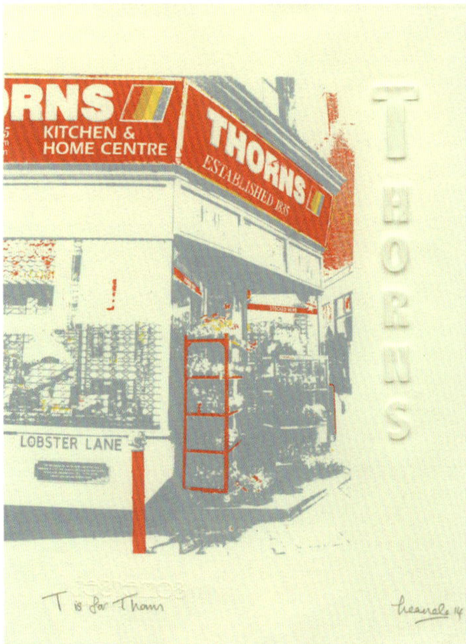
RNS
KITCHEN &
HOME CENTRE
THORNS
ESTABLISHED 1835
LOBSTER LANE
THORNS
T is for Thorns

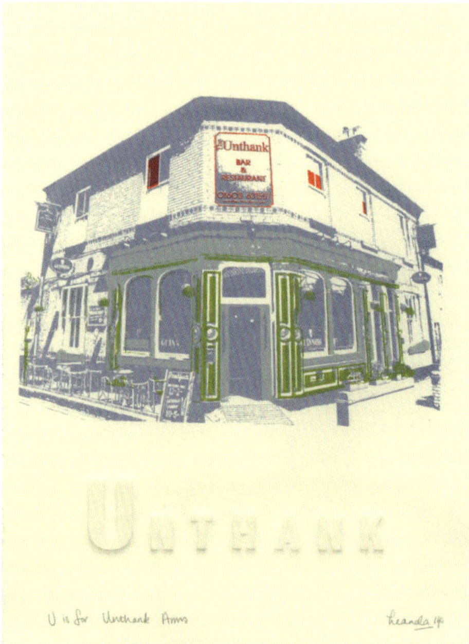
Unthank
BAR & RESTAURANT
UNTHANK
U is for Unthank Arms

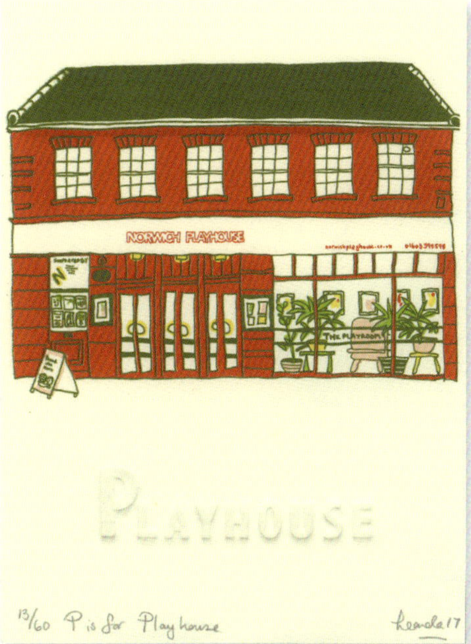
NORWICH PLAYHOUSE
PLAYHOUSE
13/60 P is for Playhouse

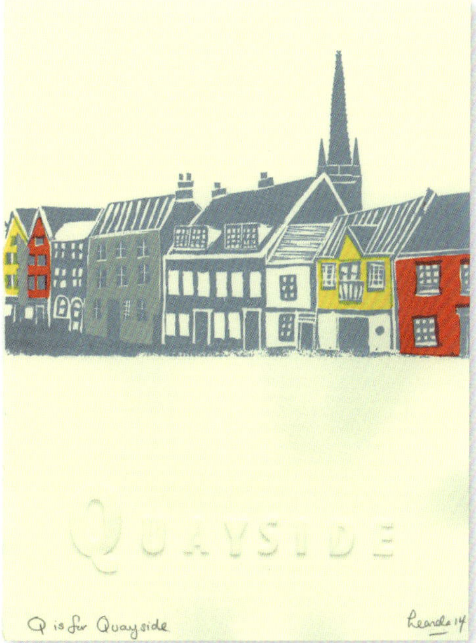
QUAYSIDE
Q is for Quayside

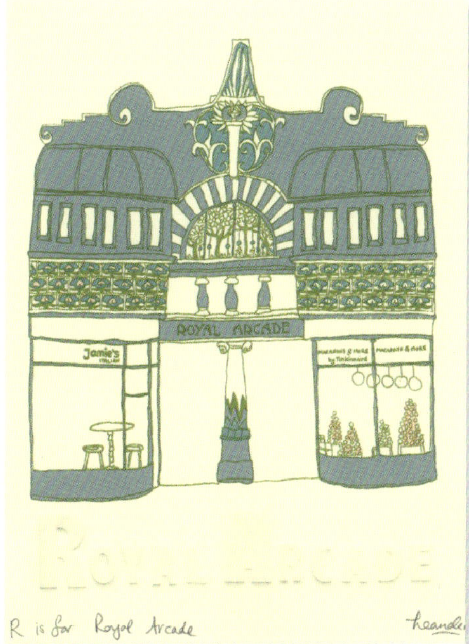
ROYAL ARCADE
R is for Royal Arcade

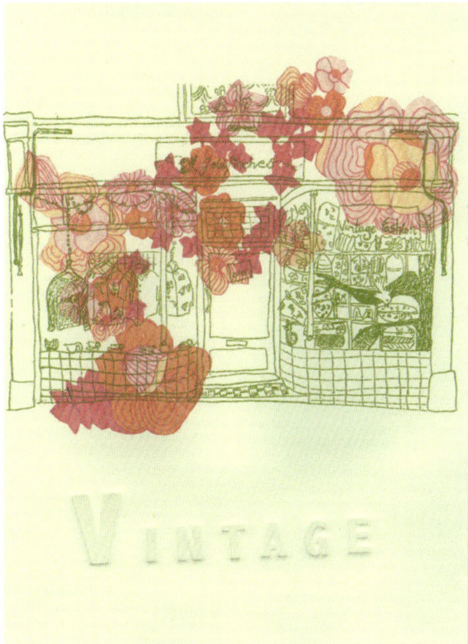
VINTAGE

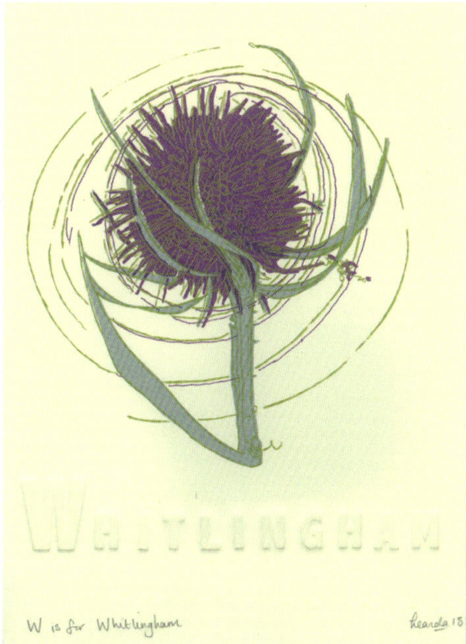
WHITLINGHAM
W is for Whitlingham

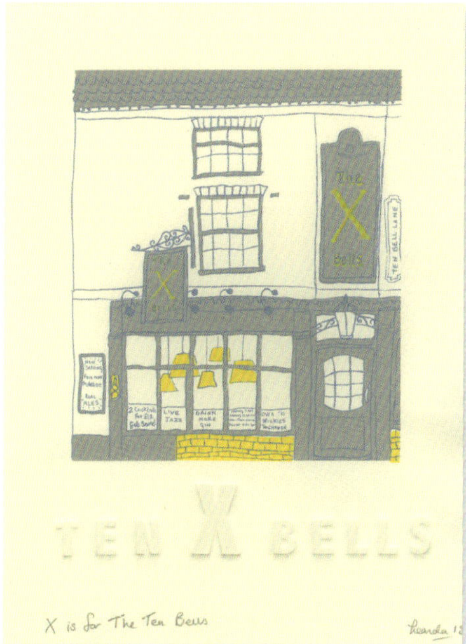
TEN X BELLS
X is for The Ten Bells

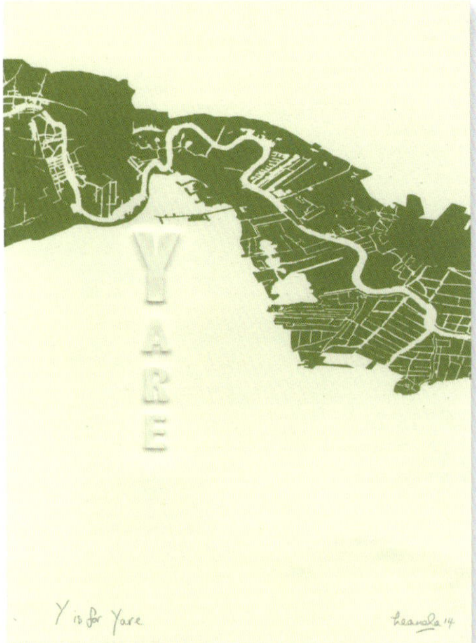
YARE
Y is for Yare

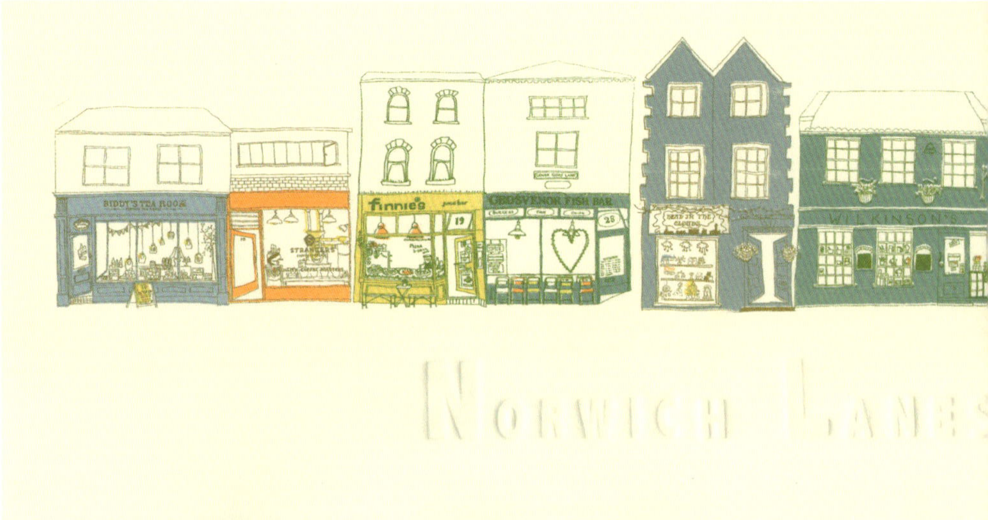
NORWICH LANES

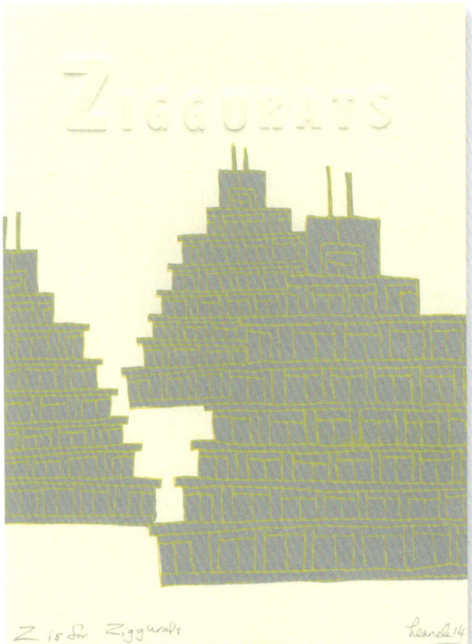
ZIGGURATS
Z is for Ziggurats

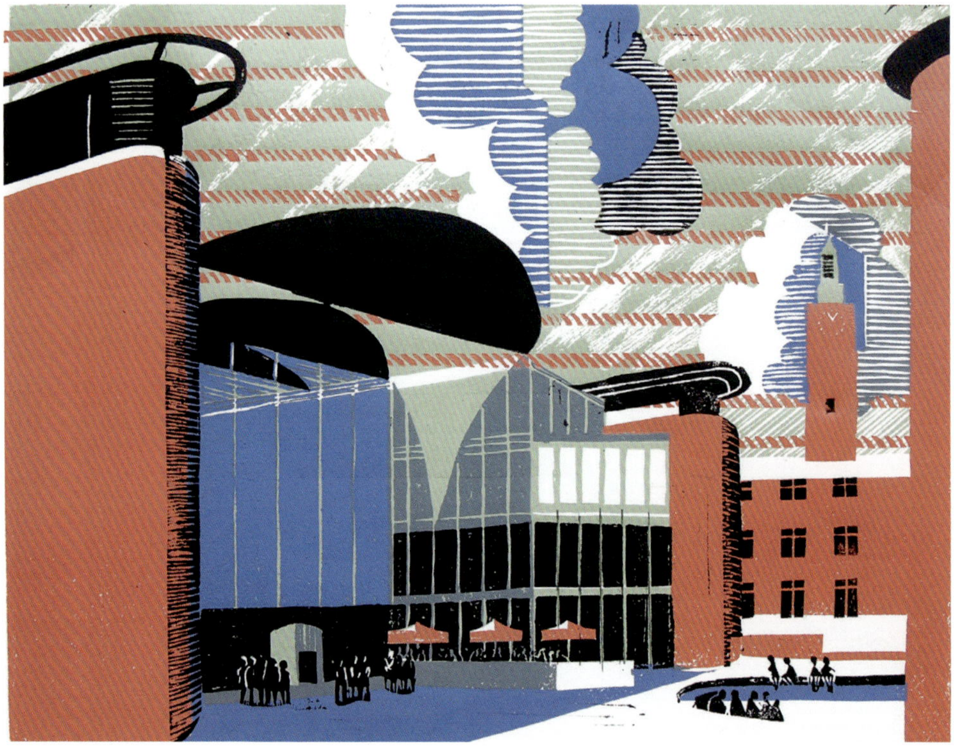

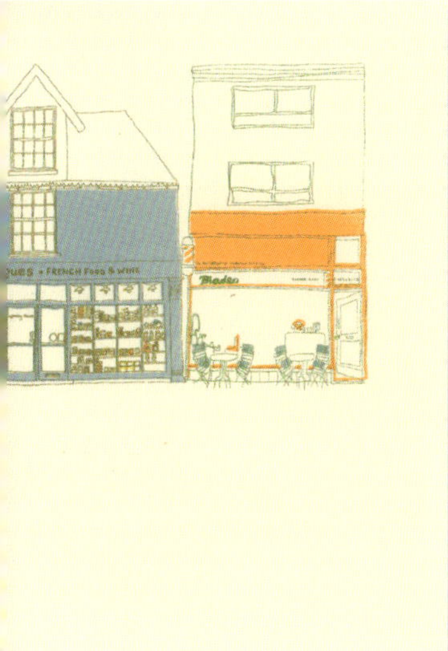

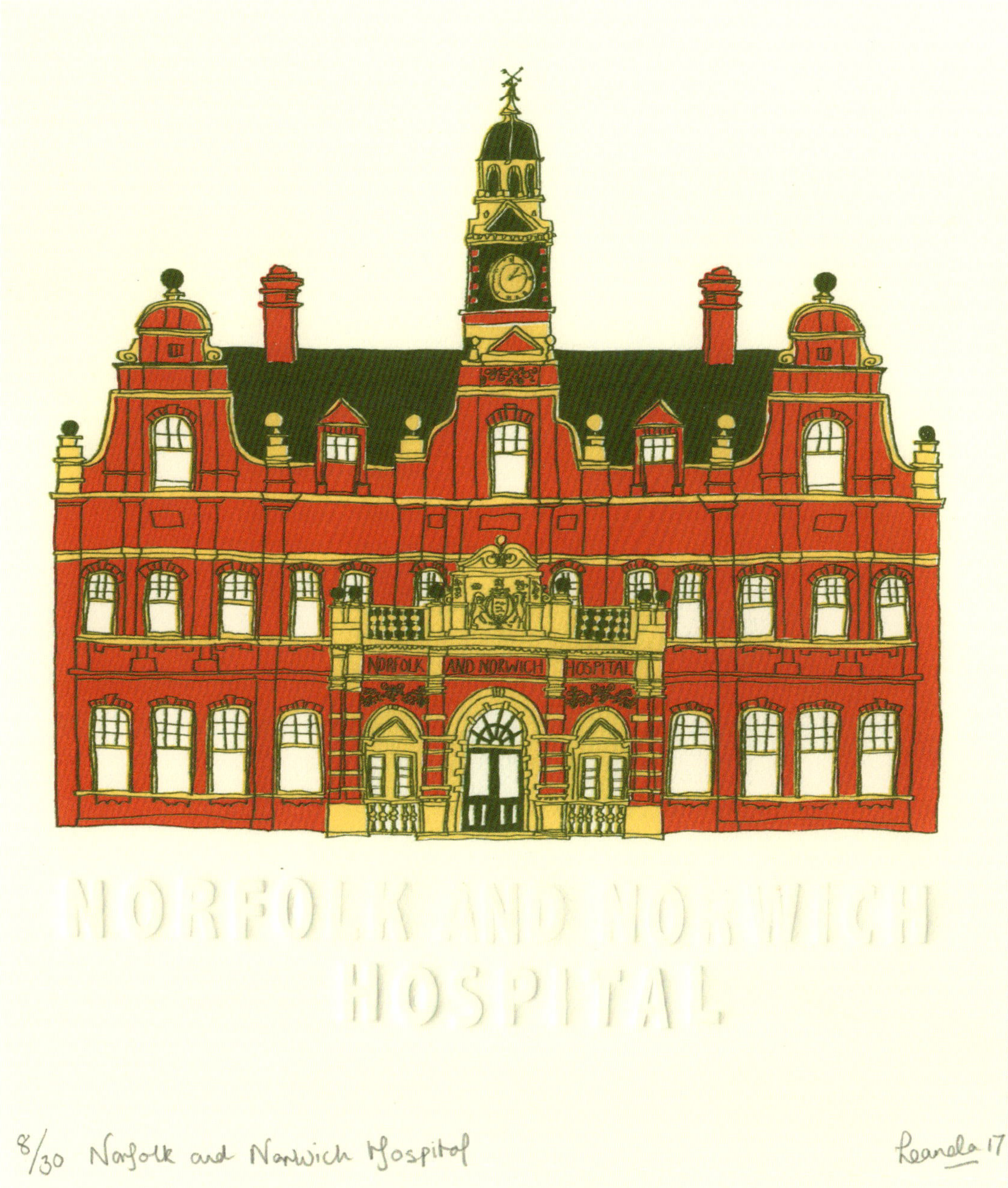

***Far left**: Y and Z from the Leanda Jaine Hughes Norwich alphabet. **Above**: Leanda Jaine Hughes – Norwich Lanes (embossed screenprint). **Left**: David Jones – The Forum (linocut). **Right**: Leanda Jaine Hughes – Norfolk and Norwich Hospital (embossed screenprint).*

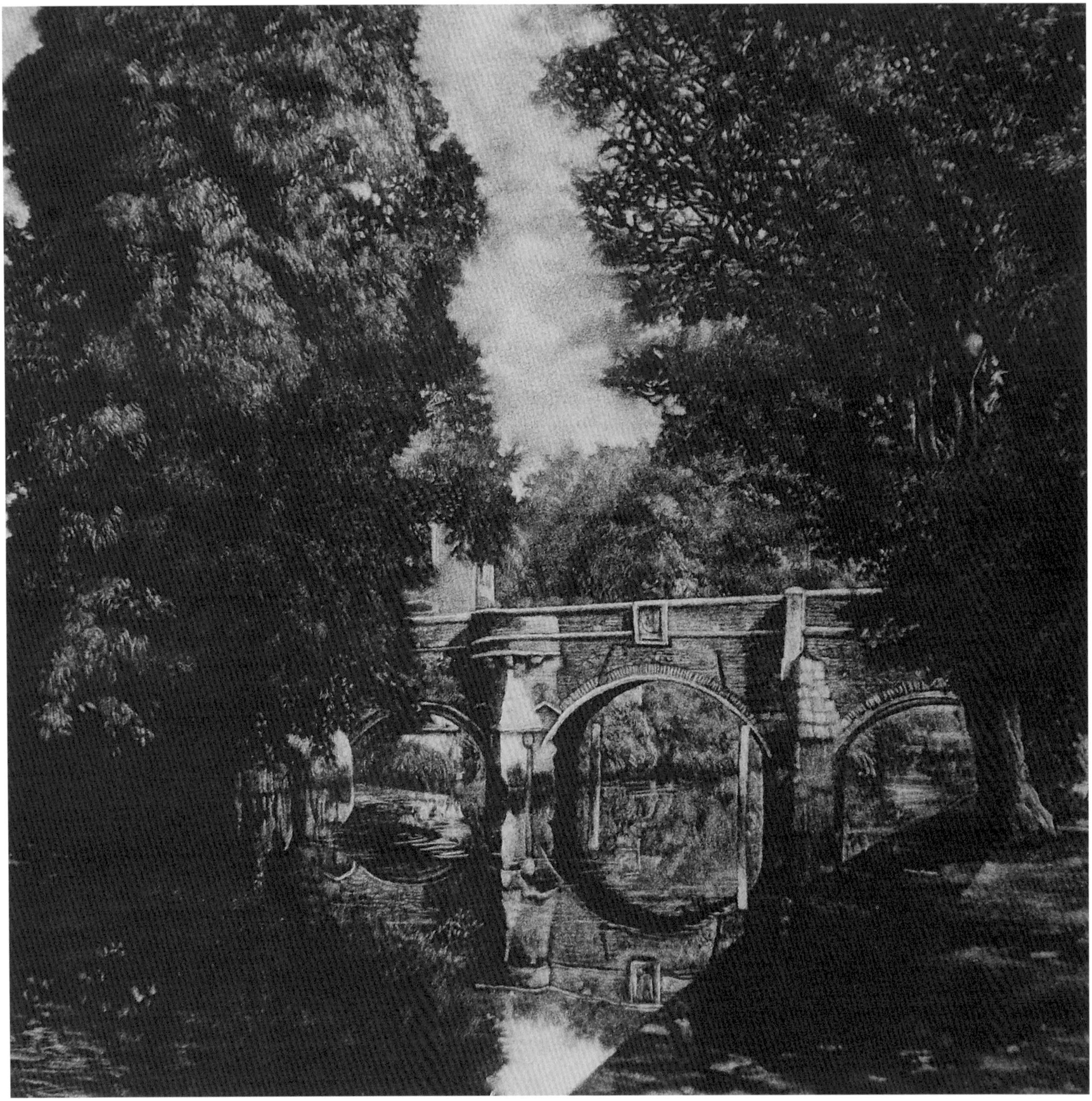

to them. The majority of his work is landscape, with some examples here. We have also reproduced, on the left, his powerful mezzotint of *Bishop Bridge* in Norwich, while another mezzotint of Norwich Cathedral's *Erpingham Gate* appears on page 127. Below right is *Marriott's Morning*, a mezzotint of the long-distance walking and cycling trail from Norwich to Aylsham. On the right is *Whitlingham Broad #2*, a mezzotint of the reclaimed body of recreational water on the outskirts of the city.

"For me, art is combining the aesthetics of the image and the dexterity of the craft skills of the artist," says Martin. "This can be best exemplified in the techniques of printmaking, and especially mezzotint."

Norfolk linocut specialist Rob Barnes is responsible for the colourful print *The Hostry* on page 126 that helps show the marriage of architecture old and new at the Anglican cathedral in Norwich. Alongside it is one of the 'Revolutionary Norwich' series of screenprints by local artist Richard Horne. The subject here is *City Hall*, overlooking the market in the centre of Norwich. The cathedral and the castle get similar treatment by Richard and his Japanese Gocco printing process. He admires greatly Chinese and Russian revolutionary posters, which he reinterpreted for his images of iconic Norwich buildings.

Norwich is blessed with more than its fair share of ancient, important and interesting buildings. During the 11th century it was the largest city in England after London, and one of its most important. It remained the capital of the most populous English county until the Industrial Revolution created northern powerhouses and left Norfolk to plough its lonely agricultural furrow.

The Domesday Book states that Norwich had approximately 25 churches and a population of between 5,000 and 10,000. It also records the site of an Anglo-Saxon church in Tombland, the site of the Saxon marketplace and the later Norman cathedral. Norwich Castle was founded soon after the Norman Conquest, and the Domesday Book records that 98 Saxon homes were demolished to make way for the structure. The Normans established a new settlement around the castle and the area to the west of it, where their marketplace

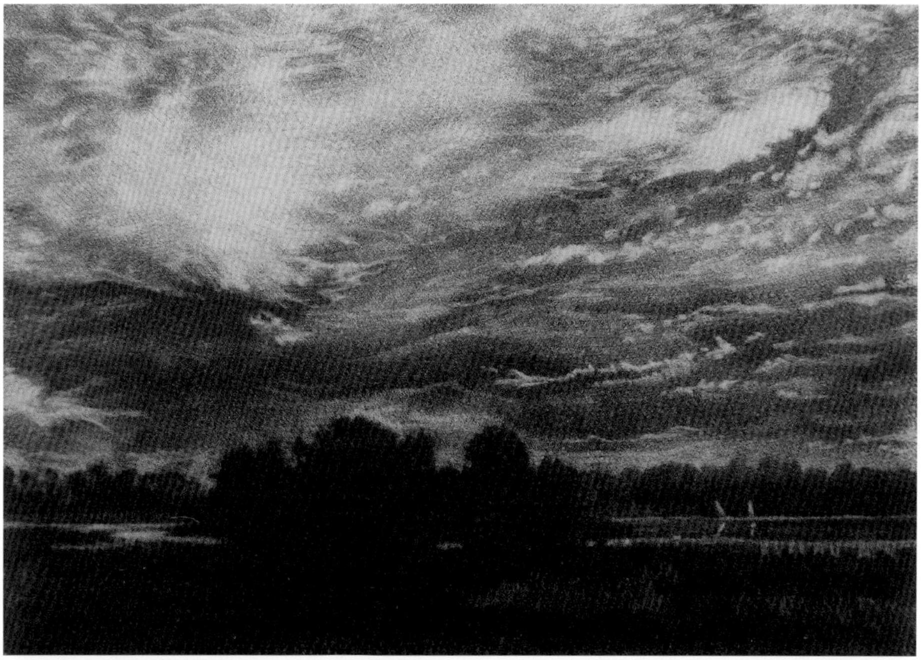

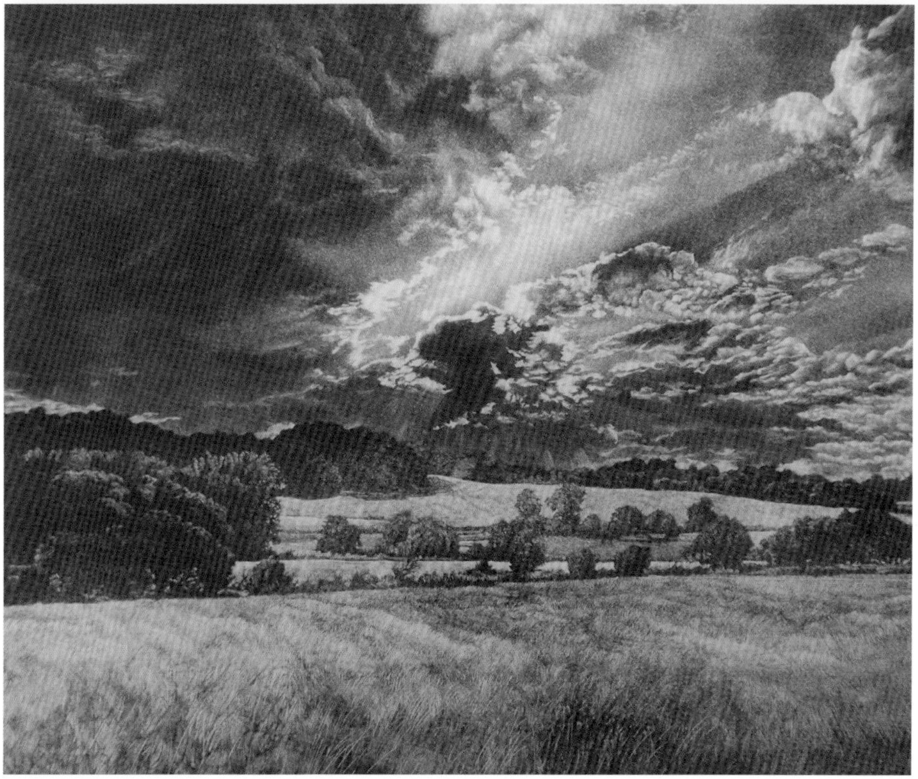

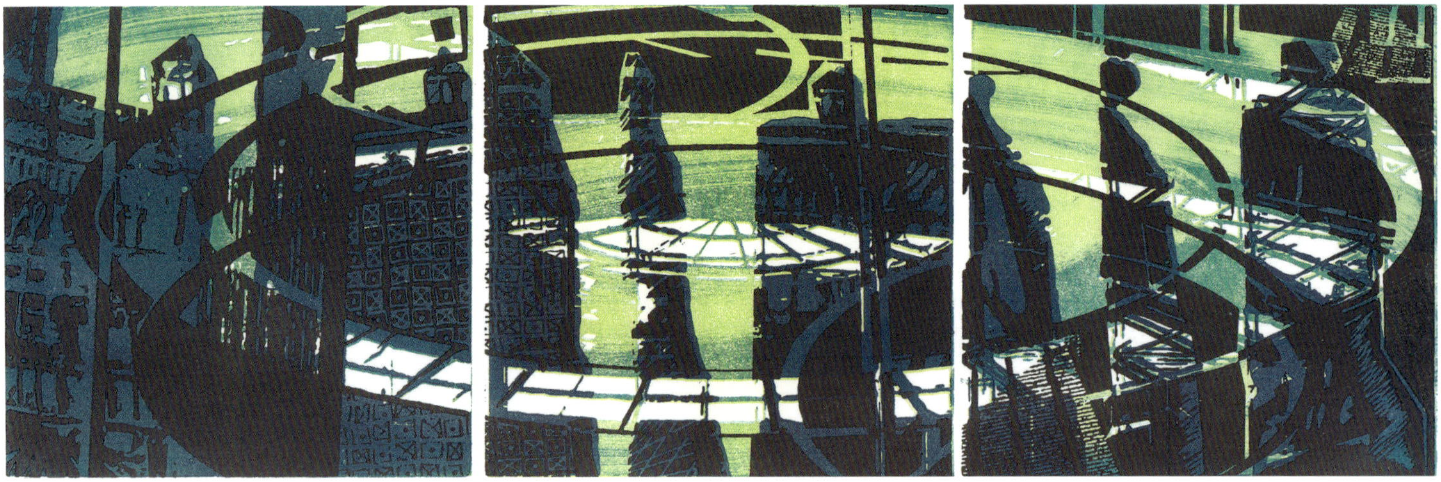

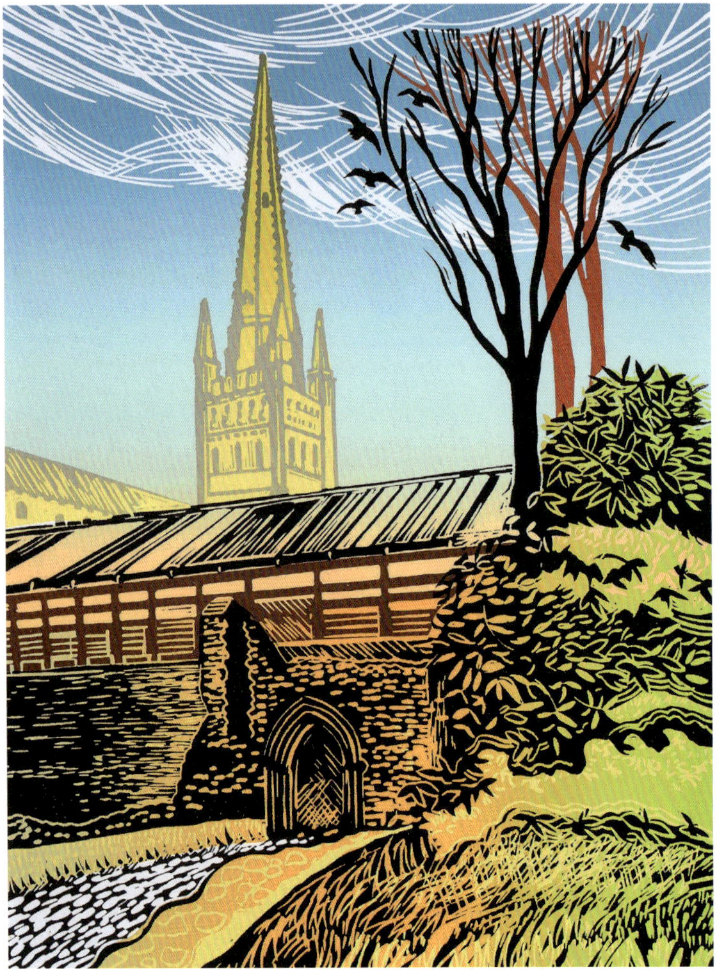

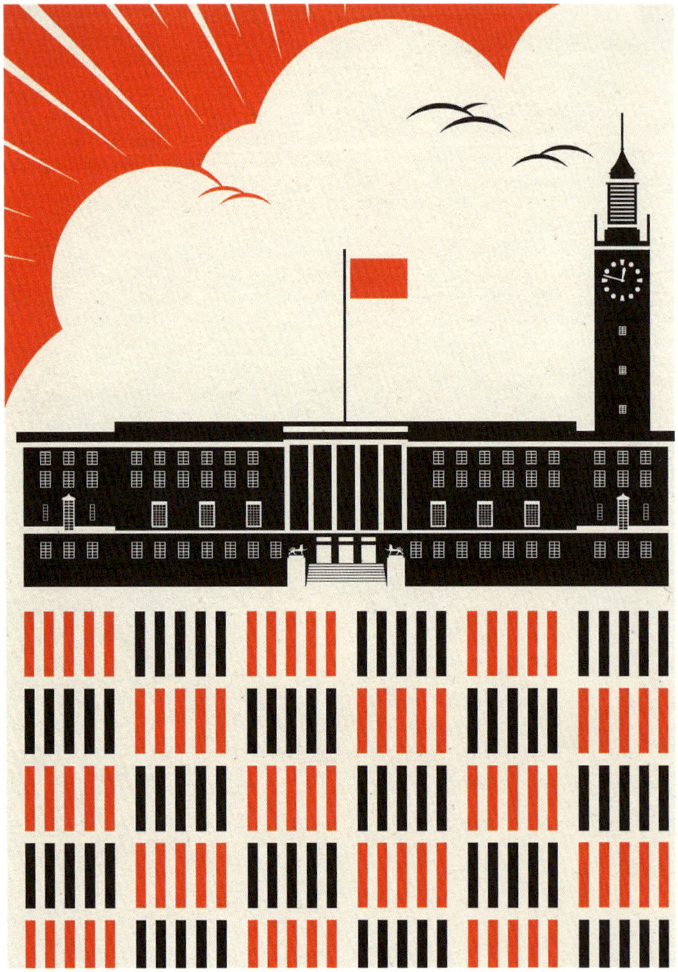

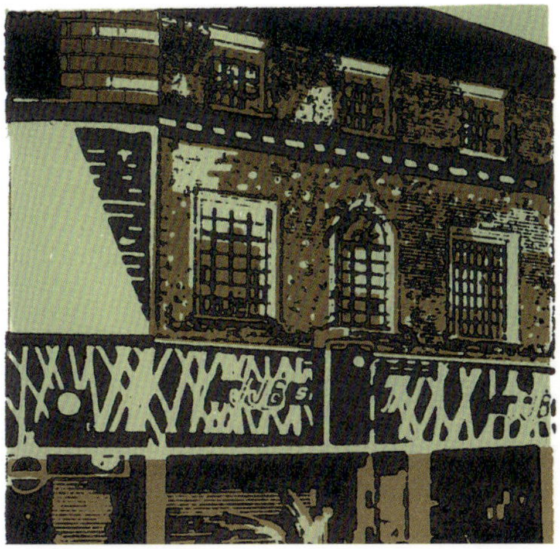

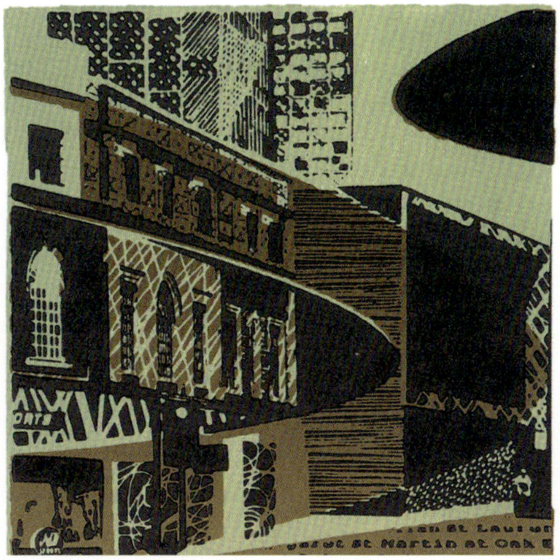

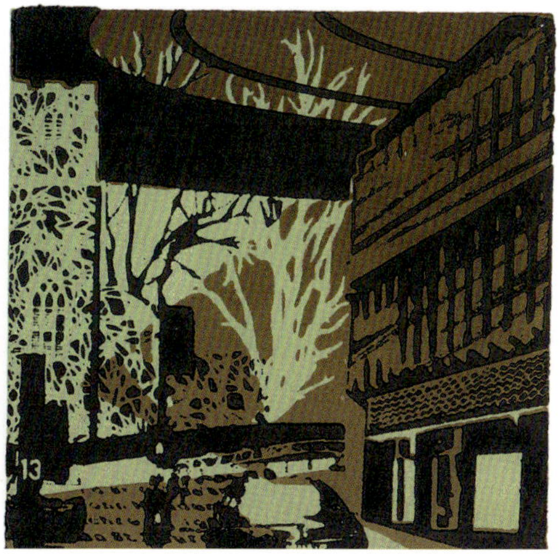

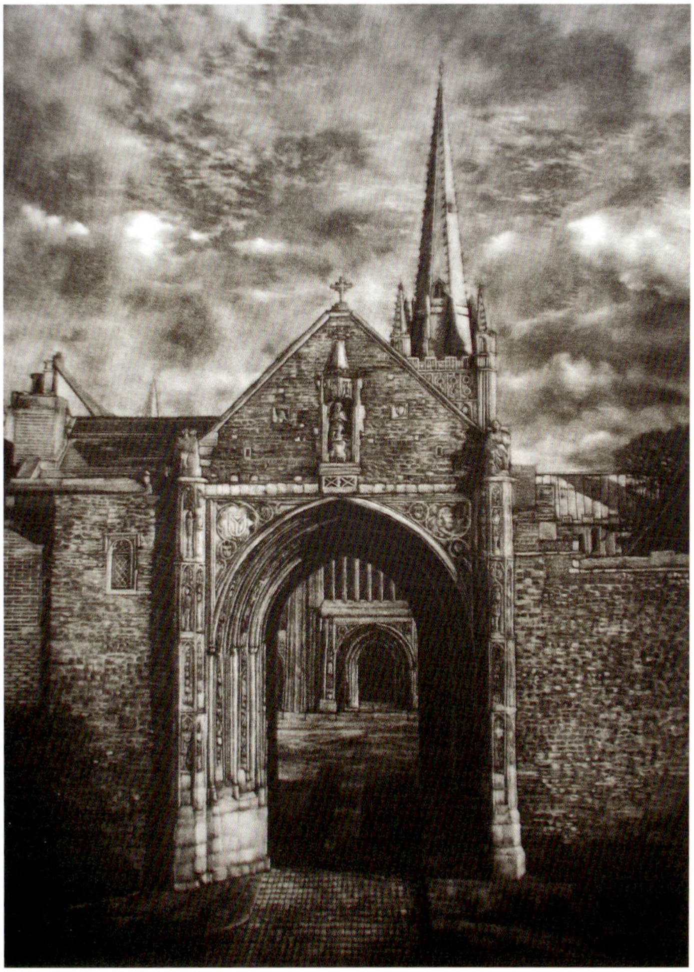

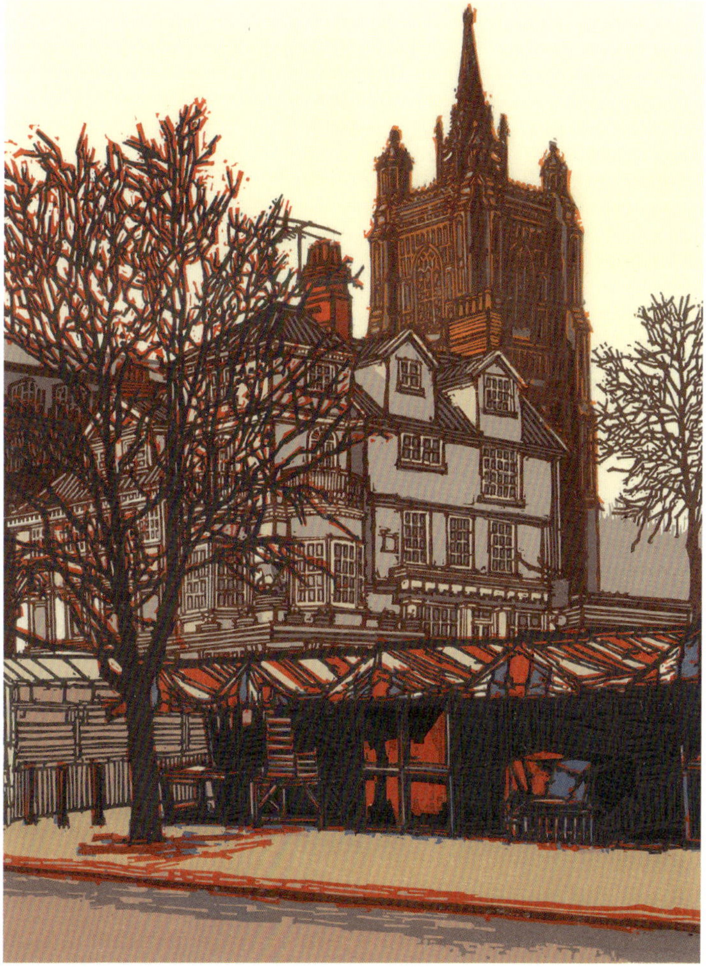

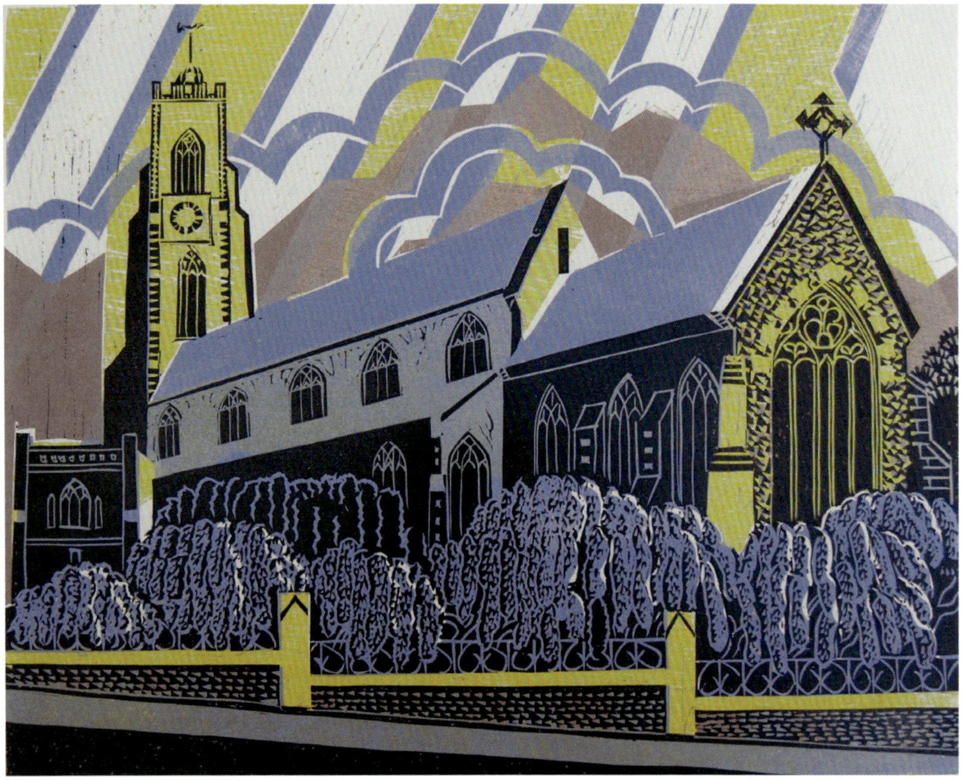

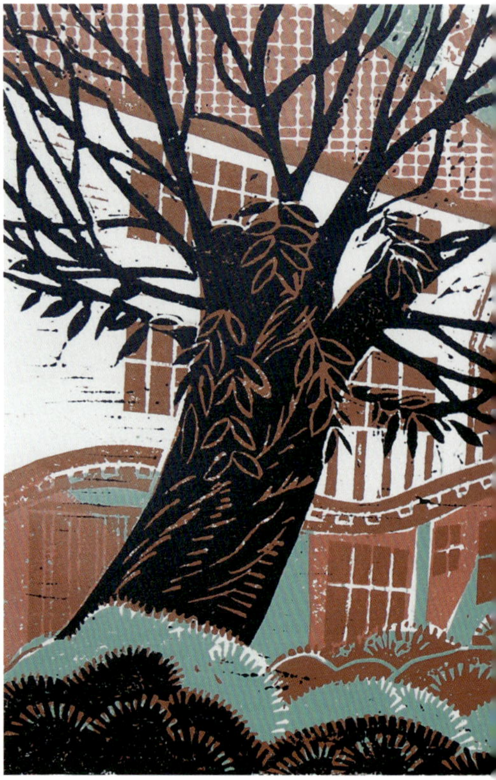

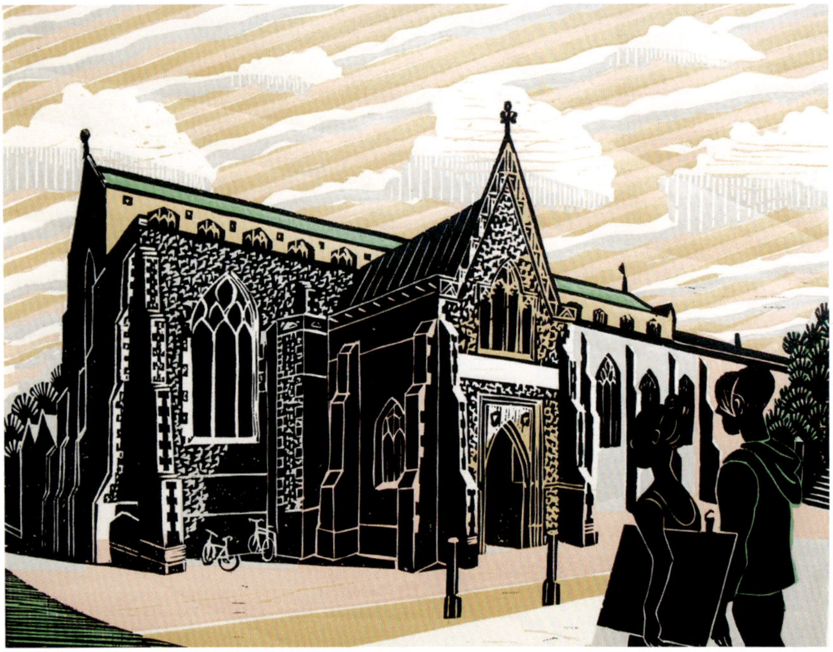

has survived as the site of the current Norwich Market.

In 1096, Herbert de Losinga, Bishop of Thetford, began construction of Norwich Cathedral. The chief building material was limestone from Caen, and a canal was cut from the river (from the site of Pull's Ferry) all the way up to the east wall. Norwich received a royal charter from Henry II in 1158, and another from Richard the Lionheart in 1194. Following a riot in the city in 1274, Norwich has the distinction of being the only complete English city to be excommunicated by the Pope. The city has in recent times been described as somewhat 'ungodly', which seems surprising given the number of churches – and two cathedrals – it boasts!

The city walls were built between 1280 and 1340. At around 4km, the walls (part of which remain standing) and the river enclosed an area larger than the City of London. The wool trade funded much of the city's development, including many of the grand buildings and churches, and for a period in the 18th century Norwich was the wealthiest town in Britain. Theatres were built, alehouses flourished and a surprisingly large number of booksellers emerged during the golden age of cloth.

By the 1790s, the wool trade was experiencing intense

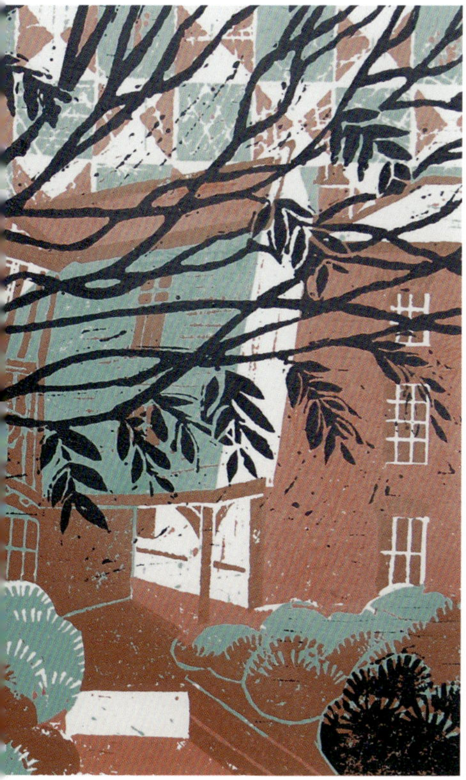

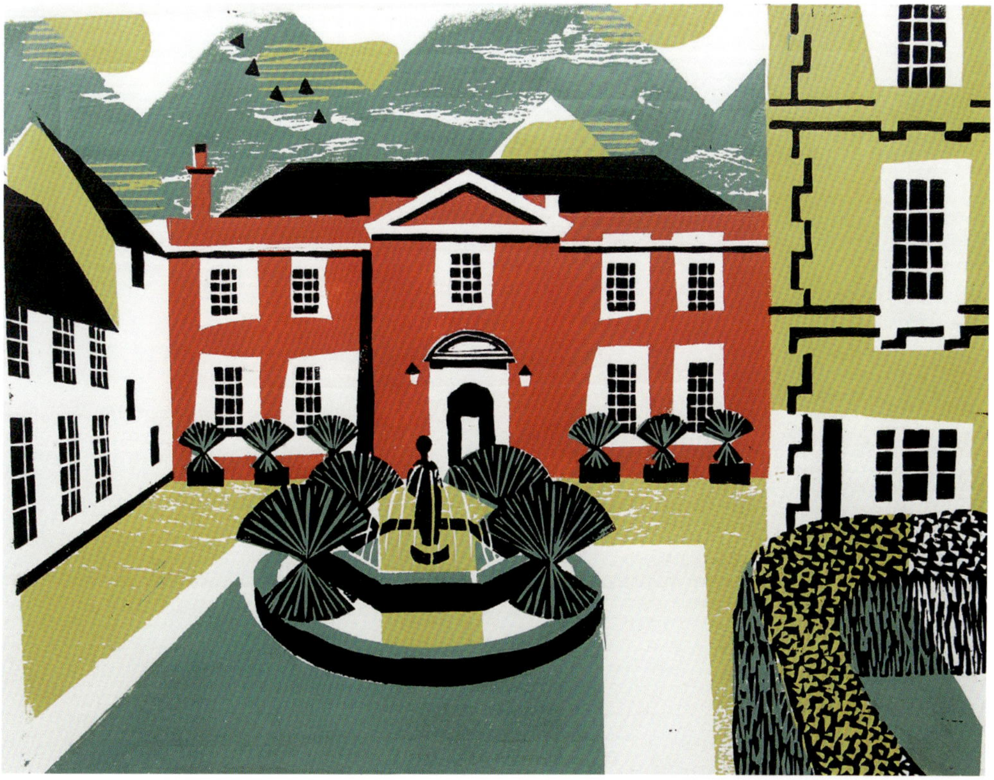

competition from Yorkshire woollens and, increasingly, from Lancashire cottons. The impact was exacerbated as Britain went to war with France. De-industrialisation began in the early 19th century, and Norwich saw its fortunes eroded and its people become poor and angry. Without a rail connection until 1845, the city became increasingly isolated. Business came and went, from shoe-making and brewing to chocolate and furniture manufacture.

Norwich suffered extensive bomb damage during World War II, affecting large parts of the old city centre and Victorian terraced housing around the centre. Industry and the rail infrastructure also suffered. Lord Haw-Haw made reference to the imminent destruction of Norwich's new City Hall (completed in 1938), although it survived unscathed – unlike the Morgan's Brewery building, the Wincarnis works, City Station and the Mackintosh chocolate factory.

Nowadays, Norwich is a pleasing mixture of medieval and modern. Its centre may have become a little confused, with unpopular decisions such as the market redevelopment and shopping malls that have hurt established outlets in the 'old' part of town, but the castle, cathedral and churches

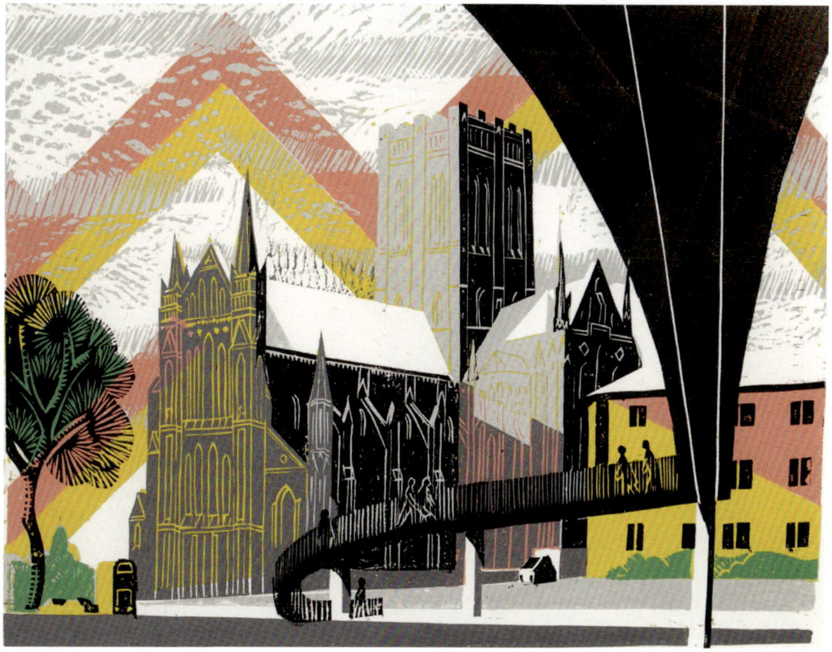

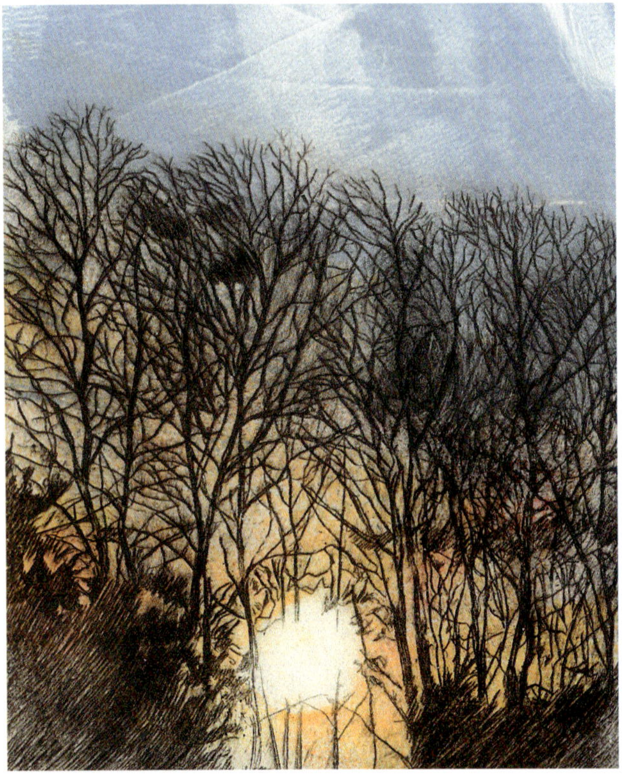
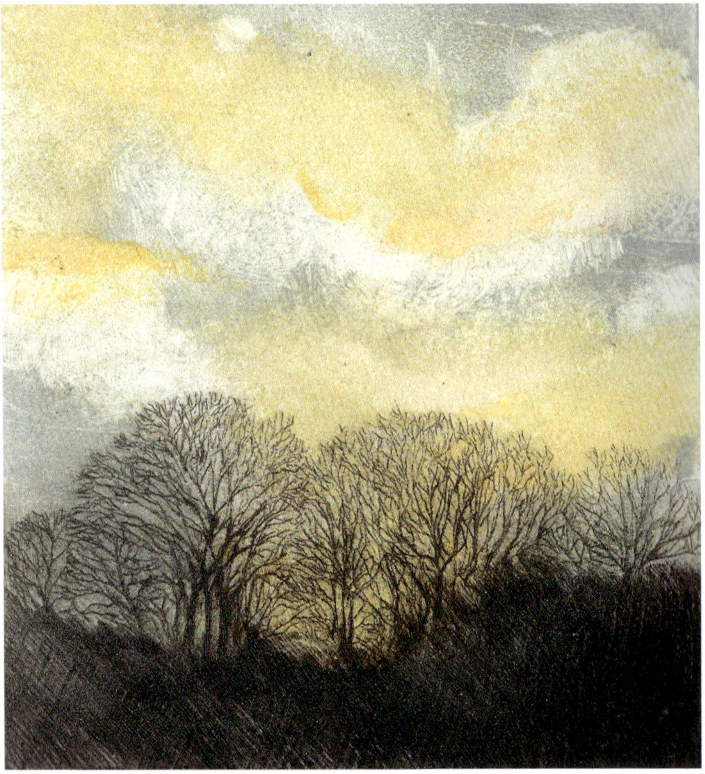
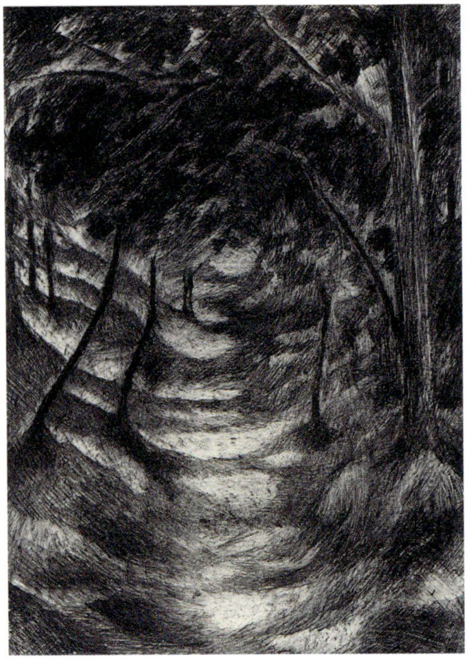
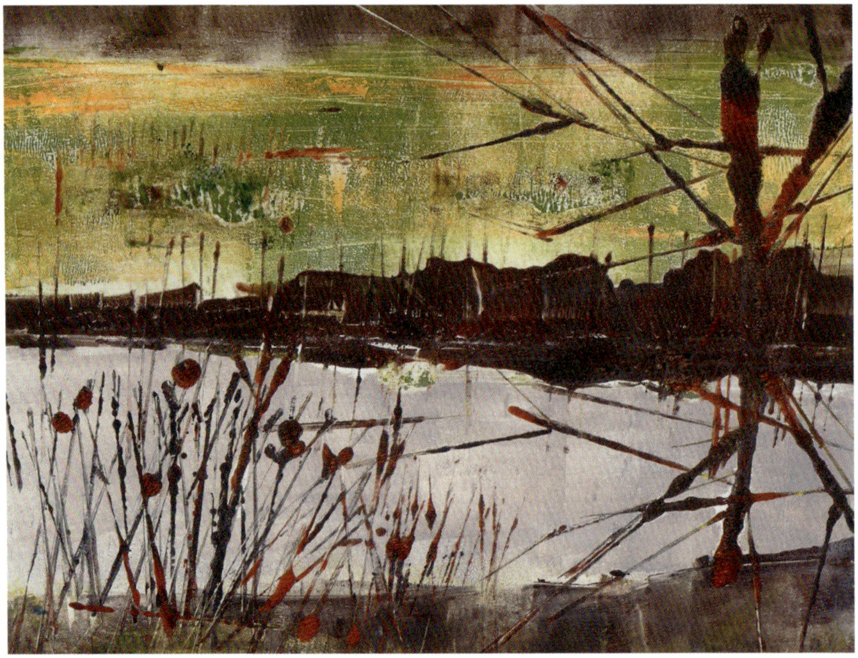

ensure that Norwich continues to deserve its 'fine city' epithet.

Expansion has seen villages become suburbs, then get absorbed into the city. Green spaces have, however, survived. Mousehold Heath is the subject of *Sunrise* (facing page, top left), a monotype/drypoint print by Norwich artist Sarah Bays from 2014 (10cm x 9.5cm). "One of the places my dog and I enjoy for our morning walk is Mousehold Heath – a nature reserve made up of heathland and woodland to the north-east of Norwich. It is especially inspiring in the stillness of early morning with the sun rising through the trees and birds flying through the mist to land on dew-laden branches."

First Light is a print using the same technique from the same artist (facing page, top right), while *Through the Woods* (bottom left) is one of Sarah's drypoint prints from 2012. The Marriott's Way path from Norwich to Aylsham is depicted earlier by Martin Mitchell, and appears again here (facing page, bottom right) in a Sarah Bays monotype *Under the Bridge* from 2016. "Following the route of the old M&GN railway line, this path- and cycleway has plenty to inspire in all seasons. At the Norwich end of the route it passes through Sweet Briar Marsh, a Site of Special Scientific Interest teeming with wildlife. It has provided inspiration for many of my prints, including monotypes." Sarah's print *Sweet Briar Marsh* is reproduced overleaf (19cm x 24cm).

On the right of this page is one of the older parts of Norwich receiving the unusual treatment meted out by imaginative Suffolk-based painter and printmaker Mandy Walden. Through many years of Norwich Print Fair membership, Mandy has been a regular visitor to the city and here captures the cobbled streets of Elm Hill complete with rampant hares.

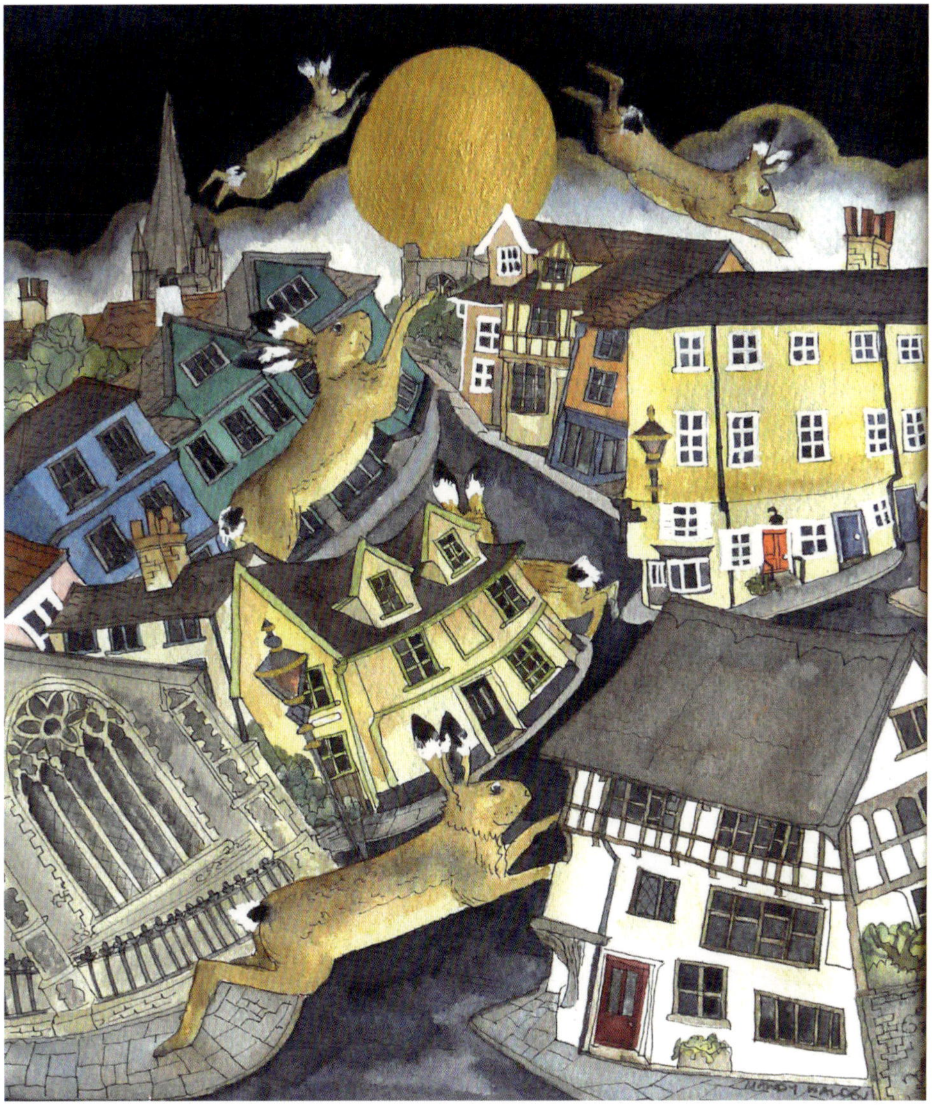

Mandy's collagraph print is entitled *That First Day of Spring the Hares Would Come to Leap and Run by Timbers Old*. "Narrative has become of great importance in my work, both in composition and also in the ever-increasing passages of text that accompany each image," she explains. "I am not concerned with portraying an exact realistic copy of a particular place, person or animal but rather its essence by using a distortion of scale or perspective, a patchwork of unconnected parts found in a landscape... to communicate an atmosphere of place and the feelings of folk – a story of magical ordinariness!"

Elm Hill, the subject of her print, is a historic cobbled lane with many buildings dating back to the Tudor period. It today extends from the Church of St Peter Hungate, where the top of Elm Hill meets Princes Street, to the Church of St Simon and St Jude, situated at the bottom of Elm Hill on the corner with Wensum Street. It was realigned in the 15th century to permit the construction of St Andrew's & Blackfriars Halls (depicted earlier by David Jones), which were originally the home of the Dominican friars.

The lane acquired its name from the elm trees that had stood successively in the square since the first quarter of the 16th century when the churchwardens of St Peter Hungate planted the first one. Sadly, like most British elms, disease has since wiped them out. Very few buildings now standing in Elm Hill date from earlier than 1507, when a disastrous fire destroyed more than 700 houses in the city.

The north side of Elm Hill runs parallel with

the river Wensum, and in the past many of the merchant houses had their own quays. During the 15th and 16th centuries, Elm Hill and the river were important commercial thoroughfares. The river was the route from which raw materials were imported and finished products exported via Great Yarmouth.

However, with the gradual decline of Norwich as a centre of the weaving industry in the 19th century, Elm Hill lost its importance and slowly degenerated into a slum area. By 1926 the fine houses of the merchants were no more. The areas leading down to the river were instead scenes of poverty and squalor.

In 1927, the Norwich Society carried out a detailed survey and report on Elm Hill, forwarding this, with its recommendations, to the Norwich Corporation for its consideration. The report made it clear that, in spite of the appalling condition of the Elm Hill area, there still remained much of historic and architectural value. The Norwich Corporation wanted to demolish and build a swimming pool on the north side of the street but, at the last minute, was persuaded to adopt the ideas from the Norwich Society. Renovation work commenced in 1927. The Corporation purchased some of the properties, the slums were largely demolished and further purchases were made after the war. Today, Norwich City Council still owns most of the buildings.

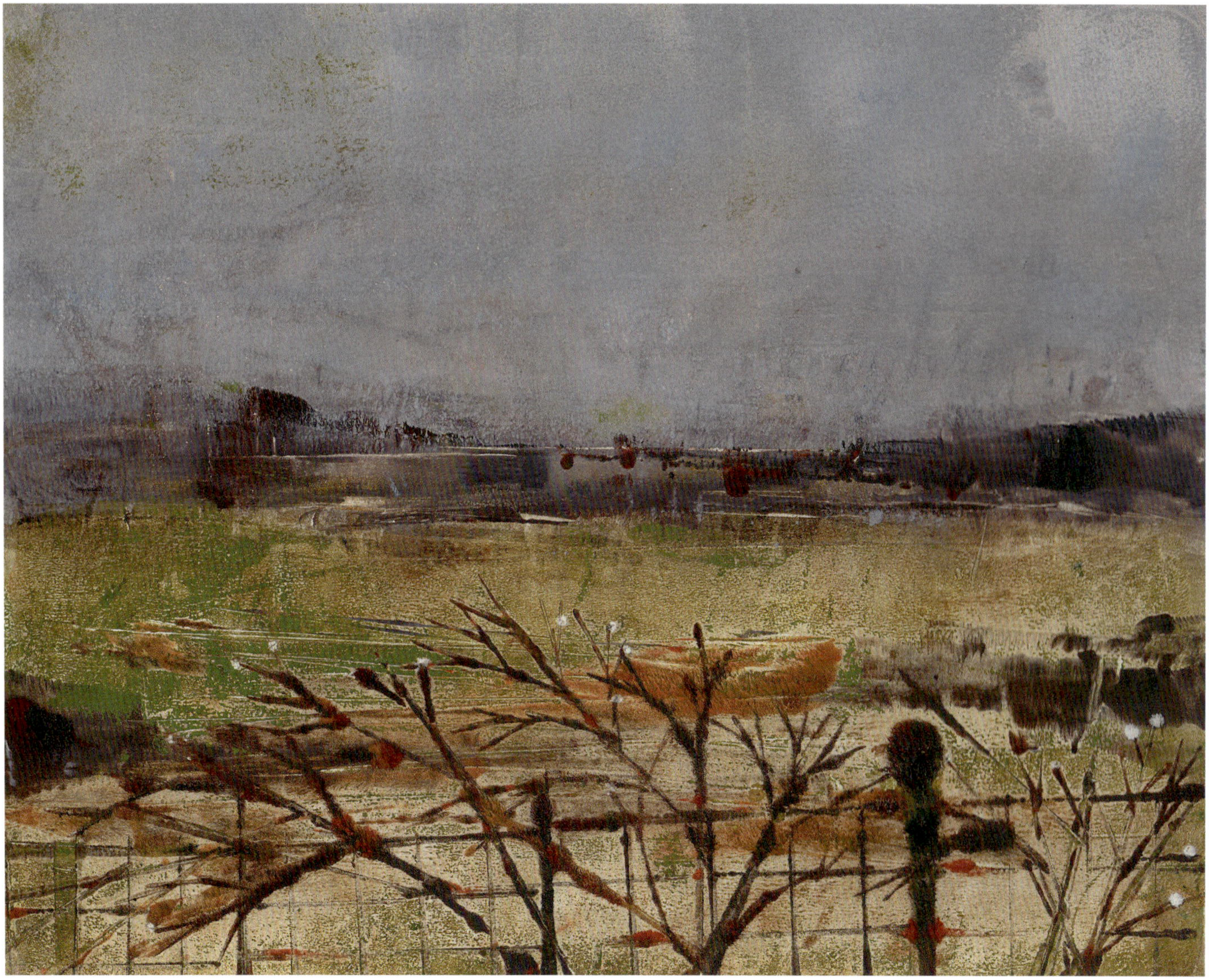

Reedham

Mention Reedham to most Norfolk residents and visitors and it will conjure up visions of the river and the small car ferry service that crosses it. However, Suffolk-based artist Chris Evans has chosen to focus on the village's railway junction.

His 2011 etching *Reedham Junction* (15cm x 20cm) shows the point at which the Norwich to Lowestoft and Norwich to Great Yarmouth via Berney Arms lines connect.

"I always find railways and trains of great interest. In this print I liked the way the track disappears through the dominant shape of the bridge – also the quaintness of the signal box and the random pile of sleepers."

The post-1885 Great Eastern design signal box is much admired by railway enthusiasts. The junction itself dates back to 1904.

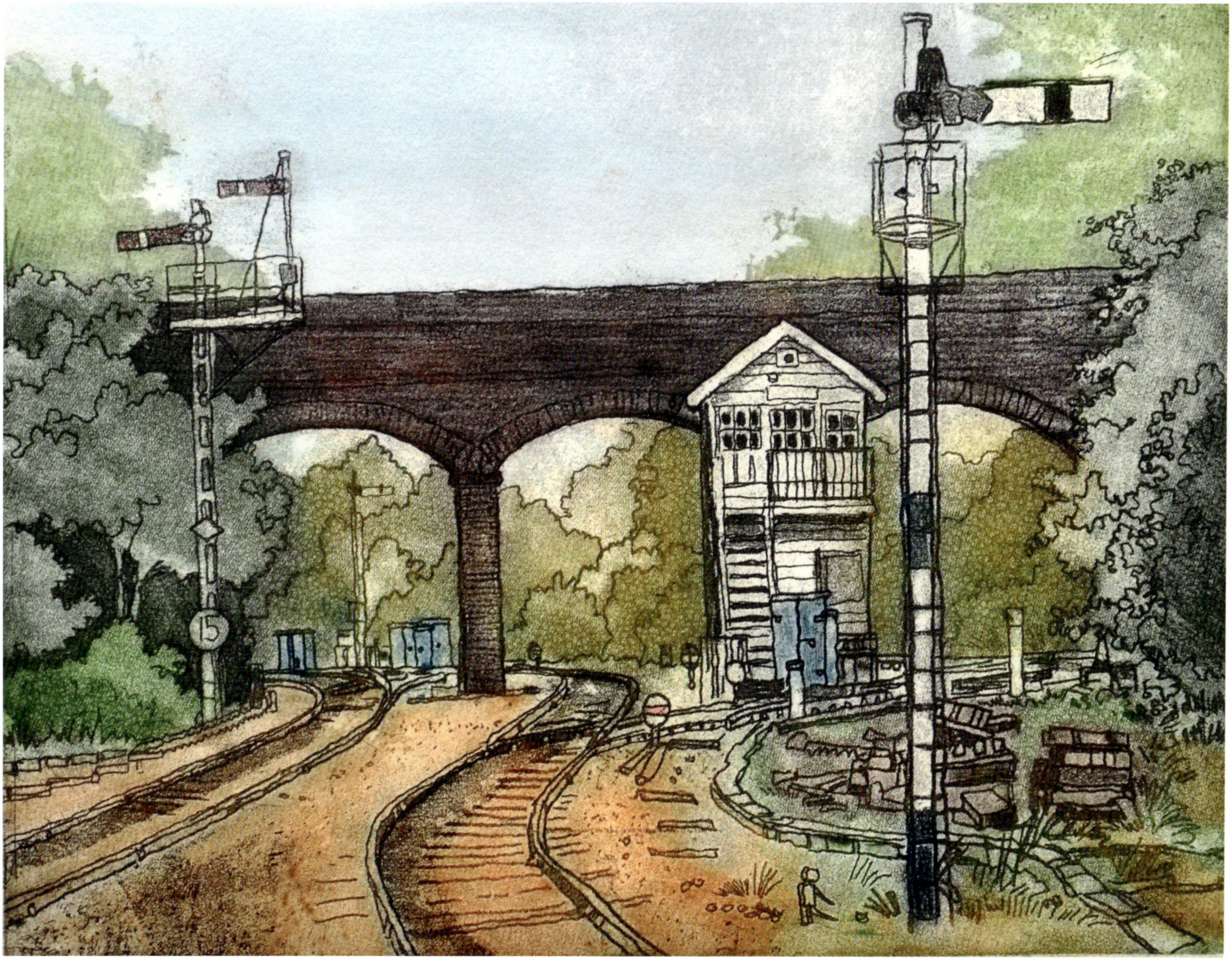

Salthouse

The name of this popular north Norfolk coastal village comes from the once valuable commodity of salt, from which the word 'salary' is derived. The Domesday Book of 1086 describes it as a 'house for the storing of salt'. Salthouse is now famed for its unspoilt beauty and the thousands of birds attracted to the marshes. Some 66 hectares of coastal grazing marsh and salt-rich lagoons are managed as a nature reserve by the Norfolk Wildlife Trust.

Lying between Walsey Hills and Kelling Hard, the marshes are of international importance for wildlife, particularly birds. Glynn Thomas here manages to fit in a few familiar species such as avocet, curlew and oystercatcher, as well as passing geese forming a skein in the far left of his etching, entitled *Salthouse* (42cm x 13cm, edition of 200) from 2003.

St Nicholas Church looms large in Glynn's print. It is a handsome example of late Perpendicular style, having been rebuilt by Sir Henry Heydon in the late 15th century. The west tower is from the earlier church, traces of which can be seen to the north, and has bell openings. The interior is full of light – with tall, narrow aisles and windows (including an

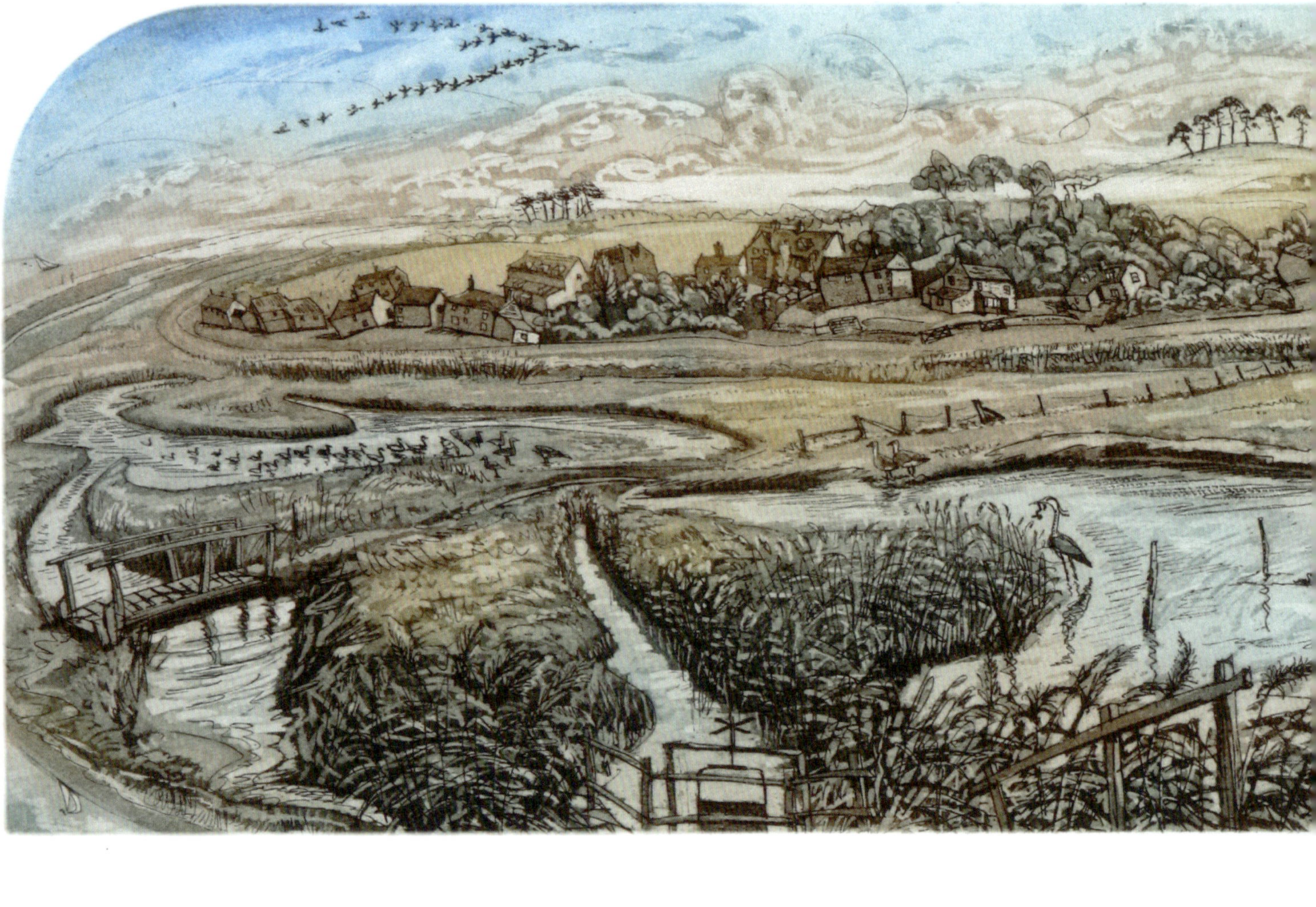

enormous east window). Most of the tiled floor is original.

The well-preserved 15th-century carved octagonal font has evangelist and passion symbols on its faces and smiling lions at the angles. The remains of a repositioned screen has painted saints; and, on the rear, graffiti of ships, which can also be seen on the choir stalls. In the graveyard outside, a ruined chapel was excavated in the 1930s.

The church has become a popular venue for art exhibitions. Its elevated position makes it far safer from flooding than most low-lying parts of the village. North Norfolk's storm surges have done plenty of damage to Salthouse over the years, and the village remains at risk from the infrequent but threatening combination of high tides and strong winds.

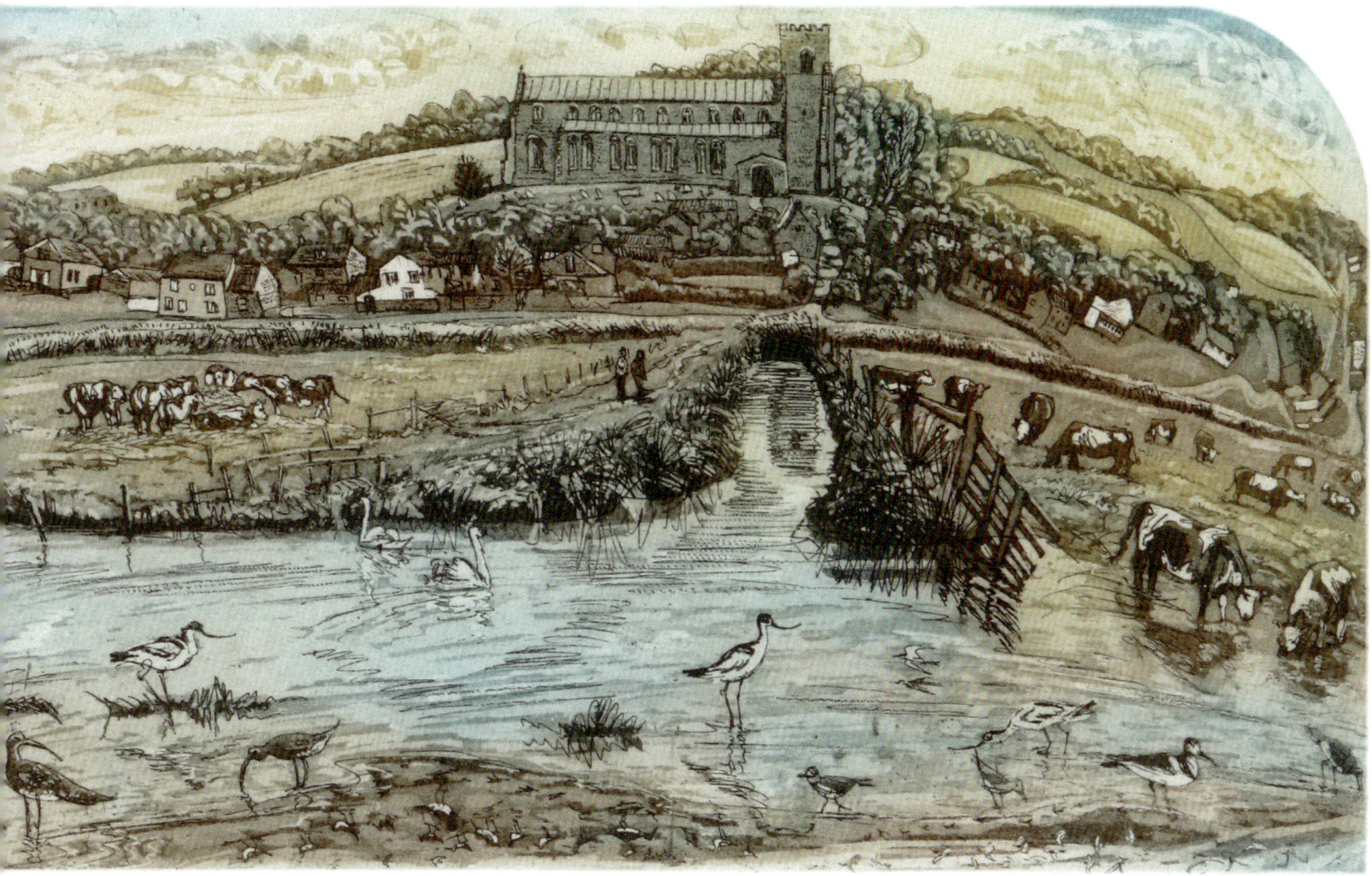

Sheringham

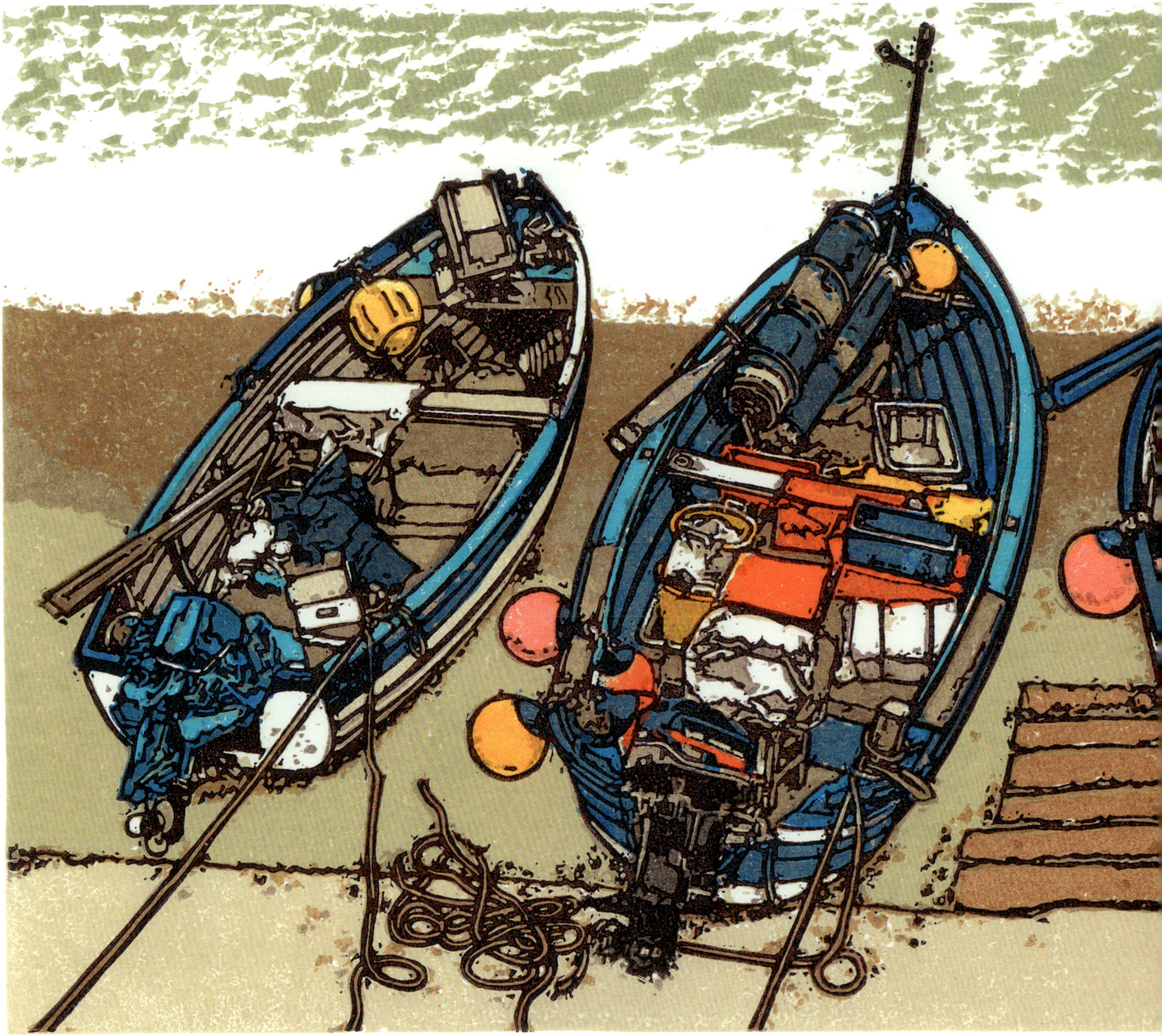

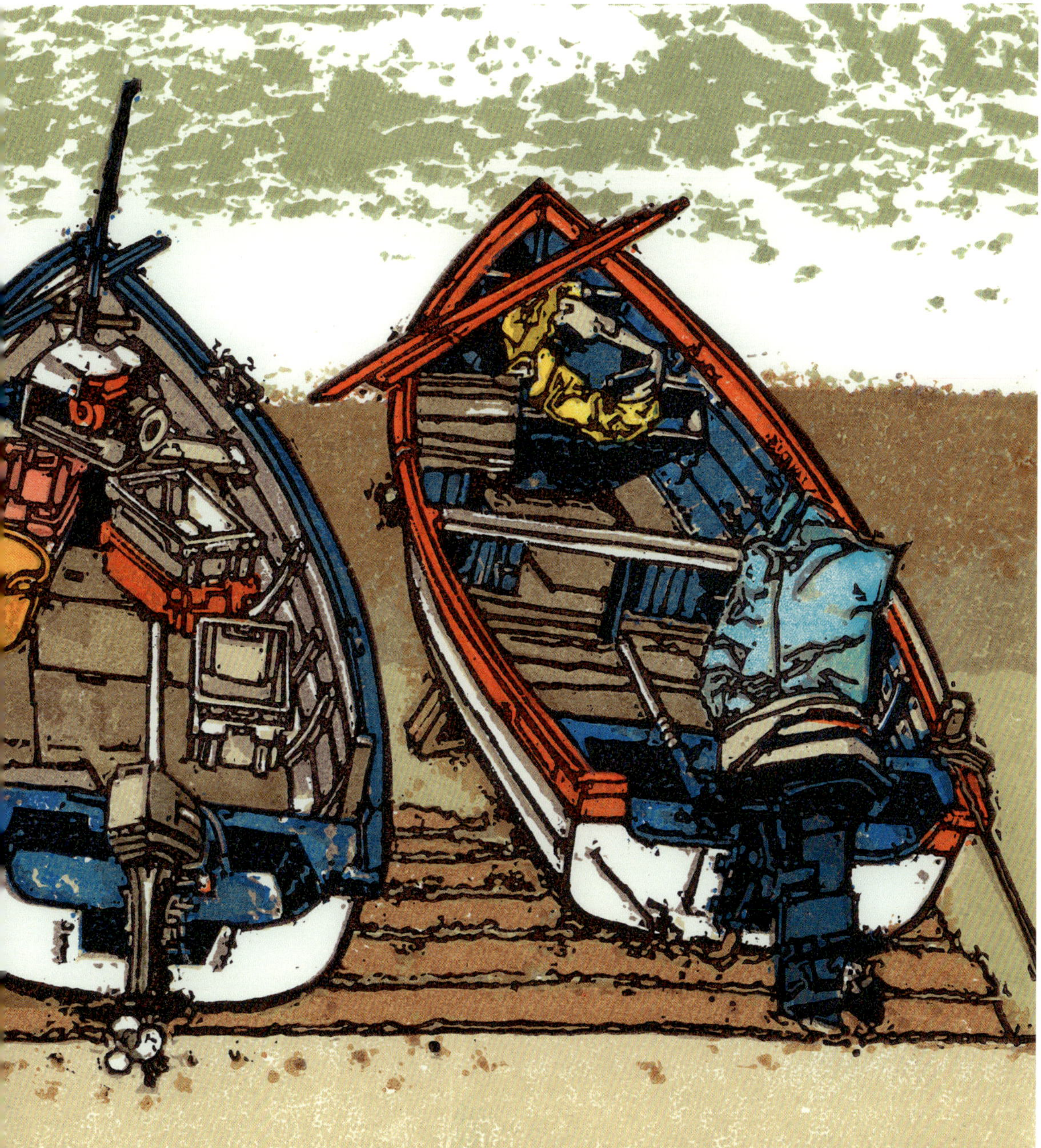

HJ Jackson – On the Foreshore (linocut, 2016)

Norfolk printmaker HJ Jackson's linocut print *High Tide,* below, is a print from 2013 of an earlier Sheringham fishing scene. It captures the few remaining commercial fishing boats beached in front of the town, waiting to be launched in their daily quest to bring crab and lobster to the local restaurants and shops. The artist has made a career out of fishing boats, packing his images with the streaks of discolouration, rust, worn paint and the frayed rope ends that are entirely representative of the elderly fleet of traditional vessels.

The newest of Jackson's Sheringham offerings is reproduced on the opening spread of this section, in the form of the 2016 linocut print *On the Foreshore*. His third contribution appears on page 140. *Boats and Cottages* is a linocut of far earlier vintage, dating back to 1971 and demonstrating perhaps the subtle changes in the artist's colour palette and technique.

Sheringham does not qualify as a fishing port. The handful of boats adds charm to the north Norfolk seaside town that nowadays owes its living to tourism and steam trains, plus the nearby National Trust property Sheringham Park. The latter is seen below in an aquatint etching (*The Path, Sheringham Park I*) by fellow Norfolk artist Colin Bygrave, who demonstrates further his technique and love of the park's trees and paths overleaf with *The Path Under the Snow, Sheringham Park*; *Sunlit Tree, Sheringham Park*; and *The Path, Sheringham Park* – all aquatint etchings.

After the Rain (10cm x 11cm), a 2012 drypoint by Norwich artist Sarah Bays (far

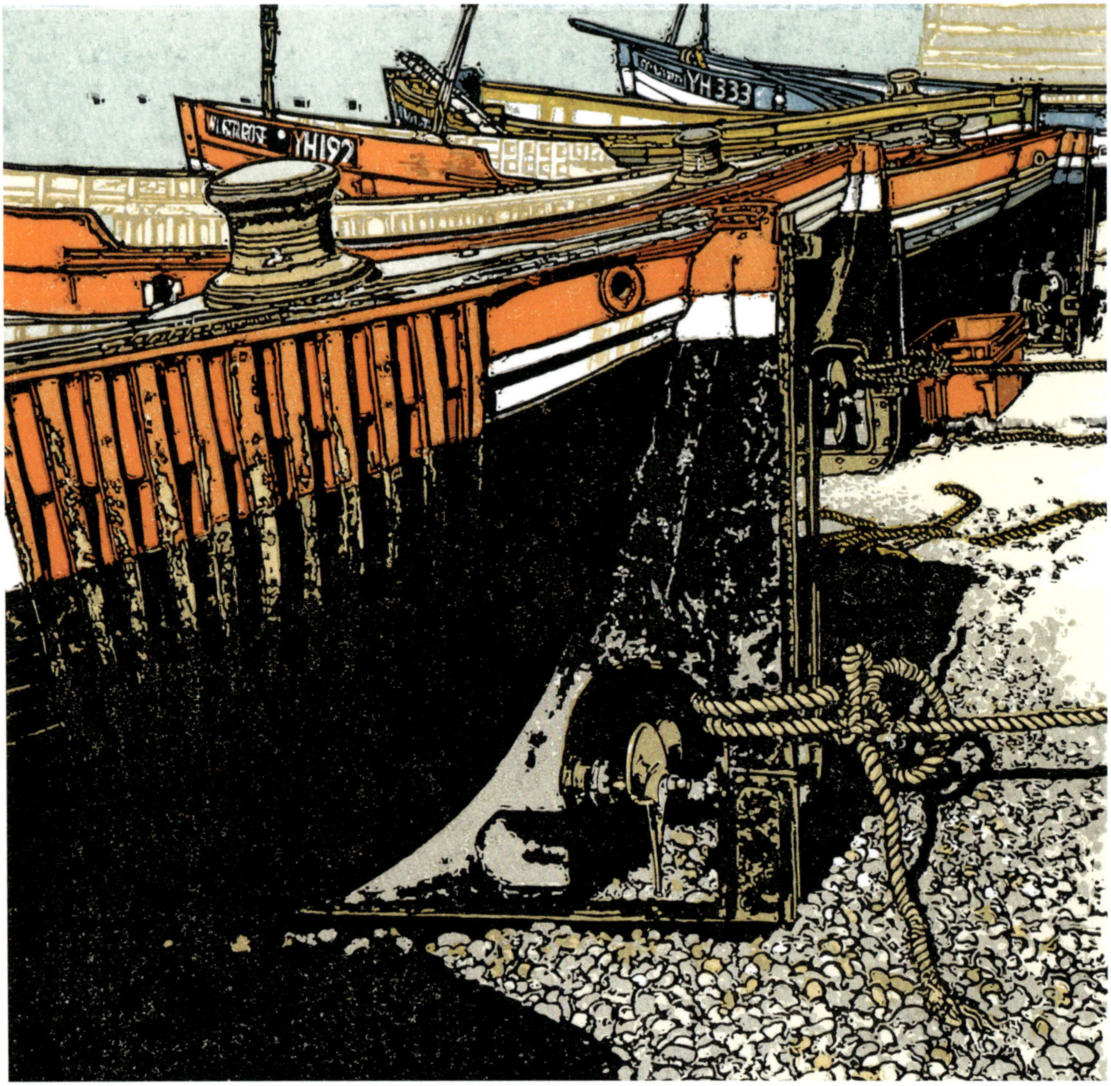

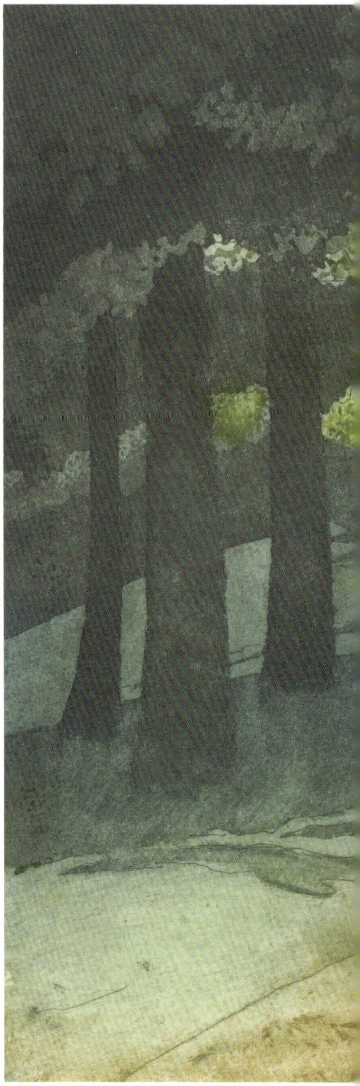

right, top) was inspired by the sun breaking through the clouds and the sunlight reflected in the puddles left by a sudden torrential downpour. "The figure is my husband looking longingly out to sea, dreaming of fishing no doubt," adds Sarah.

Sheringham Shoal, a Jeremy James linocut of Red-throated Divers (bottom right) shows the striking birds against a backdrop of the Sheringham Shoal offshore wind farm that has now altered the view from the town out to sea.

Historically, the parish of Sheringham comprised the two villages of Upper Sheringham, a farming community, and Lower Sheringham, which combined farming with fishing. The fishing industry was at its peak in the late 19th and early 20th centuries, as the arrival of the railways made it possible for fish to be transported more efficiently to market. Today, from a peak of perhaps 200 vessels, Sheringham has eight boats – each operated by just one man.

The current town of Sheringham was once Lower Sheringham, a fishing station for the main village. It developed as a railway town with the coming of the Midland and Great Northern Joint Railway line in the late 19th century. The railway is still operational, but as a specialist moving museum rather than as a commercial service. Steam and veteran diesel engines pull restored carriages up the line via Weybourne to the outskirts of Holt. The hugely popular recreational line has been linked across the town's main road to the existing Cromer to Norwich branch line, allowing excursion trains to travel farther in Norfolk.

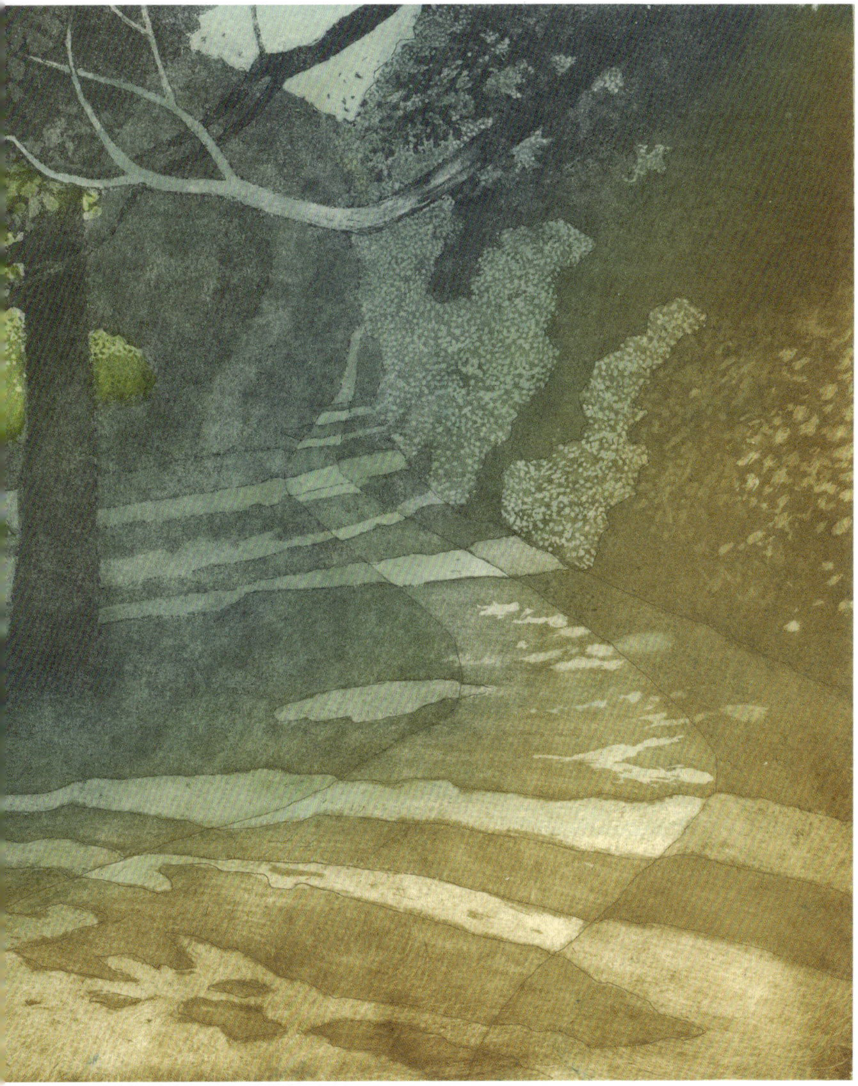

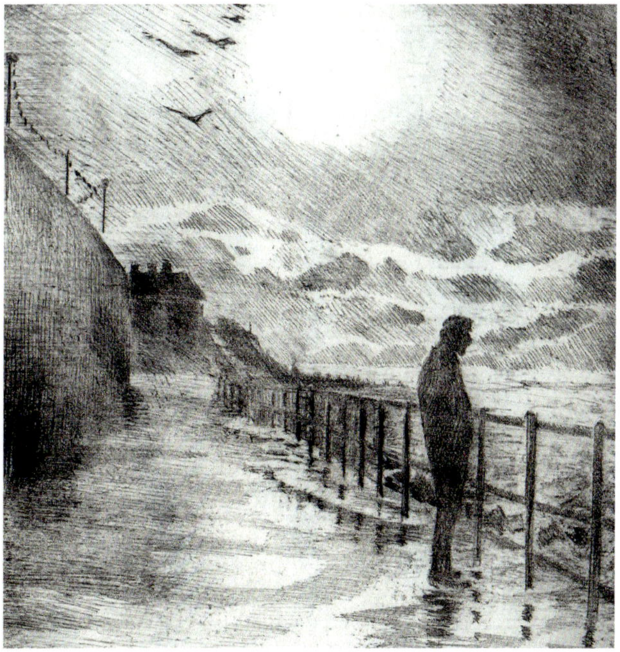

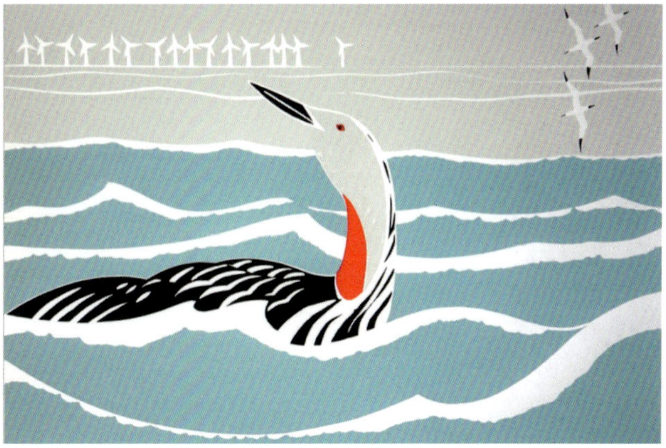

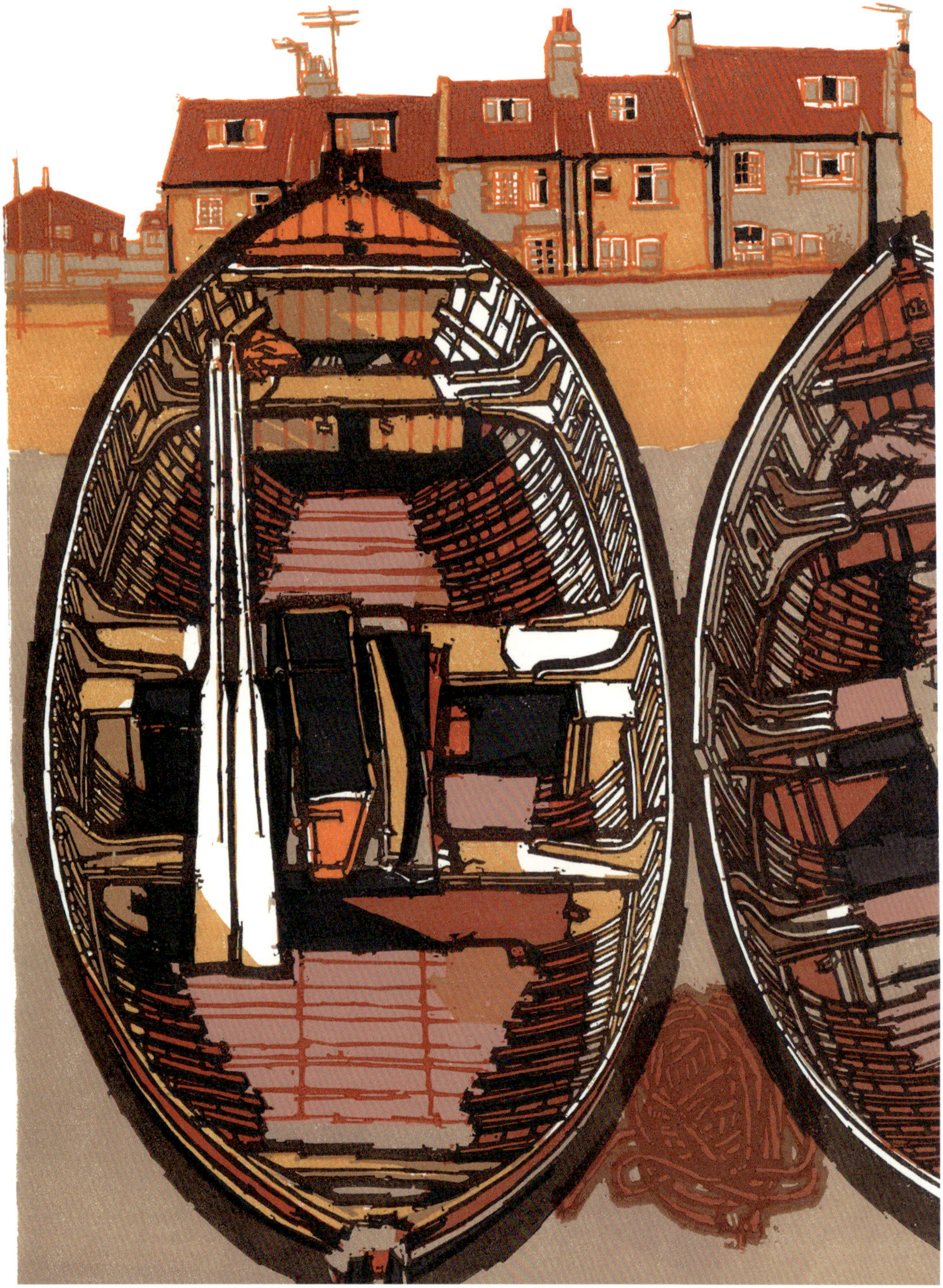

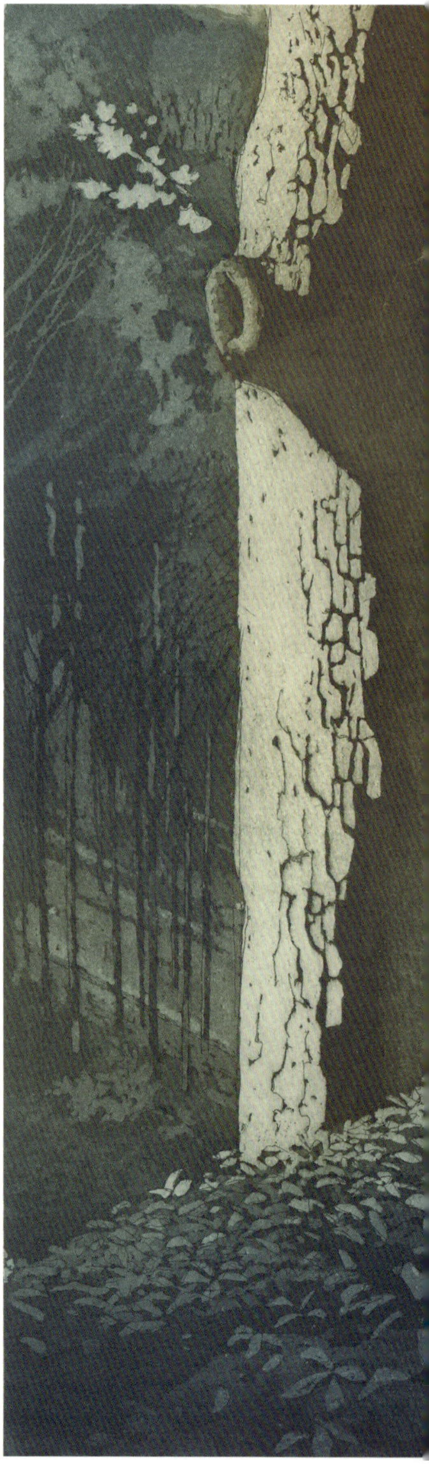

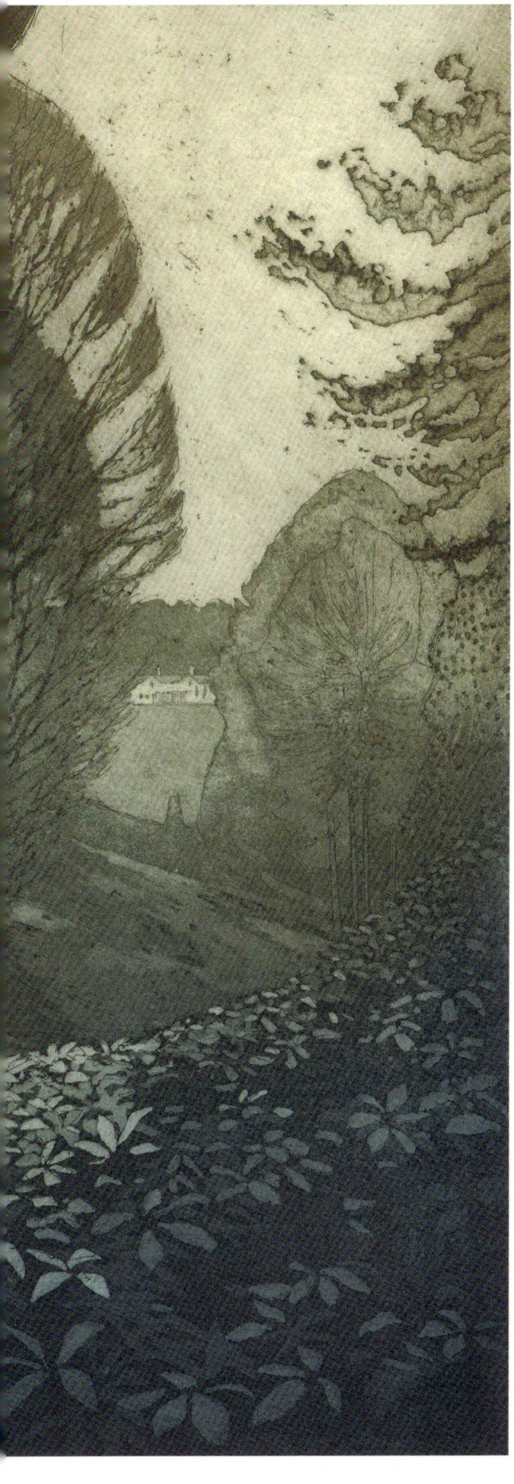

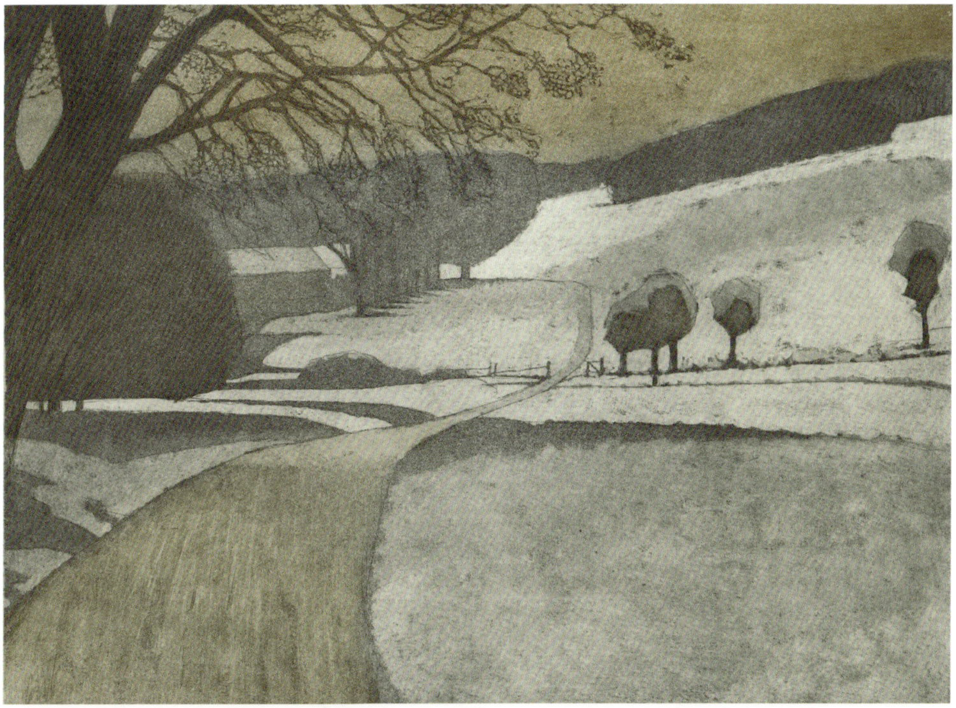

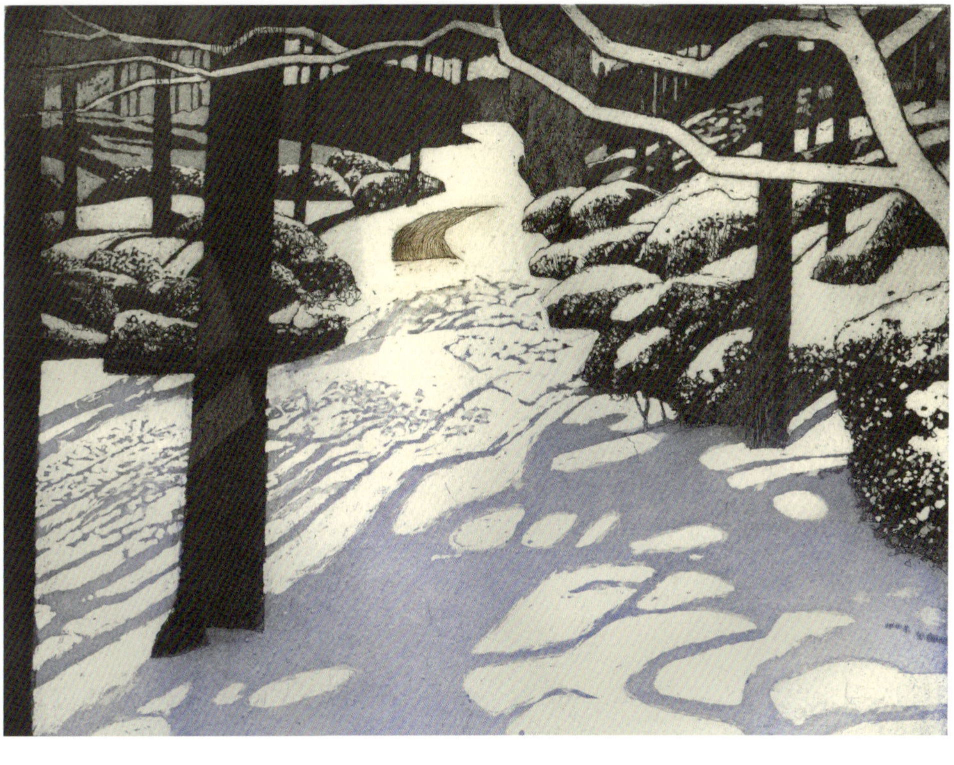

Stiffkey

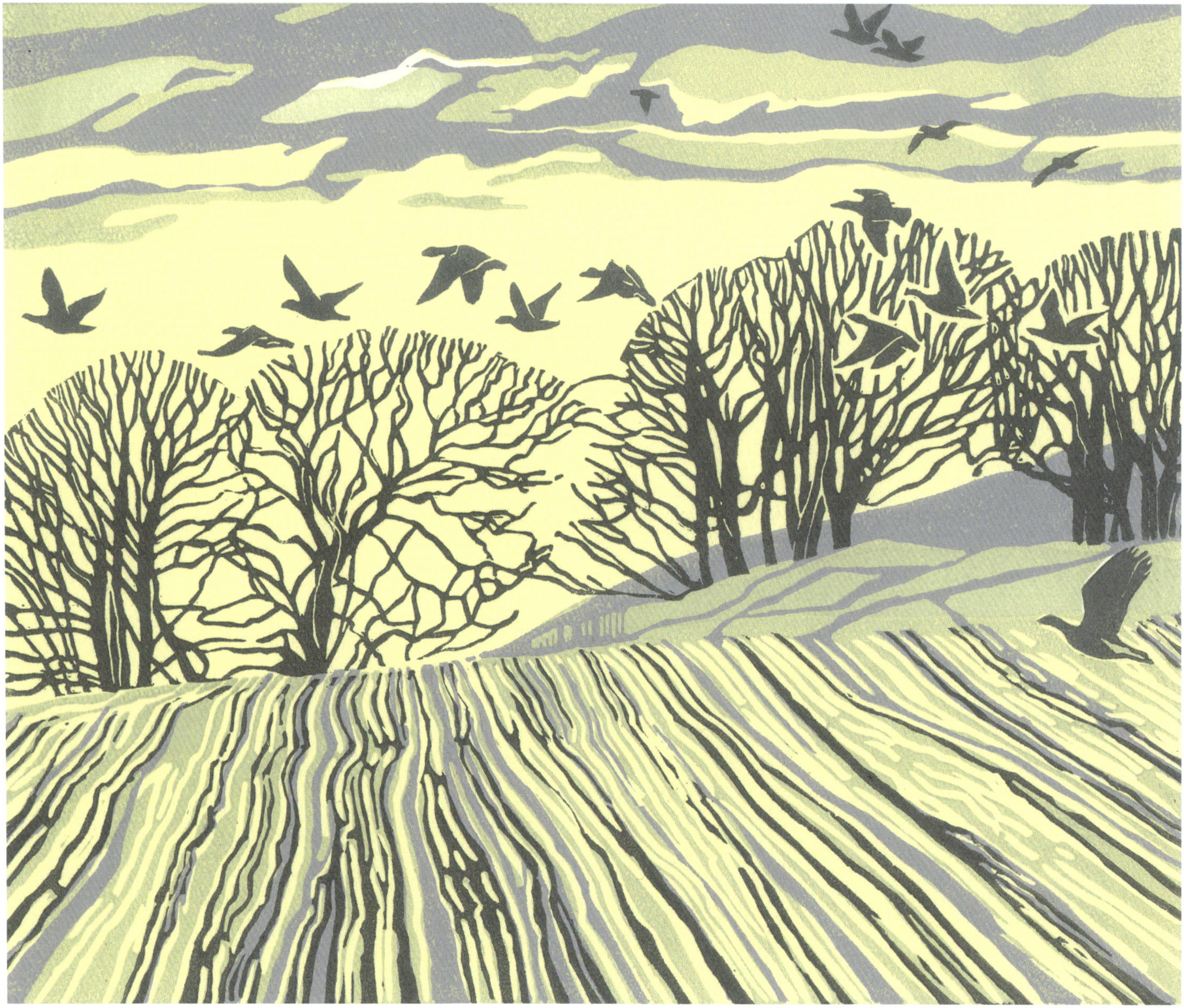

Stiffkey shares its name with the narrow Norfolk river that runs through it, and is one of a scattering of small coastal villages along the north coast between Blakeney and Wells. It is the scene for wildlife artist Max Angus's linocut *Pinkfeet Cinder Sky* on the left, which blends her interest in landscape with her love of birds and mammals.

Max's description of the area reveals her powers of observation. "The main north Norfolk coastal road passes through the centre of Stiffkey. Many of the old flint cottages lining the road have turned their backs to the traffic. Driving through can be challenging. Keeping eyes on the oncoming traffic detracts from the hidden charm of the village. Staying in the village is very different.

"The landscape around the village is breathtaking. On the coastal side, there is a footpath following the edge of the saltmarsh to Wells. On the right, the footpath meanders to Morston and on to Blakeney. Inland from the coastal path, Stiffkey has spectacular rolling countryside.

"On winter mornings, the Pinkfoot Geese fly high over the village in their distinctive skeins. They travel from their overnight roost to their daytime sugar beet fields. They return before dark. During the day, the geese will fly in small groups looking for new opportunities and inspecting the fields."

The 2016 print on the right is by Annette Sykes. *Crabbing at Stiffkey* (40cm x 30cm) brings back memories for the artist of her grandchildren fishing for crabs on the bridge. Annette sketched them happy with their twine and bait, converting the result directly to lino with her cutting tools. She added carborundum and dribbled PVA glue "to give the impression of sand and mud".

The river powered the 16th-century Stiffkey watermill until 1881, when it was auctioned as a warehouse. Only a few low ruined walls remain.

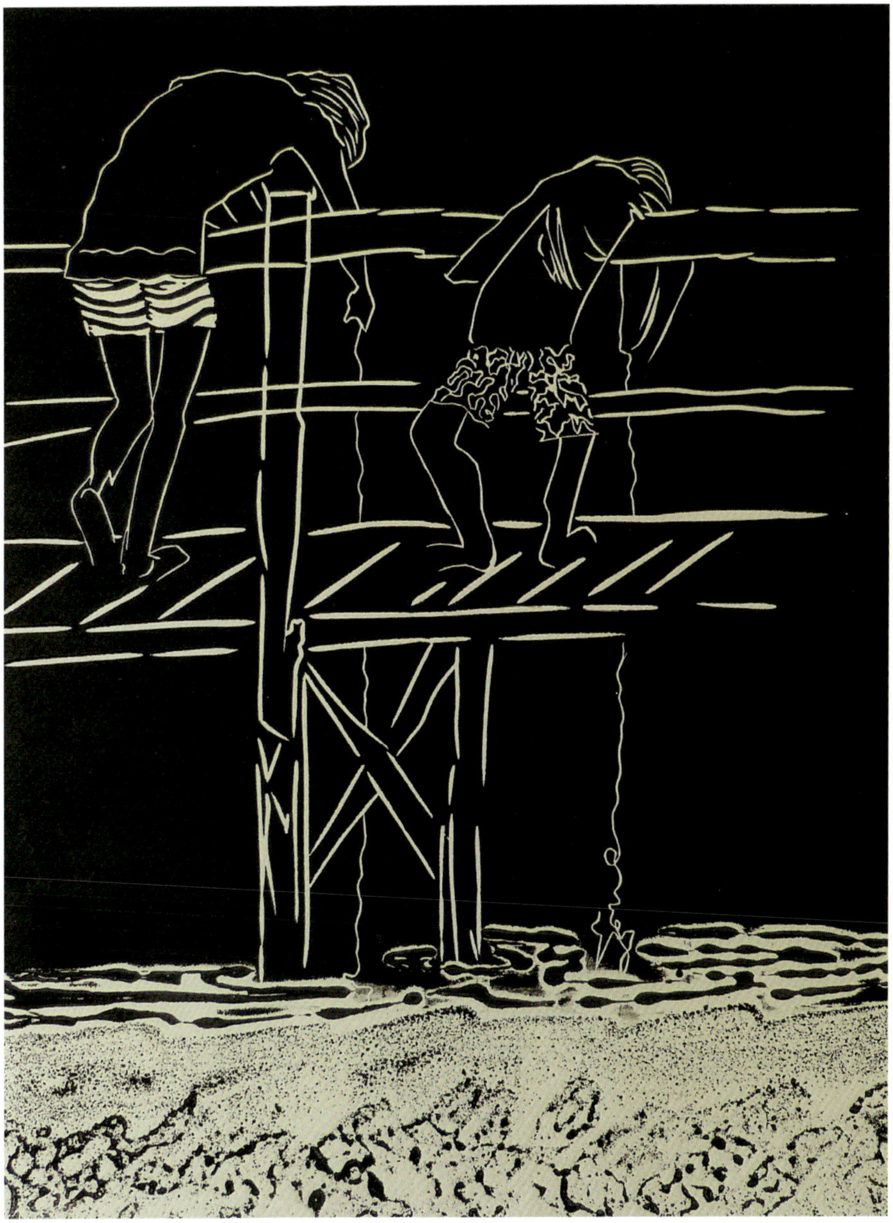

Thornham

Kate Heiss provides us with two linocut prints inspired by the Norfolk village of Thornham, just inland from the coast in prime birdwatching country. *Goldcrests at Thornham* (30cm x 20.5cm, 2015) is a 5-block print in an edition of eight.

"I spotted the Goldcrests high in the trees while walking through the pines at Holme Dunes nature reserve. I was following the coastal path to Thornham harbour. It is a beautiful walk where you meander through the dunes and the tidal creeks that nestle beside the beds of sea lavender and reeds. The print

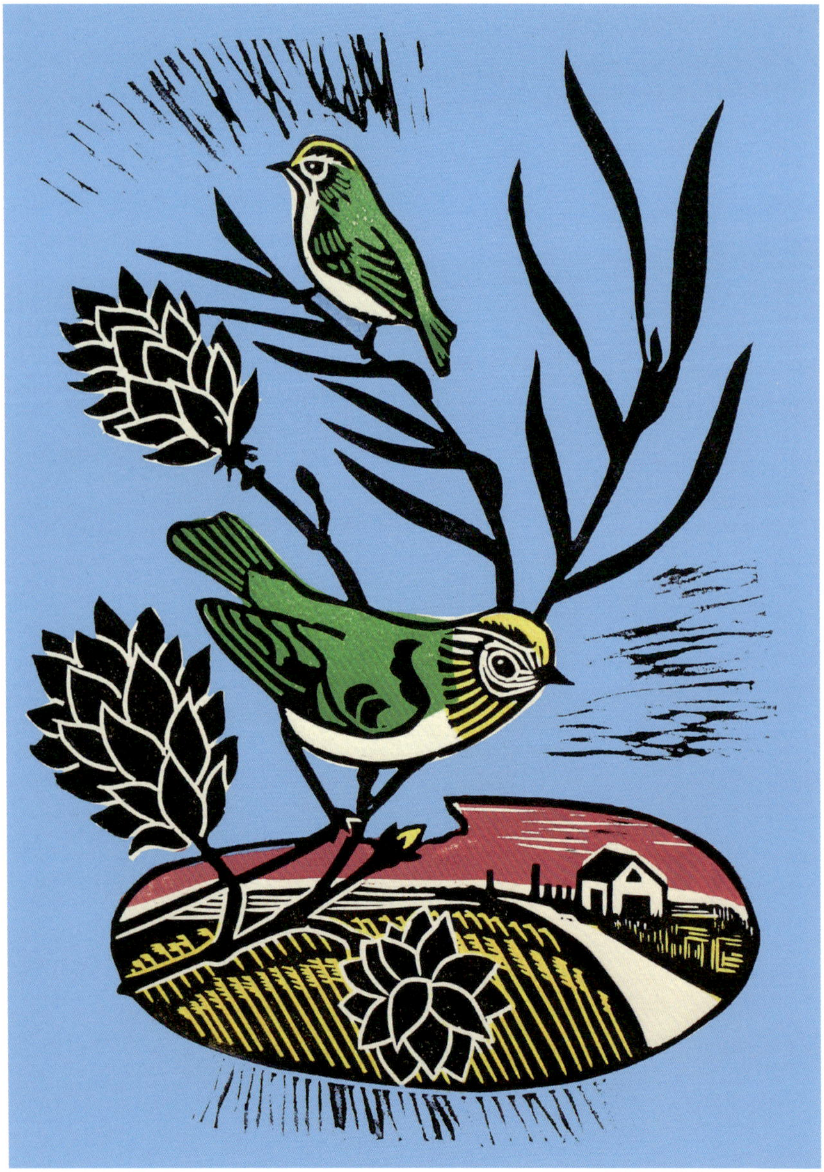

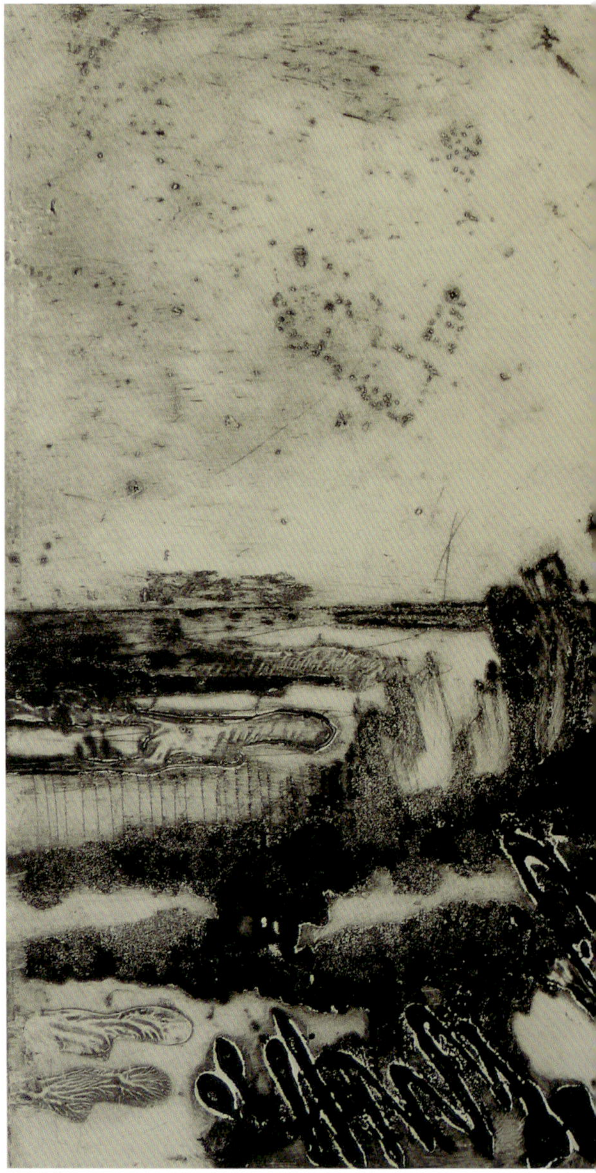

juxtaposes the birds against the evocative landscape of Thornham harbour featuring the coal barn and the reed beds.

Her second image on the right is *Birdwatchers* – a monoprint (45cm x 40cm) formed from stencilled screen-printed colours with black linocut. "Birdwatchers were gathering on top of the bank at Thornham harbour. It was dusk, and the sun silhouetted their bodies. In front of me an oystercatcher was hopping around the muddy creek."

In the centre, from Annette Sykes, is a 30cm x 30cm print entitled *Thornham Marshes* from 2016. It is from an edition of just seven, and the printmaking process is drypoint on aluminium with added carborundum for texture.

The village of Thornham is around 7km north-east of Hunstanton; the parish includes Titchwell, site of a major RSPB reserve. From the small harbour it is possible to walk alongside the sea and saltmarsh to Holme Dunes.

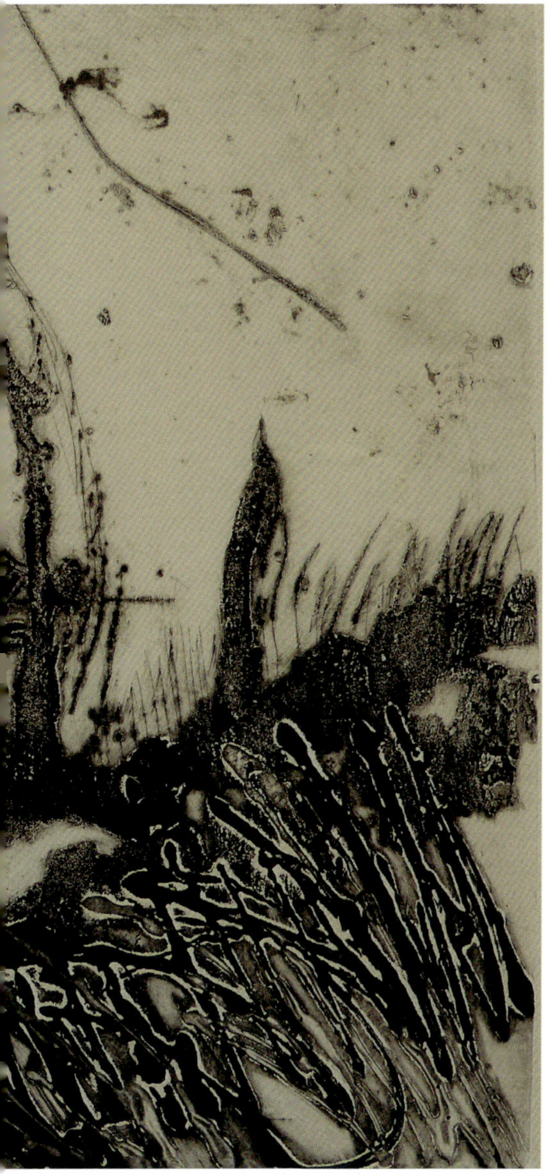

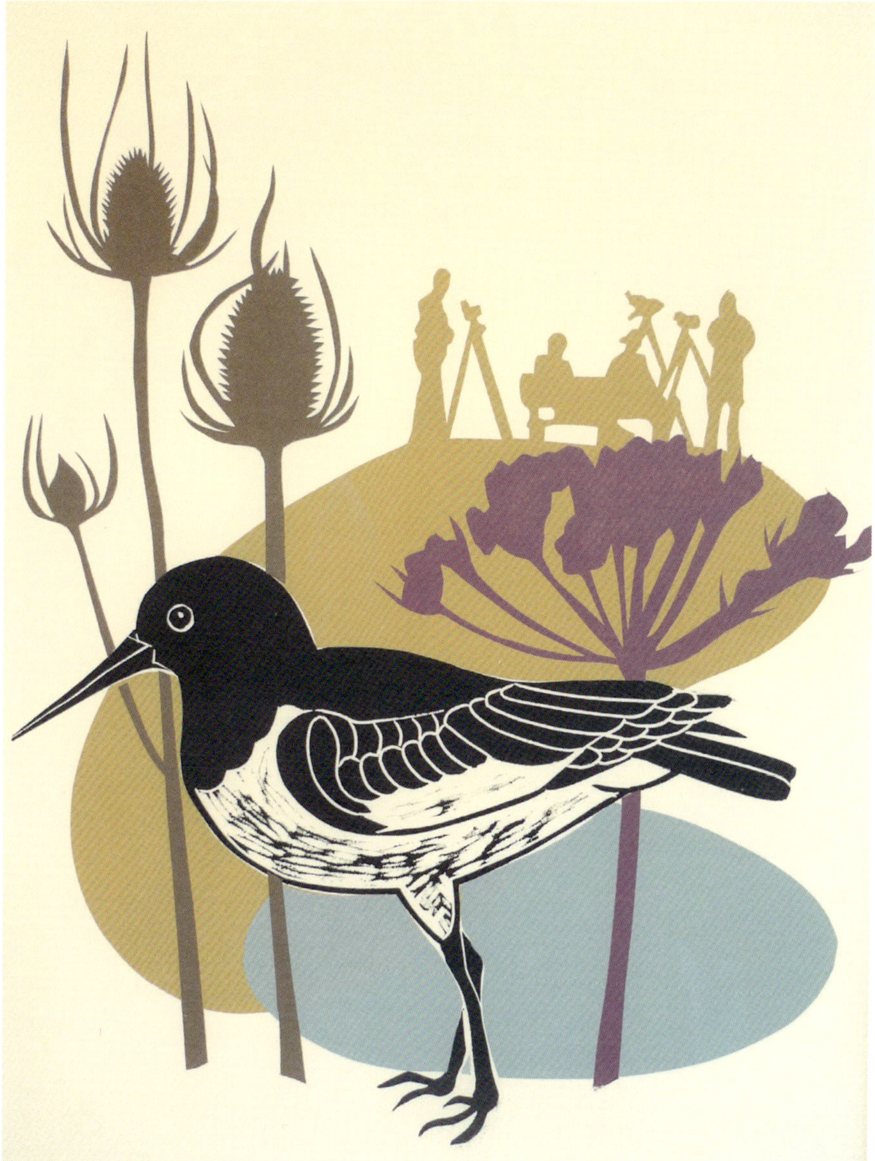

Titchwell

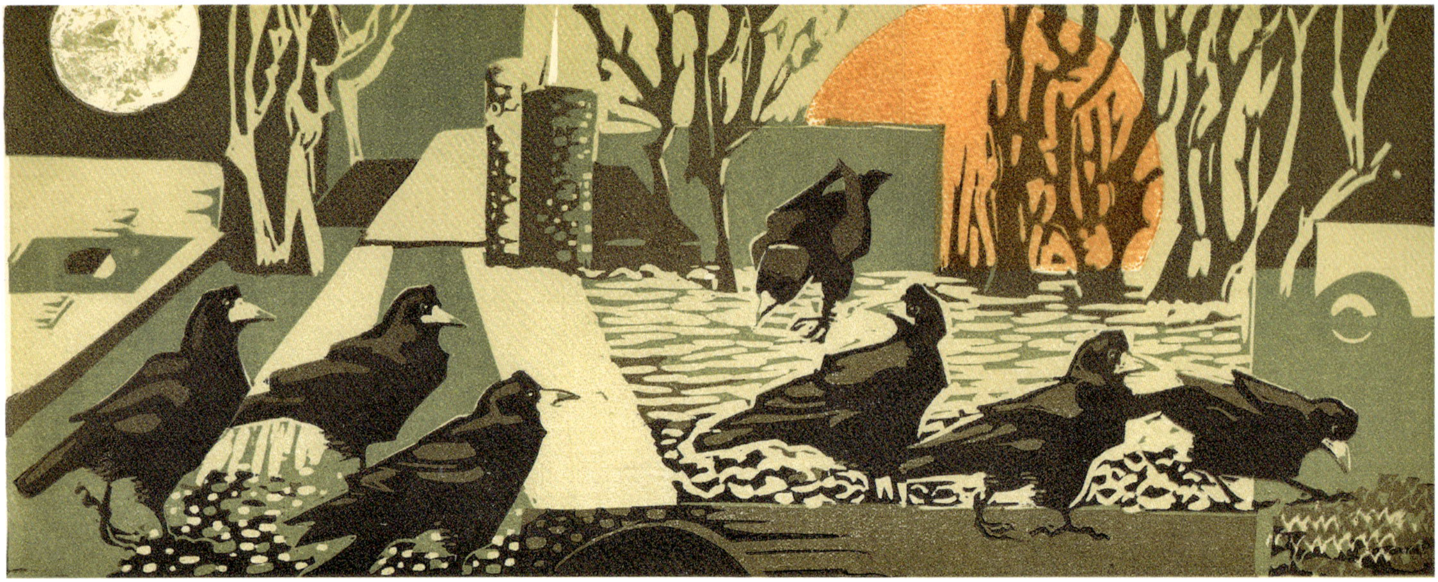

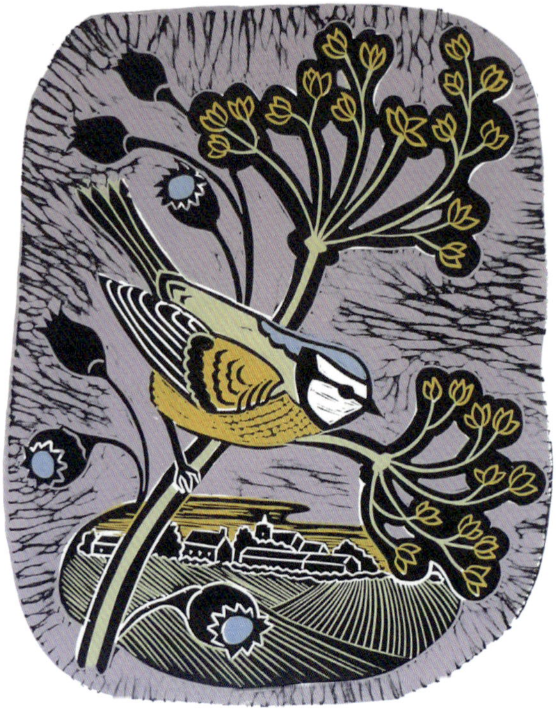

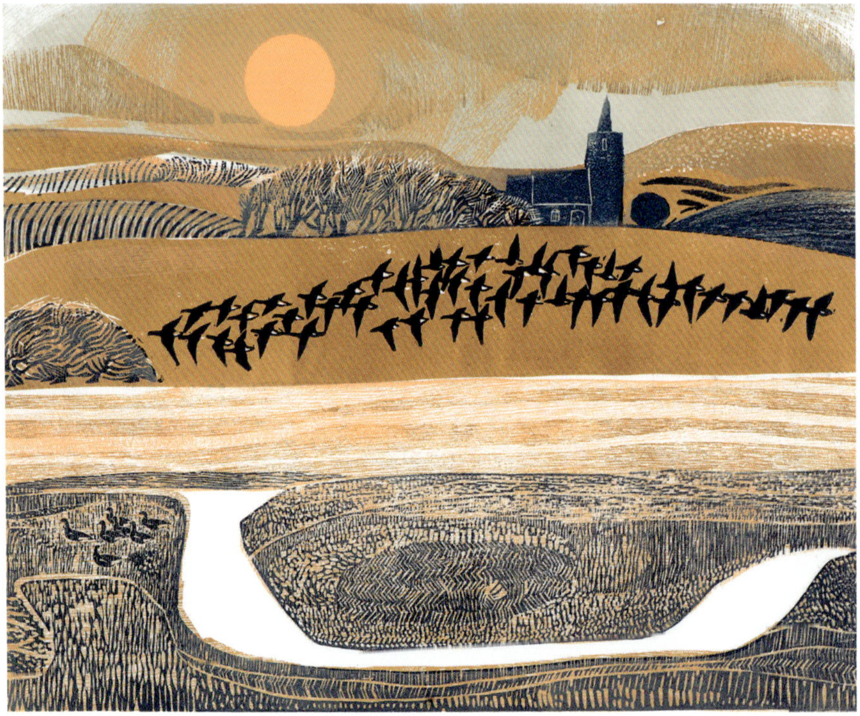

Thelma Sykes provided the image on the top left named *Flintstone and Furrow* of rooks in Norfolk, foraging near Titchwell on the north coast. It is a multiple-reduction block linocut (13cm x 33cm) from 2003 and from an edition of just 14.

"Moon and sun together in the sky: it is evocative yet disturbing, it fractures the sequence, changes perspective. Similarly, I skewed elements of this north Norfolk landscape to search for the rhythms of the place and to try to unravel what draws me back at different seasons.

"There is ice in the furrows: the salt-scarred trees look wintry now, but their skeletons spring no leaf and they will echo winter all summer through. Flints gleam from dark earth and from the church tower as if the building, by geological right, becomes part of the natural history.

"I want to celebrate rooks alongside elements seeped into me from this landscape: the ice-filled furrows, the enormous sun rising alongside a relic moon from dawn walks along Thornham's sea wall. My landscape is formed of geometric blocks punctuated by the trees where cormorants, and now egrets, roost at Titchwell with its church beyond."

Kate Heiss combines wildlife, vegetation and landscape in two Titchwell prints here. Far left is *Titchwell Village*, a linocut edition of just five prints (26cm x 21cm) from 2015, made using five blocks and printed with caligo inks.

"I made this print after we walked along the coastal path between Thornham and Brancaster. The path here moves inland, giving fantastic elevated views down across the fields and marshes to the sea. It was autumn so all the hedgerows were full of seed heads; and the fields, recently ploughed, were a patchwork of patterns."

Kate's print on the right, *Geese Over the Marsh*, is another 2015 linocut, this time just two blocks (20cm x 20cm). "One of my favourite things about Norfolk is seeing and hearing the geese flying in over the marshes during the autumn and winter months. The geese in this print were flying in over Titchwell nature reserve. In the foreground I have featured two wild flowers that I think epitomise Norfolk coastal waysides, a marsh thistle and an Alexanders seed head."

Sticking with the wildlife theme, Robert Greenhalf is the provider of the print to the right of Kate's Blue Tit. The Sussex-based artist explains that this 1974 four-block linocut and woodcut (*Brents*, 30cm x 39cm) is a remembered view inspired by a visit to Titchwell before the RSPB took over adjoining land to become an internationally renowned nature reserve. Plywood was used for some of the blocks to give a grain effect.

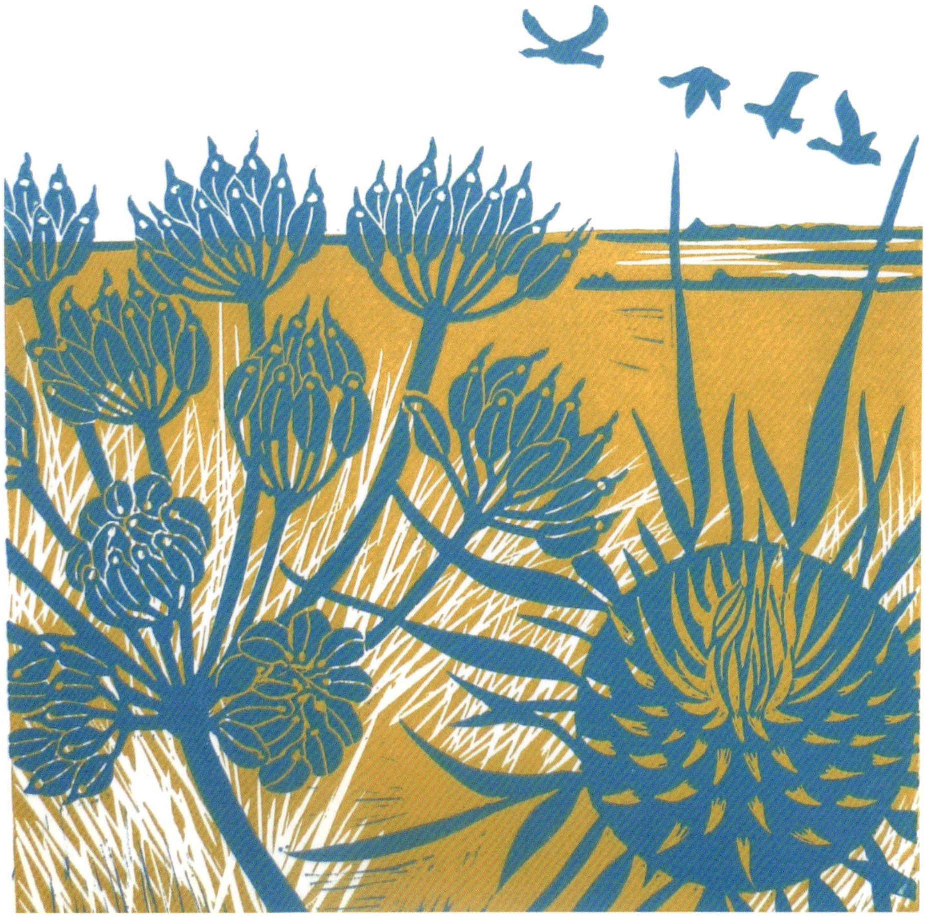

Walcott

Neil Bousfield lives close to the north-east coast of Norfolk, and is more familiar than most with the endangered landscape around Happisburgh and Walcott. The uneasy relationship between these communities and their environment is a theme explored in his printmaking, with thought-provoking wood engravings depicting this area and, more recently, the Broads.

Walcott, which lies 19km south-east of Cromer, is in places only a few feet from the North Sea as the village is the only point where the B1159 coast road actually runs along the water's edge – making it a key spot for storm watchers and the reckless or suicidal.

On the night of 31 January 1953, a combination of a high spring tide and a severe wind storm caused a storm tide that partly

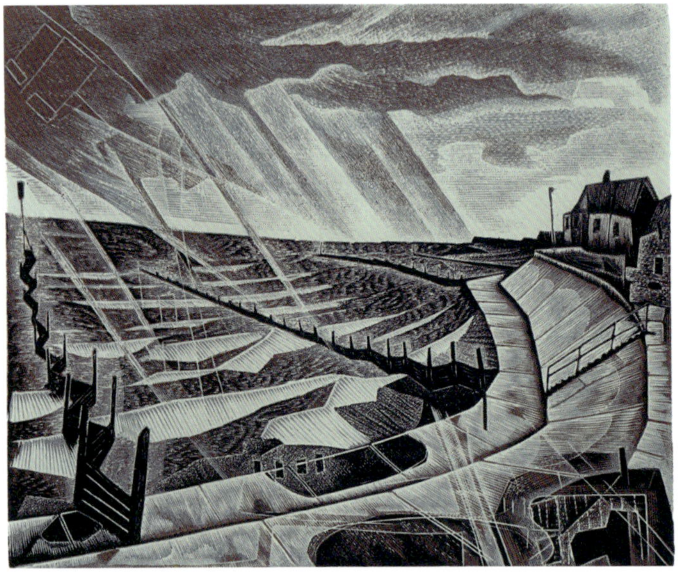

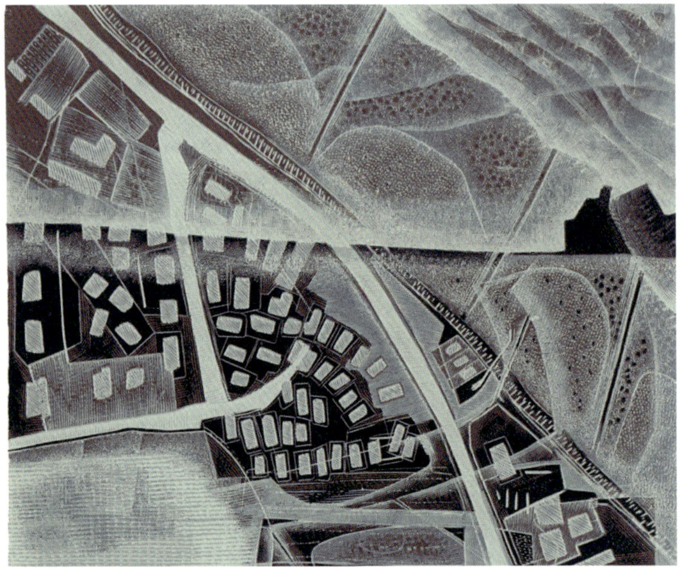

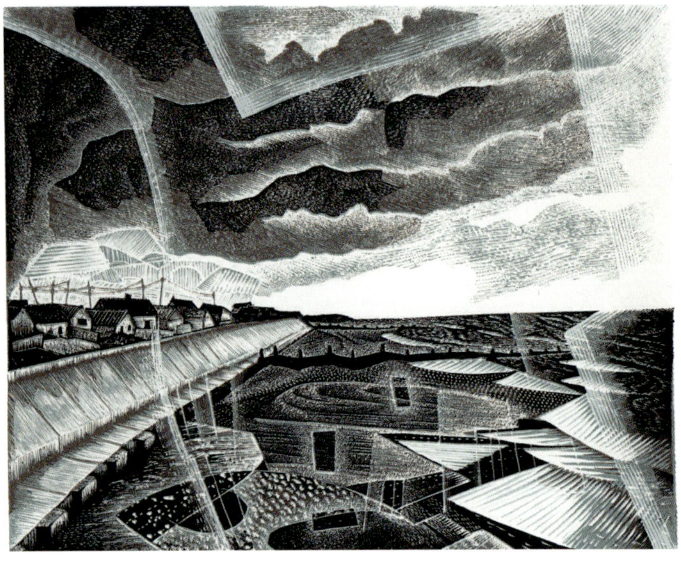

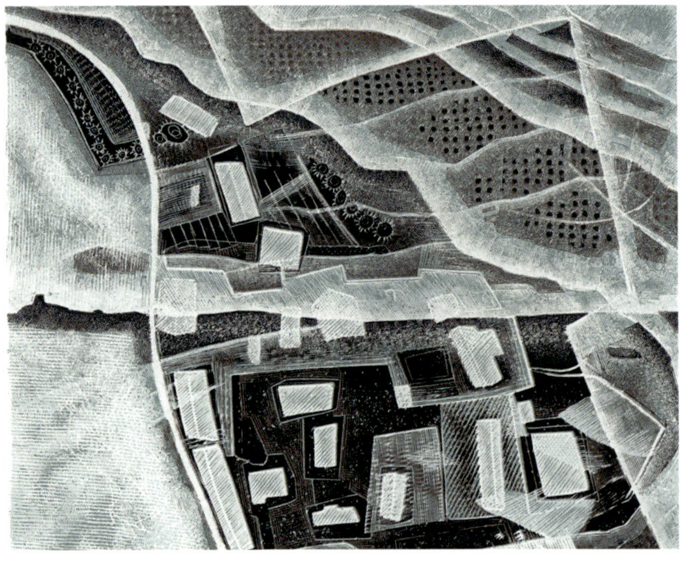

devoured Walcott and neighbouring Keswick.

November 2007 saw another damaging surge that breached the sea wall, and homes and businesses were again badly damaged by the marauding wind and sea in December 2013.

The prints shown here, completed in March 2017, began a mapping and recording process that explores the notion of place and the narratives that make it. Entitled (clockwise from top left) *Walcott – Sea Rising*, *Walcott – Land and Sea*, *Walcott – Fragile Coast* and *Walcott – Vanishing Land*, they are all 10cm x 26cm wood engravings in editions of 50.

Neil is a member of the Society of Wood Engravers, and a number of his imaginative and highly original prints have won prizes and the admiration of his peers.

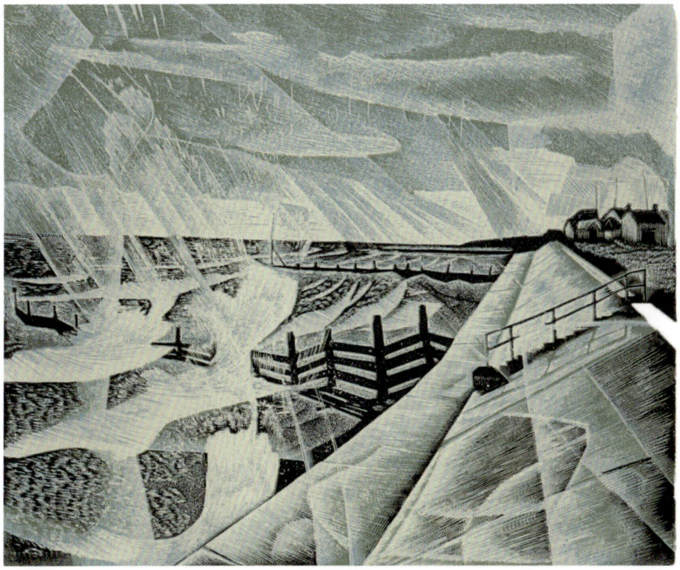

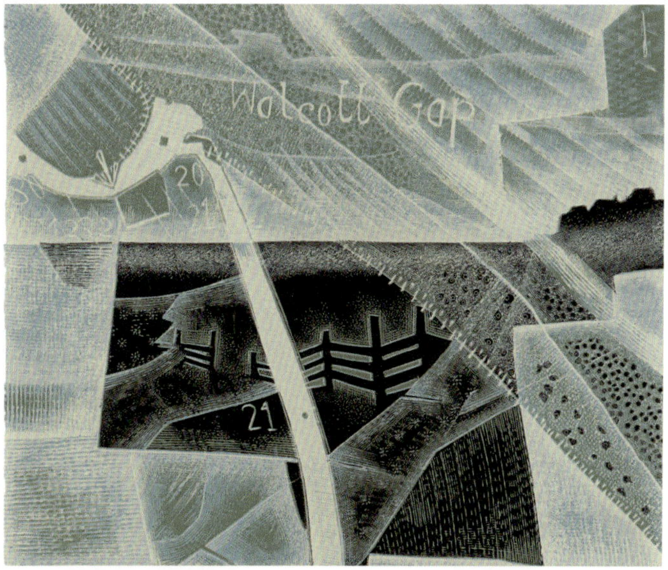

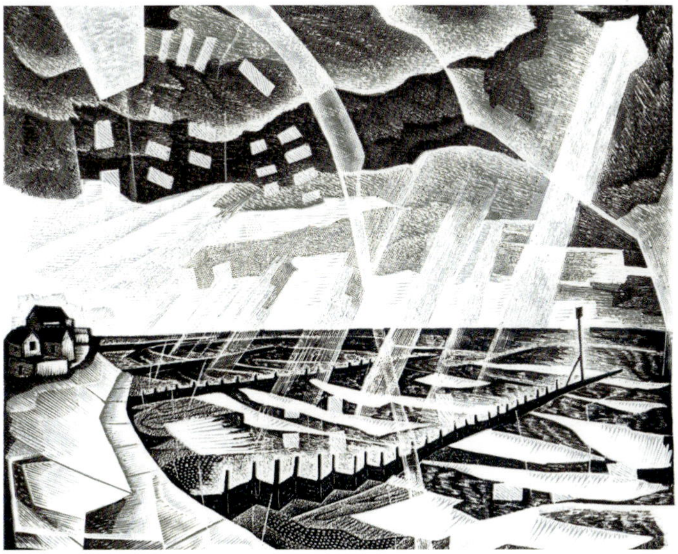

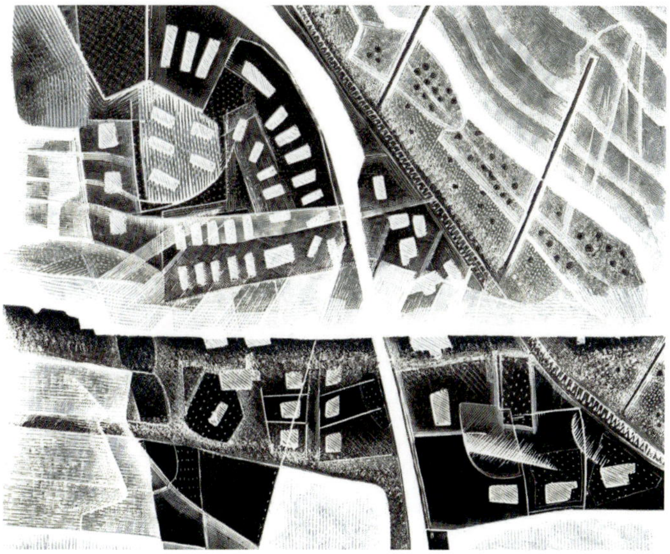

Walsingham

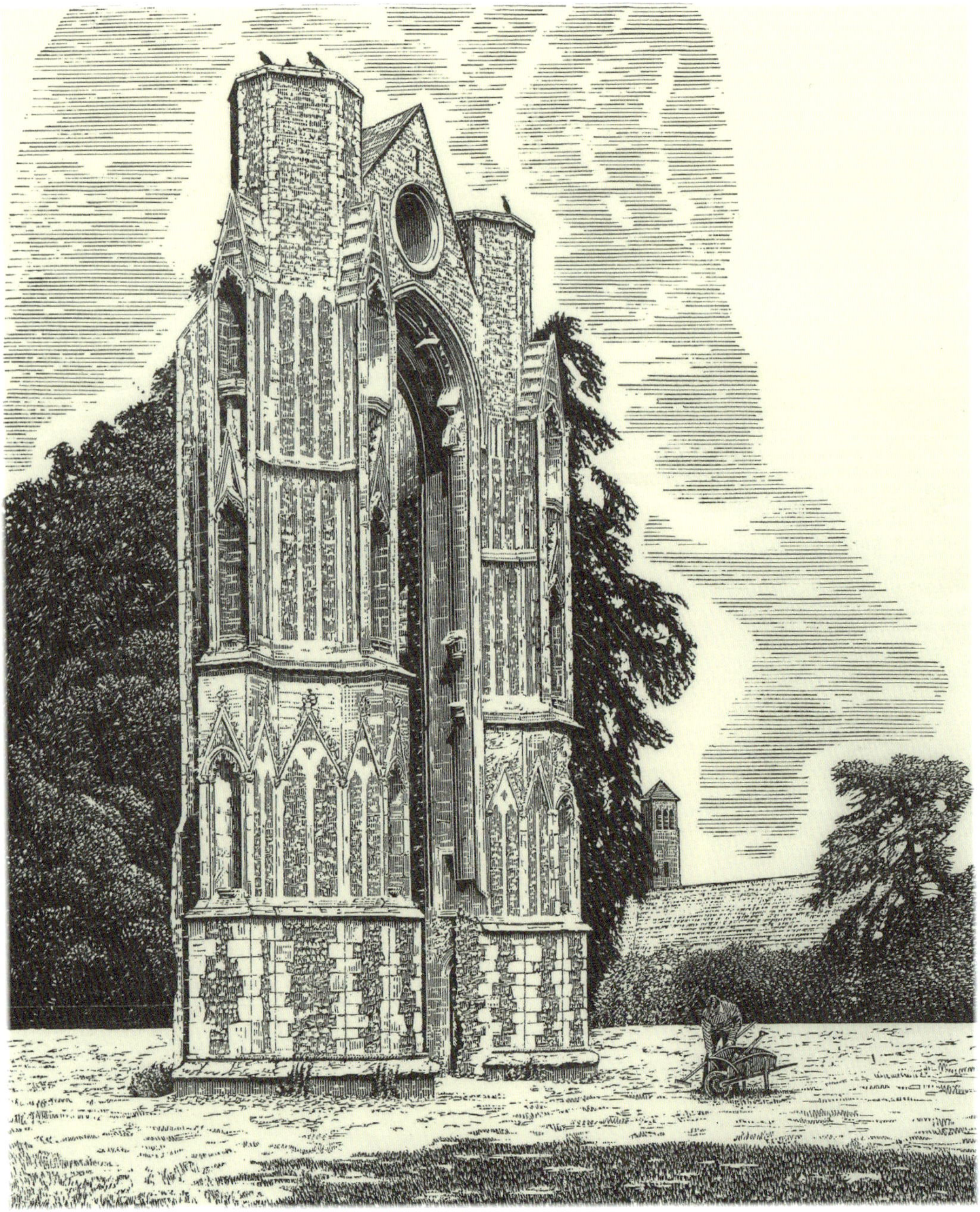

Among the ruins of the Augustinian Priory at *Walsingham* is the East Window, which engraver Anthony Dunigan describes as "magnificent". He tells us that it was a complicated subject to draw and engrave (in reverse, of course) from this viewpoint. "I have framed it against the dark trees for clarity and to lessen the pictorial dominance of all the straight lines and angles."

The 37cm x 30cm print, created using engraver's plastic, was made by Anthony in 2006 as part of an edition of 40.

The Monastery at Walsingham was always a priory. But in the late 17th or early 18th century the house on the site, originally the Prior's lodging, was enlarged into a mansion, and became known as 'The Abbey'.

The house is still called The Abbey and is privately occupied, but the surrounding grounds are open to the public. They contain the ruins of the Augustinian Priory of The Annunciation of the Blessed Virgin Mary. The Priory was founded circa 1153.

Little remains of the original buildings that were altered in the 13th and 14th centuries, but the most striking feature is undoubtedly the East Window featured in Anthony's print.

Warham

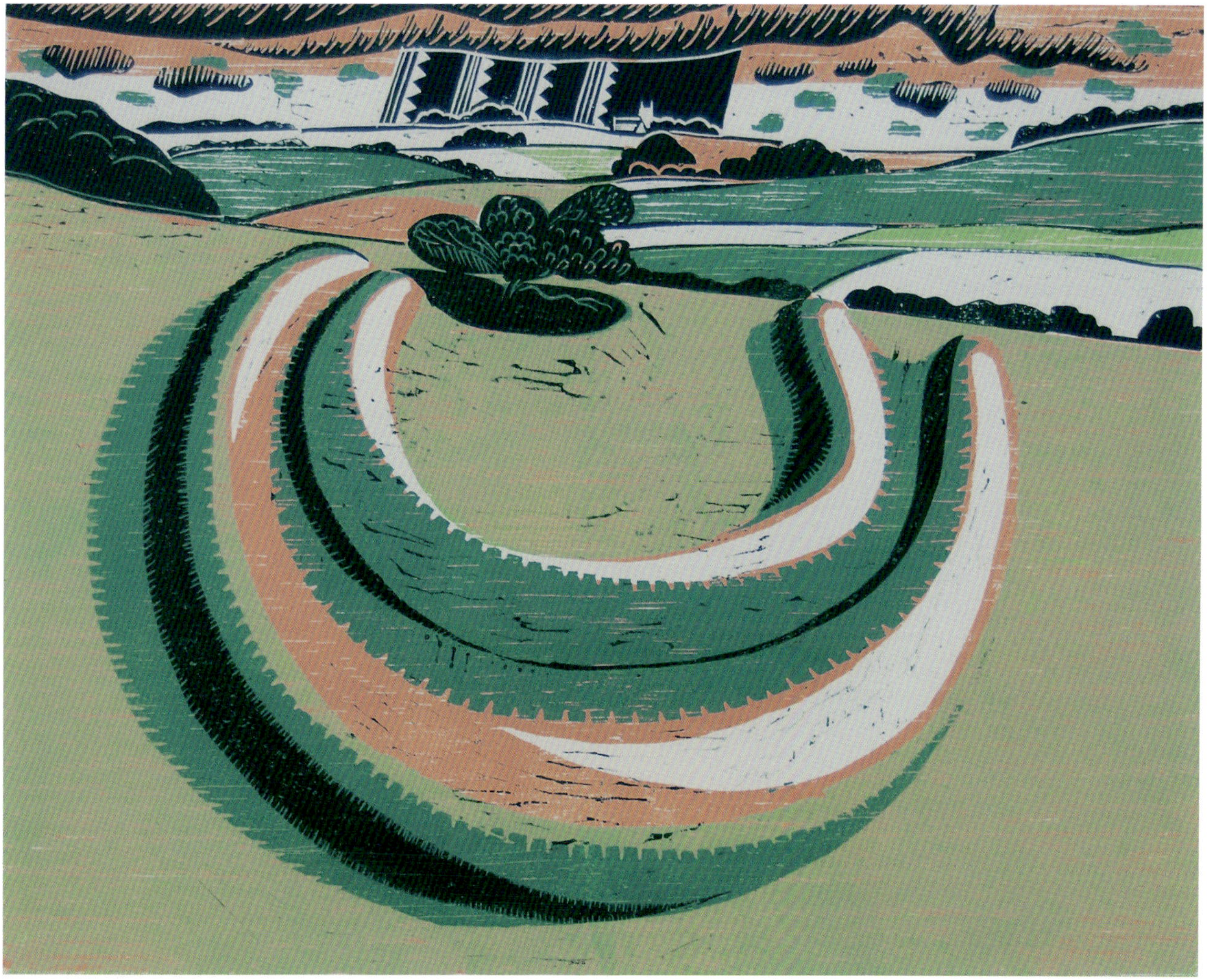

Norfolk-based David Jones is responsible for this linocut print of *Warham Camp* (30cm x 38cm) near the county's north coast. Warham Camp is an Iron Age circular hill fort close to the River Stiffkey. The ramparts remain after more than 2,000 years.

Warham Camp is circular and has been surveyed repeatedly from the air to confirm an overall diameter of 212 metres, with a 3m-high double bank and ditch.

The course of a channel of the River Stiffkey cuts across the south-western edge of the earthworks, but this is an 18th-century alteration and the original river ran in a curve to the west. Excavation in 1914 and 1959 produced evidence of a timber palisade and platform at the rear and timber revetment on the inner face. Iron Age and Roman pottery shards have been recovered.

Warham Camp dates to the last few centuries before the Roman invasion of Britain, with evidence of post-occupation activity. The University of East Anglia has described it as the best-preserved hill fort in Norfolk.

The Wash

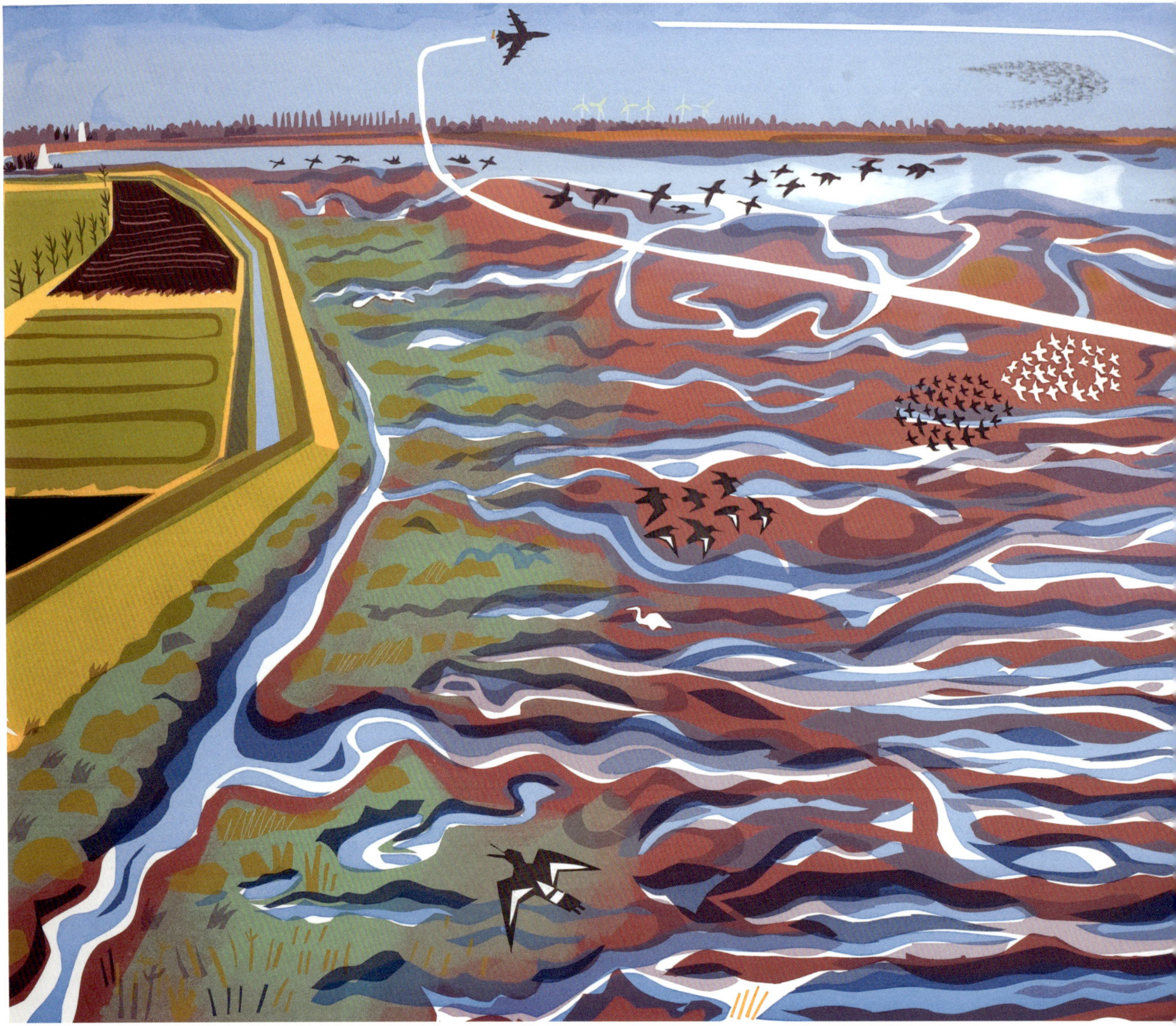

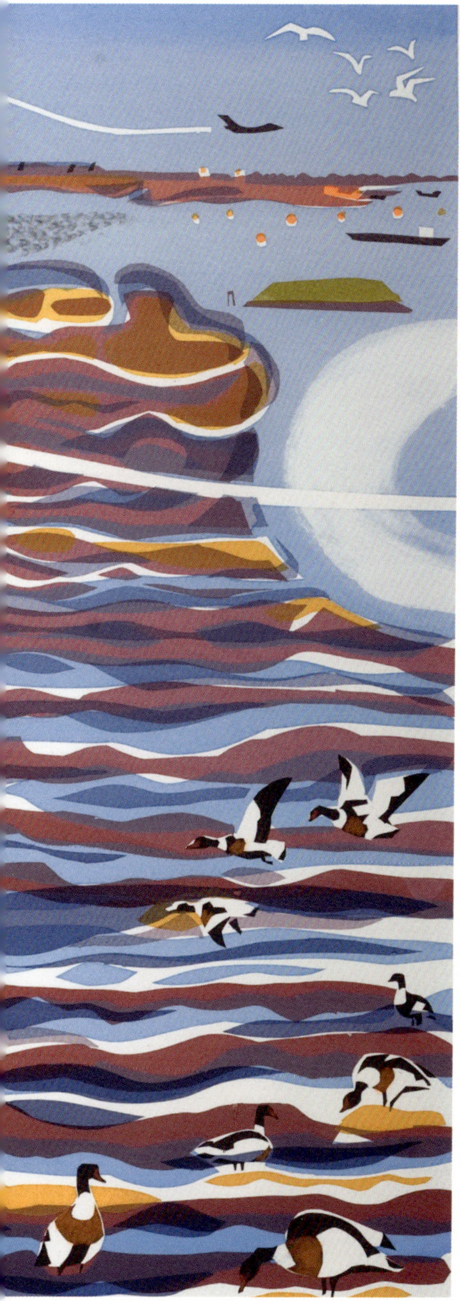

Northamptonshire-based artist Carry Akroyd provided us with this spectacular serigraph (screenprint) entitled *Winter Day at The Wash*. Her paintings and prints favour wildlife and the environment, peppered occasionally with the less natural trappings of modern Britain such as wind turbines and passing military jets.

Shelduck, an Oystercatcher, Little Egret and various waders and geese are enjoying the special habitat of The Wash, which links the counties of Norfolk and Lincolnshire.

Carry shows the twin lighthouses in the top left of the picture that mark the mouth of the River Nene. The green wedge of island on the right hand side is a trial bank created to experiment with a barrage, superseded then by the creation of Rutland Water.

The Wash is a large bay with three roughly straight sides meeting at right angles, each about 25km in length. The eastern coast of the Wash is entirely within Norfolk, and extends from a point a little north of Hunstanton in the north to the mouth of the River Great Ouse at King's Lynn in the south.

The opposing coast, which is roughly parallel to the east coast, runs from Gibraltar Point nature reserve to the mouth of the River Welland, all within Lincolnshire.

The southern coast runs roughly north-west to south-east, connecting these two river mouths; and is punctuated by the mouth of a third river, the Nene.

Owing to deposits of sediment and land reclamation, the coastline of The Wash has altered markedly over the centuries. King's Lynn, for example, is now some distance inland. Much of The Wash itself is very shallow, with several large sandbanks – such as Breast Sand, Bulldog Sand, Roger Sand and Old South Sand – exposed at low tide, especially along the south coast. For this reason, navigation in The Wash can be hazardous.

A re-survey of the coastline of The Wash carried out by The Ordnance Survey in 2011 revealed that an estimated additional 12sq km on the coastline had been created by accretion since the previous surveys were carried out between 1960 and 1980.

The Wash is a Special Protection Area (SPA) under European Union legislation. It is made up of very extensive salt marshes, major inter-tidal banks of sand and mud, shallow waters and deep channels. The seawall at Freiston has been breached in three places to increase the saltmarsh area in order to provide an extra habitat for birds, particularly waders, and also as a natural flood prevention measure. The extensive creeks in the salt marsh, and the vegetation that grows there, help dissipate wave energy – thus improving the protection afforded to land behind the saltmarsh.

On the eastern side of The Wash are Hunstanton's low chalk cliffs with their famous stratum of red chalk. There are also gravel pits at Snettisham RSPB reserve, which are an important roost for waders at high tide. This SPA borders on to the North Norfolk Coast Special Protection Area. To the north-west, The Wash extends to Gibraltar Point, another Special Protection Area.

The unusual nature of The Wash habitats, coupled with the ample tidal flows, allows shellfish to breed, especially shrimp, cockles and mussels. Many water birds feed on shellfish, and it is also an important breeding area for Common Terns, and a feeding area for Marsh Harriers. Migrating birds, such as geese, ducks and wading birds, come to The Wash in huge numbers to spend the winter, with an average of around 400,000 birds present at any one time. It has been estimated that around two million birds will use The Wash for feeding and roosting during their annual migrations.

The Wash is recognised as being internationally important for 17 species of bird. These include Pink-footed Goose, Dark-bellied Brent Goose, Shelduck, Pintail, Oystercatcher, Ringed Plover, Grey Plover, Golden Plover, Lapwing, Knot, Sanderling, Dunlin, Black-tailed Godwit, Bar-tailed Godwit, Curlew, Redshank and Turnstone.

Wells-next-the-Sea

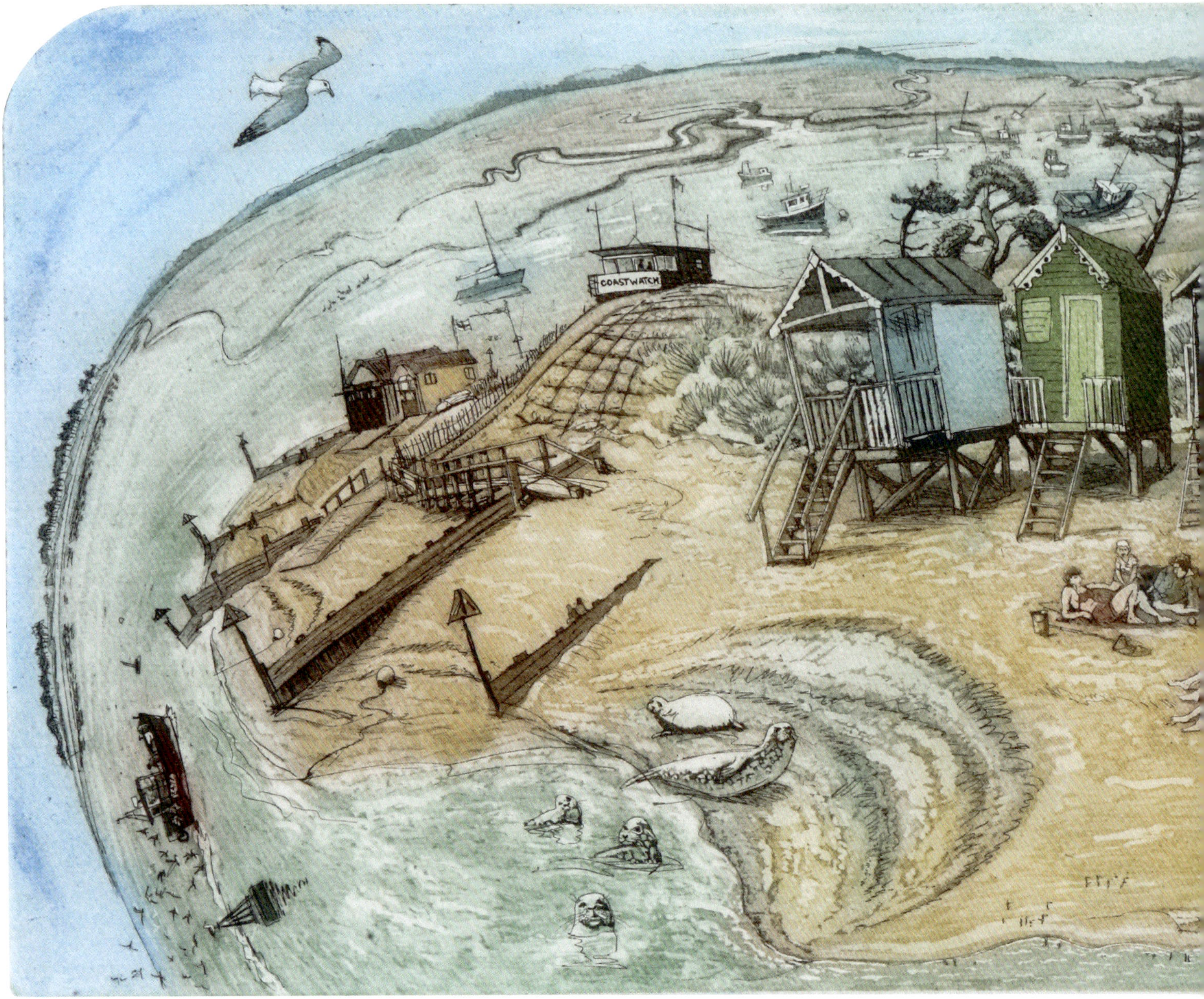

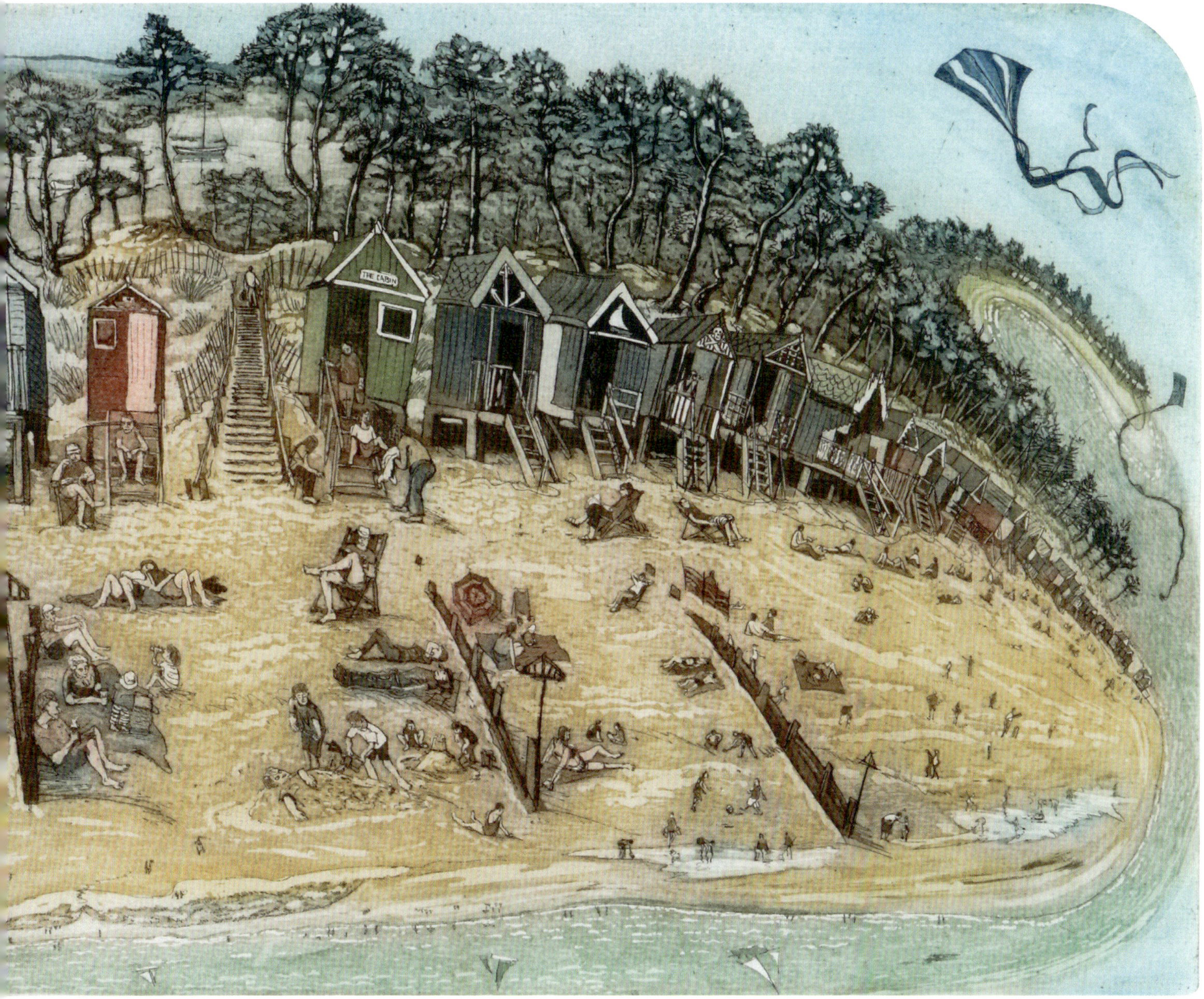
THE CABIN

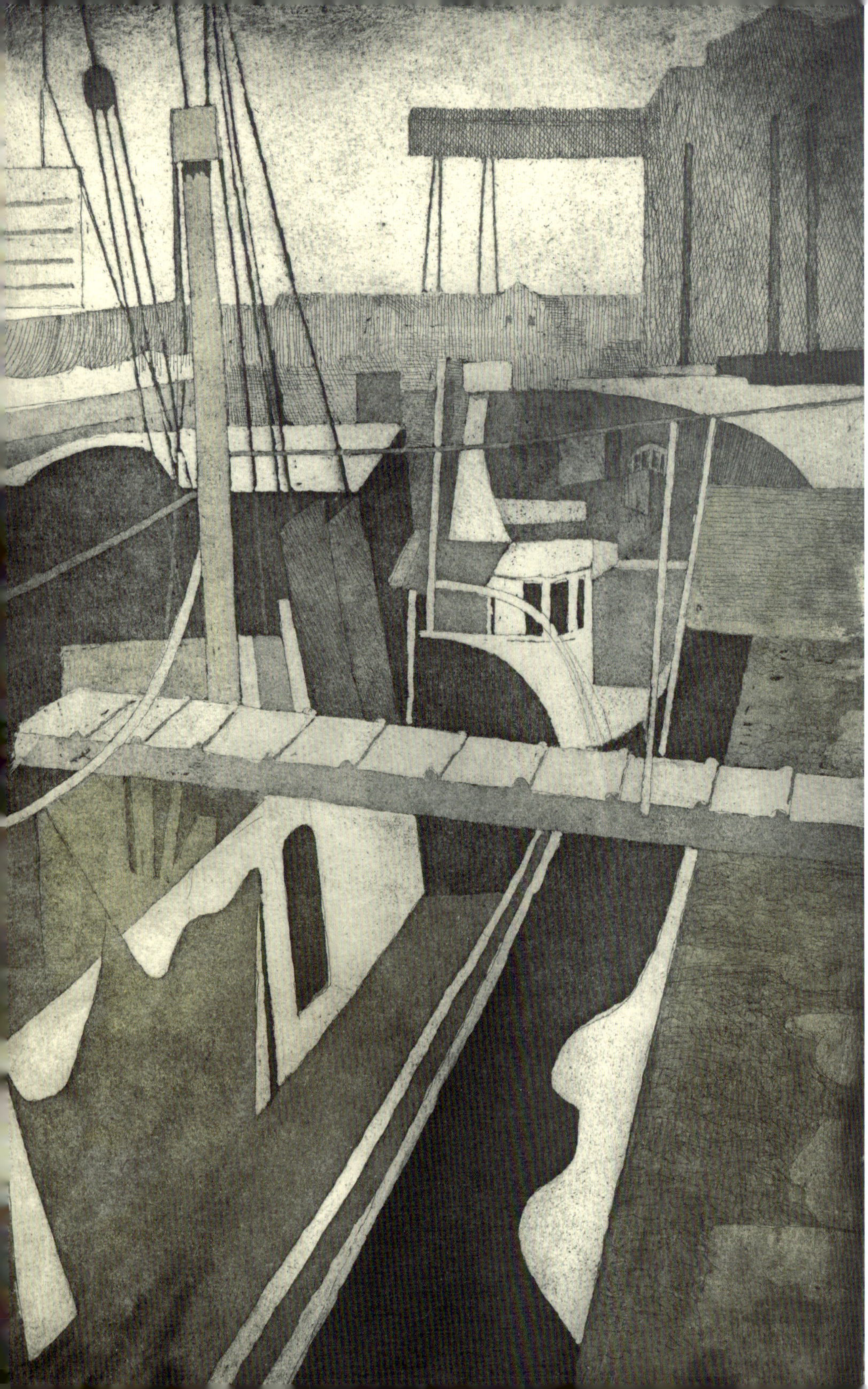

Beach huts and pine trees form the basis of the spectacular 2009 Glynn Thomas etching (24cm x 63cm) that opens this section. Both line the sand at one of Norfolk's most popular coastal resorts, the quaintly named Wells-next-the-Sea. The brightly coloured huts are some of the most expensive real estate in East Anglia, and can be found after a brisk walk from the bustling town. Wander for a mile and a half along the beautiful sandy beach and you'll end up in Holkham. Actress Gwyneth Paltrow walked across the very same stretch of sand during the closing scenes of *Shakespeare in Love*. This is a designated Area of Outstanding Natural Beauty, allowing visitors to catch a glimpse of Shore Larks, Ringed Plovers, Oystercatchers and Terns during the summer.

The name Wells derives from the many clear spring wells that were found in the area. The town became known as Wells-next-the-Sea in the early 1800s, to distinguish it from other places in Norfolk of the same name. In 1956, this became the town's official title. Located more than a mile from open water, the name nowadays may seem to be a slight exaggeration. In the late 16th century, however, the town benefited from much easier access to the sea, and was one of the major ports in the area. A handful of fishing boats still go crabbing, shrimping and whelking from the quay, which sits in front of a network of narrow streets, old alleys and yards, boasting some impressive Georgian and Victorian architecture.

On the left is an aquatint etching by Norfolk artist Colin Bygrave, which takes him away from his preferred subject of trees and winding lanes to the quayside at Wells. From an edition of 30, the print (40cm x 26cm) is entitled *Wells Quay* and shows the cantilever loading gantry on the granary building. This pops up in a number of prints, including in Amelia Bowman's 2017 collagraph on page 160 and in the 2011 three-block linocut overleaf by Colin Moore entitled *Wells Morning*.

"Wells offers you a different selection of

Pages 154-155: Glynn Thomas – Wells next the Sea (copperplate etching); ***Far left:*** *Colin Bygrave – Wells Quay (aquatint etching); Right: HJ Jackson – LN96, Dry Dock (linocut)*

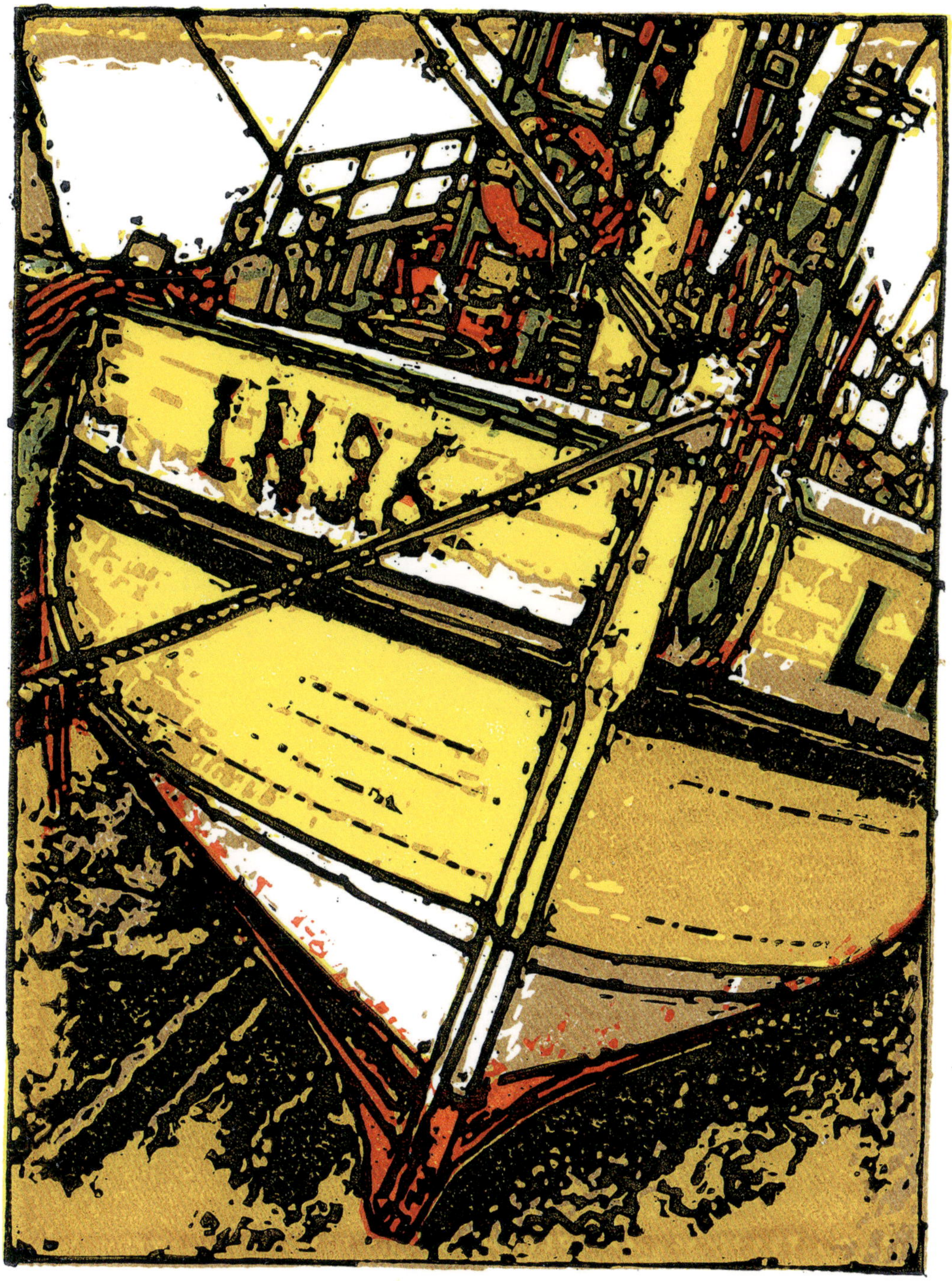

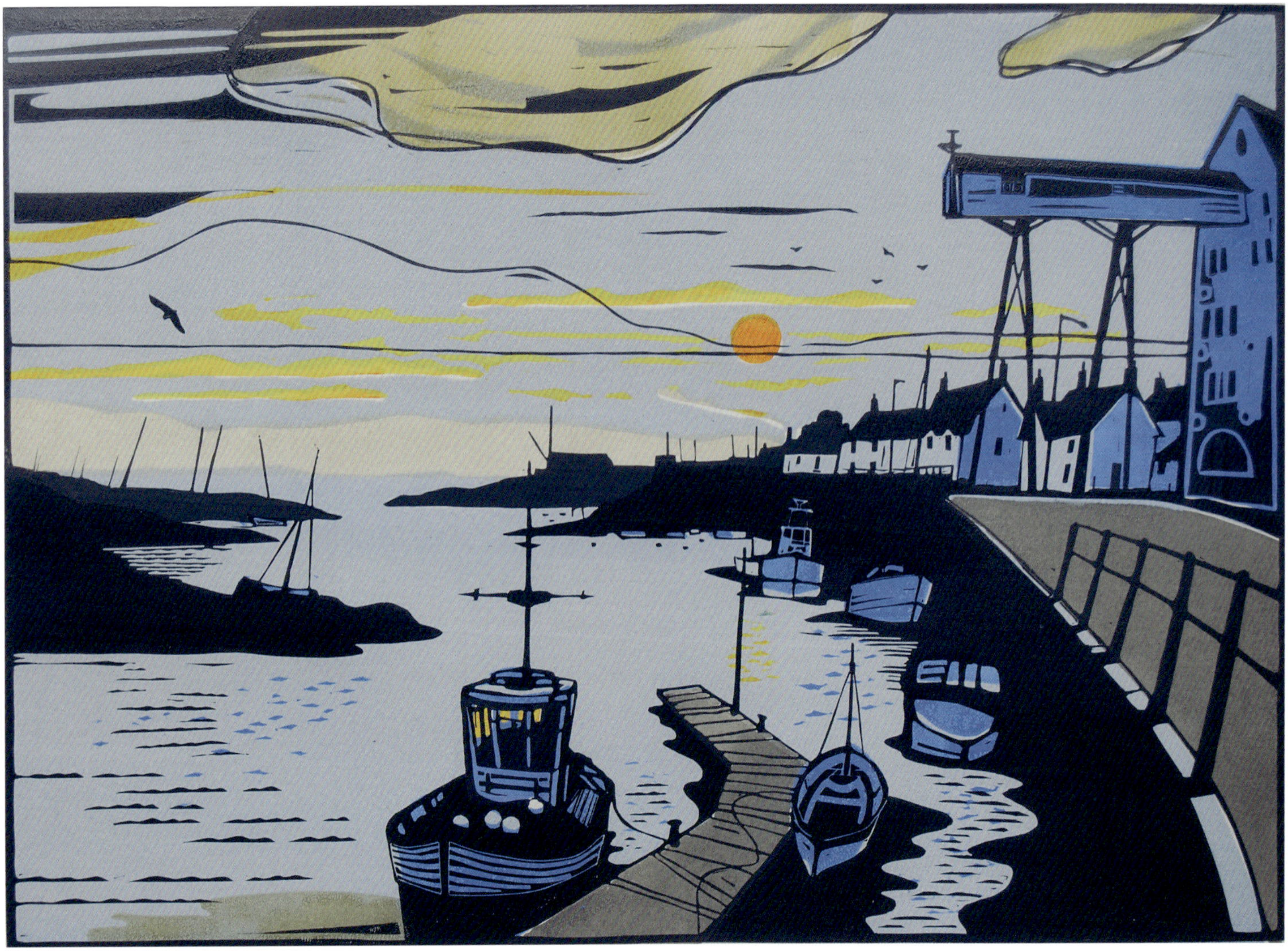

floating subjects every time you go there," says Colin. "And there is the old granary building, one of the strangest structures on the Norfolk coast and irresistible to artists, especially ones who used to be architects."

On page 157 is a 1998 linocut by veteran Norfolk printmaker HJ Jackson. As ever, he avoids the predictable and delivers a colourful image entitled *LN96 – Dry Dock*, featuring one of a small number of local fishing boats undergoing repair at Wells.

On page 159, Norwich-based Sarah Bays offers an atmospheric take on the beach at Wells with her monotype *Receding Tide* (14cm x 14cm) from 2015. "The wide, open spaces of the beach at Holkham and Wells that seems to stretch on forever often inspires my monotypes," says Sarah. "The sands can be dotted with people and dogs or completely empty – both of which offer ample artistic inspiration." Another of the artist's prints appears on page 162, this time a 2012 drypoint entitled *The Beach at Wells* (11cm x 15cm) from an edition of 20.

Walking the concrete causeway from the town towards the beach, lifeboat station and beach huts provides a view of the dozens of boats stranded by the tide on the mud of this once important port. Wading birds scuttle among the sailing boats, fishing vessels and dinghies, probing the damp mud for insects and crustaceans.

Wells has been a port for at least 700 years, and was at its peak in the middle of the 19th century, when the quay was built. The primary trade was the import of coal, timber and salt,

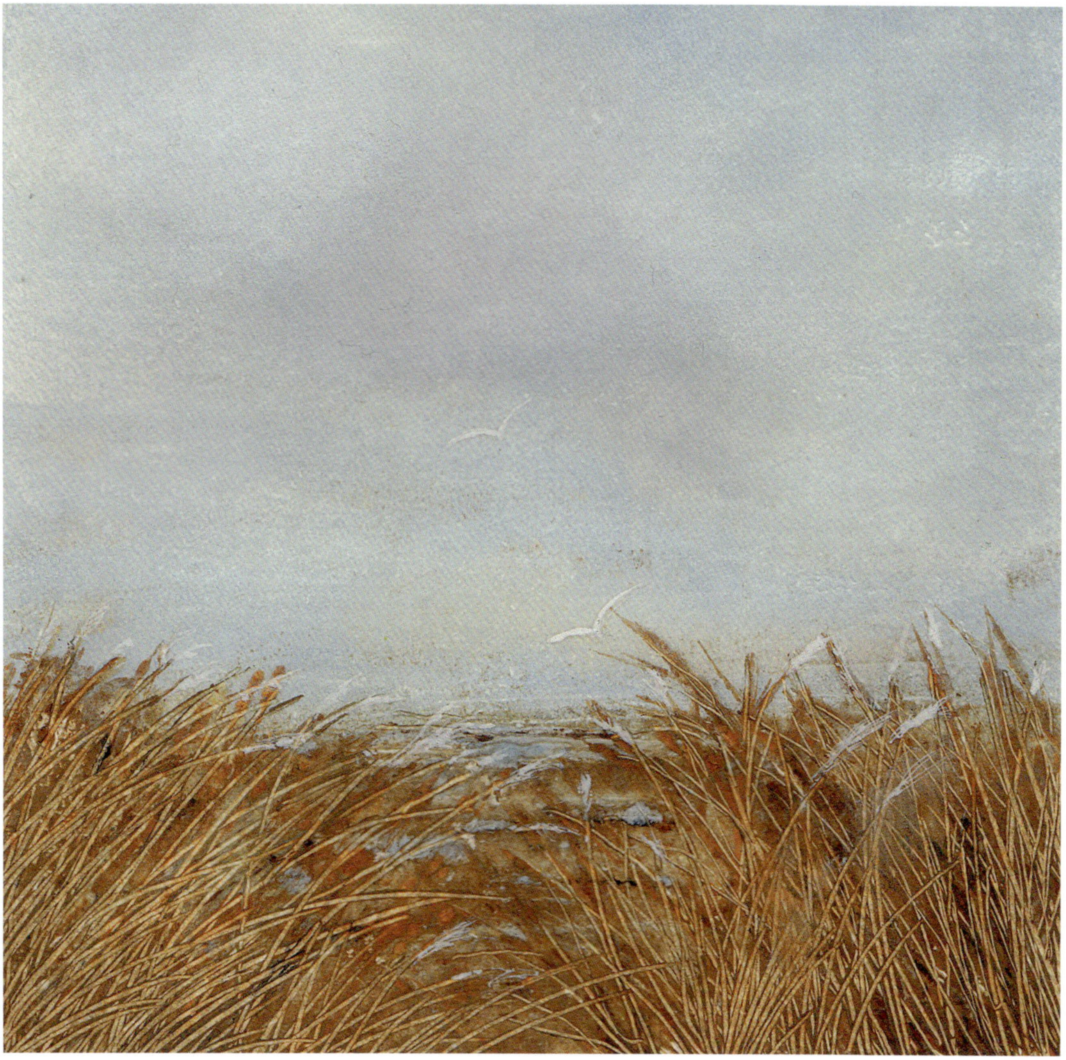

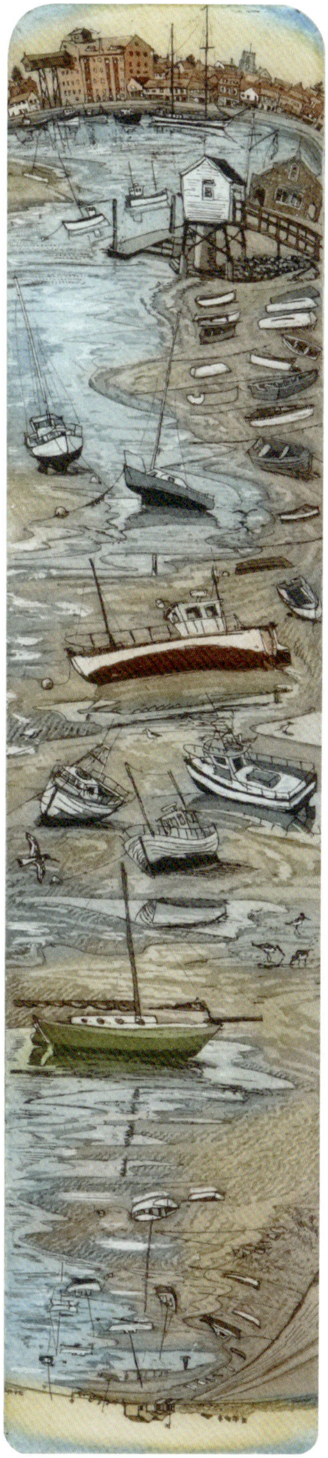

Facing page: Colin Moore – Wells Morning (linocut).
Above: Sarah Bays – Receding Tide (monotype).
Right: Glynn Thomas – Ebb Tide (etching).

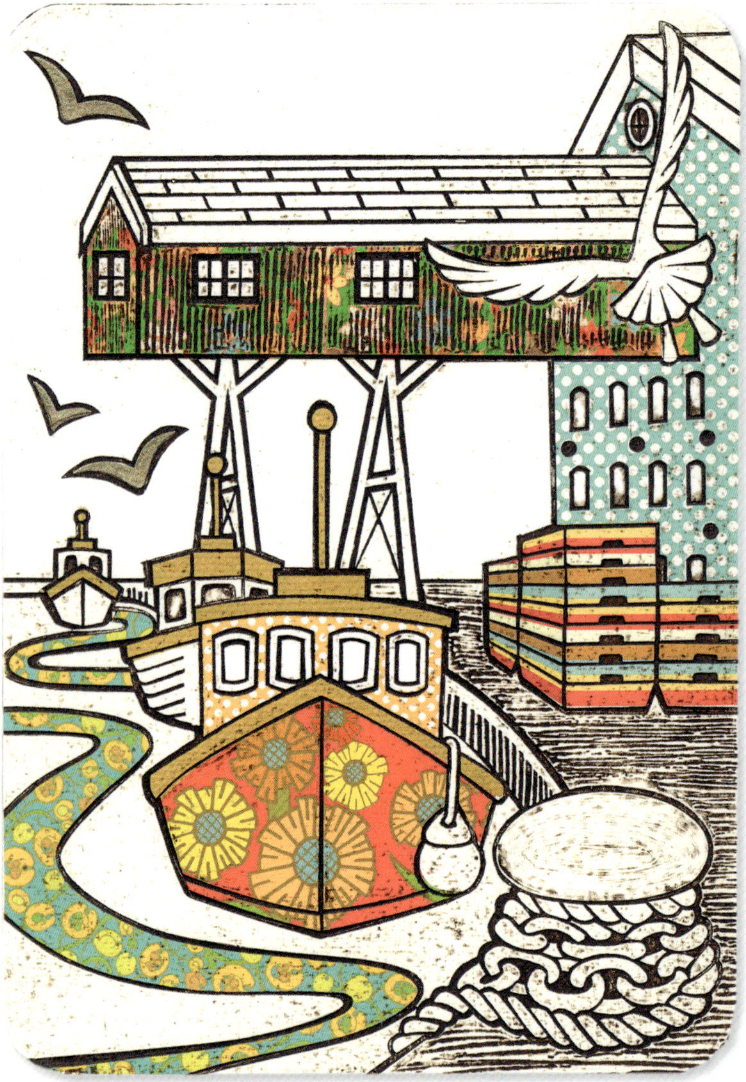

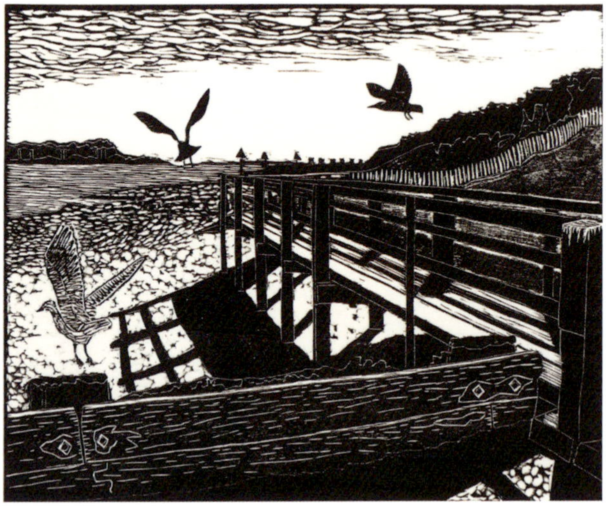

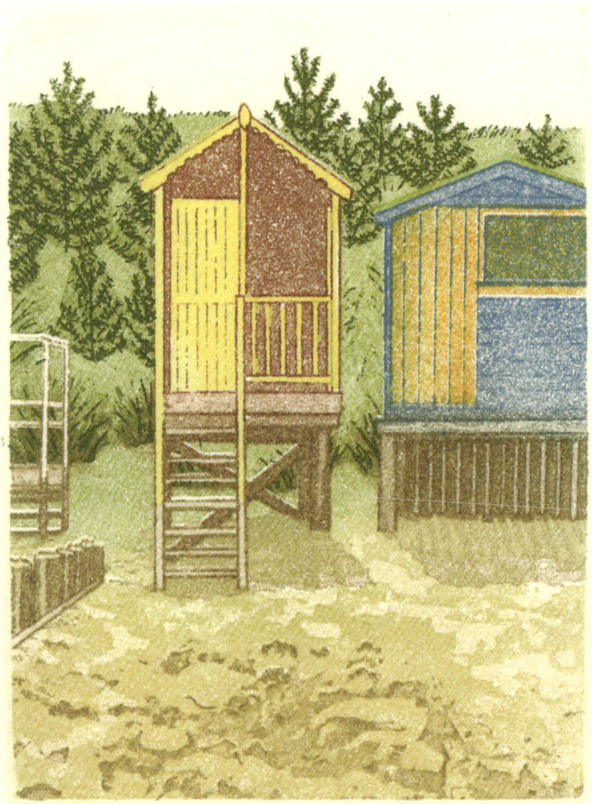

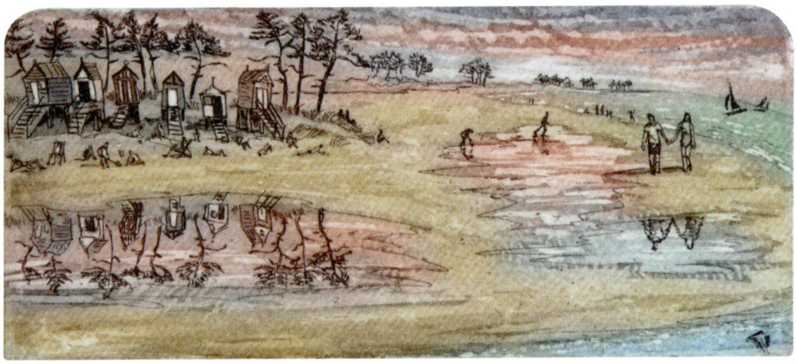

From top left, clockwise: *Amelia Bowman – Wells-Next-The-Sea (Ixia II), collagraph; Valerie Sims –Walkway (woodcut); Jan Dingle – High Dive (etching); Glynn Thomas – Norfolk Sunset (etching).* ***Facing page:*** *Vanessa Burroughes – Beach Huts at Wells (collaged screenprint).*

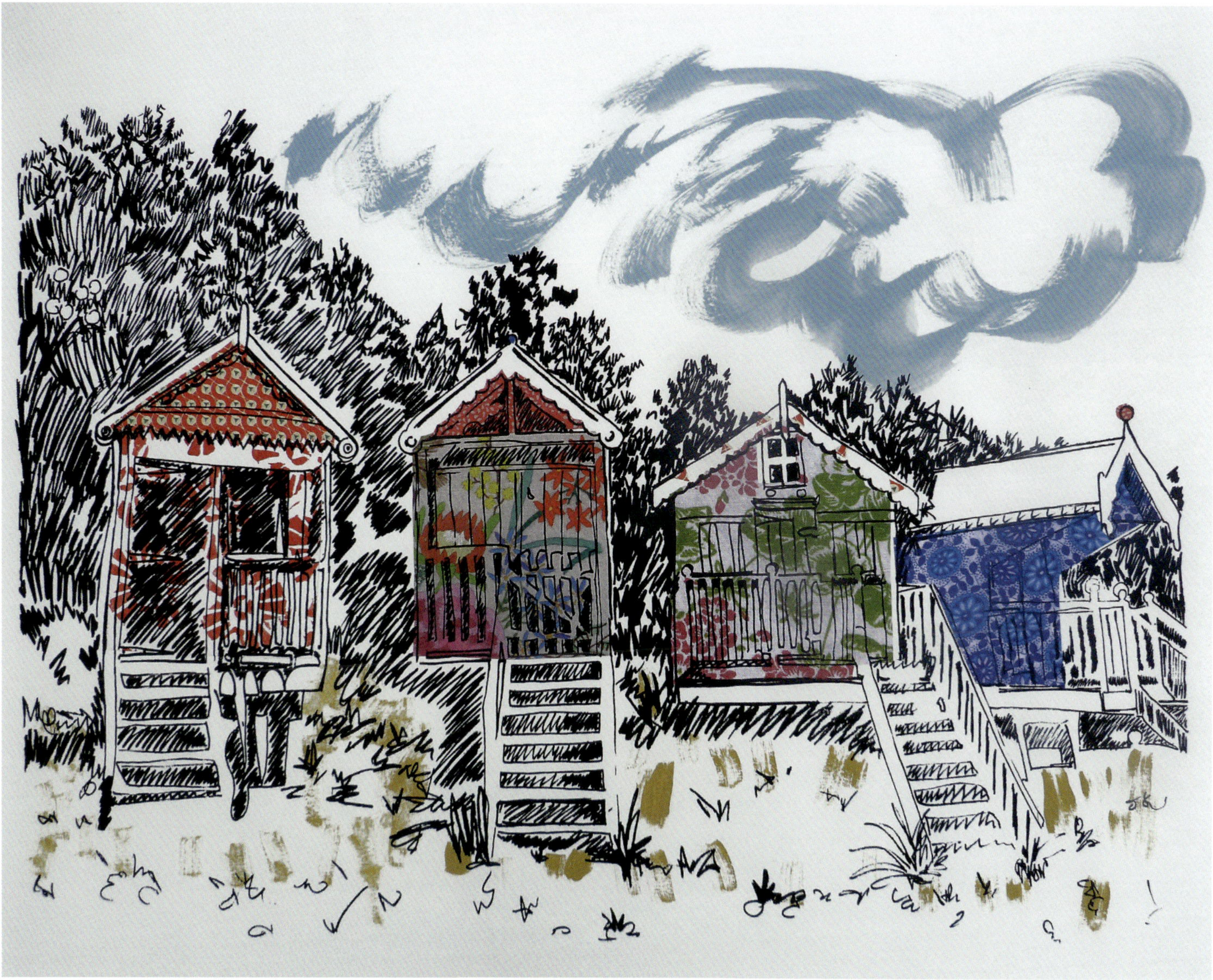

and the export of corn, barley and malt for breweries. Once again featured in the Glynn Thomas etching *Ebb Tide* (42cm x 9cm) on page 159 is the afore-mentioned granary building with its distinctive overhanging gantry. Completed in 1904, the granary (which ceased operations in 1990) now provides apartment owners with magnificent views of the harbour.

Suffolk-based Glynn also provides the 2009 etching on page 160 called *Norfolk Sunset* (62cm x 19cm). As you reach the last few huts on the long stretch of sand at Wells-next-the-Sea, shown here, you turn the corner and start heading for Holkham Beach, forming part of the Holkham estate.

As suggested by the picture title, this is a particularly good spot from which to observe the Norfolk sunset, with nothing to spoil the view but miles of clean sand and the occasional stand of pine trees. It may be a long, hot walk from Wells town or from Holkham itself, but it is well worth the trip.

More pinewoods exist to the east of the beach over the shipping channel at an area called the East Hills. This can be accessed on foot at low tide, although all of the tidal sands in the area

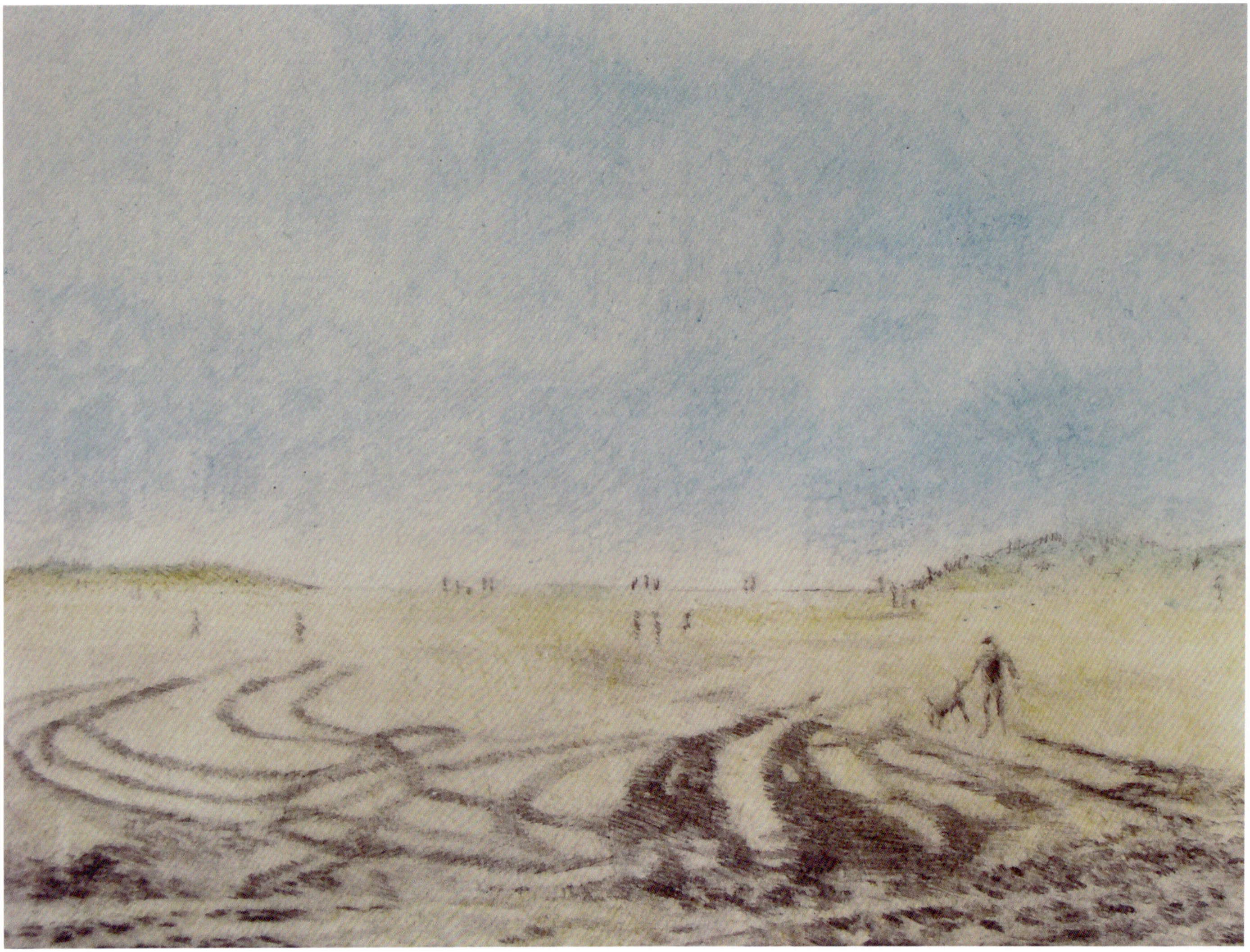

are extremely dangerous due to the speed and currents of the rising tide.

The beach huts at Wells are the subject of Jan Dingle's 9cm x 7cm etching *High Dive* on page 160, as well as of fellow Norfolk artist Vanessa Burroughes' large collaged screenprint (*Beach Huts at Wells*) on the facing page. Jan's work more typically features sailing scenes on the Broads, but the prints on pages 160 and 164 show that she enjoys the occasional day at the seaside. Vanessa has a background in fabric design, which shows through in her bold and colourful prints.

Cambridgeshire artist Valerie Sims on page 160 provides us with a 2012 woodcut entitled *Walkway* (26cm x 32cm) that forms part of an edition of just 20. Another secret corner of the town's beach is portrayed, complete with gulls.

Amelia Bowman takes us back to the quayside with her 2015 collagraph print *Wells Harbour (Anemone)* on page 163 (27cm x 38cm, edition of 10). "I made my first sketch for this piece while enjoying a coffee sitting in the window seat at Wells Deli. It wasn't planned but the view just had to be captured and I set to making the collagraph plate as quickly as if I had been asked if it could be used on a local magazine cover!"

The final Wells print, on page 164, is another by HJ Jackson. *Shadows* from 1999 is a linocut showing some of the town's doorways. The town stretches nearly a mile inland, and the majority of shops and other businesses are now found on Staithe Street. Another feature of the town is the area known as The Buttlands, a sizeable green ringed by lime trees and overlooked by large, elegant Georgian houses.

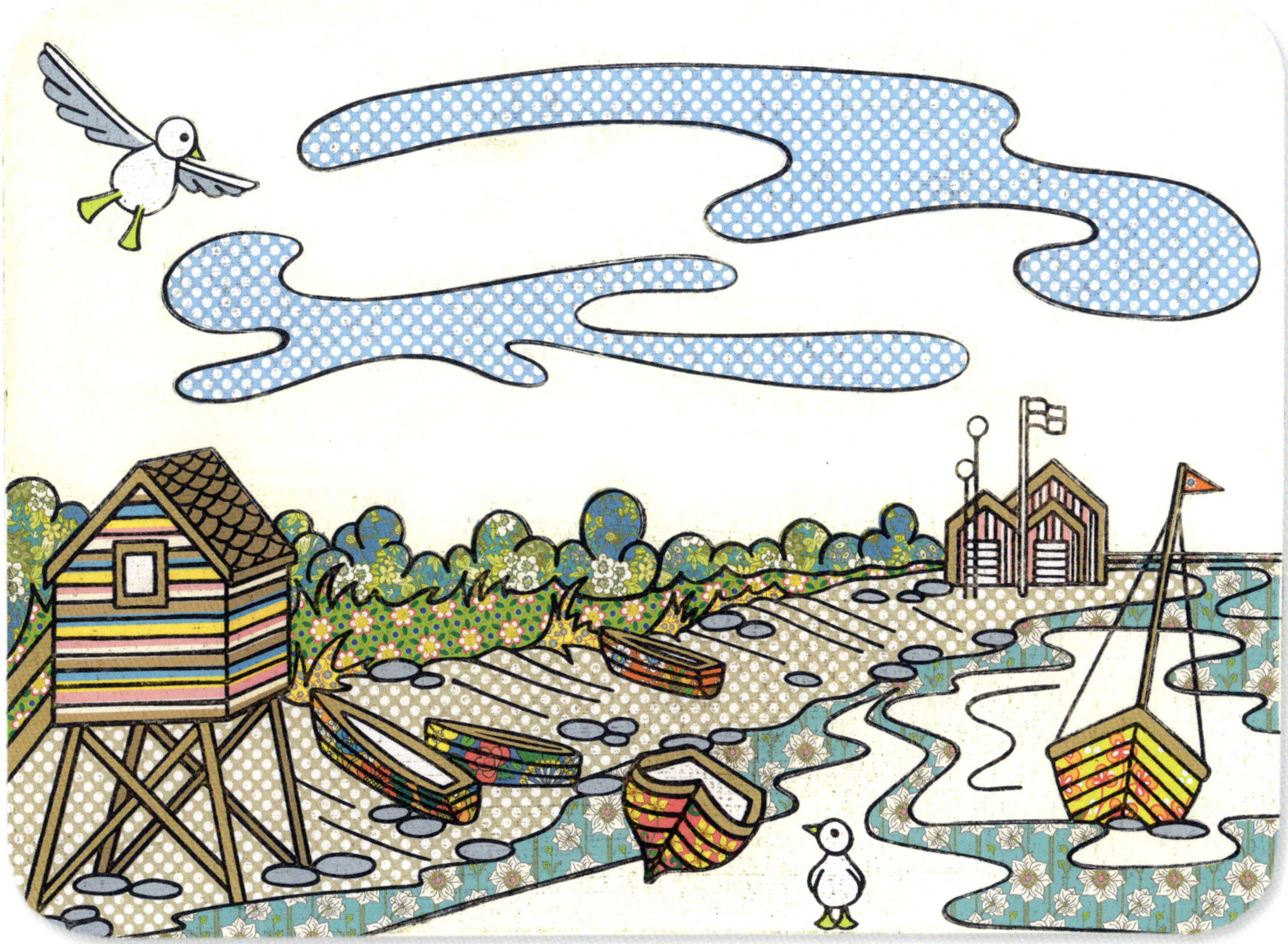

Facing page: *Sarah Bays – The Beach at Wells (drypoint).*
Above: *Amelia Bowman – Wells Harbour (Anemone), collagraph.*
Overleaf: *Jan Dingle – The Beach (etching); HJ Jackson – Shadows (linocut).*

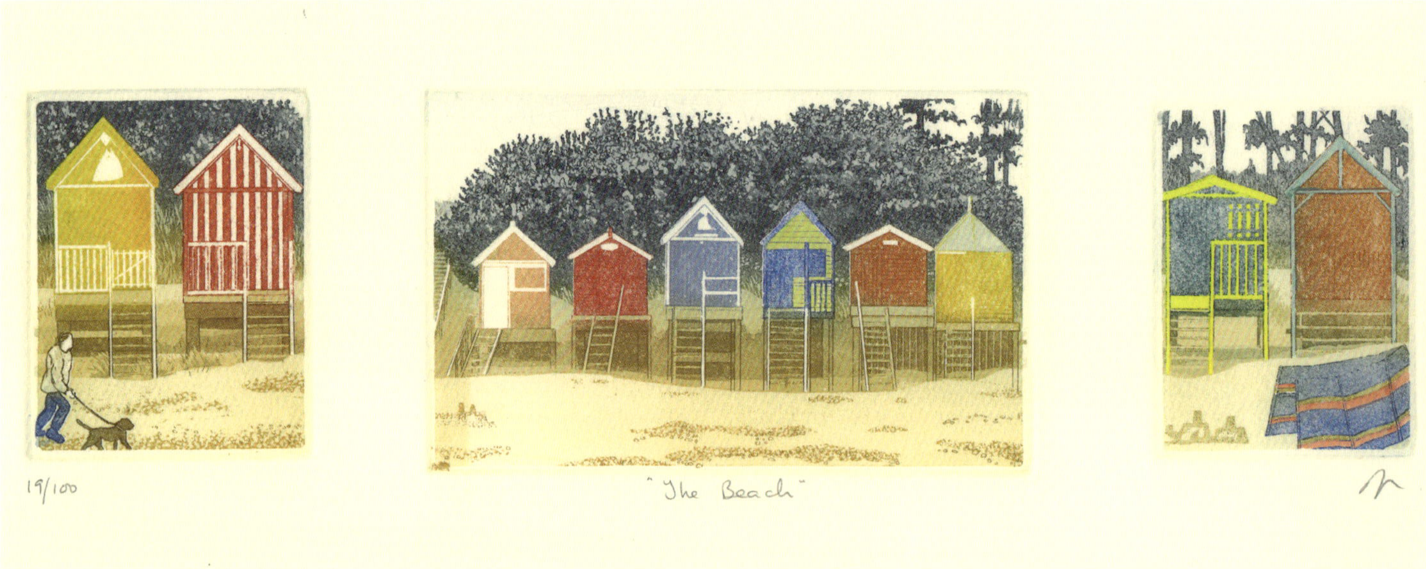
19/100
"The Beach"

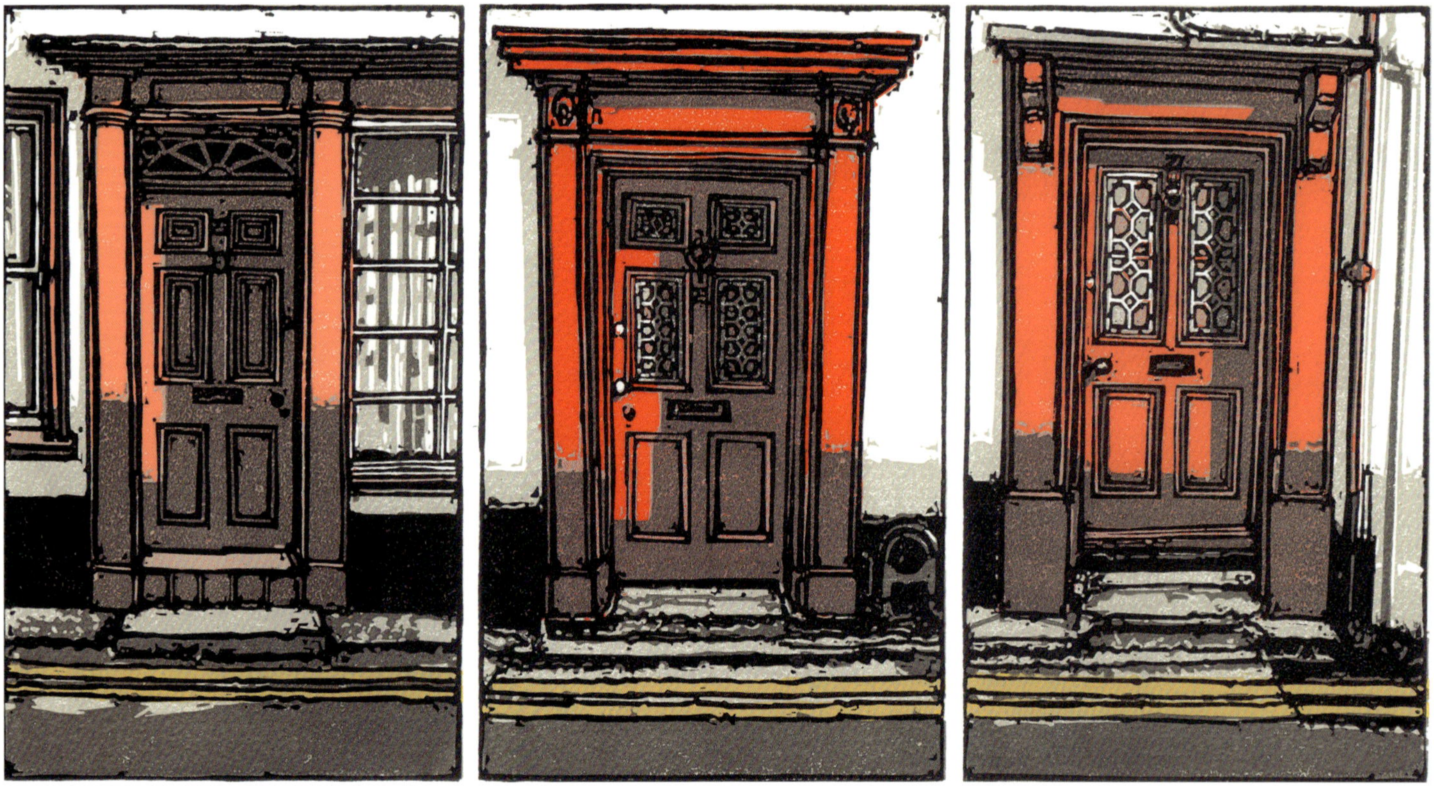

Wheatacre Church

Anthony Dunigan explains that the obvious attraction here is the striking pattern on the church tower of squares of red brick and knapped flint. "As this was to be a black-and-white print, I chose to have strong sunlight on the scene and heighten the tone on the brick as much as possible to contrast it with the flint squares."

The artist's 32cm x 38cm print is from a block made of engraver's plastic created in 2006. Anthony produced an edition of 40 featuring Wheatacre's early 16th-century All Saints church – which, along with its handsome tower, has fine brickwork in the west doorway, the west window and the nave. Aldeby, Wheatacre and Burgh St Peter are in the south-east corner of Norfolk, bounded by the River Waveney on two sides in well-farmed countryside with good grazing marshes bordering the river.

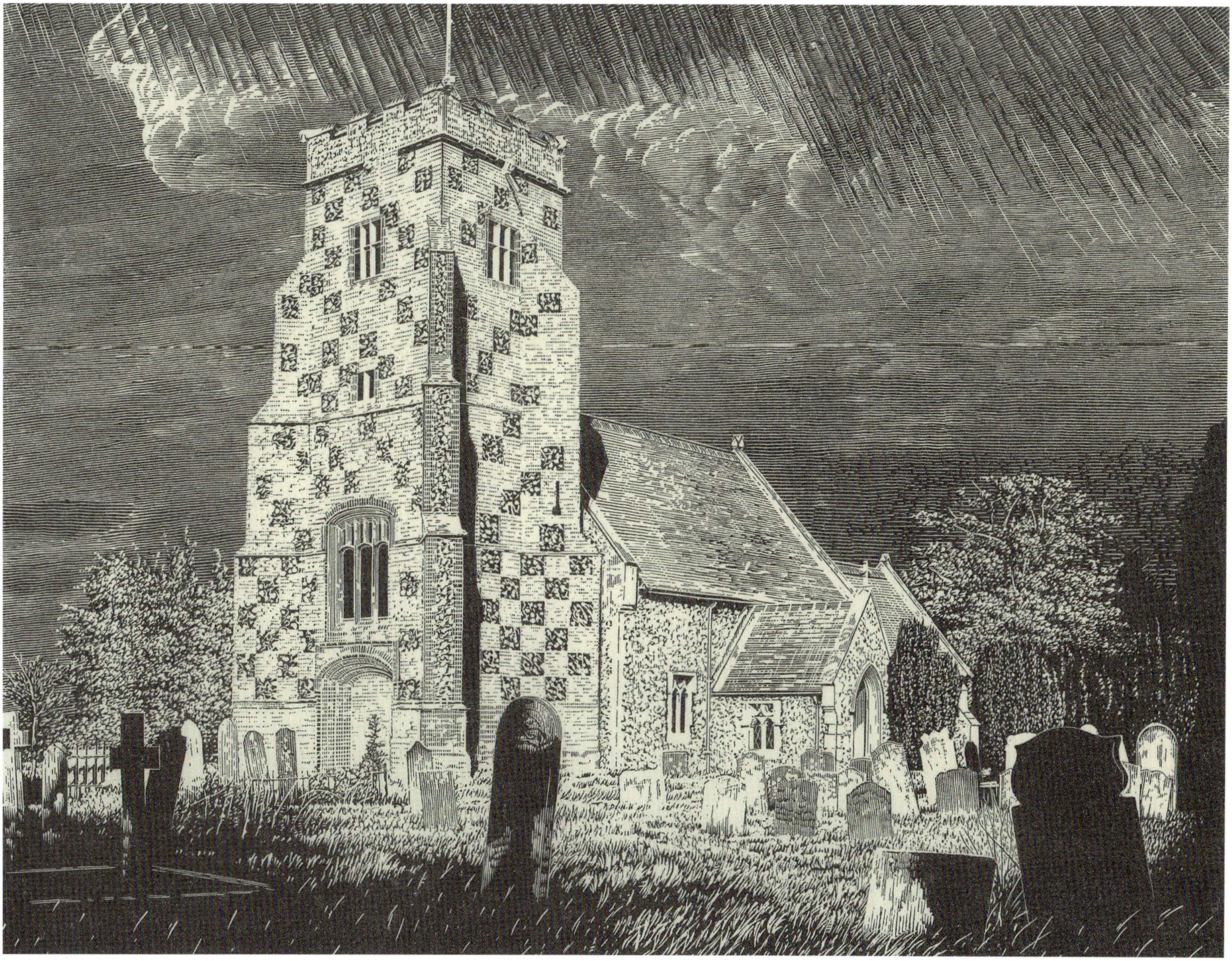

Wiveton

Robert Gillmor's *Norfolk Night* (18cm x 30cm) is a linocut print from 1998/99 that features St Mary's church at Wiveton, as well as the hares silhouetted in the foreground. Robert is first and foremost a wildlife artist, being awarded an MBE for his services to the genre in 2015. He inherited a taste for printmaking from his grandfather Allen W Seaby, and now specialises in linocut printmaking from his studio and home in Cley.

His prints generally feature Norfolk species set in their natural surroundings, so familiar locations will often accompany the wildlife. In this instance, Robert observed these particular trees alongside the road between Weybourne and Sheringham on the north coast. They were sketched from his car while parked in a field entrance. The church at Wiveton, like the moon benefiting from a pale yellow watercolour wash, is one of three visible from the green at Cley. This is a two-block print from an edition of 26.

Wiveton is a village and civil parish situated on the west bank of the River Glaven, 3km inland from the coast and directly across the river from Cley. The villages of Blakeney and Morston are just a few miles to the west.

Until the 17th century, the River Glaven was navigable and Wiveton was a port. The outline of the former harbour can still be seen in the fields between Wiveton and Cley. Alongside this, marks from mooring ropes belonging to large transport barges can still be seen etched into the wall on the east side of the church.

Fellow wildlife artist Robert Greenhalf on page 64 has contributed the etching *Norfolk Barn Owl*, inspired by the view from just outside Cley on the road south to Wiveton, looking towards Blakeney Church.

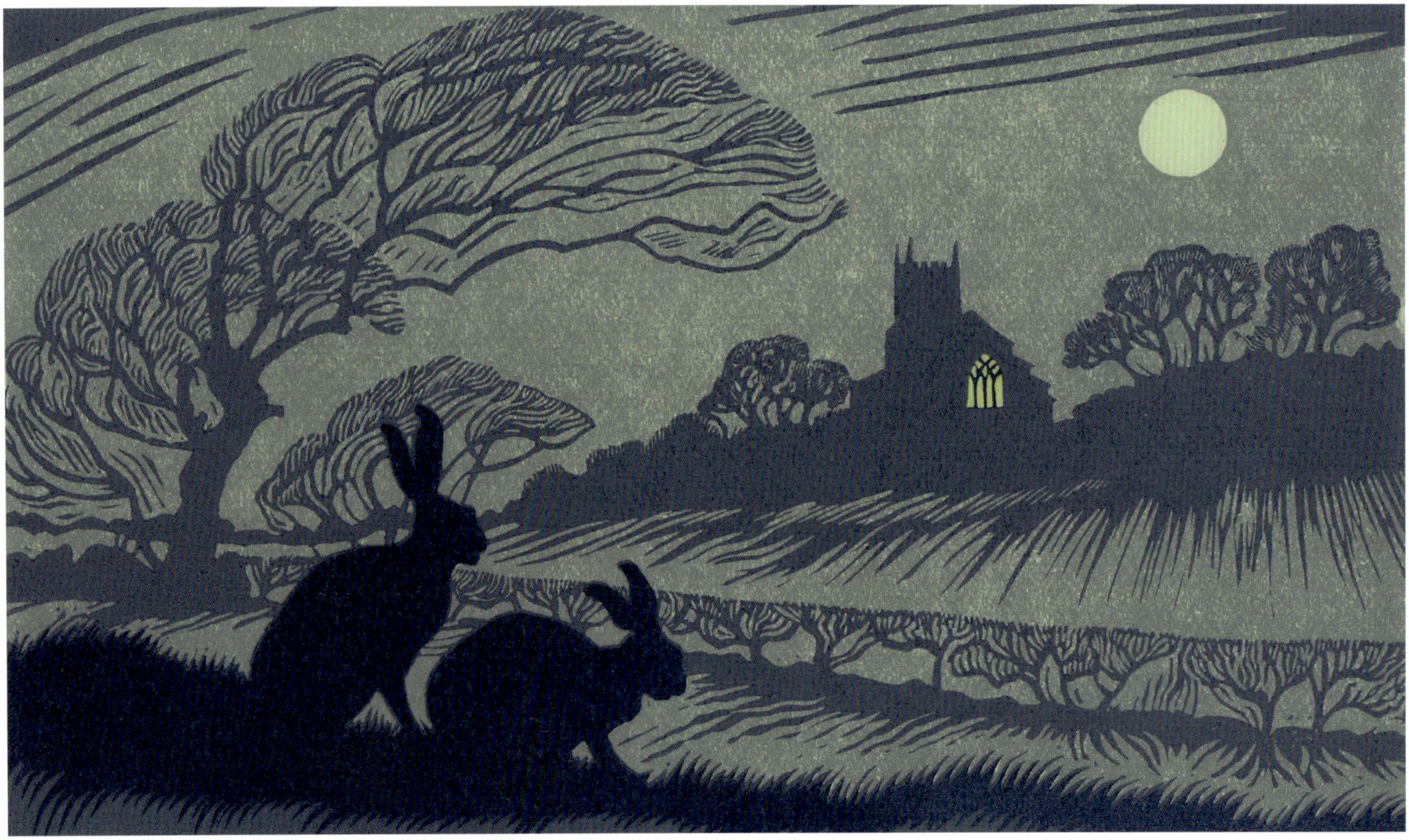

Wymondham

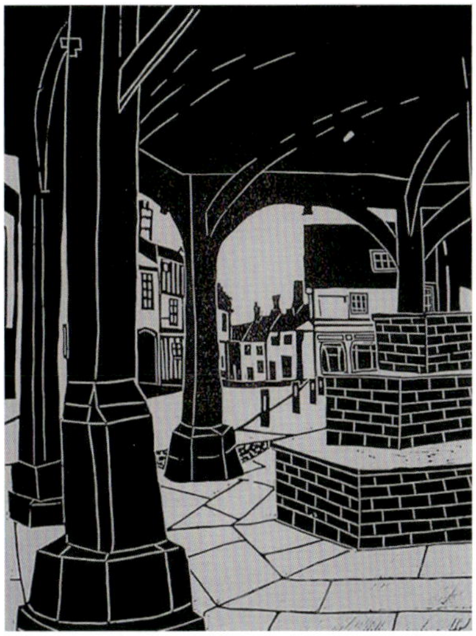

A popular south Norfolk market town, Wymondham is home to Amelia Bowman who pays tribute overleaf with her collagraph print *Market Cross (Clover)*. The 2013 image shows the iconic structure, as does Suffolk printmaker/bookbinder Janet Watson's linocut above.

On the right, David Jones has chosen to portray the magnificent *Wymondham Abbey* (35cm x 27cm) in his lino- and woodcut print. The Abbey today serves as the parish church of Wymondham, but it started life as a Benedictine priory with roots back to 1107 and Henry I's chief butler William d'Aubigny.

Wymondham Priory was relatively small, initially for some 12 monks, but grew in influence and wealth over the centuries. In 1448, following a successful petition from the King, the Pope granted Wymondham the right to become an Abbey.

The monastery church was completed by about 1130, and originally was dedicated to the Virgin Mary. Later, following the murder of St Thomas

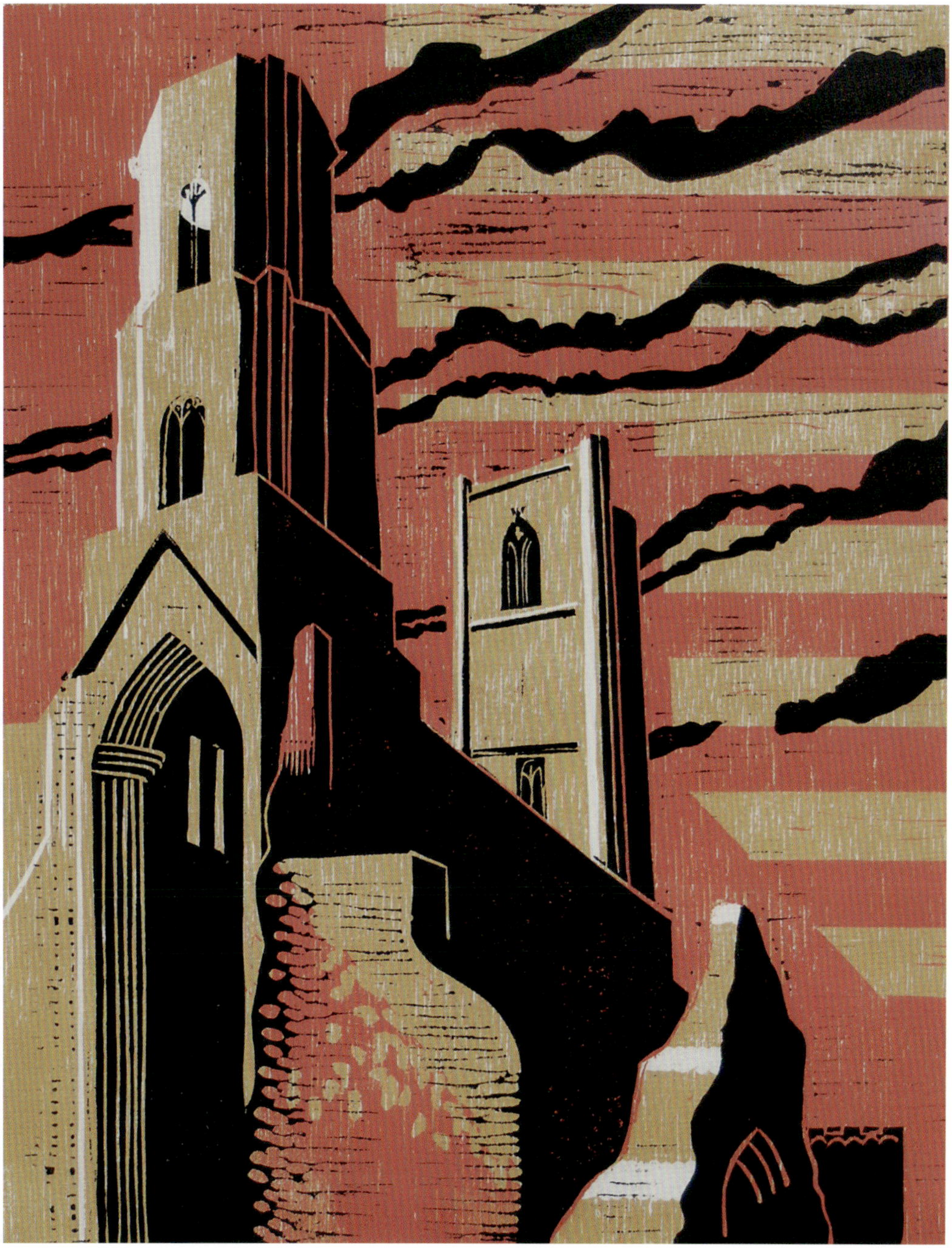

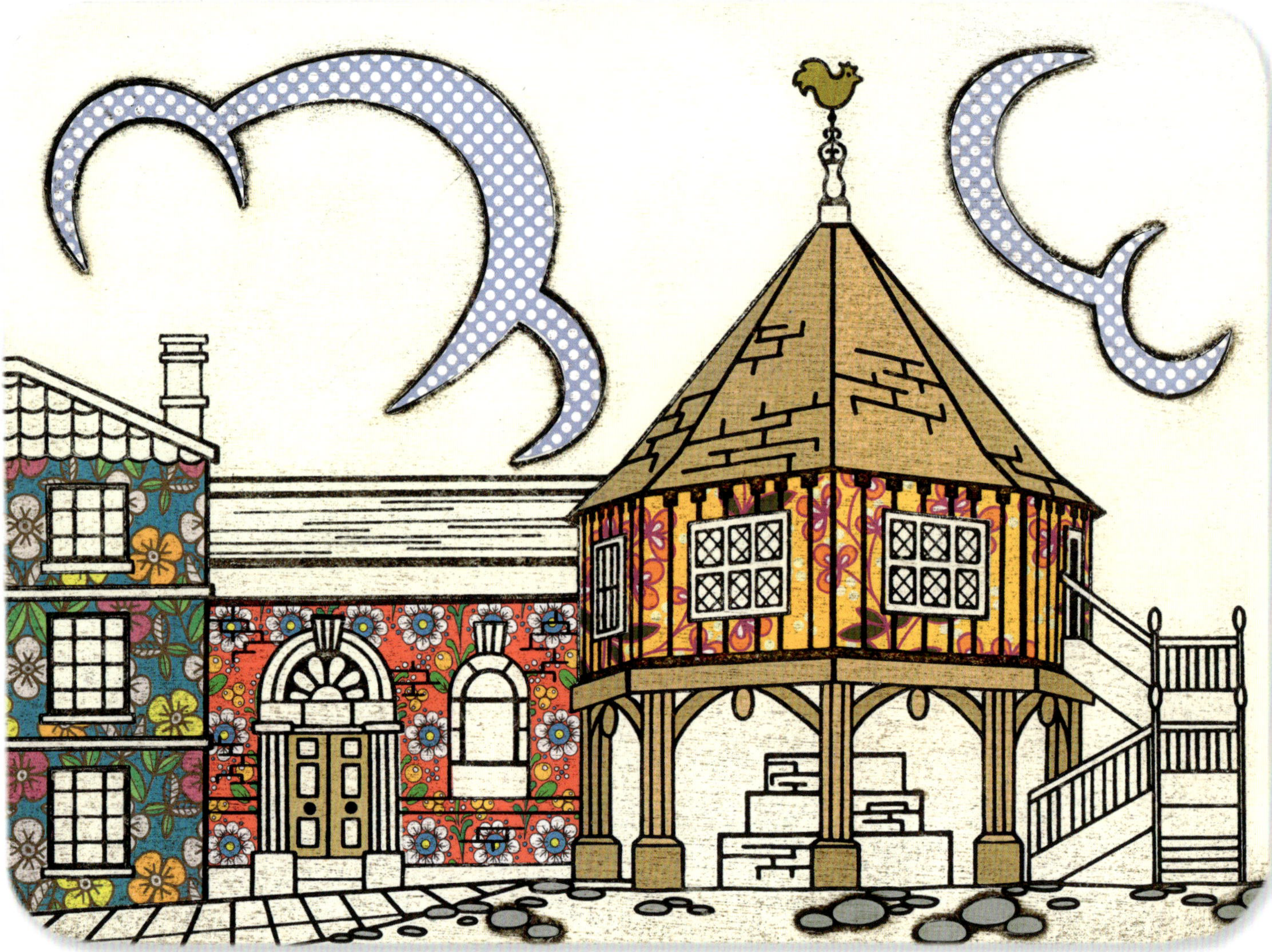

Becket in 1170, Becket's name was added to the dedication. The church was originally cruciform in shape, with a central tower and twin west towers. When it was built, stone from Caen in Normandy was shipped across the English Channel to face the walls. The central tower was replaced in about 1376 with a tall octagonal tower (now ruined) that held the monks' bells. In 1447, work on a much taller single west tower began. This replaced the original Norman towers and held the townspeople's bells.

King Henry VIII's dissolution of the monasteries brought about the closure of Wymondham Abbey, which was surrendered to the King in 1538. The following years saw the gradual demolition of the monastic buildings for re-use of the stone. The eastern end of the church was destroyed, leaving the present building. Repairs to the church were carried out following Queen Elizabeth I's visit in 1573.

Notable features of the church are the twin towers (a landmark for miles around), the Norman nave, the splendid 15th-century angel roof in the nave and fine north aisle roof.

As for Wymondham's market cross, there was an earlier one in the marketplace during the Middle Ages, but it was destroyed with many other buildings in the Great Fire of Wymondham in 1615. The present Market Cross was built in 1617-18 and is now owned by the Town Council, housing Wymondham's Tourist Information Centre and hosting many events during the summer months.

Amelia Bowman describes the Market Cross as being at the heart of the town and, conveniently, "opposite my favourite cafe where I sat and made my initial sketch for the 2013 edition of 10 prints!".